Essays in Honor of Edmond Malinvaud

volume 1: Microeconomics

Essays in Honor of Edmond Malinvaud

volume 1: Microeconomics (with introduction by J.-C. Milleron)

volume 2: Macroeconomics

volume 3: Empirical Economics (with bibliography)

Essays in Honor of Edmond Malinvaud

volume 1: Microeconomics

edited by
Paul Champsaur
Michel Deleau
Jean-Michel Grandmont
Roger Guesnerie
Claude Henry
Jean-Jacques Laffont
Guy Laroque
Jacques Mairesse
Alain Monfort
Yves Younès

The MIT Press
Cambridge, Massachusetts
London, England

Published in French as part of a single volume entitled *Mélanges économiques: Essais en l'honneur de Edmond Malinvaud* (Paris: Economica, 1988). Translations provided by the authors.

Set in Palatino by Asco Trade Typesetting Ltd. in Hong Kong. Printed and bound in the United States of America.

Library of Congress Cataloging-in-Publication Data

Essays in honor of Edmond Malinvaud.

Includes bibliographical references.
Contents: v. 1. Microeconomics.
1. Economics. 2. Malivaud, Edmond. I. Malinvaud, Edmond.
II. Champsaur, Paul.
HB173.M4213 1990 330 89-48826
ISBN 0-262-03158-2 (v. 1)

volume 1
ISBN 0-262-03158-2

volume 2
ISBN 0-262-03159-0

volume 3
ISBN 0-262-03160-4

3-volume set
ISBN 0-262-03174-4

Contents

Introduction

Jean-Claude Milleron

This three-volume festschrift for Edmond Malinvaud was designed as a miscellany. No constraint other than format, and no objective other than excellence, was imposed on the contributors. Like Malinvaud's own work (see bibliography at end of volume 3), the papers assembled here cover a very wide spectrum, ranging from theoretical analysis to applied project evaluation, from the formalization of basic concepts to analyses more directed toward policy planning and assessment, and from examples of pure statistical methodology to empirical studies that aim to be as "clean" as possible. With the exception of one sociologist, all the authors are economists.

The breadth of the topics covered is hardly surprising. This is a collective tribute to a man who has often reminded us that, in the economic and social sciences, no approach must be neglected. It is the role of the introduction writer to define an order amid the diversity of these papers. Such an attempt is obviously reductionist. However, we hope it will offer some advantages over a purely alphabetical listing. For convenience, we have grouped this partial classification under three broad headings. Although each of these subjects is indeed represented in Malinvaud's own writings, our choice is far from providing exhaustive coverage.

From Equilibrium to Disequilibrium

The question of unemployment—one of the basic issues in much of Malinvaud's work—is an underlying leitmotif here. Unemployment, he argues, cannot be interpreted simply as the natural outcome of transitory disadjustments. One must look beyond, and come to grips with the dimension of disequilibrium.[1] This approach enables us to deal with the old "Keynes versus Pigou or Rueff" dispute in a single conceptual framework and therefore to supersede it. Accordingly, we have included a number of valuable studies that, on the whole, relativize the significance of certain approaches such as rational expectations. They report significant advances in the theory of disequilibrium and related approaches.

The debate on expectation formation remains one of the central aspects of any dynamic study. J.-M. Grandmont and G. Laroque show in their paper the existence of a "relatively large" set of cases where "the stability of a steady state for the dynamics with learning implies its instability for the dynamics with perfect foresight."

The paper by R. Guesnerie and J.-J. Laffont focuses on the random "noise" introduced in forecasts by extrinsic uncertainty ("sunspots"). One of the potential consequences of this feature is that equilibria with rational expectations may differ from intertemporal Arrow-Debreu equilibria, which are Pareto-efficient. These authors review in detail the restrictive conditions defined in the literature in order to make the two concepts of equilibrium coincide. They broaden the conditions for the existence of "sunspot" equilibria. They confirm that an equilibrium of this sort is not generally a first-best optimum.

The simplest formalizations of the disequilibrium approach are often criticized for the "sharpness" of their results. Depending on the parameter values, it is argued, we get either "Keynesian unemployment" or "Classical unemployment." Several of the contributions here show that, by postulating what are often more realistic assumptions, we can make Classical unemployment and Keynesian unemployment coexist. P. A. Muet and H. Sterdyniak, for example, introduce a random demand for firms' output as well as adjustment costs that allow the construction of an original and interesting dynamics of "mixed unemployment." In the same vein, A. d'Autume's contribution is explicitly entitled "The Dynamics of Mixed Unempolyment." F. Gagey, J.-P. Lambert, and B. Ottenwaelter estimate a disequilibrium model that takes into account the business-survey data pertaining to firms' direct perception of disequilibrium situations. As the authors themselves put it, this leads to a "smoothing" of the "Min" condition (between supply and demand) that characterizes the response of the model in terms of states of unemployment (Keynesian or Classical). Another fertile and innovative approach is that of C. Gouriéroux and G. Laroque, who examine a market for a single good in terms of physical characteristics. The good is exchanged in different locations, however, generating travel costs for the agents. The model seeks to formalize explicitly the "encounter" between sellers and buyers.

The detailed empirical study of firms' investment behavior by P. Artus and P. Sicsic inspires modesty in the light of the persistent difficulties we face when trying to make our investment equations fit the most recent past. In particular, the authors report their inability to corroborate the impact on investment of factors often cited in the theoretical literature—especially the factors that "rise" from the financial sphere to the real sphere. Another, more theoretical attempt to accommodate certain financial factors in the investment decision is made by X. Freixas and J.-J. Laffont. Their paper offers an interesting characterization of the information asymmetry affecting banks, and of the potential effects of this incomplete information on fluctuations in economic activity, notably through investment decisions.

Closer to economic policy but "downstream" from the disequilibrium approach is the contribution by P. Nasse, who provides a highly articulate analysis of wage stickiness—notably in France—and its impact on investment and employment. In addition to wage policies, economic policies should also take into account certain factors that are too often neglected, such as profit sharing and time management, in particular with a view to a more intensive utilization of equipment.

J.-P. Laffargue bravely departs from the closed-economy hypothesis that too often characterizes theoretical macroeconomic work. Using a model with two industries and two regions, Laffargue discusses the implementation of "demand-side" policies in a conceptual framework where "external constraints" come rather naturally into play.

The link between the long term and the short term is one of the most complex aspects of macroeconomic modeling. As M. Deleau, C. Le Van, and P. Malgrange point out in a stimulating essay, one should perhaps speak of *several* "nested" long terms rather than *the* long term when discussing macroeconomic models. In any event—and this point is relevant to some of the preceding discussions—it would be a mistake to think, as is so often rashly asserted, that the short term is Keynesian and the long term Walrasian.

Moving away somewhat from the disequilibrium approach, but not from the issue of unemployment, we come to S.-C. Kolm's study on the consequences in terms of inefficiency of the *direct* introduction of wages as an argument of the agents' utility function. Kolm seeks to show how, in such a context, suitable economic policies could remedy the inefficiencies resulting from the set of assumptions adopted.

Microeconomics: Beyond Conventional Assumptions

Malinvaud's *Leçons de théorie microéconomique* provides a deep understanding of the Walrasian construction à la Arrow-Debreu. Of all the works in that field, it is also perhaps the one that places the greatest emphasis on the assumptions—and therefore the limits—of conventional analysis, and urges us to "look beyond." Malinvaud points out the limits of the standard microeconomic theory under specific assumptions: various forms of externality, nonconvexities, and disequilibrium situations. He insists on the problems raised by the choice of the time horizon and the need to make greater allowance in our normative analyses for the actual behavior of agents and for the strict limits imposed on our choice of truly incentive mechanisms. He also stresses the need to question the analyses of market functioning and to push them forward. These analyses cover imperfect competition, the foundations of competition "policies," the stability of monopoly situations, the choice of product quality, and even the study of planning procedures (sometimes understood as an alternative to market mechanisms).

The article by N. Curien and M. Gensollen on the microeconomic modeling of a telephone network seeks to provide an effective combination of descriptive aspects (telephone demand) and normative aspects (optimal pricing). The perspective adopted is that of a second-best optimum, which is well suited to a case of positive externality (linked to the network's existence) where the operator is required to make a positive profit.

A contribution of a distinctly more theoretical nature sheds some light on nonconvex production sets. B. Cornet's paper is a vigorous attempt to accommodate nonconvexities, particularly those related to the presence of increasing returns in the productive sector. By replacing profit maximization by a suitably defined marginal pricing behavior, Cornet demonstrates the existence of a price system associated with an efficient program. But, in general, the conventional optimality properties are not preserved in an equilibrium "with marginal pricing."

Taking into account disequilibrium situations leads to questions about certain rules of decentralized project evaluation. Using a model that openly formalizes a concept of foreign-trade constraint, D. Bureau offers some interesting and subtly argued conclusions regarding the use of shadow prices (below-market shadow wages and above-market import prices). P. Michel, adopting an ultimately rather similar approach, formalizes a "classical unemployment" situation by means of a Ramsey growth model in which he sets a lower limit to marginal labor productivity (thereby implying that the real wage is "too" high). He then shows how, in the search for a second-best optimum, a divergence appears between the private and public valuations of capital, which could entail a government intervention in the form of an investment subsidy.

The implementation of second-best optimum solutions requires a knowledge of direct- and cross-price elasticities. But, except for particular specifications, econometrics is incapable of estimating these accurately given the data generally available. In a simple framework often encountered in the economics of transportation, A. Bernard shows how a strong specification of preferences (CES utility functions) provides a way to overcome this difficulty.

J. Tirole offers a profound, highly stimulating analysis of the not-so-obvious relationships between the search for efficiency, intertemporal redistribution (in particular, the debt problem), and asset prices. This paper bears directly on a basic theme in Malinvaud's work (see his article of 1953 on intertemporal efficency in models with infinite horizons and his subsequent contributions in the field of capital theory). The underlying issues of Tirole's paper are debt neutrality ("Ricardo's theorem")—the answer here being that in most cases debt is not neutral—and the valuation of nonproducible resources. On the latter subject, Malinvaud supplied certain insights at a very early stage in his work, in particular at the request of Pierre Massé. Tirole's essay epitomizes his often luminous personal reflections on one of the most difficult areas of microeconomic theory.

In a lucid, pioneering contribution, D. Cohen seeks to formalize the behavior of an indebted country faced with the temptation—overlooked by the theory—to "repudiate" its debt in the event that the debt-servicing charges set by the lender are deemed exorbitant. Cohen shows that the awareness of this risk incites private lending banks to reduce debt maturity; he also points out that this market inefficiency leaves scope for specific action by international institutions such as the IMF and the World Bank.

Next come a fairly coherent group of essays that provide an excellent sample of recent advances in market analysis. C. Henry invites us to a close scrutiny of the very concept of a contestable monopoly. His starting point is that "potential competition" is nonexistent unless it constitutes a *credible* threat. From this, Henry derives a notion that must, however, be accurately formalized: the credibility of a potential competition cannot be assessed without taking into account an effective competition, the effectiveness of which depends on market structures in the most conventional sense. Such an analysis leads to complex conclusions regarding competition policy. This is an area in which economists are alerting politicians with increasing clarity to the dangers of simplistic statements and choices. Perhaps the warnings have not yet been properly heeded.

P. Champsaur and J.-C. Rochet tackle a technically challenging subject and fill a major gap in conventional analyses of quality differentiation in oligopoly situations. The weakness of these analyses stems from the implicit or explicit assumption that each firm chooses a single quality. It was naturally tempting to try to determine how the outcome might be affected if firms were not restricted *a priori* in their choice of qualities. The authors' basic finding is that, within a reasonable framework of assumptions, firms have an incentive to reduce their quality range, so that the hypothesis of one quality per firm is an acceptable approximation.

The subject examined by G. Laffond and J. Lesourne—"the dynamics of a market with information transmission via prices"—is also technically difficult, but it is just as important for our understanding of market mechanisms. The study of market dynamics thus defined aims to clarify the market's actual functioning. Here, the market is seen not as an abstraction—where one rarely finds an auctioneer—but as a place where buyers and sellers meet to conclude transactions. The paper analyzes the realistic case in which the sellers and some buyers know the product's quality but the rest of the buyers do not. Laffond and Lesourne show that, under these conditions, the market dynamics can vary widely, depending particularly on the assumptions about the manner in which buyers enter the market.

Malinvaud was one of the first to stress the unrealistic character of the attempts to integrate uncertainty through a complete system of contingent markets. D. Henriet and J.-C. Rochet furnish an interesting analysis of insurance markets that are subjected to the phenomenon of "adverse selection," now well identified by economists. This situation occurs in particular when the asymmetry of information prevents the market from spontaneously reaching an efficient allocation of resources. The novelty of Henriet and Rochet's approach is that it spells out the properties of a "regulated" market equilibrium in which the government intervenes in a manner very similar to that employed by French supervisory bodies in the automobile-insurance market.

Another interesting case where a certain asymmetry of information is at work is that of research contracts, notably for undertakings of a cooperative nature such as the Esprit and Eureka programs. The information of the initiators of such projects is obviously incomplete, both as regards the effective contribution of each contracting party and also, often, as regards the performance of the firms involved (for example, their profitability). P. Picard and P. Rey analyze the development of cooperation programs of this type and show the ways in which one can offer optimal contractual rules that make it possible to avoid collective welfare losses.

Other types of solutions have been sought for well-identified cases in which the market does not lead to an optimum (externalities, public goods, and so on). These solutions involve the application of planning procedures that formalize information exchanges between a center and more or less decentralized units in a conceptual framework where information is not the same for everyone. Edmond Malinvaud himself has made a significant contribution to developing the literature in this field, as regards production procedures and the markets for public goods. J. Crémer's paper offers fairly general formalizations suited to the planning of production programs in cases where the planning center is able to pre-define an order of preference for all the programs. Crémer reports convergence results arrived at under minimally restrictive hypotheses.

The article by Y. Younès aims to develop a generalized approach encompassing a very wide range of the cases in economic analysis discussed so far, where an optimum does not result spontaneously from individual decisions. Examples include the "overlapping-generations" model, fixed-price models, and models with incomplete market structure. Using game-theory concepts (core and Cournot equilibrium), Younès seeks to "fit" each model of this type into a larger model in order to attain a unified formalization. This would afford a better understanding of the role played by various inefficiency factors such as market structures, modes of contact between operators, and specific difficulties linked to the irreversible nature of the time parameter.

Statistical Methods for the Economist

The first edition of Malinvaud's *Méthodes statistiques de l'économétrie* (1964), which was hailed by the entire profession,[2] gave a generation of French students and researchers the privilege of using a reference work regarded by many foreign experts as the best in its field. This gave rise to a preference for a method that takes concrete problems and issues as its starting point and then seeks to develop a transparent, well formalized, "clean" statistical procedure. The papers gathered under the present heading may be read in this spirit. They contain the elements of solutions to highly practical questions, such as data "adjustment"—an issue that, although "upstream" from econometrics in the usual sense, is being recognized as crucial by an ever-wider audience. The reader will also discover the significant advances of econometrics in such difficult areas as the application of test theory to complex nonlinear cases, the fundamentals of estimation under more realistic hypotheses, and panel-data studies.

The work of Y. Aït-Sahalia, M. Balinski, and G. Demange on the adjustment of contingency tables is a fine example of how to reorganize a method, notably by constructing a reasonable axiomatics. Indeed, making explicit what is implicit in the choice of a particular method lies at the very heart of a scientific approach.

The sociologist C. Baudelot draws on a sociological survey to answer some of the challenging questions put to him in 1972 by the economists who authored a volume on French growth.[3] Baudelot agrees that the relationship to the future is a "decisional dimension of social behavior." He rests his case on the "value" content of statements by pupils at a French vocational secondary school. These findings incite the economist to modesty, so much does the object studied seem to resist confinement in oversimplified categories.

Next come four studies that make significant contributions to statistical methods in econometrics. The paper by C. Fourgeaud, C. Gouriéroux, and J. Pradel departs from the traditional framework of estimation theory by reporting maximum-likelihood estimates that do not exhibit the standard asymptotic properties (asymptotic biases and non-normality). More specifically, the authors work on a simple, two-state Markovian model. One of its basic parameters corresponds to the limit probability of the occurrence of either state, the other to the speed of convergence toward that limit probability. The parameters are estimated from individual observations made on two different dates. This paper provides an explicit study of estimation accuracy, notably in terms of the time interval between the observations.

An equally important contribution from G. Gouriéroux, A. Monfort, and E. Renault deals with the case in which constraints on parameters (under test, or to be estimated) may be expressed in bilinear form (linear with respect to the parameters under study and linear with respect to a set of auxiliary *ad hoc* parameters). The authors show that formalizations of this type apply to a fairly wide range of problems identified in the literature. This bilinear formalization serves to implement ordinary least-squares (OLS) or generalized least-squares (GLS) methods, thereby allowing the use of appropriate software for estimation and testing.

A. Trognon and C. Gouriéroux explore the "two-step" estimation procedures—such as GLS methods—whose asymptotic efficiency is inadequate. The authors show that one can find an alternative objective function to the initial objective function (for example, likelihood) that preserves the simplicity of the two-step calculation without loss of efficiency. The method is applied to various classes of models and to a few estimation methods, including a two-step estimation method for the Tobit model.

J.-P. Florens examines a topic that is purely theoretical and methodological: the empirical researches regarding the choice of model specifications. Florens applies the "encompassing" concept to a comparison of two models. This concept, which is of a very partial nature, provides a criterion for preferring one of the models if its findings can explain the other model's findings. The demonstration is supported with examples drawn from the standard literature.

It is all too rare for an article to contain insightful economic analysis cogently related to an empirical study. The contribution by F. Bourguignon and P.-A. Chiappori deserves special praise on this score. These authors provide a well-argued discussion of the workings of an internal labor market (within a firm, from a "descriptive" angle) and perform an econometric estimate under "Logit"-type specifications appropriate to the problem analyzed.

Equally praiseworthy on this count is the paper by J. Mairesse and Z. Griliches, who examine estimates of simple production functions using firm panels in three major countries. The basic issue tackled by these authors is whether the high scatters observed in panel-data estimates are indeed "real." The evidence leads the authors to regard the observed heterogeneity as implausible and to question the adequacy of the specifications. They conclude that it "seems difficult to estimate stable production functions at firm level on samples for which a number of important economic variables are unavailable." For the statistician, this amounts to an invitation to get to work.

These volumes are intended as a testimonial for the scholarly community of the intellectual debt that French economists owe to Edmond Malinvaud. The harvest of essays gathered has fulfilled the editors' expectations. May it also be judged worthy of the man it seeks to honor.

Notes

1. This point of view was superbly expressed by Don Patinkin back in the 1950s: "Thus, our first task in studying involuntary unemployment is to free ourselves of the mental habit—long ingrained by the methods of static analysis—of seeing only the points *on* the demand or supply curves" (*Money, Interest and Prices*, second edition, 1965, p. 323).

2. See, for example, the review by Franklin M. Fisher in *Econometrica*, April 1965.

3. J. J. Carré, P. Dubois and E. Malinvaud, *La croissance française. Un essai d'analyse causale économique de l'après-guerre* (Seuil, 1972).

I

Microeconomics and Economic Dynamics

1

Marginal Cost Pricing and Pareto Optimality

Bernard Cornet

1. Introduction

The presence of increasing returns and of fixed costs in various production sectors is widely recognized in the economics literature, and the failure of the competitive mechanism in such an environment has been known since Marshall. The theories of monopoly or imperfect competition assume that the producers behave strategically in fixing the prices and/or choosing the quantities of goods that they produce. In contrast, this article is mainly concerned with the pricing policy of public monopolies presenting increasing returns to scale, such as railways or electricity production, for which the state intervention is often suggested.

In *"Etudes d'économie politique appliquée,"* Léon Walras states:

> l'état peut et doit intervenir dans l'industrie des chemins de fer et cela à double titre: 1° parce que le service des chemins de fer, en ce qui concerne les transports des services ou produits publics, est lui-même un service public; 2° parce que le service des chemins de fer en ce qui concerne le transport des services ou produits d'intérêt privé, est un monopole naturel et nécessaire qui, comme monopole privé ne serait fondé ni en droit, ni en intérêt, et qui, par conséquent, doit être érigé en monopole d'état économique.

For a public monopoly of this type, the fundamental problem is to determine at which prices the goods and services that it provides should be sold, assuming that the inputs it uses are accessible at the market prices. An answer to this question is provided by the doctrine of "sale at marginal cost," which was elaborated in the 1930s and 1940s, mainly by Allais, Hotelling, Lange, Lerner, and Pigou, but which in fact dates back to Jules Dupuit and his work in 1844 on public utility pricing.

The aim of this article is to reexamine the optimality properties of the doctrine of sale at marginal cost and to study this question in a framework with the same level of generality as the Walrasian model as presented, for example, in Gérard Debreu's *"Theory of value"* or Edmond Malinvaud's *Leçons de théorie microéconomique,"* but in which no convexity assumption is made on the production sector. Each firm j ($j = 1, \ldots, n$) is represented by its production set Y_j, an arbitrary subset of the commodity space R^ℓ, and, in this article, no convexity assumption will be made on the sets Y_j, or on the total production set $\sum_{j=1}^n Y_j$, or on their iso-output sets. This clearly allows for increasing returns but also for more general types of "nonconvexities" in the production sector.

The first question, addressed in section 2, concerns the generalization of the doctrine of sale at marginal cost in the general framework described previously. We follow Guesnerie (1975) by saying that the firm j follows the *marginal pricing rule* if its equilibrium condition for a couple $(p, y_j) \in R^\ell \times Y_j$ corresponds to the first-order necessary conditions for profit maximization, in a precise mathematical sense formalized by the normal cone defined by Clarke (1975) or a related notion. It is worth pointing out that if the production set Y_j is convex, then the necessary conditions are also sufficient; in other words, the marginal pricing rule coincides with profit maximization. The main result of section 2 [Lemma 1] shows that the marginal pricing rule coincides with the classical doctrine of sale at marginal cost under standard assumptions, such as the differentiability of the cost function and the convexity of the iso-output sets. The relationship between this formalization and the different one considered by Guesnerie is discussed in section 5.

In section 3, we provide a general formulation of the second fundamental theorem of welfare economics in the absence of convexity and of differentiability assumptions on the production sets Y_j. The main result (Corollary 1) generalizes the classical theorem of Arrow (1951) and Debreu (1951), by removing the convexity assumption on the production sets Y_j when the profit maximization rule is replaced by the marginal pricing one. This result is proved in section 4 by a direct argument. Finally, in section 5, we show that our main result can be strengthened in two cases of particular economic interest. The first case applies to firms with fixed costs set up and constant marginal costs and, more generally, production sets with "simple inward kinks," in a precise sense which will be defined later. The second case concerns the framework considered by Guesnerie (1975), who uses a different formalization of the marginal pricing rule with Dubovickii-Miljutin's normal cone.

Finally, in section 6, we study the optimality properties of marginal (cost) pricing equilibria, when consumers' revenue structure is exogenously fixed. In other words, we examine whether or not an analogue of the first fundamental theorem of welfare economics holds in a nonconvex framework when the profit maximization rule for the firms is replaced by the marginal pricing one. As shown by Guesnerie (1975) (see also Brown and Heal 1979), results in this area are essentially negative, unless one considers very specific situations as in the articles by Dierker (1986) and Quinzii (1988). Moreover, a recent counterexample, due to Beato and Mas-Colell (1985), shows that in the absence of convexity assumption on the production sets Y_j, a marginal pricing equilibrium is not productive efficient in general.

The questions in this article have been studied in a general equilibrium framework by numerous authors, most of whom are mentioned in the bibliography. The bibliography also provides references to two important problems related to marginal (cost) pricing, which are not considered in this article; specifically, the existence of marginal pricing equilibria, and the existence of such an equilibrium which is also Pareto optimal. The treatment of these different questions has benefited from the recent development of new mathematical techniques, known as "Nonsmooth Analysis," which are expounded in the books by Clarke (1983) and Rockafellar (1981). This article, however, can be read without any previous knowledge of these techniques; the main results used here are reviewed in section 2.

The General Equilibrium Model

We end this introduction by describing the general framework of this article, which is the same as that in Debreu's "Theory of value" with one major difference, being that we assume neither the convexity of firms' production sets, nor of the total production set of the economy, nor of the firms' iso-output sets. We consider an economy $\mathscr{E}$ with finite numbers, ℓ of commodities, m of consumers, and n of producers. The technological possibilities of each producer j ($j = 1, \ldots, n$) are represented by a subset Y_j of R^{ℓ}. An element $y_j = (y_{jh})$ in Y_j represents a possible production plan of the producer j and the good h is an input (resp. output) for this plan if $y_{jh} \leqslant 0$ (resp. $y_{jh} \geqslant 0$).

We make the following assumption on the production sets:

Assumption P. For every j, Y_j is closed, nonempty and $Y_j - R^{\ell}_{+} \subset Y_j$ (free disposal).[1]

This assumption implies that if a plan y_j is possible for the producer j, this is also true for every plan z_j verifying $z_{jh} \leqslant y_{ih}$ for every commodity h, that is, which does not use fewer inputs than y_j (in absolute value) and does not produce more outputs than y_j. It is important to notice that, under Assumption P, the boundary, ∂Y_j, of the production set Y_j coincides with the set of (weakly) efficient production plans, that is,

$$\partial Y_j = \{y_j \in Y_j | \nexists z_j \in Y_j, z_j \gg y_j\}.$$

For each consumer i ($i = 1, \ldots, m$), we denote by X_i, the subset of R^ℓ of consumption plans that are possible for this consumer; we suppose that his (her) preferences are represented by a complete, reflexive, transitive binary relation $\preceq_i$ on the set X_i. We denote by $P_i(x_i) = \{x \in X_i | x_i \preceq x$ and not $[x \preceq_i x']\}$ the set of strictly preferred elements to x_i in X_i.

We make the following basic assumption on the consumption sector:

Assumption C. For every i, X_i is nonempty, closed, convex, bounded inferiorly, and the preference relation $\preceq_i$ is continuous, convex, and nonsatiated.[2]

To complete the description of the economy $\mathscr{E}$, we denote by $\omega = (\omega_h)$ the vector of initial endowment ω_h in commodity h of the economy. Thus to summarize, $\mathscr{E} = ((X_i, \preceq_i), (Y_j), \omega)$.

2. Marginal Cost Pricing and Marginal Pricing

The aim of this section is to show how the doctrine of marginal cost pricing can be integrated into the general framework described previously, regardless of whether the cost function of each producer is defined.

Marginal Cost Pricing

We first recall the classical definition of marginal cost pricing which requires distinction between the inputs and the outputs of each producer. For every j, we assume that there is a partition of the set of commodities $\{1, \ldots, \ell\}$ into two nonempty subsets I_j and O_j such that $y \in Y_j$ and $h \in I_j$ imply $y_h \leqslant 0$. In other words, every commodity h in I_j is an input of the producer j. At this stage, it is worth noticing that no assumption is made for the commodities h in O_j.

We let $R^{I_j} = \{p \in R^\ell | p_h = 0$ if $h \notin I_j\}$, $R^{O_j} = \{p \in R^\ell | p_h = 0$ if $h \notin O_j\}$, and, for every x in R^ℓ, we denote by $x|_{I_j}$ (or simply x_{I_j}) the orthogonal projection of x onto R^{I_j}, that is, x_{I_j} is the vector of R^ℓ with coordinates $(x_{I_j})_h = x_h$ if $h \in I_j$, and $(x_{I_j})_h = 0$ if $h \notin I_j$. We then define the iso-output sets and the cost function as follows. We let, for $(r, b) \in R_+^{I_j} \times R^{O_j}$,

$$Y_j(b) = \{-y_{I_j} | y \in Y_j \text{ such that } y_{O_j} = b\},$$

$$c_j(r, b) = \inf\{r \cdot a | a \in Y_j(b)\} \qquad \text{if} \qquad Y_j(b) \neq \emptyset.$$

The following lemma characterizes geometrically the marginal cost pricing condition for the firm j (condition TCM hereafter), in terms of "exterior normal vectors" to the set Y_j, under classical assumptions of convexity of the isoquants and of differentiability of the cost function with respect to the (output) vector b.

Lemma 1. Let Y_j be a closed subset of R^ℓ, let $(y_j^*, p^*) \in Y_j \times R_+^\ell$, we note $a_j^* = -y_j^*|_{I_j}$, $b_j^* = y_j^*|_{O_j}$, and we make the following assumptions: (i) for every $b_j \in R^{O_j}$, the iso-output set $Y_j(b_j)$ is a nonempty, convex, subset of $R_+^{I_j}$, such that $Y_j(b_j) + R_+^{I_j} \subset Y_j(b_j)$,[3] (ii) for every fixed $r \in R_+^{I_j}$, the cost function $c_j(r, \cdot)$ is twice continuously differentiable on a neighborhood of b_j^*, and (iii) the mapping $\nabla_{O_j} c_j(\cdot, \cdot)$[4] is continuous on a neighborhood of $(p_{I_j}^*, b_j^*)$.

Then the following four conditions are equivalent:

Condition TCM:

(i) $p_{I_j}^* \cdot a_j^* \leqslant p_{I_j}^* \cdot a$ for every $a \in Y_j(b_j^*)$, (cost minimization)

and

(ii) $p_{O_j}^* = \nabla_{O_j} c_j(p_{I_j}^*, b_j^*)$; (marginal cost)

Condition $(\perp)$: p^* is a perpendicular vector (or a proximal normal vector) to Y_j at y_j^*, in the sense that p^* belongs to the set

$$\perp_{Y_j}(y_j^*) \stackrel{\text{def}}{=} \{p \in R^\ell | \exists \rho > 0, \forall y_j \in \text{cl}Y_j, p^* \cdot y_j^* \geqslant p^* \cdot y_j - \rho \| y_j - y_j^* \|^2\}.$$

Condition $(\hat{\beta})$: p^* is a limiting normal vector to Y_j at y_j^*, in the sense that p^* belongs to the set

$$\hat{N}_{Y_j}(y_j^*) \stackrel{\text{def}}{=} \{\lim_\nu p^\nu | (y_j^\nu) \subset \text{cl}Y_j, (y_j^\nu) \to y_j^* \text{ and } \forall \nu, p^\nu \in \perp_{Y_j}(y_j^\nu)\}.$$

Condition (β): p^* is a normal vector in the sense of Clarke (1975) to Y_j at y_j^*, that is, p^* belongs to the set

$$N_{Y_j}(y_j^*) \stackrel{\text{def}}{=} \text{clco}\hat{N}_{Y_j}(y_j^*),$$

i.e., the smallest closed convex subset of R^ℓ containing $\hat{N}_{Y_j}(y_j^*)$.

The proof of the lemma is given in the appendix.

Condition TCM formalizes the standard behavioral rule of marginal cost pricing for the producer j [cf. Allais 1953 and Malinvaud 1972 (Ch. 4.6)] and can be interpreted as follows. Given the market prices of its inputs (p_h^*; $h \in I_j$) and given the quantities of its outputs ($y_{jh}^* = b_{jh}^*$; $h \in O_j$), the producer j first chooses the quantities of its inputs ($a_{jh}^* = |y_{jh}^*|$; $h \in I_j$) by minimizing its costs and then fixes the prices of its outputs (p_h^*; $h \in O_j$) according to their marginal costs.

Marginal Pricing

We first note that the definitions of the sets $\perp_{Y_j}(y_j^*)$, $\hat{N}_{Y_j}(y_j^*)$, and $N_{Y_j}(y_j^*)$ given previously are valid for an arbitrary subset (not necessarily closed) Y_j of R^ℓ at a point $y_j^* \in \mathrm{cl}\, Y_j$. Furthermore, these sets verify the following inclusions:

$$\perp_{Y_j}(y_j^*) \subset \hat{N}_{Y_j}(y_j^*) \subset N_{Y_j}(y_j^*).$$

We say that the producer j follows the *marginal pricing rule* (resp. in a strong sense, resp. in a weak sense) if its behavioral rule is formalized by the condition ($\hat{\beta}$) [resp. the stronger condition ($\perp$), resp. the weaker condition ($\hat{\beta}$)]—in other words, if the couples (y_j^*, p^*) of a production plan y_j^* and of a price system p^* that are in "equilibrium" for the producer j are those that satisfy the condition

$$p^* \in \hat{N}_{Y_j}(y_j^*) \quad [\text{resp. } p \in \perp_{Y_j}(y_j^*), \text{ resp. } p^* \in N_{Y_j}(y_j^*)].$$

Under the assumptions of Lemma 1, the above three definitions of the marginal pricing rule coincide with that of marginal *cost* pricing; thus they all allow the classical definition of marginal cost pricing to be extended to a framework where the cost function may not be differentiable (and, in fact, may not be defined) and where the producer j is characterized by its production set Y_j, an arbitrary subset of R^ℓ. Note also that, even if the cost function is defined for the producer j (which necessitates a priori distinction between the inputs and the outputs of this producer) and if this producer follows the *marginal pricing* rule, in the absence of convexity assumption on its iso-output sets, its costs are no longer minimized, in general (Arrow and Hurwicz 1960; Guesnerie 1989). It is essentially for this reason that we have preferred to introduce a new term (with no reference to the cost function) to be able to distinguish the classical notion from the above one.

The term "marginal pricing rule" is justified by the fact that the stronger condition ($\perp$) [and thus also the conditions ($\hat{\beta}$) and (β)] is a first-order necessary condition for profit maximization. Indeed, if y_j^* maximizes the profit $p^* \cdot y_j$ over the production set Y_j, it also maximizes, for every $\rho \geqslant 0$, the function $p^* \cdot y_j - \rho \| y_j - y_j^* \|^2$ over the set Y_j; thus the condition ($\perp$) is satisfied. We shall see below that if Y_j is convex, we can take $\rho = 0$ in the ($\perp$), that is, the necessary condition ($\perp$) for profit maximization is also sufficient.

Of the three conditions ($\perp$), (β), and ($\hat{\beta}$), Condition ($\perp$) has the clearest economic and geometric interpretations. The condition $p^* \in \perp_{Y_j}(y_j^*)$ means that, given the price system p^*, the plan y_j^* maximizes the quadratic function $p^* \cdot y_j - \rho \| y_j - y_j^* \|^2$ over the production set Y_j, i.e., the profit $p^* \cdot y_j$ up to the perturbation "$-\rho \| y_j - y_j^* \|^2$." This condition can also be interpreted in terms of "nonlinear prices" by noting that it is equivalent to saying that y_j^* maximizes the quadratic function

$$\pi_j(y_j) = [p^* - \rho(y_j - y_j^*)] \cdot (y_j - y_j^*)$$

over the production set Y_j.

Moreover, the condition ($\perp$) formalizes in a natural way the notion of "orthogonality" to a set; indeed, it is easily shown that ($\perp$) is equivalent to the following geometric condition, illustrated in figure 1:

$$(\perp') \quad \exists \varepsilon > 0 \quad \mathrm{int} B(y_j^* + \varepsilon p^*, \varepsilon \| p^* \|) \cap \mathrm{cl} Y_j = \emptyset.$$

Condition ($\perp$), however, is too restrictive in many situations [cf. the plan y_1^* on figure 1 for which $\perp_{Y_1}(y_1^*) = \{0\}$] and it is essentially for this reason that, in the following, we consider the weaker notions of orthogonality defined by conditions ($\hat{\beta}$) and (β). These two conditions are discussed in the next subsection, which also summarizes the properties of the three sets $\perp_{Y_j}(y_j^*)$, $\hat{N}_{Y_j}(y_j^*)$, and $N_{Y_j}(y_j^*)$.

Properties of the Normal Cones

To familiarize the reader with notions he may not be accustomed to, the three definitions of orthogonality (in dimension 2) are illustrated in figure 2.

Proposition 1. Let $C \subset R^\ell$ and $x^* \in \mathrm{cl} C$. (a) The sets $\perp_C(x^*)$, $\hat{N}_C(x^*)$, and $N_C(x^*)$ are all cones of vertex 0 and satisfy the following inclusions:

$$\perp_C(x^*) \subset \hat{N}_C(x^*) \subset N_C(x^*).$$

(b) If $x^* \in \mathrm{int\,cl} C$, then $\perp_C(x^*) = \hat{N}_C(x^*) = N_C(x^*) = \{0\}$. Conversely, if $\hat{N}_C(x^*) = \{0\}$, then $x^* \in \mathrm{int\,cl} C$, but the implication $\perp_C(x^*) = \{0\} \Rightarrow x^* \in$

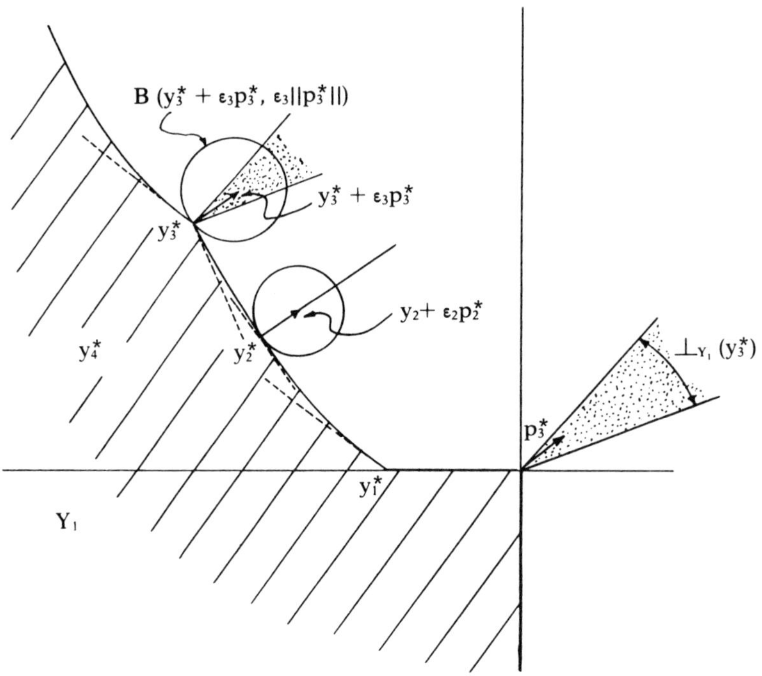

Figure 1.

int cl$C$ is not true in general [cf. figure 1 and the plan $y_1^* \in \partial Y_1$ for which $\perp_{Y_1}(y_1^*) = \{0\}$].

(c) Let U be an open set containing C and let f: $U \mapsto R$ be a differentiable function at a point x^* in C [resp. twice continuously differentiable on a neighborhood of x^*]. If x^* is a maximum of the function f on the set C, then the following necessary condition is satisfied:

$$\nabla f(x^*) \in \hat{N}_C(x^*) \quad [\text{resp. } \nabla f(x^*) \in \perp_C(x^*)].$$

(d) Let $\hat{G} = \{(x, p) \in \text{cl}C \times R^\ell | p \in \hat{N}_C(x)\}$ be the graph of the correspondence $\hat{N}_C(\cdot)$, then $\hat{G}$ is closed (in cl$C \times R^\ell$). Moreover $\hat{G}$ is the closure (in cl$C \times R^\ell$) of the graph $G = \{(x, p) \in \text{cl}C \times R^\ell | p \in \perp_C(x)\}$ of the correspondence $\perp_C(\cdot)$.

For the proof of Propositions 1 and 2, we refer to Clarke (1983).

It is essentially due to Property (b) that the cones $\hat{N}_{Y_j}(\cdot)$ and $N_{Y_j}(\cdot)$ are well adapted to the formalization of the marginal pricing rule and to the questions that are considered in this article. In other words, if Y_j is closed,

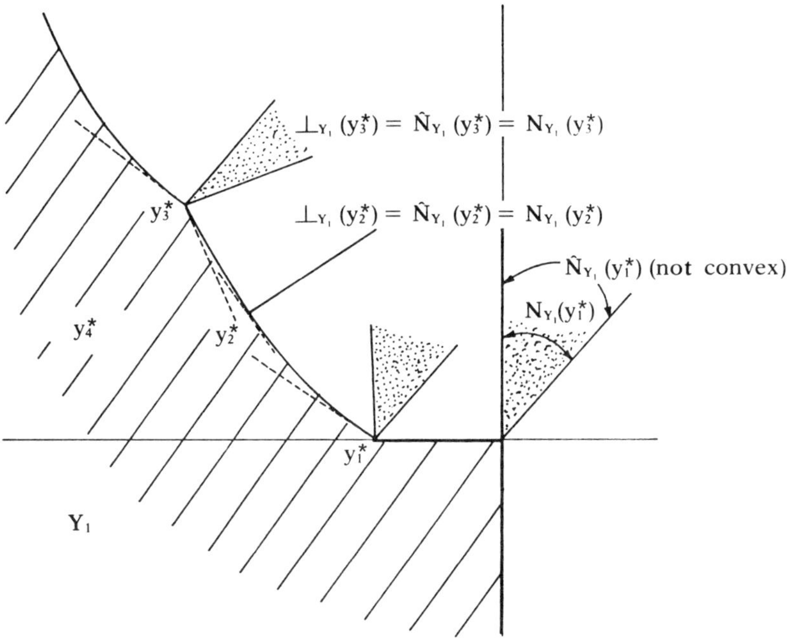

Figure 2.

to every element $y_j^* \in \partial Y_j$ [which coincides with the set of (weakly) efficient production plans, under assumption P] one can associate a *nonzero* price system p^* that *sustains* the plan y_j^* (in Koopmans' words), in the sense that (y_j^*, p^*) verifies Condition $(\hat{\beta})$ [and thus also Condition (β)]; but this property does not hold, in general, for the cone of perpendicular vectors. Moreover, the definition of Clarke's normal cone allows the recovery of a convexity property which is not satisfied, in general, by the cone $\hat{N}_{Y_j}(y_j^*)$ (cf. the point y_1^* in figure 2), and that will be of fundamental use in analyzing the problem of existence of equilibria (cf. Remark 6.1).

The next proposition states that the above three definitions of outward normal vectors coincide with the classical notions when C is convex or when C has a smooth boundary.

Proposition 2. (a) If $C \subset R^\ell$ is convex and if $x^* \in \mathrm{cl}C$, then $\perp_C(x^*) = \hat{N}_C(x^*) = N_C(x^*) = \{p^* \in R^\ell | p^* \cdot x^* \geqslant p^* \cdot x \text{ for all } x \in C\}$.

(b) If $C \subset R^\ell$ can be written as follows $C = \{x \in R^\ell | g(x) \leqslant 0\}$, where $g\colon R^\ell \to R$ is twice continuously differentiable, and if x^* is an element of C such that $g(x^*) = 0$ and $\nabla_g(x^*) \neq 0$, then

$$\perp_C(x^*) = \hat{N}_C(x^*) = N_C(x^*) = \{\lambda \nabla_g(x^*) | \lambda \geqslant 0\}.$$

Finally, we give a consequence of the free disposal Assumption P. We denote by $S = \{p \in R^\ell_+ | \sum_{h=1}^\ell p_h = 1\}$, the simplex of R^ℓ.

Proposition 3. Let C be a nonempty, closed subset of R^ℓ such that $C - R^\ell_+ \subset C$. Then

$$\{0\} \neq \hat{N}_C(x) \subset N_C(x) \subset R^\ell_+ \quad \text{for every } x \in \partial C.$$

Moreover, the correspondences $x \to \hat{N}_C(x) \cap S$ and $x \to N_C(x) \cap S$ are both upper semicontinuous, from ∂C to S, with nonempty compact values (and the second one is also convex valued).

The proof of this property is given in Cornet 1982.

We end this section with a remark, which shows the relationship between the previous definitions of normal vectors and another notion often encountered in the literature, introduced by Bouligand (1932), and which will enable us to give an equivalent definition of the cone of limiting normal vectors.

Remark 3.1. Let $C \subset R^\ell$ and $x^* \in \text{cl}C$, we call *normal vector in the sense of Bouligand*, every element p^* of the set

$$N_C^B(x^*) \stackrel{\text{def}}{=} \{p \in R^\ell | \forall \varepsilon > 0, \exists r > 0, \forall x \in \text{cl}C \cap B(x^*, r):$$
$$p \cdot x^* \geqslant p \cdot x - \varepsilon \|x - x^*\|\}.$$

It is clear that $\perp_C(x^*) \subset N_C^B(x^*)$ and, moreover (cf. Ioffe 1984 for the proof),

$$\hat{N}_C(x^*) = \{p = \lim_\nu p^\nu | (x^\nu) \subset \text{cl}C, (x^\nu) \to x^* \text{ and } \forall \nu, p^\nu \in N_C^B(x^\nu)\};$$

that is, in the definition of $\hat{N}_C(\cdot)$, one can replace the cone $\perp_C(\cdot)$ by the larger cone $N_C^B(\cdot)$. However, the use of Bouligand's cone leads to the same difficulties as those associated previously with the cone of perpendicular vectors [cf. the point y_1 on figure 1 for which $N_1^B(y_1) = \{0\}$].

3. The Second Theorem of Welfare Economics

The model that we consider hereafter is slightly more general than the one presented in the introduction, since we shall allow consumers to have noncomplete and nontransitive preferences.

We follow the classical presentation of Gale and Mas-Colell (1977) by associating to each consumer i ($i = 1, \ldots, m$) and to each vector $x = (x_1, \ldots, x_i, \ldots, x_m) \in X_1 \times \cdots \times X_i \times \cdots \times X_m$ of the possible consumption plans of the different consumers, the set $P_i(x)$ of the elements in X_i that the consumer i prefers to x. If the preferences of this consumer are represented by a preference relation $\precsim_i$, then the set $P_i(x)$ coincides with the definition given in the introduction (and in this case it depends only upon the consumption x_i of the ith consumer). The economy $\mathscr{E}$ is now described by the m-list (X_i, P_i), by the n-list (Y_j) of the production sets, and by the vector ω in R^ℓ of total initial endowments. More concisely: $\mathscr{E} = ((X_i, P_i), (Y_j), \omega)$.

An *attainable allocation* of this economy is an element $((x_i^*), (y_j^*)) \in R^{\ell m} \times R^{\ell n}$ verifying the three following conditions: (a) $x_i^* \in X_i$ for every i, (b) $y_j^* \in Y_j$ for every j, and (c) $\sum_{i=1}^m x_i^* \leqslant \sum_{j=1}^n y_j^* + \omega$.

A *Pareto optimum*[5] is an attainable allocation $((x_i^*), (y_j^*))$ for which there exists no attainable allocation $((x_i), (y_j))$ such that, $x_i \in P_i(x_1^*, \ldots, x_m^*)$ for every i.

An Optimum Is a Quasi-equilibrium

We now state our main result; no convexity and no differentiability assumption are made with respect to either the production sets or consumers' preferences.

Theorem 3.1. Let $((x_i^*), (y_j^*))$ be a Pareto optimum such that, for each consumer i, $x_i^* \in \mathrm{cl}P_i^*$, where $P_i^* \stackrel{\text{def}}{=} P_i(x_1^*, \ldots, x_m^*)$ (nonsatiation). Then there exists a *nonzero* price system p^* in R^ℓ such that

($\hat{\alpha}$) for every i, $\quad -p^* \in \hat{N}_{P_i^*}(x_i^*)$;

($\hat{\beta}$) for every j, $\quad p^* \in \hat{N}_{Y_j}(y_j^*)$;

(γ) $p^* \geqslant 0, \quad \sum_{i=1}^m x_i^* - \sum_{j=1}^n y_j^* - \omega \leqslant 0,$

$$\text{and} \quad p^* \cdot \left(\sum_{i=1}^m x_i^* - \sum_{j=1}^n y_j^* - \omega \right) = 0.$$

In the next section we prove Theorem 3.1 directly. This theorem extends a previous result by Cornet (1986), in which the marginal pricing rule was formalized by Clarke's normal cones $N_{P_i^*}(\cdot)$, $N_{Y_j}(\cdot)$. Khan (1987) then noticed that the same proof allowed consideration of the cones $\hat{N}_{P_i^*}(\cdot)$, $\hat{N}_{Y_j}(\cdot)$, of limiting normal vectors, as in the above theorem. We refer to these two papers for a more detailed discussion on the relationship with other results on this subject.

Finally, we note that Theorem 3.1 does not hold, in general, if the cones $\hat{N}_{P_i^*}(\cdot)$ and $\hat{N}_{Y_j}(\cdot)$ of limiting normal vectors are replaced, in the above conditions ($\hat{\alpha}$) and ($\hat{\beta}$), by the cones $\perp_{P_i^*}$ and $\perp_{Y_j}(\cdot)$ or by Bouligand's cones (cf. Remark 3.2 below for a counterexample).

An attainable allocation $((x_i^*), (y_j^*))$ satisfying, for some nonzero price system p^*, the conditions ($\hat{\alpha}$), ($\hat{\beta}$), and (γ), is called a *marginal pricing quasi-equilibrium with respect to a price system* or, simply a *quasi-equilibrium.* This definition is essentially the same as Guesnerie's notion of a *P.A. equilibrium*, the only difference being that we use here the cones $\hat{N}_{P_i^*}(\cdot)$ and $\hat{N}_{Y_j}(\cdot)$ of limiting normal vectors, instead of the cones of Dubovickii and Miljutin (1965) as does Guesnerie (cf. section 5).

Following Guesnerie, in the statement of the theorem we have kept the symmetry between the consumption and production sectors for which no convexity assumption is made. However, the presence of nonconvexities in these two sectors is of a different nature. For example, by considering a continuum of consumers, all infinitely small, the convexity assumption on consumers' preferences can be dropped (cf. Hildenbrand 1974). Analogous treatment of the production sector, however, is not very realistic on economic grounds, since the presence of increasing returns (and other types of nonconvexities) commonly characterizes large firms.

The Case of Convex Preferences

Under the standard Assumption C on the consumption sector, we can state the following result.

Corollary 1. Let $((x_i^*), (y_j^*))$ be a Pareto optimum such that, for each consumer i, the set $P_i^* \overset{\text{def}}{=} P_i(x_1^*, \ldots, x_m^*)$ is convex, and $x_i^* \in \text{cl}P_i^*$. Then there exists a *nonzero* price system p^* in R^ℓ such that

(α') for every i, $p^* \cdot x_i^* \leqslant p^* \cdot x_i$ for every $x_i \in P_i^*$;

($\hat{\beta}$) for every j, $p^* \in \hat{N}_{Y_j}(y_j^*)$;

(γ) $p^* \geqslant 0$, $\sum_{i=1}^{m} x_i^* - \sum_{j=1}^{n} y_j^* - \omega \leqslant 0$,

and $p^* \cdot \left(\sum_{i=1}^{m} x_i^* - \sum_{j=1}^{n} y_j^* - \omega \right) = 0$.

Moreover, if each consumer i is represented by a preference relation $\preceq_i$ verifying Assumption C and if $p^* \cdot x_i^* \neq \min p^* \cdot X_i$, then the following holds:

(α) for every i, x_i^* is a greatest element for $\preceq_i$ in the budget set:

$$\{x_i \in X_i | p^* \cdot x_i \leqslant p^* \cdot x_i^*\}.$$

Proof. The first part of Corollary 1 is a consequence of Theorem 3.1 and of the fact that the convexity of P_i^* implies that the conditions ($\hat{\alpha}$) and (α') are equivalent by Proposition 2.a. The second part of the Corollary is a consequence of the first part and of Debreu (1959; Proposition (1) of 4.9). ∎

The interpretation of this result is the same as of the second fundamental theorem of welfare economics in the convex case (consumers and producers), the only difference being that here the producers are striving to follow the marginal pricing rule (or the marginal cost pricing rule, under the assumptions of Lemma 1) rather than maximizing their profits as in the convex case.

More precisely, under Assumption C and for arbitrary production sets Y_j, to every Pareto optimum $((x_i^*), (y_j^*))$, one can associate a nonzero price system $p^* \geqslant 0$ and a revenue $r_i^* = p^* \cdot x_i^*$ for each consumer i such that $((x_i^*), (y_j^*))$ is a *quasi-equilibrium* with respect to $(p^*, (r_i^*))$ in the following sense: given the price system p^* and the revenues r_i^* ($i = 1, \ldots, m$), at x_i^*, each consumer i minimizes his (her) expenditure $p^* \cdot x_i$ among the consumption plans that are preferred to x_i^* [Condition (α')], each producer follows the marginal pricing rule [Condition ($\hat{\beta}$)], the excess demand is nonpositive for every commodity h, with equality if the price p_h^* is positive [Condition (γ)]. Under the additional assumption that $p^* \cdot x_i^* \neq \min p^* \cdot X_i$ [i.e., $p^* \cdot x_i^*$ is not the least expenditure with respect to p^* in the consumption set X_i], then the quasi-equilibrium is in fact an *equilibrium* with respect to $(p^*, (r_i^*))$; that is, at x_i^*, each consumer i maximizes his (her) preferences in his (her) budget set $\{x_i \in X_i | p^* \cdot x_i \leqslant r_i^*\}$ [Condition (α)], and the conditions ($\hat{\beta}$) and (γ) are satisfied.

We now state the standard version of the second fundamental theorem of welfare economics in the convex case (compare with the statements in Debreu 1959, Gale and Mas-Colell 1977, and Malinvaud 1972).

Corollary 2. Let $((x_i^*), (y_j^*))$ be a Pareto optimum such that, for each consumer i, the set $P_i^* \stackrel{\text{def}}{=} P_i(x_1^*, \ldots, x_m^*)$ is convex, $x_i^* \in \mathrm{cl}P_i^*$, and, for each producer j, Y_j is convex. Then there exists a nonzero price system p^* in R^ℓ such that

(α') for every i, $p^* \cdot x_i^* \leqslant p^* \cdot x_i$ for every $x_i \in P_i^*$;

(β) for every j, $p^* \cdot y_j^* \geqslant p^* \cdot y_j$ for every $y_j \in Y_j$;

(γ) $p^* \geqslant 0, \quad \sum_{i=1}^{m} x_i^* - \sum_{j=1}^{n} y_j^* - \omega \leqslant 0,$

and $p^* \cdot \left(\sum_{i=1}^{m} x_i^* - \sum_{j=1}^{n} y_j^* - \omega \right) = 0.$

Moreover, if each consumer i is represented by a preference relation $\preceq_i$ verifying assumption (C), and if $p^* \cdot x_i^* \neq \min p^* \cdot X_i$, then the following holds:

(α) for every i, x_i^* is a greatest element for $\preceq_i$ in the budget set

$$\{x_i \in X_i | p^* \cdot x_i \leqslant p^* \cdot x_i^*\}.$$

Remark 3.1. Theorem 3.1 and Corollary 1 do not hold, in general, if the cones $\hat{N}_{Y_j}(\cdot)$ of limiting normal vectors are replaced by the cones of perpendicular vectors $\perp_{Y_j}(\cdot)$ [or by Bouligand's cones $N_{Y_j}^B(\cdot)$ defined previously].

Indeed, let us consider the following counterexample (Bonnisseau and Cornet 1988a, Remark 3.3) of an economy with two commodities, one consumer, two producers, with the vector of total initial endowments $\omega = (1, 1)$. The consumption set of this consumer is $X_1 = R_+^2$, and his (her) preferences are represented by the utility function $u(x_1, x_2) = \min\{x_1, x_2\}$; the production sets Y_1 and Y_2 are represented in figure 3.

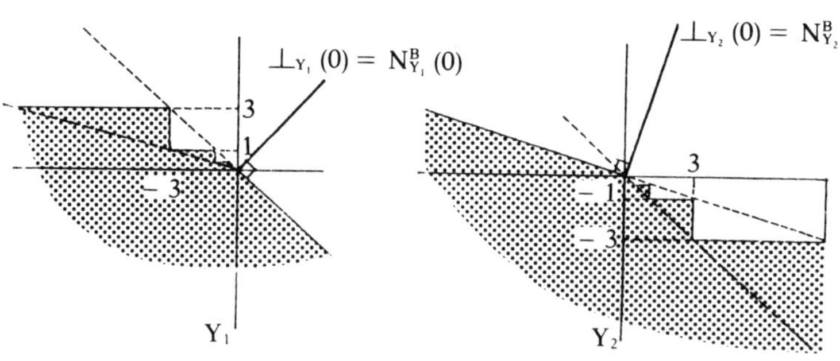

Figure 3.

One verifies that the triple (x_1^*, y_1^*, y_2^*), where $x_1^* = (1, 1)$, $y_1^* = 0$, $y_2^* = 0$ is a Pareto optimum and that $\perp_{Y_1}(y_1^*) \cap \perp_{Y_2}(y_2^*) = \{0\}$ [and also $N_{Y_1}^B(y_1^*) \cap N_{Y_2}^B(y_2^*) = \{0\}$]. Thus there exists no nonzero price system p^* verifying the conclusion of Corollary 1 with the cones $\perp_{Y_j}(\cdot)$ [or with Bouligand's cones].

Remark 3.2. In Theorem 3.1 and in the Corollaries 1 and 2, no assumption is made on the production sets Y_j. Actually, a free disposal assumption is implicitly made in the previous definitions of attainable allocations and Pareto optima.

We now call *Pareto optimum with no free disposal* an element

$$((x_i^*), (y_j^*)) \in \prod_{i=1}^{m} X_i \times \prod_{j=1}^{n} Y_j$$

such that $\sum_{i=1}^m x_i^* - \sum_{j=1}^n y_j^* - \omega = 0$ (instead of $\leqslant 0$ previously) and for which there exists no element $((x_i), (y_j)) \in \prod_{i=1}^m X_i \times \prod_{j=1}^n Y_j$ such that $\sum_{i=1}^m x_i - \sum_{j=1}^n y_j - \omega = 0$ (instead of $\leqslant 0$ previously) and $x_i \in P_i(x_1^*, \ldots, x_m^*)$ for every i.

Clearly, every Pareto optimum $((x_i^*), (y_j^*))$ verifying $\sum_{i=1}^m x_i^* - \sum_{j=1}^n y_j^* - \omega = 0$ is a Pareto optimum with no free disposal[6] and we refer to Cornet (1986) for a counterexample showing that it is not possible, in general, to replace the notion of a Pareto optimum in Theorem 3.1 by that of a Pareto optimum with no free disposal.

We point out, however, that, if *one* of the production sets Y_j satisfies the free disposal assumption $Y_j - R_+^\ell \subset Y_j$, then every Pareto optimum with no free disposal is a Pareto optimum; thus, under the additional Assumption P, both Theorem 3.1 and Corollary 1 hold for the two notions of Pareto optimality.

Remark 3.3. Note that, in the example of Remark 3.1, $\hat{N}_{Y_1}(0) = N_{Y_1}(0) = R_+^2$; hence the marginal pricing conditions $(\hat{\beta})$ and (β) do not restrict the choice of the price system p^* [recall that, under Assumption P, $\hat{N}_{Y_1}(0) \subset N_{Y_1}(0) \subset R_+^2$, by Proposition 3]. However, in section 5, we shall indicate two important situations (which include the previous example) in which it is possible to shrink significantly the cones $\hat{N}_{Y_j}(\cdot)$ in the marginal pricing conditions $(\hat{\beta})$ of Theorem 3.1 (and thus obtain a stronger conclusion).

4. Proof of Theorem 3.1

The structure of the proof of Theorem 3.1 is to show that the Pareto optimum $((x_i^*), (y_j^*))$ is the solution of a maximization problem (that we define explicitly below) and that its associated Kuhn-Tucker multiplier p^* (a vector in R^ℓ) verifies the conclusion of the theorem. This approach is standard in a differentiable framework (cf., for example, Samuelson 1947) but it was abandoned after the work by Arrow (1951) and Debreu (1951) in the convex case, and has been replaced by an argument using a separation theorem (cf., however, Malinvaud 1972).

The maximization problem defined below is very similar to the one considered in our previous article (cf. Cornet 1986). But, rather than using a sophisticated version of the Kuhn-Tucker Theorem [Clarke 1983 (Theorem 6.1.1) as in Cornet 1986, or Ioffe 1984 (Proposition 12) as in Khan 1987], we shall give a direct proof. This proof shows that the price system p^* can be obtained as the derivative *in a weak sense* of the value function of the maximization problem. In the following, we denote by $e = (1, \ldots, 1)$ the vector of R^ℓ whose coordinates are all equal to 1.

Step 1. $z^* = (0, (x_i^*), (y_j^*))$ is the unique[7] solution of the following maximization problem:

$P(\omega)$: maximize: $t - \|z - z^*\|^2$

subject to: $\sum_{i=1}^{m} x_i - \sum_{j=1}^{n} y_j + te \leqslant \omega$

and $z = (t, (x_i), (y_j)) \in Z \overset{\text{def}}{=} R \times \prod_{i=1}^{m} \text{cl}P_i^* \times \prod_{j=1}^{n} \text{cl}Y_j$.

Proof. Indeed, if z^* is not the unique solution of $P(\omega)$, there exists $z = (t, (x_i), (y_j)) \in Z$ different from z^* such that $0 \leqslant t - \|z - z^*\|^2$ and $u \overset{\text{def}}{=} -\sum_{i=1}^m x_i + \sum_{j=1}^n y_j - te + \omega \geqslant 0$. But, for every i, $x_i \in \text{cl}P_i^*$, hence there exists a sequence $(x_i^\nu) \subset P_i^*$ converging to x_i; similarly, for every j, $y_j \in \text{cl}Y_j$, hence there also exists a sequence $(y_j^\nu) \subset Y_j$ converging to y_j. We shall contradict the fact that $((x_i^*), (y_j^*))$ is a Pareto optimum by showing that, for ν large enough,

$$u^\nu \overset{\text{def}}{=} -\sum_{i=1}^{m} x_i^\nu + \sum_{j=1}^{n} y_j^\nu + \omega \geqslant 0.$$

We first notice that, for every ν,

$$u^\nu = u + te + \sum_{i=1}^{m} (x_i - x_i^\nu) - \sum_{j=1}^{n} (y_j - y_j^\nu)$$

and that the sequence (u^ν) converges to $u + te$. But $u + te \in \text{int}\, R_+^\ell$, since $u \geqslant 0$ and $t \geqslant \|z - z^*\|^2 > 0$ (this last inequality being strict since z is different from z^*). Hence, for ν large enough, $u^\nu \in \text{int}\, R_+^\ell \subset R_+^\ell$ and this ends the proof of Step 1. ■

We denote by $v(s)$ the value of the maximization problem $P(s)$ for every $s \in R^\ell$, that is,

$$v(s) = \sup\left\{t - \|z - z^*\|^2 \,\middle|\, \sum_{i=1}^{m} x_i - \sum_{j=1}^{n} y_j + te \leqslant s \right.$$
$$\left. \text{and} \quad z = (t, (x_i), (y_j)) \in Z \right\},$$

with the convention that $v(s) = -\infty$ if the set of constraints of the problem $P(s)$ is empty.

The value function $s \to v(s)$ is not, in general, differentiable at $s = \omega$, and we cannot interpret the price p^* as the gradient $\nabla v(\omega)$ of the function $v(\cdot)$ at ω. However, we show below that this property is true, in a "weak sense." We first note that for every $\omega^1 \geqslant \omega$, the problem $P(\omega^1)$ admits a solution z^1 and thus $v(\omega^1) \neq -\infty$ and $v(\omega^1) \neq +\infty$; indeed, this is a consequence of the facts that, first, for every $\omega^1 \geqslant \omega$, the set of constraints of the problem $P(\omega^1)$ contains z^* and, second, that the set $\{z | t - \|z - z^*\|^2 \geqslant \alpha\}$ is compact for every real number α.

Furthermore, the value function $v(\cdot)$ is increasing, in the sense that $v(\omega^1) \geqslant v(\omega^2)$ for every $\omega^1 \geqslant \omega^2$. Hence, by Ward's theorem (cf. Ward 1934, Chabrillac and Crouzeix 1987), the value function $v(\cdot)$ is differentiable almost everywhere (for the Lebesgue measure) on the open set $\Omega = \{\omega^1 \in R^\ell | \omega^1 \gg \omega\}$. Consequently, there exists a sequence $(w^\nu) \subset \Omega$ converging to ω such that the function $v(\cdot)$ is differentiable at ω^ν for every ν. We let $p^\nu = \nabla v(w^\nu)$ be the gradient of the value function $v(\cdot)$ at ω^ν, and we shall show below, first, that the sequence (p^ν) admits a subsequence, which converges to an element p^*, and, second, that such an element p^* verifies the conclusion of the theorem.

From above we deduce that, for every ν, there exists a solution (not necessarily unique) $z^\nu = (t^\nu, (x_i^\nu), (y_j^\nu))$ of the maximization problem $P(\omega^\nu)$, since $\omega^\nu \gg \omega$. We now show two intermediate properties of the sequences (z^ν) and (p^ν).

Step 2. The sequence (z^ν) converges to z^*.

Proof. Since the sequence (z^ν) remains in the compact set $\{z | t - \|z - z^*\|^2 \geqslant 0\}$, it suffices to show that, for every subsequence of (z^ν) (denoted identically in the following), converging to some element $z = (t, (x_i), (y_i))$, then $z = z^*$. Indeed, for every ν, we let $\alpha^\nu = \max_h(\omega_h^\nu - \omega_h) > 0$, then

$$0 = v(\omega) \leqslant t^\nu - \|z^\nu - z^*\|^2 = v(\omega^\nu) \leqslant v(\omega + \alpha^\nu e),$$

since the value function $v(\cdot)$ is increasing and since $\omega \leqslant \omega^\nu \leqslant \omega + \alpha^\nu e$.

On the other hand, one can easily show that $v(\omega + \alpha^\nu e) \leqslant v(\omega) + \alpha^\nu + (\alpha^\nu)^2$. Taking the limit, when $\nu \to \infty$, one gets $z \in Z$, $\sum_{i=1}^m x_i - \sum_{j=1}^n y_j - \omega \leqslant 0$, and, from the two above inequalities, one deduces that $t - \|z - z^*\|^2 = 0[= v(\omega)]$. Thus we have shown that z is a solution of $P(\omega)$ and since z^* is the unique solution of this problem, one deduces that $z = z^*$. ■

Step 3. The sequence (p^ν) verifies the following four conditions:

$$1 - 2t^\nu - p^\nu \cdot e = 0;$$

$$-p^\nu - 2(x_i^\nu - x_i^*) \in \hat{N}_{P_i^*}(x_i^\nu) \quad \text{for every } i;$$

$$p^\nu - 2(y_j^\nu - y_j^*) \in \hat{N}_{Y_j}(y_j^\nu) \quad \text{for every } j;$$

$$p^\nu \geqslant 0, \quad \text{and} \quad p^\nu \cdot \left(\sum_{i=1}^m x_i^\nu - \sum_{j=1}^n y_j^\nu - \omega\right) = 0.$$

Proof. Indeed, for $z = (t, (x_i), (y_j)) \in R^{1+\ell m+\ell n}$, $u \in R^\ell$, and $s = (z, u)$, we let

$$L(s) = t - |t|^2 - \sum_{i=1}^m \|x_i - x_i^*\|^2 - \sum_{j=1}^n \|y_j - y_j^*\|^2$$
$$- v\left(\sum_{i=1}^m x_i - \sum_{j=1}^n y_j + te + u\right),$$

where $v(\cdot)$ is the value function defined above.

We let $u^\nu = -\sum_{i=1}^m x_i^\nu + \sum_{j=1}^n y_j^\nu - te + \omega^\nu$ and one can easily check that $s^\nu = (z^\nu, u^\nu)$ is a maximum of the function L over the set $Z \times R_+^\ell$, that is, $L(s^\nu)[= 0] \geqslant L(s)$ for every $s \in Z \times R_+^\ell$.

But the function $L(\cdot)$ is differentiable at s^ν, since the value function $v(\cdot)$ is differentiable at ω^ν from our choice of the sequence (ω^ν). Noticing that the cone of limiting normal vectors to a Cartesian product of sets is equal to the Cartesian product of the cones of limiting normal vectors, from Proposition l.c, one deduces that:

$$\nabla L(s^\nu) \in \hat{N}_R(t^\nu) \times \prod_{i=1}^{m} \hat{N}_{P_i^*}(x_i^\nu) \times \prod_{j=1}^{n} \hat{N}_{Y_j}(y_j^\nu) \times \hat{N}_{R_+^\ell}(u^\nu).$$

From above, using the fact that $\hat{N}_R(t^\nu) = \{0\}$ [by Proposition 1.b, since $t^\nu \in \operatorname{int} R$] and $\hat{N}_{R_+^\ell}(u^\nu) = \{p \leqslant 0 | p \cdot u^\nu = 0\}$ [by Proposition 2.a], one deduces that the sequence (p^ν) verifies the above four conditions. ■

Step 4. We now end the proof of Theorem 3.1. Since (z^ν) converges to z^*, the sequence (t^ν) converges to 0, and the conditions $p^\nu \geqslant 0$ and $p^\nu \cdot e = 1 - 2t^\nu$ imply that the sequence (p^ν) is bounded. Hence, there exists a subsequence of (p^ν) (denoted identically in the following) which converges to some element $p^* \in R^\ell$. Taking the limit, when $\nu \to +\infty$, in the fourth and the first conditions of Step 3, one gets $p^* \geqslant 0$, $p^* \cdot (\sum_{i=1}^m x_i^* - \sum_{j=1}^n y_j^* - \omega) = 0$, and $p^* \cdot e = 1$. Hence p^* is a nonzero vector verifying Condition (γ) of the theorem. From the second condition of Step 3 and from Proposition 1.d, one deduces that, for every i, $-p^* \in \hat{N}_{P_i^*}(x_i^*)$ since (x_i^ν) converges to x_i^* and (p^ν) converges to p^*. Hence Condition ($\hat{\alpha}$) is satisfied. Similarly, one shows that Condition ($\hat{\beta}$) is also satisfied. ■

5. Some Consequences of Theorem 3.1

In this section we consider two situations in which it is possible to strengthen the conclusion of Theorem 3.1; in other words, the price system p^* will belong to a smaller set than the cones $\hat{N}_{Y_j}(\cdot)$ $(j = 1, \ldots, n)$ of limiting normal vectors.

The results presented below have their origins in the two following remarks. Firstly, if $((x_i^*), (y_j^*))$ is a Pareto optimum of the economy $\mathscr{E} = ((X_i, P_i), (Y_j), \omega)$, then it is also a Pareto optimum of every economy $\mathscr{E}^\nu = ((X_i, P_i), (Y_j^\nu), \omega)$ having production sets Y_j^ν smaller or equal to Y_j, and containing y_j^* for every j (and an analogous result can also be stated for the consumption sector). Then we shall choose the sets Y_j^ν so that the conclusion of Theorem 3.1 is stronger for the new production sets than for the original ones.

To summarize, the sets Y_j^ν are chosen to verify the following conditions:[8]

$$y_j^* \in Y_j^\nu \subset Y_j \qquad \text{and} \qquad \hat{N}_{Y_j^\nu}(y_j^*) \subsetneqq \hat{N}_{Y_j}(y_j^*).$$

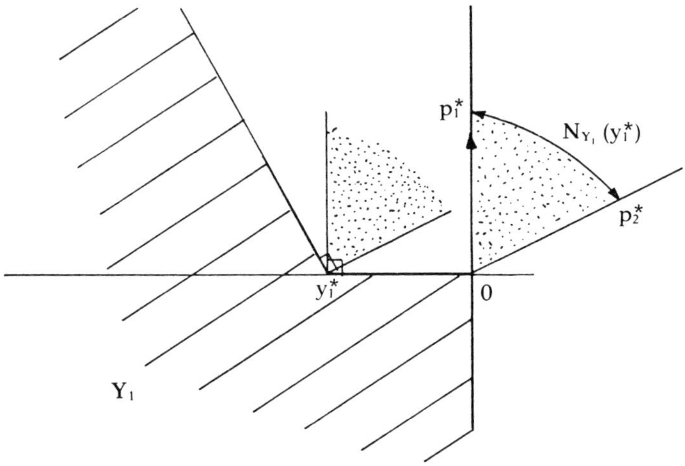

Figure 4.
$\hat{N}_{Y_1}(y_1^*) = \{\lambda p_1^* | \lambda \geqslant 0\} \cup \{\mu p_2^* | \mu \geqslant 0\}$;
$N_{Y_1}(y_1^*) = \{\lambda p_1^* + \mu p_2^* | \lambda \geqslant 0, \mu \geqslant 0\}$;
$\perp_{Y_1}(y_1^*) = k_{Y_1}(y_1^*)^0 = \{0\}$.

There exists many ways to choose the sets Y_j^ν so as to verify the above property; we consider only two of them.

A Simple Example of Inward Kinks: The Case of a Producer Having a Fixed Cost and Then a Linear One

We state a first result that will allow us to strengthen the conclusion of Theorem 3.1 for the important case of the production set of figure 4, that is, when a firm has a fixed set up cost and constant marginal costs.

If the production plan y_1^* of figure 4 corresponds to a Pareto optimum $((x_i^*), (y_j^*))$, from Theorem 3.1 we deduce the existence of a nonzero price system p^* satisfying, for the first producer, the condition $p^* \in \hat{N}_{Y_1}(y_1^*)$. The following result shows that, in this case, every nonzero price system in $\hat{N}_{Y_1}(y_1^*)$ (that is, the two open half-lines spanned by the vectors p_1^* and p_2^* represented on figure 4) verifies the conclusion of Theorem 3.1 and, moreover, every nonzero price system p^* in $\mathrm{clco}\hat{N}_{Y_1}(y_1^*)$, Clarke's normal cone also verifies the conclusion of Theorem 3.1, with the exception of the marginal pricing condition $(\hat{\beta})$ of the first producer.

In the following, we in fact consider a more general situation than the one of figure 4. We say that a subset Y_j of R^ℓ admits a *simple inward kink* at $y_j^* \in Y_j$ if, locally, the set Y_j can be written as a finite union of sets having smooth boundaries; formally, if there exist an open neighborhood V_j of y_j^* (in R^ℓ) and a finite number T of twice continuously differentiable functions $g_j^t\colon V_j \to R$ $(t = 1, \ldots, T)$ such that $\nabla g_j^t(y_j^*) \neq 0$ for every t, and if $Y_j \cap V_j$ can be written as follows:

$$Y_j \cap V_j = \bigcup_{t=1}^{T} \{y \in V_j | g_j^t(y) \leqslant 0\}.$$

A simple inward kink y_j^* is said to be *smooth* if there exist real numbers $\lambda^1 > 0, \ldots, \lambda^T > 0$ such that

$$\lambda^1 \nabla g_j^1(y_j^*) = \cdots = \lambda^T \nabla g_j^T(y_j^*).$$

Corollary 3. Let $((x_i^*), (y_j^*))$ be a Pareto optimum such that, for each consumer i, $x_i^* \in \mathrm{cl}P_i^*$ where $P_i^* = P_i(x_1^*, \ldots, x_m^*)$.

(a) If one of the production sets, say Y_1, admits at y_1^* a simple inward kink, then:

$$\{0\} \neq N_{Y_1}(y_1^*) \subset N \subset \bigcap_{i=1}^{m} \hat{N}_{P_i^*}(x_i^*) \cap \bigcap_{j=2}^{n} \hat{N}_{Y_j}(y_j^*),$$

where $N \overset{\text{def}}{=} \{\sum_{t=1}^{T} \lambda^t \nabla g_j^t(y_1^*) | \lambda^t \geqslant 0 \text{ for every } t\}$.

(b) The set $\{j = 1, \ldots, n | y_j^*$ is a simple inward kink of Y_j which is *not smooth*$\}$ has at most one element.

Part (a) of the corollary can be equivalently rewritten by saying that, for every nonzero price system p^* in the set N [which contains Clarke's normal cone $N_{Y_1}(y_1^*)$], $((x_i^*), (y_j^*), p^*)$ satisfies the conditions $(\hat{\alpha})$, $(\hat{\beta})$, (γ) of Theorem 3.1 (with the exception of the marginal pricing condition of the first producer). This implies, in particular, that $((x_i^*), (y_j^*), p^*)$ is a quasi-equilibrium for every nonzero price system p^* in $\hat{N}_{Y_1}(y_1^*)$.

Proof. Part (a). We first show that the set N contains Clarke's normal cone $N_{Y_1}(y_1^*)$. Indeed, from Rockafellar (1985, Corollary 6.3.1), $\hat{N}_{Y_1}(y_1^*) \subset N$ and by Farkas' lemma, we know that N is a closed convex cone. Consequently, $N_{Y_1}(y_1^*) = \mathrm{clco}\hat{N}_{Y_1}(y_1^*) \subset \mathrm{clco}N = N$.

Let p^* be a nonzero price system in the set N; then there exist real numbers $\lambda^t \geqslant 0$ $(t = 1, \ldots, T)$ such that $p^* = \sum_{t=1}^{T} \lambda^t \nabla g_j^t(y_1^*)$. We let

$g(y) = \sum_{t=1}^{T} \lambda^t g_j^t(y)$ and $\tilde{Y}_1 = \{y \in V_1 | g(y) \leqslant 0\}$. We now show that $\tilde{Y}_1 \subset Y_1$; indeed, if it is not true there exists an element $y \in \tilde{Y}_1$ which does not belong to Y_1, that is, such that $g_j^t(y) > 0$ for every t. Since $p^* = \sum_{t=1}^{T} \lambda^t \nabla g_j^t(y_1^*)$ is nonzero, the λ^t cannot be all equal to 0. Hence, $g(y) = \sum_{t=1}^{T} \lambda^t g_j^t(y) > 0$, which contradicts the fact that $y \in \tilde{Y}_1$.

We now consider the economy $\tilde{\mathscr{E}} = ((X_i, P_i), (\tilde{Y}_1, Y_2, \ldots, Y_n), \omega)$, which differs from the original economy $\mathscr{E}$ only with respect to the production set of the first producer, which we now take to be equal to $\tilde{Y}_1$ as defined above. Clearly, $((x_i^*), (y_j^*))$ is a Pareto optimum of the economy $\tilde{\mathscr{E}}$ since $y_1^* \in \tilde{Y}_1 \subset Y_1$ and we deduce from Theorem 3.1 that there exists a nonzero price system $\tilde{p}$ verifying the conditions $(\hat{\alpha})$, $(\hat{\beta})$, (γ) associated with the economy $\tilde{\mathscr{E}}$. In particular, the first producer verifies the marginal pricing condition: $\tilde{p} \in \hat{N}_{\tilde{Y}_1}(y_1^*)$ and $\hat{N}_{\tilde{Y}_1}(y_1^*) = \{\lambda \nabla g(y_1^*) | \lambda \geqslant 0\}$ [by Proposition 2.b]. Consequently, there exists $\tilde{\lambda} \geqslant 0$ such that $\tilde{p} = \tilde{\lambda} \nabla g(y_1^*)$ and, moreover, $\tilde{\lambda} > 0$ since $\tilde{p} \neq 0$. But $p^* = \nabla g(y^*)$, thus $p^* = (1/\tilde{\lambda})\tilde{p}$ and $p^* \in \bigcap_{i=1}^{m} \hat{N}_{P_i^*}(x_i^*) \cap \bigcap_{j=2}^{n} \hat{N}_{Y_j}(y_j^*)$. ■

Part (b). Suppose that two production sets, say the two first ones Y_1 and Y_2, admit simple inward kinks which are not smooth, respectively at y_1^* and y_2^*. We consider the economy $\tilde{\mathscr{E}}$ obtained from $\mathscr{E}$ by replacing each of the production sets Y_1 and Y_2, respectively, by one of their components with a smooth boundary that we note:

$$\tilde{Y}_1 = \{y \in V_1 | g_1^t(y) \leqslant 0\} \quad \text{and} \quad \tilde{Y}_2 = \{y \in V_2 | g_2^\tau(y) \leqslant 0\}.$$

By a similar argument to the one in Part (a), one shows that there exist real numbers $\lambda_1^t > 0$ and $\lambda_2^\tau > 0$ such that $\lambda_1^t \nabla g_1^t(y_1^*) = \lambda_2^\tau \nabla g_2^\tau(y_2^*)$ and that this vector verifies the conclusion of Theorem 3.1. But, since t is arbitrary in the set $\{1, \ldots, T\}$, we have shown that there exist real numbers $\lambda_1^t > 0$ $(t = 1, \ldots, T)$ such that $\lambda_1^t \nabla g_1^t(y_1^*) = \ldots = \lambda_1^T \nabla g_1^T(y_1^*)$, which contradicts the fact that the simple inward kink y_1^* is not smooth.

Guesnerie's Version of the Second Welfare Theorem

We first recall the definitions of the tangent and normal cones in the sense of Dubovickii and Miljutin (1965) denoted, respectively, $k_{Y_j}(y_j^*)$ and $n_{Y_j}(y_j^*)$, and which were used by Guesnerie (1975) to formalize his notion of *P.A. equilibrium* (the analogue of our notion of quasi-equilibrium). If C is a subset of R^ℓ and if $x^* \in \text{cl}C$, we let

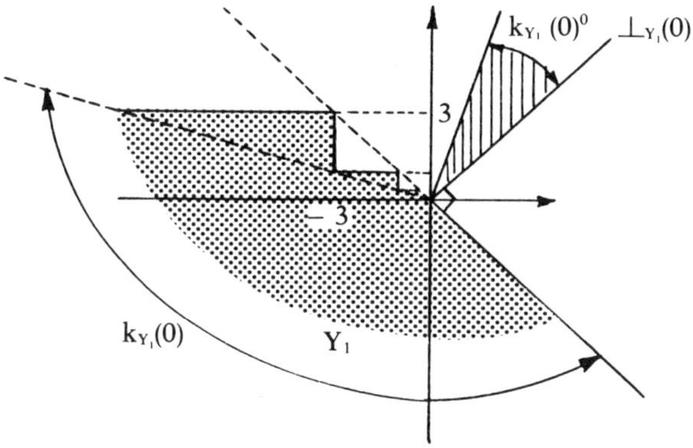

Figure 5.

$$k_C(x^*) = \{v \in R^\ell \mid \exists \varepsilon > 0,\ \forall t \in (0, \varepsilon]: x^* + tB(v, \varepsilon) \subset C\},$$

$$n_C(x^*) = [k_C(x^*)]^o \stackrel{\text{def}}{=} \{p \in R^\ell \mid p \cdot v \leqslant 0 \text{ for every } v \in k_C(x^*)\}$$

[i.e., the negative polar cone of $k_C(x^*)$].[9]

One can easily show that $k_C(x^*)$ is an open cone of vertex 0 (eventually empty and/or nonconvex) and that $n_C(x^*)$ is a closed convex cone of vertex 0 that contains the cone $\perp_C(x^*)$) [and also Bouligand's cone $N_C^B(x^*)$].

The two above definitions are illustrated in figure 5 (for the production set Y_1 defined previously in figure 3). In this example, one sees that the cone $k_{Y_1}(0)$ is convex, nonempty and that

$$\perp_{Y_1}(0) = N_{Y_1}^B(0) \subsetneqq n_{Y_1}(0) \subsetneqq N_{Y_1}(0) = N_{Y_1}(0) = R_+^\ell.$$

The following result shows that if the cones $k_{Y_j}(y_j^*)$ and $k_{P_i^*}(x_i^*)$ are all convex and nonempty, one can replace the cones of limiting normal vectors $\hat{N}_{Y_j}(\cdot)$, $\hat{N}_{P_i^*}(\cdot)$, in the conclusion of Theorem 3.1, by the normal cones of Dubovickii-Miljutin. For the production set Y_1 in figure 5, this permits to have a more precise result than that of Theorem 3.1.

Corollary 4. (Guesnerie 1975) Let $((x_i^*), (y_j^*))$ be a Pareto optimum such that, for each consumer i, $x_i^* \in \mathrm{cl}P_i^*$, where $P_i^* = P_i(x_1^*, \ldots, x_m^*)$. If the sets $k_{P_i^*}(x_i^*)$ $(i = 1, \ldots, m)$ and $k_{Y_j}(y_j^*)$ $(j = 1, \ldots, n)$ are all convex and nonempty, then there exists a nonzero price system p^* in R^ℓ such that

(α^k) for every i, $\quad -p^* \in [k_{P_i^*}(x_i^*)]^o$;

(β^k) for every j, $\quad p^* \in [k_{Y_j}(y_j^*)]^o$;

$$(\gamma) \quad p^* \geqslant 0, \quad \sum_{i=1}^{m} x_i^* - \sum_{j=1}^{n} y_j^* - \omega \leqslant 0,$$

$$\text{and} \quad p^* \cdot \left(\sum_{i=1}^{m} x_i^* - \sum_{j=1}^{n} y_j^* - \omega \right) = 0.$$

Remark 5.1. We note that the above result excludes the case considered previously, of a firm with a fixed set up cost and constant marginal costs (and, more generally, the case of simple inward kinks that are not smooth). Indeed, the convexity assumption of Corollary 4 is not satisfied by the production plan y_1^* of figure 5, i.e., the tangent cone of Dubovickii-Miljutin $k_{Y_1}(y_1^*)$ is not convex.

We shall deduce Corollary 4 from the second welfare theorem in the convex case (Corollary 2). We prepare the proof by a lemma which shows that, under the convexity assumption of the Dubovickii-Miljutin's tangent cones, on a neighborhood of x_i^* [resp. $_j^*$], one can define an interior approximation of the set P_i^* [resp. Y_j] by a convex one.

Lemma 2. Let $Z \subset R^\ell$, let $z^* \in \mathrm{cl}Z$, and let Q be a nonempty open convex cone of vertex 0 such that $Q \subset k_Z(z^*)$. Then there exists a sequence of closed convex cone (Q^ν) of vertex 0, and a sequence (ε^ν) of positive real numbers, verifying the three following conditions:

(i) $Q^\nu \subset Q^{\nu+1}$;

(ii) $Q \backslash \{0\} = \bigcup_\nu Q^\nu \backslash \{0\}$;

(iii) $\{z^*\} + [Q^\nu \backslash \{0\}] \cap B(0, \varepsilon^\nu) \subset Z$.

We note that the above property (iii) is not true, in general, if the cone Q^ν is replaced by the cone Q.

Proof of Lemma 2. The existence of an interior approximation of the cone Q by a sequence (Q^ν) of closed convex cones is standard; it suffices to choose an arbitrary element v_0 in the set $Q \cap -Q^o$ (which is easily shown to be nonempty) and to define, for every integer $\nu > 0$, $Q^\nu = \{v + \lambda_{u_0} \mid v \in \mathrm{cl}Q \text{ and } \lambda \geqslant (1/\nu)\,\|v\|\}$. We let the reader check that the sequence (Q^ν) verifies the conditions (i) and (ii) and we now show that the third one is satisfied. Indeed, for every fixed integer $\nu > 0$, the set $K = Q^\nu \cap \{v \in R^\ell \mid \|v\| = 1\}$ is a compact subset of $k_Z(z^*)$. From the definition of $k_Z(z^*)$, for every $v \in K$, there exist a positive real number $\varepsilon(v) > 0$ such that, for every $t \in (0, \varepsilon(v)]$, $z^* + tB(v, \varepsilon(v)) \subset Z$. Since K is compact, there exists a finite subset $\{v_1, \dots, v_q\}$ of K such that $K \subset \bigcup_{i=1}^{q} B(v_i, \varepsilon(v_i))$. One then verifies that condition (iii) holds for $\varepsilon^\nu = \min\{\varepsilon(v_i) \mid i = 1, \dots, q\}$. ■

We now prove Corollary 4.

Proof of Corollary 4. We first consider, for every integer ν, the economy $\mathscr{E}^\nu = ((X_i, P_i^\nu), (Y_j^\nu), \omega)$ where

$$P_i^\nu(x_1^*, \dots, x_m^*) = \{x_i^*\} + [Q_i^\nu \backslash \{0\}] \cap B(0, \varepsilon_i^\nu),$$

$$P_i^\nu(x) = P_i(x) \quad \text{if } x \neq (x_1^*, \dots, x_m^*) \ (i = 1, \dots, m);$$

$$Y_j^\nu = \{y_j^*\} + Q_j^\nu \cap B(0, \varepsilon_j^\nu) \ (j = 1, \dots, n),$$

where (Q_i^ν), (ε_i^ν) $(i = 1, \dots, m)$, (Q_j^ν), (ε_j^ν) $(j = 1, \dots, n)$ are associated by Lemma 2, respectively, to the sets $Z = P_i^*$, $Q = k_{P_i^*}(x_i^*)$ and $Z = Y_j$, $Q = k_{Y_j}(y_j^*)$.

Clearly, $((x_i^*), (y_j^*))$ is a Pareto optimum of the economy $\mathscr{E}^\nu$ for every ν, since $P_i^\nu(x_1^*, \dots, x_m^*) \subset P_i^*$ $(i = 1, \dots, m)$ and $y_j^* \in Y_j^\nu \subset Y_j$ $(j = 1, \dots, n)$ by Lemma 2. From Corollary 2, one deduces that, for every ν, there exists a price system $p^\nu \in R^\ell$ verifying $\| p^\nu \| = 1$ and such that for every i and j

$$p^\nu \cdot x_i^* \leqslant p^\nu \cdot x_i \quad \text{for every } x_i \in P_i^\nu(x_1^*, \dots, x_m^*),$$

$$p^\nu \cdot y_j^* \geqslant p^\nu \cdot y_j \quad \text{for every } y_j \in Y_j^\nu,$$

$$p^\nu \geqslant 0, \quad \sum_{i=1}^{m} x_i^* - \sum_{j=1}^{n} y_j^* - \omega \leqslant 0,$$

$$\text{and} \quad p^\nu \cdot \left(\sum_{i=1}^{m} x_i^* - \sum_{j=1}^{n} y_j^* - \omega \right) = 0.$$

Without any loss of generality, one can suppose that the sequence (p^ν) (which belongs to the unit sphere) converges to some nonzero element p^* in R^ℓ. We first show that $((x_i^*), (y_j^*), p^*)$ verifies Condition (α^k), or equivalently that, for every i and every $v \in k_{P_i^*}(x_i^*) \backslash \{0\}$, one has $p^* \cdot v \geqslant 0$. Indeed, from Lemma 2, for every $v \in k_{P_i^*}(x_i^*) \backslash \{0\}$ there exists an integer ν such that $v \in Q_i^\nu \backslash \{0\}$ and $x_i^* + \varepsilon_i^k v / \|v\| \in P_i^\nu(x_1^*, \dots, x_m^*)$. One then deduces from the first of the above conditions that $p^\nu \cdot x_i^* \leqslant p^\nu \cdot [x_i^* + \varepsilon_i^k v / \|v\|]$, hence $p^\nu \cdot v \geqslant 0$. Taking the limit, when $\nu \to \infty$, one gets $p^* \cdot v \geqslant 0$, which ends the proof of (α^k). Condition (β^k) is shown in a similar way and the condition (γ) is obtained from the last of the above three conditions, at the limit when $\nu \to \infty$. ■

6. Optimality of Marginal Pricing Equilibria

The aim of this section is to examine whether an analogue of the first fundamental theorem of welfare economics is satisfied in a nonconvex framework when the profit maximization rule for the firms is replaced by the marginal pricing rule. As we shall see, results in this area, however, are generally negative, unless one considers very specific situations.

Marginal Pricing Equilibrium

We again consider the model presented in the introduction, to which we add the description of the revenue of each consumer which, in contrast with the previous sections, is now given exogenously. We shall consider general revenue structures so as to finance firms' deficits.[10]

In the Walrasian model, the economy is privately owned; the revenue $r_i(p, (\pi_j))$ of the ith consumer is equal to $p \cdot \omega_i + \sum_{j=1}^{n} \theta_{ij}\pi_j$, that is, the sum of $p \cdot \omega_i$, the value of his (her) initial endowment ω_i, and of his (her) share $\theta_{ij}\pi_j$ of the profit π_j of the jth producer; in this case it is assumed that $\theta_{ij} \geqslant 0$ for every $i = 1, \ldots, m$, $j = 1, \ldots, n$, and that $\sum_{i=1}^{m} \theta_{ij} = 1$ for every j. Firms that follow the marginal (cost) pricing rule are usually publicly owned and the (eventual) deficits of these firms are covered by a tax system. Consequently, we need to consider more general revenue structures than that of private ownership.

We assume that the revenues $r_i(p, (\pi_j))$ of the ith consumer depend upon the price system p and of the profit/losses π_j of each producer j. We make the following basic assumption on the revenue functions r_i:

Assumption R. For every i, the function $(p, \pi) \rightarrow r_i(p, \pi)$ is continuous on $R_+^\ell \times R^n$, and verifies the following conditions for every p and $\pi = (\pi_j)$: (i) $\sum_{i=1}^{m} r_i(p, \pi) = p \cdot \omega + \sum_{j=1}^{n} \pi_j$, (ii) $r_i(\lambda p, \lambda \pi) = \lambda r_i(p, \pi)$ for every $\lambda > 0$, and (iii) $p \cdot \omega + \sum_{j=1}^{n} \pi_j > 0$ implies that $r_i(p, \pi) > 0$ for every i.

A *marginal pricing equilibrium* of the economy $\mathscr{E} = ((X_i, \preceq_i, r_i), (Y_j), \omega)$, is an element $((x_i^*), (y_j^*), p^*) \in R^{\ell m} \times R^{\ell n} \times [R^\ell \backslash \{0\}]$ verifying the following conditions:

(α) for every i, x_i^* is a greater element of $\preceq_i$ in the budget set $\{x \in X_i | p^* \cdot x \leqslant r_i(p^*, (p^* \cdot y_j^*))\}$;

(β) for every j, $y_j^* \in Y_j$ and $p^* \in N_{Y_j}(y_j^*)$; *(Clarke's normal cone)*

$$(\gamma) \quad p^* \geqslant 0, \quad \sum_{i=1}^{m} x_i^* - \sum_{j=1}^{n} y_j^* - \omega \leqslant 0,$$

$$\text{and} \quad p^* \cdot \left(\sum_{i=1}^{m} x_i^* - \sum_{j=1}^{n} y_j^* - \omega \right) = 0,$$

and a *production equilibrium* (for the marginal pricing rule) is an element $((y_j^*), p^*) \in R^{\ell n} \times [R^{\ell} \setminus \{0\}]$ satisfying only Condition (β). It is important to notice that, in these two definitions, the price system p^* is *the same* for each producer j.

The concept of marginal pricing equilibrium is essentially the one of *W.A. equilibrium* introduced by Guesnerie (1975) and often called marginal cost pricing equilibrium by various authors (cf. the references). The only difference between these two notions of equilibria comes from the way the marginal pricing condition (β) is formalized. Guesnerie (1975) was using Dubovickii-Miljutin's normal cone whereas we use here Clarke's one [as in the articles devoted to the existence problem of marginal pricing equilibria (cf. Cornet 1982, Bonnisseau and Cornet 1990, and the references of these papers)].

At the end of this section we show that if, in the above definition of equilibria, Clarke's normal cone is replaced by the cone of limiting normal vectors there may not exist equilibria in simple and nonpathological economic situations.[11]

Finally, we note that, for a private ownership economy $\mathscr{E}$, the notions of marginal pricing equilibria and of Walras equilibria coincide when each production set Y_j is convex (cf. Proposition 2.a).

The Example of Beato and Mas-Colell

In his 1975 article, Guesnerie shows that, in the absence of convexity assumption on the production sets Y_j, a marginal pricing equilibrium is not, in general, a Pareto optimum (see also Brown and Heal 1979). In this section, we shall present another counterexample, due to Beato and Mas-Colell (1986), which further shows that a marginal pricing equilibrium may not be aggregate productive efficient (and thus is not a Pareto optimum) in general.

The example of Beato and Mas-Colell (1985) consists of an economy with two commodities, two producers with production sets: $Y_1 = \{(y^1, y^2) \in R^2 | y^1 \leqslant 0 \text{ and } y^2 \leqslant -y^1\}$, which is convex, and $Y_2 = \{(y^1, y^2) \in R^2 | y^1 \leqslant 0 \text{ and } y^2 \leqslant (1/16)(y^1)^2\}$, which admits increasing returns to scale, and two consumers with consumption sets $X_1 = X_2 = R_+^2$, utility functions $u_1(x^1, x^2) = x^2$ and $u_2(x^1, x^2) = \min\{6x_1, x_2\}$, initial endowments $\omega_1 = (0, 50)$, $\omega_2 = (20,0)$, and revenue functions $r_1(p, \pi_1, \pi_2) = p \cdot \omega_1 + \pi_1 + \pi_2$, $r_2(p, \pi_1, \pi_2) = p \cdot \omega_2$, where π_1 (resp. π_2) denotes the profit/losses of the first (resp. second) producer. One checks that the economy $\mathscr{E} = ((X_i, u_i, r_i), (Y_1, Y_2), \omega)$ admits three marginal pricing equilibria $(x_1^\nu, x_2^\nu, y_1^\nu, y_2^\nu, p^\nu)$, $\nu = 1, 2, 3$, indicated in table 1.

One can verify that none of these three equilibria is aggregate productive efficient, that is, for $\nu \in \{1, 2, 3\}$, the total production plan $y_1^\nu + y_2^\nu$ does not belong to $\partial(Y_1 + Y_2)$, the boundary of the total production set (cf. figure 6, which represents the total production set $Y = Y_1 + Y_2$, its boundary, and the total equilibrium production plans $y^\nu = y_1^\nu + y_2^\nu$ for $\nu = 1, 2, 3$).

We refer to the articles by Bonnisseau and Cornet (1990a,c) for conditions that guarantee the existence of a marginal pricing equilibrium.

Marginal Pricing: Individual and Aggregate Levels

We first recall the following fundamental result for the profit maximization rule (Debreu 1959, ch. 3; Malinvaud 1972, p. 87). Let $y_j^* \in Y_j$ $(j = 1, \ldots, n)$ then, given the price system $p^* \in R^\ell$, the production plan $y^* = \sum_{j=1}^n y_j^*$ maximizes the profit $p^* \cdot y$ over the total production set $Y = \sum_{j=1}^n Y_j$ if and only if, for every j, the plan y_j^* maximizes the profit $p^* \cdot y_j$ over the individual production set Y_j.

We shall see below that, in a nonconvex framework, the analogue of this decentralization property is not satisfied, in general, when the profit maximization rule is replaced by the marginal pricing rule. Thus, in a nonconvex environment, it is important to be very precise in the definitions of the notions of "producer," of "unit of production," or of "technique of production."

To illustrate this situation we again consider the example of Beato and Mas-Colell and assume that the two producers of this economy are merged; in other words the sets Y_1 and Y_2 now represent the technological possibilities of the two "units of production" of the unique firm, whose production set is now $Y = Y_1 + Y_2$ (cf. figure 6). One can then check that the new economy $\tilde{\mathscr{E}} = ((X_i, \preceq_i, r_i), Y, \omega)$ has a unique marginal pricing equilibrium (x_1^*, x_2^*, y^*, p^*), for which $y^* = (-16, +16)$ and $p^* = (p_1^*, p_2^*)$ with $p_2^* \neq 0$ and $p_1^*/p_2^* = 3/2$. That is, y^* corresponds to the simple inward kink of the production set $Y = Y_1 + Y_2$.

We further note that the unique equilibrium (x_1^*, x_2^*, y^*, p^*) cannot be derived from any of the three marginal pricing equilibria of the original economy $\mathscr{E} = ((X_i, \preceq_i, r_i), (Y_1, Y_2), \omega)$, that is, $y^* \neq y_1^\nu + y_2^\nu$, for $\nu = 1, 2,$

Table 1

	x_1^ν	x_2^ν	y_1^ν	y_2^ν	p^ν
$\nu = 1$	$(0, 50)$	$(\frac{20}{7}, \frac{120}{7})$	$(-\frac{120}{7}, \frac{120}{7})$	$(0, 0)$	$(1, 1)$
$\nu = 2$	$(0, 46)$	$(\frac{20}{7}, \frac{120}{7})$	$(-\frac{64}{7}, \frac{64}{7})$	$(-8, 4)$	$(1, 1)$
$\nu = 3$	$[0, 50 - 4(33 - 12\sqrt{6})]$	$[\frac{4}{3}(33 - 12\sqrt{6}), 8(33 - 12\sqrt{6})]$	$(0, 0)$	$[-8(2\sqrt{6} - 3), 4(33 - 12\sqrt{6})]$	$(2\sqrt{6} - 3, 1)$

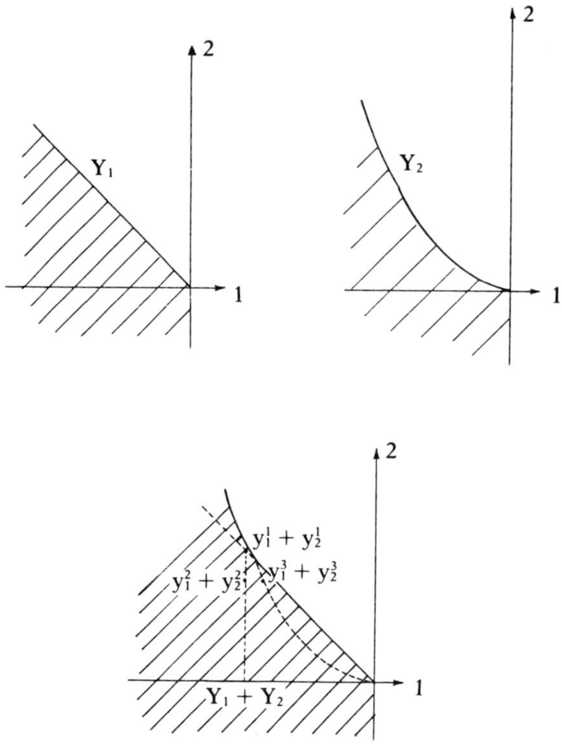

Figure 6.

3. In other words, one obtains different marginal pricing equilibria, in the two following situations: (i) by letting Y_1 and Y_2 represent the technological possibilities of two different producers, which both follow the marginal pricing rule, and (ii) by letting Y_1 and Y_2 represent two "units of production" of the same firm, which also follows the marginal pricing rule.

Remark 6.1. Note that if Y_j $(j = 1, \ldots, n)$ is a convex subset of R^ℓ and if y^* belongs to $Y = \sum_{j=1}^n Y_j$ then the above decentralization property and Proposition 2.a imply that

$$N_Y(y^*) \subset \bigcap_{j=1}^{n} N_{Y_j}(y_j^*) \qquad \text{for every } y_j^* \in Y_j$$

which implies the weaker property:

$$N_Y(y^*) \subset \bigcap_{j=1}^{n} N_{Y_j}(y_j^*) \qquad \text{for some } y_j^* \in Y_j.$$

However, in the absence of convexity assumptions, none of the two above inclusion holds in general. Consider the unique marginal pricing equilibrium (x_1^*, x_2^*, y^*, p^*) of the economy $\tilde{\mathscr{E}}$ then $p^* \in N_Y(y^*)$, but there exists no $y_1^* \in Y_1$, $y_2^* \in Y_2$ such that $y_1^* + y_2^* = y^*$, $p^* \in N_{Y_1}(y_1^*)$ and $p^* \in N_{Y_2}(y_2^*)$. Indeed, it suffices to verify that, for $y^* = (-16, +16)$, the only possible choices for y_1^* are $y_1^* = (-16, +16)$ and $y_1^* = (0, 0)$ [resp. for y_2^* are $y_2^* = (0, 0)$ and $y_2^* = (-16, +16)$] and that in these two cases p^* does not belong to $N_{Y_1}(y_1^*) \cap N_{Y_2}(y_2^*)$.

For a more detailed study of this problem, we refer to the article by Cornet and Rockafellar (1988).

Nonexistence of Equilibria When (β) Is Replaced by $(\hat{\beta})$

Remark 6.2. The economy $\tilde{\mathscr{E}} = ((X_i, \leq_i, r_i), Y, \omega)$ defined previously is a simple and nonpathological economic situation in which marginal pricing equilibria may not exist if, in the above definition of equilibria, the condition (β) is replaced by the stronger one $(\hat{\beta})$: "for every j, $p^* \in \hat{N}_{Y_j}(y_j^*)$" (cone of limiting normal vectors) [or by the condition "for every j, $p^* \in [k_Y(y^*)]^0$" (normal cone of Dubovickii-Miljutin)].

Indeed, as noted above the economy $\tilde{\mathscr{E}}$ admits a unique marginal pricing equilibrium (x_1^*, x_2^*, y^*, p^*) for which $p^* \in N_Y(y^*)$ but p^* does not belong to $\hat{N}_Y(y^*)$, noticing that

$$\hat{N}_Y(y^*) = \{\lambda(1, 1) | \lambda \geqslant 0\} \cup \{\mu(2, 1) | \mu \geqslant 0\}$$

[and $p^* \notin k_Y(y^*)^0$ since $k_Y(y^*)^0 = \{0\}$].

7. Appendix: Proof of Lemma 1

$[(TCM) \Rightarrow (\perp)]$. Condition TCM and the fact that the function $c_j(p_{I_j}^*, \cdot)$ is twice continuously differentiable imply that there exist real numbers $\hat{\rho} > 0$ and $\varepsilon > 0$ such that, for every $b_j \in B(b_j^*, \varepsilon)$:

$$\begin{aligned} p^* \cdot y_j^* &= p_{I_j}^* \cdot (-a_j^*) + p_{O_j}^* \cdot b_j^* = -c_j(p_{I_j}^*, b_j^*) + \nabla_{O_j} c_j(p_{I_j}^*, b_j^*) \cdot b_j^* \\ &\geqslant -c_j(p_{I_j}^*, b_j) + \nabla_{O_j} c_j(p_{I_j}^*, b_j^*) \cdot b_j - \hat{\rho} \| b_j - b_j^* \|^2. \end{aligned}$$

Let $y \in Y_j \cap B(y_j^*, \varepsilon)$, we define $a_j = -y|_{I_j}$ and $b_j = y|_{O_j}$. From the above inequality, noticing that $c_j(p_{I_j}^*, b_j^*) \leqslant p_{I_j}^* \cdot a_j$ since $a_j \in Y_j(b_j)$, and since $p_{O_j}^* = \nabla_{O_j} c_j(p_{I_j}^*, b_j^*)$ by Condition TCM, one deduces that

$$p^* \cdot y_j^* \geqslant p_{I_j}^* \cdot (-a_j) + p_{O_j}^* \cdot b_j - \hat{\rho} \| b_j - b_j^* \|^2 \geqslant p^* \cdot y - \hat{\rho} \| y - y_j^* \|^2.$$

We now let $y \in Y_j$ such that $y \notin B(y_j^*, \varepsilon)$. Then

$$p^* \cdot (y_j^* - y) \geqslant -\|p^*\| \cdot \|y - y_j^*\| \geqslant -(1/\varepsilon)\|p^*\| \cdot \|y - y_j^*\|^2.$$

The two above inequalities imply that the Condition ($\perp$) holds for $\rho = \max\{\hat{\rho}, \|p^*\|/\varepsilon\}$. ■

[($\perp$) $\Rightarrow$ (TCM)(i)]. Let $a_j \in Y_j(b_j^*)$, for every $t \in [0, 1]$, we let $a_j(t) = (1-t)a_j^* + ta_j$; then $a_j(t) \in Y_j(b_j^*)$ from the convexity of $Y_j(b_j^*)$. Hence Condition ($\perp$) implies [by taking $y_j = -a_j(t) + b_j^*$] that

$$tp^* \cdot [y_j^* - y_j] = p_{I_j}^* \cdot [-a_j^* + a_j(t)] \geqslant -\rho\|y_j^* - y_j\|^2$$
$$= -\rho\|a_j(t) - a_j^*\|^2 = -\rho t^2\|a_j - a_j^*\|^2.$$

Dividing by $t > 0$, taking the limit when $t \to 0$, one deduces that $p_{I_j}^* \cdot a_j^* \leqslant p_{I_j}^* \cdot a_j$. ■

We prepare the proof of the implication [($\perp$) $\Rightarrow$ (TCM)(ii)] with a Lemma.

Lemma 3. We make the assumptions of Lemma 1. (a) The correspondence $Y_j(\cdot)$ is lower semicontinuous (l.s.c.) at b_j^*.
(b) Let $v \in R^{O_j}$ and let $\rho > 0$ be given. For $t > 0$ small enough, there exists $a_j(t) \in R^{I_j}$ verifying the three following conditions:

(i) $a_j(t) \in Y_j(b_j^* + tv)$,

(ii) $\lim_{t \to 0} a_j(t) = a_j^*$,

(iii) $r(t) \cdot a_j(t) = c_j(r(t), b_j^* + tv)$,

where $r(t) \stackrel{\text{def}}{=} p_{I_j}^* + \rho[a_j(t) - a_j^*] \geqslant 0$.

Proof of Lemma 3. Part (a). Suppose that the correspondence $Y_j(\cdot)$ is not l.s.c. at b_j^*, then there exist $a_j^* \in Y_j(b_j^*)$, a real number $\varepsilon > 0$, and a sequence $(b^\nu) \subset R^{O_j}$ converging to b_j^* such that, for every ν, the sets $Y_j(b^\nu)$ and $B(a_j^*, \varepsilon)$ have an empty intersection. Since these two sets are convex and nonempty, they can be separated by a nonzero vector r^ν (say of norm one), that is, satisfying the inequality:

$$r^\nu \cdot a_j^* + \varepsilon \leqslant \sup\{r^\nu \cdot v | v \in B(a_j^*, \varepsilon)\} \leqslant \inf\{r^\nu \cdot a | a \in Y_j(b^\nu)\}.$$

Furthermore, the assumption that $Y_j(b^\nu) = Y_j(b^\nu) + R_+^\ell$ implies that $r^\nu \geqslant 0$. But the separation inequality and the fact that $a_j^* \in Y_j(b_j^*)$ imply that $c_j(r^\nu, b_j^*) + \varepsilon \leqslant r^\nu \cdot a_j^* + \varepsilon \leqslant c_j(r^\nu, b^\nu)$. From the Mean Value Theorem one then deduces that there exists $\lambda \in]0, 1[$ such that

$$\varepsilon \leqslant c_j(r^\nu, b^\nu) - c_j(r^\nu, b_j^*) = \nabla c_j(r^\nu, \lambda b^\nu + (1 - \lambda) b_j^*) \cdot (b^\nu - b_j^*).$$

Taking the limit, when $\nu \mapsto \infty$, one gets $\varepsilon \leqslant 0$, which contradicts the fact that ε is positive. ■

Part (b). We consider (for fixed a_j^*, b_j^*, $p_{I_j}^*$, $t \geqslant 0$, $v \in R^{O_j}$) the following minimization problem (in the variable a):

$$\begin{array}{lll} & \text{minimize:} & q_j(a) \stackrel{\text{def}}{=} p_{I_j}^* \cdot a + (\rho/2) \|a - a_j^*\|^2 \\ Q_j(t) & \text{subject to:} & a \in Y_j(b_j^* + tv). \end{array}$$

This problem admits a unique solution, denoted by $a_j(t)$, for $t \geqslant 0$ small enough, i.e., for every $t \geqslant 0$ such that $Y_j(b_j^* + tv)$ is convex and nonempty, since the criterion $q_j(\cdot)$ is quadratic and positive definite (cf. Rockafellar 1970). Moreover, the solution $a_j(t)$ verifies the first-order necessary and sufficient condition associated with the problem $Q_j(t)$, that is,

$$0 \geqslant \nabla q_j(a_j(t)) \cdot [a_j(t) - a] \qquad \text{for every} \qquad a \in Y_j(b_j^* + tv),$$

which is exactly Condition (iii) since $\nabla q_j(a_j(t) = p_{I_j}^* + \rho[a_j(t) - a_j^*]$. Furthermore one verifies that Assumption (i) of the lemma implies that $\nabla q_j(a_j(t)) \geqslant 0$.

We end the proof of Part (b) by showing that $a_j(t) \to a_j^*$ when $t \to 0_+$. Indeed, for $t > 0$ small enough, $a_j(t)$ is bounded since the criterion $q_j(\cdot)$ of the minimization problem is quadratic positive definite. Hence it suffices to show that if (t^ν) is a sequence converging to 0 and if $(a_j(t^\nu))$ converges to some element a_j^{**}, then $a_j^{**} = a_j^*$. Since the correspondence $Y(\cdot)$ is l.s.c. at b_j^* [Part (a)], there exists a sequence (a^ν) converging to a^* such that, for every ν, $a^\nu \in Y_j(b_j^* + t^\nu v)$, and thus $q_j(a_j(t^\nu)) \leqslant q_j(a^\nu)$. Taking the limit when $\nu \to +\infty$, one gets $q_j(a_j^{**}) \leqslant q_j(a^*)$ and the equality holds since $a_j^{**} \in Y_j(b_j^{**})$.

Consequently, a_j^{**} is a solution of the minimization problem $Q_j(0)$ and the uniqueness property implies that $a_j^{**} = a_j^*$.

$[(\perp) \Rightarrow (\text{TCM})(\text{ii})]$ Let $v \in R^{O_j}$. Condition $(\perp)$ implies that, for every $t > 0$ and every $a_j \in Y_j(b_j^* + tv)$,

$$\begin{aligned} p^* \cdot y_j^* = p_{I_j}^* \cdot (-a_j^*) + p_{O_j}^* \cdot b_j^* &\geqslant p_{I_j}^* \cdot (-a_j) + p_{O_j}^* \cdot (b_j^* + tv) \\ &\quad - \rho[\|a_j - a_j^*\|^2 + t^2 \|v\|^2]. \end{aligned}$$

Let $a_j(t)$ be the function defined by Lemma 3.b; from the above inequality, taking $a_j = a_j(t)$, one deduces that, for t small enough,

$$r(t)\cdot a_j^* \leqslant r(t)\cdot a_j(t) - tp_{O_j}^*\cdot v + \rho t^2\|v\|^2.$$

But $a_j^* \in Y_j(b_j^*$ and $a_j(t) \in Y_j(b_j^* + tv)$ [Lemma 3.b], hence,

$$c_j(r(t), b_j^*) \leqslant r(t)\cdot a_j^* \leqslant c_j(r(t), b_j^* + tv) - tp_{O_j}^*\cdot v + \rho t^2\|v\|^2.$$

From the Mean Value Theorem, there exists a real number $\lambda(t) \in]0, t[$ such that

$$p_{O_j}^*\cdot v \leqslant \nabla_{O_j} c_j(r(t), b_j^* + \lambda(t)v)\cdot v + \rho t\|v\|^2.$$

Taking the limit when $t \to 0$, one deduces that $p_{O_j}^*\cdot v \leqslant \nabla_{O_j} c_j(p_{I_j}^*, b_j^*)\cdot v$, since the mapping $\nabla_{O_j} c_j(\cdot\,,\cdot)$ is continuous [Assumption (iii)] and since $r(t) \to p_{I_j}^*$ (Lemma 3.b). But v is an arbitrary vector in R^{O_j}, hence, replacing v by $-v$, one deduces that the above inequality is in fact an equality. This shows that $p_{O_j}^* = \nabla_{O_j} c_j(p_{I_j}^*, b_j^*)$. ■

$(TCM) \Leftrightarrow (\hat{\beta})$. The implication $[(TCM) \Rightarrow (\hat{\beta})]$ is a consequence of the one $[(TCM) \Rightarrow (\perp)]$, shown previously and of the fact that the condition $(\perp)$ implies $(\hat{\beta})$.

Conversely, let (y_j^*, p^*) verify Condition $(\hat{\beta})$. Then there exist sequences $(y_j^\nu) \subset \mathrm{cl}Y_j$ and $(p^\nu) \subset R^\ell$ converging, respectively, to y_j^* and p^* and such that $p^\nu \in \perp_{Y_j}(y_j^\nu)$ for every ν. From above, one deduces that (y_j^ν, p^ν) verifies Condition (TCM), that is, denoting $a_j^\nu = -y_j^\nu|_{I_j}$ and $b_j^\nu = y_j^\nu|_{O_j}$, one has $c_j(p_{I_j}^\nu, b_j^\nu) \leqslant p_{I_j}^\nu\cdot a_j^\nu$ and $p_{O_j}^\nu = \nabla_{O_j} c_j(p_{I_j}^\nu, b_j^\nu)$. Taking the limit in the previous equality when $\nu \to \infty$, from the continuity assumption made on $\nabla_{O_j} c_j(\cdot\,,\cdot)$ one deduces that $p_{O_j}^* = \nabla_{O_j} c_j(p_{I_j}^*, b_j^*)$, that is, the second condition of (TCM) is satisfied.

Since the correspondence $Y_j(\cdot)$ is l.s.c. at b_j^* (Lemma 3.b), for every $a \in Y_j(b_j^*)$, there exists a sequence $(a^\nu) \in R^\ell$ converging to a and such that, for every ν, $a^\nu \subset Y_j(b_j^\nu)$. Hence $p_{I_j}^\nu\cdot a_j^\nu = c_j(p_{I_j}^\nu, b_j^\nu) \leqslant p_{I_j}^\nu\cdot a^\nu$. Taking the limit when $\nu \to \infty$, one gets $p_{I_j}^*\cdot a_j^* \leqslant p_{I_j}^*\cdot a$ for every $a \in Y_j(b_j^*)$, which shows that the first condition of (TCM) also holds. ■

$(TCM) \Leftrightarrow (\beta)$. In view of the previous equivalence and the definition of (β), it suffices to show that the set $TCM(y_j^*) \overset{\text{def}}{=} \{p \in R^\ell | (p, y_j^*) \text{ verifies } (TCM)\}$ is convex. Let p^1 and p^2 be two elements in this set, that is, for $\nu = 1, 2$, $c_j(p_{I_j}^\nu, b_j^*) = p_{I_j}^\nu\cdot a_j^*$ and $p_{O_j}^\nu = \nabla_{O_j} c_j(p_{I_j}^\nu, b_j^*)$. For every $\lambda \in [0, 1]$, we let $p(\lambda) = \lambda p_{I_j}^1 + (1-\lambda)p_{I_j}^2$ and the concavity of the function $c_j(\cdot\,, b_j^*)$ implies that

$$p(\lambda)\cdot a_j^* = \lambda p_{I_j}^1 \cdot a_j^* + (1-\lambda)p_{I_j}^2 \cdot a_j^*$$
$$= \lambda c_j(p_{I_j}^1, b_j^*) + (1-\lambda)c_j(p_{I_j}^2, b_j^*) \leqslant c_j(p(\lambda), b_j^*).$$

But the above inequality is in fact an equality, since $a_j^* \in Y_j(b_j^*)$. Hence $p(\lambda)$ verifies the first condition of (TCM).

The concavity of the function $c_j(\cdot\,, b)$, for fixed b [denoting by e_h ($h = 1, \ldots, \ell$) the vector in R^ℓ having all its coordinates null but the hth equal to one] implies that, for every $h \in O_j$,

$$\frac{\partial c_j}{\partial b_h}(p(\lambda), b_j^*) = \lim_{t\to 0_+} [c_j(p(\lambda), b_j^* + te_h) - c_j(p(\lambda), b_j^*)]/t$$
$$\geqslant \lambda \lim_{t\to 0_+} [c_j(p_{I_j}^1, b_j^* + te_h) - c_j(p_{I_j}^1, b_j^*)]/t$$
$$+ (1-\lambda) \lim_{t\to 0_+} [c_j(p_{I_j}^2, b_j^* + te_h) - c_j(p_{I_j}^2, b_j^*)]/t$$
$$\geqslant \lambda \frac{\partial c_j}{\partial b_h}(p_{I_j}^1, b_j^*) + (1-\lambda)\frac{\partial c_j}{\partial b_h}(p_{I_j}^2, b_j^*).$$

By a similar argument, taking above the limit when $t \to 0_-$ instead of $t \to 0_+$, one shows that the converse inequality also holds. Hence,

$$\nabla_{O_j} c_j(p(\lambda), b_j^*) = \lambda \nabla_{O_j} c_j(p_{I_j}^1, b_j^*) + (1-\lambda)\nabla_{O_j} c_j(p_{I_j}^2, b_j^*)$$
$$= [\lambda p^1 + (1-\lambda)p^2]_{O_j} = [p(\lambda)]_{O_j},$$

which implies that $p(\lambda)$ verifies the second condition of TCM. ∎

Notes

1. If $x = (x_h)$ and $y = (y_h)$ are two vectors of R^ℓ, the notation $x \geqslant y$ (resp. $x \gg y$) means that, for every coordinate h, $x_h \geqslant y_h$ (resp. $x_h > y_h$); we let $R_+^\ell = \{x \in R^\ell | x \geqslant 0\}$ and $R_{++}^\ell = \{x \in R^\ell | x \gg 0\}$ be the interior of R_+^ℓ; if A and B are two subsets of R^ℓ, we note $A + B = \{a + b | a \in A, b \in B\}$, the sum of the sets A and B, cl$A$, the closure of A, int A, the interior of A and ∂A, the boundary of A; we denote by $x \cdot y = \sum_{h=1}^{\ell} x_h y_h$, the scalar product of R^ℓ, by $\|x\| = (x \cdot x)^{1/2}$ the Euclidean norm, and by $B(x, r) = \{y \in R^\ell | \|y - x\| \leqslant r\}$, the closed Euclidean ball of center x and of radius $r \geqslant 0$.

2. That is, for every $x_i \in X_i$, the sets $\{x \in X_i | x \precsim_i x_i\}$ and $\{x \in X_i | x_i \precsim_i x\}$ are closed, the set $P_i(x_i)$ is convex, and $x_i \in \text{cl}P_i(x_i)$.

3. Note that this assumption is a consequence of Assumption P.

4. $\nabla_{O_j} c_j(r, b) = \left[\frac{\partial c_j}{\partial b_1}(r, b), \ldots, \frac{\partial c_j}{\partial b_\ell}(r, b)\right]$ denotes the gradient of the function $c_j(r, \cdot)$

at b (for a fixed r). It is important to note that the vector $\nabla_{O_j} c_j(r, b)$ belongs to R^{O_j} since, by definition, the cost function is defined for the elements $b \in R^{O_j}$.

5. This notion is usually referred to as a weak Pareto optimum to distinguish it from the stronger notion (called a Pareto optimum), for which the condition "for every i, $x_i \in P_i(x_1^*, \ldots, x_m^*)$" is replaced by "for every i, x_i is preferred or indifferent to x_i^* and there exists i_0 such that x_{i_0} is preferred to $x_{i_0}^*$," in a precise sense that we shall not make explicit here. Since we do not use the latter notion in this article, there is no risk of confusion.

6. One shows that $((x_i^*), (y_j^*))$ is a Pareto optimum of the economy $\mathscr{E}$ if and only if $((x_i^*), (y_1^*, \ldots, y_n^*, y_{n+1}^*))$, where $y_{n+1}^* = \sum_{i=1}^{m} x_i^* - \sum_{j=1}^{n} y_j^* - \omega$ is a Pareto optimum with no free disposal of the economy $\mathscr{E}_{n+1} = ((X_i, P_i), (Y_1, \ldots, Y_n, Y_{n+1}), \omega)$ obtained from the original economy $\mathscr{E}$ by the addition of a $(n + 1)$th producer having for production set $Y_{n+1} = -R_+^\ell$.

7. The perturbation term "$-\|z - z^*\|^2$" in the criterion of the problem $P(\omega)$ is the main difference with the problem considered in our previous article. This perturbation term is introduced to get the uniqueness property which is fundamental below to show the convergence of the sequence (z^ν).

8. It is important to notice that this situation cannot happen in the convex case (i.e., if Y_j and Y_j^ν are both convex) or with the cone $\perp_{Y_j}(\cdot)$ of perpendicular vectors. Indeed, from the definition of this cone, one verifies that $y_j^* \in Y_j^\nu \subset Y_j$ implies that $\perp_{Y_j}(y_j^*) \subset \perp_{Y_j^\nu}(y_j^*)$.

9. Dubovickii-Miljutin's normal cone $n_C(x^*)$ is defined by polarity from the notion of "tangent vector," formalized by the cone $k_C(x^*)$. The normal cones in the sense of Clarke or Bouligand can also be defined by polarity from a "tangential" notion, as expounded in the book by Clarke (1983).

10. We recall that profit maximizing firms do not suffer losses; indeed if, given the price system p, the producer j maximizes at y_j^* its profit $p \cdot y_j$ over its production set Y_j, then $\pi_j = p \cdot y_j^* \geqslant p \cdot 0 = 0$ [since $0 \in Y_j$]. However, this is no longer the case when the producer j follows the marginal cost pricing rule or, more generally, the marginal pricing rule.

11. This is due to the fact that the upper semicontinuity of the correspondence $y_j \to N_{Y_j}(y_j) \cap S$ from ∂Y_j to S [Proposition 3] plays a fundamental role in the existence problem [but not in the second welfare theorem]. Furthermore, one shows that if Y_j verifies Assumption P and if the correspondence $y_j \to \perp_{Y_j}(y_j) \cap S$ [resp. $k_{Y_j}(y_j)^0 \cap S$) is upper semicontinuous from ∂Y_j to S, then $N_{Y_j}(y_j) = \perp_{Y_j}(y_j)$ [resp. $N_{Y_j}(y_j) = k_{Y_j}(y_j)^0$) (cf. Cornet 1982, 1987).

References

Allais, M., 1953, *A la Recherche d'une Discipline Economique*. Paris: Ateliers Industria, 1943. Second edition, *Traité d'Economie Pure*. Paris: Imprimerie Nationale.

Arrow, K. J., 1951, "An Extension of the Basic Theorem of Classical Welfare Economics," *Proceedings of the Second Berkeley Symposium*, University of California Press.

Arrow, K. J. and L. Hurwicz, 1960, "The Firm in General Equilibrium Theory," in R. Marris and A. Wood (eds.), *The Corporate Economy* (Harvard University Press).

Beato, P., 1982, "The Existence of Marginal Cost Pricing Equilibria with Increasing Returns," *The Quarterly Journal of Economics*, 389, 669–688.

Beato, P. and A. Mas-Colell, 1985, "On Marginal Cost Pricing with Given Tax-Subsidy Rules," *Journal of Economic Theory*, 37, 356–365.

Boiteux, M., 1956, "La vente au coût marginal," *Bulletin de l'Association Suisse des Electriciens*, 47.

Boiteux, M., 1956, "Sur le gestion des monopoles publics astreints à l'équilibre budgétaire," *Econometrica*, 24, 22–40.

Bonnisseau, J. M., 1988, "On Two Existence Results of Equilibria in Economies with Increasing Returns," *Journal of Mathematical Economics*, 17.

Bonnisseau, J. M. and B. Cornet, 1988a, "Valuation Equilibrium and Pareto Optimum in Nonconvex Economies," *Journal of Mathematical Economics*, 17, 293–308.

Bonnisseau, J. M. and B. Cornet, 1988b, "Existence of Equilibria when Firms Follow Bounded Losses Pricing Rules," *Journal of Mathematical Economics*, 17, 119–147.

Bonnisseau, J. M. and B. Cornet, 1990a, "Existence of Marginal Cost Pricing Equilibria in an Economy with Several Nonconvex Firms," *Econometrica*, forthcoming.

Bonnisseau, J. M. and B. Cornet, 1990b, "Fixed-Point Theorems and Morse's Lemma for Lipschitzian Functions," *Journal of Mathematical Analysis and Applications*, forthcoming.

Bonnisseau, J. M. and B. Cornet, 1990c, "Existence of Marginal Cost Pricing Equilibria: The Nonsmooth Case," CORE Discussion Paper, Université Catholique de Louvain.

Bouligand, G., 1932, *Introduction à la géométrie infinitésimale directe*, Vuibert, Paris.

Brown, D. J. and G. M. Heal, 1979, "Equity, Efficiency and Increasing Returns," *Review of Economic Study*, 46, 571–585.

Brown, D. J. and G. M. Heal, 1980, "Two Parts Tariffs, Marginal Cost Pricing and Increasing Returns," *Journal of Public Economics*, 13, 22–50.

Brown, D. J. and G. M. Heal, 1982, "Existence, Local Uniqueness and Optimality of a Marginal Cost Pricing Equilibrium with Increasing Returns," Social Science Working Paper 415, California Institute of Technology.

Brown, D. J., Heal, G., Khan, Ali M., and R. Vohra, 1986, "On a General Existence Theorem for Marginal Cost Pricing Equilibria," *Journal of Economic Theory*, 38, 371–379.

Chabrillac, Y. and J. P. Crouzeix, 1987, "Continuity and Differentiability Properties of Monotone Real Functions of Several Real Variables," *Mathematical Programming Studies*, 30, 1–16.

Clarke, F., 1975, "Generalized Gradients and Applications," *Transactions of the American Mathematical Society*, 205, 247–262.

Clarke, F., 1983, *Optimization and Nonsmooth Analysis*. New York: John Wiley.

Cornet, B., 1982, "Existence of Equilibria in Economies with Increasing Returns," I.P. 311, University of California, Berkeley, in *Contributions to Operations Research and Economics: the Twentieth Anniversary of C.O.R.E.*, eds. B. Cornet and H. Tulkens (MIT Press, 1989).

Cornet, B., 1986, "The Second Welfare Theorem in Nonconvex Economies," CORE Discussion Paper 8630, Université Catholique de Louvain.

Cornet, B., 1987, "Regularity Properties of Open Tangent Cones," *Mathematical Programming Study*, 30, 17–33.

Cornet, B., 1988, "Topological Properties of the Set of Attainable Production Plans in a Nonconvex Production Economy," *Journal of Mathematical Economics*, 17, 275–292.

Cornet, B. and R. T. Rockafellar, 1990, "Separation Theorems and Supporting Price Theorems for Nonconvex Sets," CORE Discussion Paper, Université Catholique de Louvain.

Debreu, G., 1951, "The Coefficient of Resource Utilization," *Econometrica*, 19, 273–292.

Debreu, G., 1954, "Valuation Equilibrium and Pareto Optimum," *Proceedings of the National Academy of Sciences of the U.S.A.*, 40, 588–592.

Debreu, G., 1959, *Theory of Value*. New York: John Wiley.

Dierker, E., 1986, "When Does Marginal Cost Pricing Lead to Pareto Efficiency," *Zeitschrift für Nationalökonomie* Suppl. 5, 41–66.

Dierker, E., Guesnerie, R. and W. Neuefeind, 1985, "General Equilibrium where Some Firms Follow Special Pricing Rules," *Econometrica*, 53, 1369–1393.

Dubovickii, A. J. and A. Miljutin, 1965, "Extremum Problems in the Presence of Restrictions," *Zh. Vychisl. Mat. Fiz.*, 5, 395–453; *USSR Comp. Math. Math. Physics*, 5, 1–80.

Dupuit, J., 1952, "On the Measurement of the Utility of Public Works" (1844), translated in *International Economic Papers*, 83–110.

Gale, D. and A. Mas-Colell, 1977, "On the Role of Complete Transitive Preferences in Equilibrium Theory," in: *Equilibrium and Disequilibrium in Economic Theory*, Schwödiauer, ed., Dordrecht: Reidel, 7–14.

Guesnerie, R., 1975, "Pareto Optimality in Nonconvex Economies," *Econometrica*, 43, 1–29.

Guesnerie, R. 1984, *Modèles de l'Economie Publique*, Monographie du Séminaire d'Econométrie, Editions du CNRS, Paris.

Guesnerie, R., 1989, "First Best Allocation of Resources with Non Convexities in Production," Working Paper: E.H.E.S.S., Paris, in *Contributions to Operations Research and Economics: The Twentieth Anniversary of C.O.R.E.* (MIT Press).

Hildenbrand, W., 1974, *Core and Equilibria of a Large Economy*, Princeton: Princeton University Press.

Hotelling, H., 1938, "The General Welfare in Relation to Problems of Taxation and of Railway and Utility Rates," *Econometrica*, 6, 242–269.

Hotelling, H., 1939, "The Relation of Prices to Marginal Costs in an Optimum System," *Econometrica*, 7, 151–155.

Ioffe, A. D., 1984, Approximate Subdifferentials and Applications. I: The finite Dimensional Theory," *Transactions of the American Mathematical Society*, 281, 389–416.

Jouini, E., 1988, "A Remark on Clarke's Normal Cone and the Marginal Cost Pricing Rule," *Journal of Mathematical Economics*, 17, 309–315.

Kamiya, K., 1988, "Existence and Uniqueness of Equilibria with Increasing Returns," *Journal of Mathematical Economics*, 17, 149–178.

Khan, Ali M., 1987, "Ioffe's Normal Cone and the Foundations of Welfare Economics," Discussion Paper, University of Illinois.

Khan, Ali M. and R. Vohra, 1987, "An Extension of the Second Welfare Theorem to Economies with Non-Convexities and Public Goods," *Quarterly Journal of Economics*, 102, 223–241.

Laffont, J.-J., 1988, *Fondements de l'économie publique*, Economica second edition, Paris.

Lange, O., 1942, "The Foundations of Welfare Economics," *Econometrica*, 10, 215–228.

Malinvaud, E., 1972, *Leçons de théorie microéconomique*, Dunod, Paris.

Mantel, R., 1979, "Equilibrio con rendimiento crecientes a escala," *Anales de la Asociation Argentina de Economia Politica*, 1, 271–283.

Quinzii, M., 1986 "Rendements croissants et équilibre général," Thèse de Doctorat: Université de Paris II.

Quinzii, M., 1988, "Efficiency of marginal cost pricing equilibria," Working Paper, University of Southern California.

Rockafellar, R. T., 1970, *Convex Analysis*. Princeton: Princeton University Press.

Rockafellar, R. T., 1979, "Clarke's Tangent Cone and the Boundary of Closed Sets in R^n," *Nonlinear Analysis*, 3, 145–154.

Rockefellar, R. T., 1981, *The Theory of Subgradients and its Application to Problems of Optimization* (Berlin: Helderman).

Rockafellar, R. T., 1985, "Extensions of Subgradient Calculus with Applications to Optimization," *Nonlinear Analysis*, 9, 665–698.

Samuelson, P. A., 1947, *Foundations of Economic Analysis*, Cambridge: Harvard University Press.

Walras, L., *Etudes d'économie politique appliquée*.

Ward, A. J., 1934, "The Differential Structure of Real Functions," *Proceedings of the London Mathematical Society*, 39, 339–362.

Yun, K. K., 1984, "Pareto Optimality in Nonconvex Economies and Marginal Cost Pricing Equilibria," *Proceedings of the First International Conference of Korean Economists*.

2 Two Planning Procedures for All Economies

Jacques Crémer

Approximately twenty-five years ago, Edmond Malinvaud wrote his now classical article "Decentralized Procedures for Planning" ([18]). This article stimulated the interest of economists in the theory of planning procedures for at least three reasons. First, it stresses that theories of planning must throw light on practice. Second, it proposes a precise classification of the desirable properties for a planning procedure. Finally, it introduces a new theoretical approach. In section V Malinvaud describes a "large step" procedure, in the terminology of Weitzman ([23])—that is, a procedure in which the center, instead of feeling its way toward the optimum, uses the answers of the firms to build a global, but approximative, representation of their production sets.

In this article, we investigate the existence of planning procedures in a very general framework where we will impose no convexity hypothesis and where we will rule out neither externalities nor public goods. We will study this question by adapting and generalizing significantly two procedures, described in previous work ([6] and [9]), that could be applied only to the planning of the productive sector when no externalities or public goods were present. One of these procedures is a local procedure of the family of Heal's procedure, while the other belongs to the "quantity-quantity" family. In this respect, this study can be seen as a commentary on the respective benefits and disadvantages of large step and gradient procedures in the presence of increasing returns to scale.

Conceptually, our approach differs from other procedures studied in the literature by our modeling technique. Traditionally, each agent i is assumed to know a set $Y_i \in \Re^m$, and a vector $y \in \Re^m$ belongs to the aggregate production set of the economy if and only if it is the sum of vectors y_i, each of them belonging to the corresponding set Y_i. Here, we will still assume that i knows Y_i, but y will belong to Y if and only if it belongs to the intersection of the sets Y_i. If externalities are present, the production sets are not really separable as the production of firm 1 may depend on the production of firm 2, and our formulation allows us to describe the fact that firm 1 knows how the production decisions of firm 2 affect its own production set. Our problem is to find an element of Y that maximizes a social utility function u.

We need to impose only a monotonicity assumption on the set of Y_i's. For simplicity, consider the case where there exists a function f_i such that y belongs to Y_i if and only if $f_i(y)$ is smaller than or equal to 0 for every i. Then, we assume that f_i is monotonic in each of the components y_h of y. Of course, f_i can be increasing in some y_h and decreasing in others. This is our only economically significant assumption.

These very general hypotheses allow us to plan with the procedures described below all the economies for which procedures have been proposed, whether in convex ([2]), [17], [18], [22]) or nonconvex ([6], [9], [12], [13], [14]) environments, in the presence of public goods ([11], [19]) or externalities ([1], [10], [16]).

In section I we present our general framework, and an example of the type of problems that can be tackled by the procedures of this paper. Sections II and III present, respectively, the global and local algorithms. Section IV is the conclusion. Most of the proofs are relegated to three appendices. Some of them are very close to proofs already published in [6] and [9] and are not reproduced.

1. The Problem

We consider an economy in which the agents are trying to solve a problem of the type

$$\max u(y) \quad \text{subject to } y \in \bigcap_{i \in N} Y_i, \tag{P1}$$

where $y \in \Re^m$ is a vector of decisions and N the set $\{1, \dots, n\}$. The set $\bigcap_{i \in N} Y_i$ will also be called Y.

As is customary in the literature on planning procedures, there is no conflict of interest and all agents agree on the general form of the problem. However, information on the function u and the sets Y_i is dispersed among the agents. Because their rationality is bounded, they are unable to transmit to each other a complete description of these data, and they must use iterative planning methods in which each agent answers simple questions about his knowledge.

The planner knows the function u, and each agent i ($i = 1, \ldots, n$) the set Y_i. In practice, the planner could know *ex ante* (before the first stage of planning) not only u but also some set Y_i, for instance the consumption set of the economy. Similarly, in order to ensure that the sets Y_i satisfy the constraints that we will impose later, we may be led to assume that a single agent knows two of these sets. In these cases, these agents behave as if they were two separate agents.

We will use the term "agents" to designate either the set of $n + 1$ agents composed of the center and agents 1 to n, or only the set of agents 1 to n. The meaning of the term will always be clear from the context.

In section III we will assume that Y_i is of the form $\{y | f_i(y) \leqslant 0\}$, where f_i is a function from $\mathfrak{R}^m$ into $\mathfrak{R}$. In this case, (P1) becomes

$$\max u(y) \quad \text{subject to } f_i(y) \leqslant 0, \quad i = 1, \ldots, n. \tag{P2}$$

The only economically restrictive assumptions that we will make throughout the paper are monotonicity assumptions. In problem P2, they state that the functions f_i are monotonic in y_h, where $h = 1, \ldots, m$. More precisely, for each i, there exists a set $H_i \subset M = \{1, \ldots, m\}$, such that f_i is monotonically increasing (in the sense not strictly decreasing) in y_h if $h \in H_i$, and monotonically decreasing (in the sense not strictly increasing) in y_h if $h \notin H_i$.

To test the generality of this setup, we consider the problem of a utilitarian planner in charge of a κ-goods economy with λ firms and μ consumers. Firm $\gamma \in \{1, \ldots, \lambda\}$ produces a vector $z_\gamma \in \mathfrak{R}^\kappa$, according to the production function $g_\gamma(z_\gamma; (z_\delta)_{\delta \neq \gamma}) \leqslant 0$. The inclusion of the vectors z_δ, where $\delta \neq \gamma$, as arguments of g_γ allows for the presence of externalities. The total net production of the economy is $\sum_\gamma z_\gamma$, which must be allocated between private and public consumption. Let x_ζ be the allocation of private goods to consumer ζ, and let π be the total amount of public goods. Then, good h can be either consumed exclusively as a private good, or exclusively as a public good, or allocated between private and public consumption. The utility of consumer ζ is $u_\zeta(x_\zeta, \pi)$, and the problem of the planner can then be written:

$$\max u(\bar{u}_1, \bar{u}_2, \ldots, \bar{u}_\kappa)$$

$$\text{subject to} \begin{cases} g_\gamma(z_\gamma; (z_\delta)_{\delta \neq \gamma}) \leqslant 0 & \text{for all } \gamma = 1, \ldots, \lambda \\ \bar{u}_\zeta - u_\zeta(x_\zeta, \pi) \leqslant 0 & \text{for all } \zeta = 1, \ldots, \mu \\ \sum_\zeta x_\zeta + \pi - \sum_\gamma z_\gamma - \omega \leqslant 0 \end{cases} \tag{P3}$$

where ω is the vector of initial endowment of the economy. If we assume that from the point of view of firms each externality is either unambiguously good or bad, and that the functions u_ζ are monotonic in all arguments, problem P3 is of the form P2 in the variable

$$y = \{(z_\gamma)_{\gamma=1,\ldots,\lambda}, (x_\zeta)_{\zeta=1,\ldots,\mu}, \pi, (\bar{u}_\zeta)_{\zeta=1,\ldots,\mu}\} \in \Re^{\{\lambda\times\kappa+\mu\times\kappa+\kappa+\mu\}}.$$

The reader will easily see how other constraints representing the presence of consumption sets, locational considerations, and externalities in consumption can be added.

The central planning board knows *a priori* only the function u and the vector of initial resources ω. The procedure will enable it to acquire information on the other parameters of the problem P3, at the same time that it solves it.

Contrary to the MDP procedure introduced by Malinvaud ([19]) and Drèze and de la Vallée-Poussin ([11]), the procedures presented here require the consumers to choose a specific utility functions (the u_ζ's) among all those which could represent their preferences. The rule for building these utility functions should be set by the center. In practice in a planned economy, the role of the consumers would be played either by politicians or by bureaucrats knowledgeable about the demands of specific sectors of the population, and explaining these rules should not be an insurmountable problem.

It would be of course preferable to use only, as the MDP procedure can, data on the marginal rates of substitution. However, MDP type procedures incur a cost for this simplification as the center has imperfect control over the final allocation of utilities among consumers. It is true that Champsaur ([4]) has proved the following neutrality result: by an appropriate choice of the rule for allocating surplus at each iteration, the center can obtain any efficient allocation that is Pareto superior to the initial allocation. However, this neutrality result does not completly answer the problem, as the weights must be chosen *a priori* before any exchange of information, and choosing them so as to maximize a specific utilitarian social-welfare function would require knowledge of the utility functions of the agents and of the production function of the firms, which are known only *a posteriori*, once information has been accumulated by the center.

When monotonicity does not hold, the problem can sometimes be rewritten to fit our framework. For instance, a firm produces good 1 from good 2 so that the following relationship holds: $h(y_1, y_2) = y_1 - g(y_2) \leqslant 0$. Assume that for some y_2' (known only to the firm) g is increasing for y_2

smaller than y_2' and decreasing for y_2 greater than y_2'. Let us define the functions g_1 and g_2 as follows:

$$g_1(y_2) = \begin{cases} g(y_2) & \text{if } y_2 \leqslant y_2' \\ g(y_2') & \text{if } y_2 \geqslant y_2' \end{cases}$$

$$g_2(y_2) = \begin{cases} g(y_2') & \text{if } y_2 \leqslant y_2' \\ g(y_2) & \text{if } y_2 \geqslant y_2'. \end{cases}$$

Let $h_i(y) = y_1 - g_1(y_2)$. The set of constraints $\{h_1(y) \leqslant 0, h_2(y) \leqslant 0\}$ is equivalent to $h(y) \leqslant 0$, and h_1 and h_2 are both monotonic. Our procedures can be applied to this case if the firm builds its responses using h_1 and h_2, as if it were two separate agents. This strategy does not work if g first decreases on $[0, y_2']$ and then increases on $[y_2', +\infty]$.

II. The Global Procedure

Assumptions

In order to study the global procedure, it is simpler to work with problem P1. We must first present a definition of monotonicity adapted to this case.

Let H be a subset of $M = \{1, \ldots, m\}$. We define preorders $\leqslant_{H_i}$ and $<_{H_i}$ as follows:

$$\{y \leqslant_H y'\} \Leftrightarrow \{y_h \leqslant y_h' \text{ for all } h \in H, \text{ and } y_h' \leqslant y_h \text{ for all } h \notin H\},$$

$$\{y <_H y'\} \Leftrightarrow \{y \leqslant_H y' \text{ and } y_h' \neq y_h \text{ for all } h \in M\}.$$

To each $i \in N$ is associated a set H_i. The preorders $\leqslant_{H_i}$ and $<_{H_i}$ will be written $\leqslant_i$ and $<_i$. The preorder $\leqslant_M$ will be written either $\leqslant$ or $\leqslant_0$, and the preorder $<_M$ will be written either $<$ or $<_0$.

The sets Y_i satisfy the following two assumptions:

Assumption G1. For all $i \in N$, Y_i is closed.

Assumption G2. For all $i \in N$, if $y \in Y_i$ and $y' \leqslant_i y$, then $y' \in Y_i$.

G2 is a modified free disposal assumption. We will use the following definition: $\tilde{Y}_i$ is the set $\{y \in Y_i | \{y <_i y_i'\} \Rightarrow y_i' \notin Y_i\}$.

Before presenting the assumptions that we require on the function u, we must introduce the definition of a (closed) rectangle. First, we define the completed set $\overline{\mathfrak{R}^m}$ as the set of m-vectors $(x_1, x_2, \ldots, x_m)$ in which some of the components can be equal to $+\infty$ or $-\infty$. Given two elements x and z of $\overline{\Re^m}$, such that $x \leqslant z$, the rectangle $\overline{x,z}$ is the set of points $y \in \overline{\Re^m}$ such $x \leqslant y \leqslant z$. We now have the following assumptions:

Assumption G3. The C.P.B. knows how to solve the problem $\{\max u(y) | y \in \overline{x,z}\}$ for any rectangle $\overline{x,z}$.

This assumption is satisfied for instance when u is monotonic, as it is then possible to solve these problems by computing the value of u at one "corner" of the rectangle. If u is not monotonic, this still seems to be a minimal assumption. It states that the C.P.B. is able to find its preferred point on a very simple set.

Assumption G4. u is upper semicontinuous.

We assume that at the outset the center has some information about one of the optimal solutions y^* of P1. It knows a rectangle Y^0 to which y^* belongs (although, of course, it does not know y^*).

We will need three assumptions which are satisfied if Y^0 is bounded. We introduce them as separate assumptions for ease of future reference, rather than for the small gain in generality.

Assumption G5. The problem $\max_{y \in Y^0} u(y)$ admits a bounded solution, y^0.

Assumption G6. The set $Y^0 \cap \{y \in \Re^m | u(y) \geqslant u(y^*)\}$ is compact.

Before introducing the last assumption, we need a little more notation. First, if A is a subset of $\Re^m$, then $\mathring{A}$ is its interior. Second, if A and B are two sets in $\Re^m$, $A \sim B$ is the set $\{y \in \Re^m | y \in A \text{ and } y \in B\}$. Assumption G2 implies that $\mathring{Y}_i$ is equal to $Y_i \sim \tilde{Y}_i$.

Assumption G7. For all $i \in N$, the set $W_i = Y^0 \sim \mathring{Y}_i$ is bounded.

The Procedure

At stage s the C.P.B. knows a set Y^s, which contains y^*. It solves

$$\max u(y) \quad \text{subject to } y \in Y^s. \qquad (\mathrm{P}_1^s)$$

Let y^s be the solution to this problem; it will be the question asked of the agents. The answer of agent i, $\overline{y}_i^s$, will be equal to y^s, if y^s belongs to Y_i; it will be some $\overline{y}_i^s \in \tilde{Y}_i$ such that $\overline{y}_i^s <_i y^s$, if y^s does not belong to Y_i (we will restrict further the choice of $\overline{y}_i^s$ later).

Let N^s be the set $\{i \in N | y^s \notin Y^i\}$. Then, for all $i \in N^s$, the center knows that no element y of $\mathfrak{R}^m$ belongs to Y_i and satisfies $\overline{y}_i^s <_i y$ (by definition of $\tilde{Y}_i$). It builds Y^{s+1} by the following formula:

$$Y^{s+1} = Y^s \sim \left\{ \bigcup_{i \in N^s} \{y | \overline{y}_i^s <_i y\} \right\}. \tag{1}$$

No element of Y is eliminated when we go from Y^s to Y^{s+1}, so that the following formula holds:

$$y^* \in \cdots \subset Y^{s+1} \subset Y^s \subset \cdots Y^0. \tag{2}$$

The first two stages of the procedure are illustrated in figure 1. As s increases the set Y is approximated from the outside by a set which is a

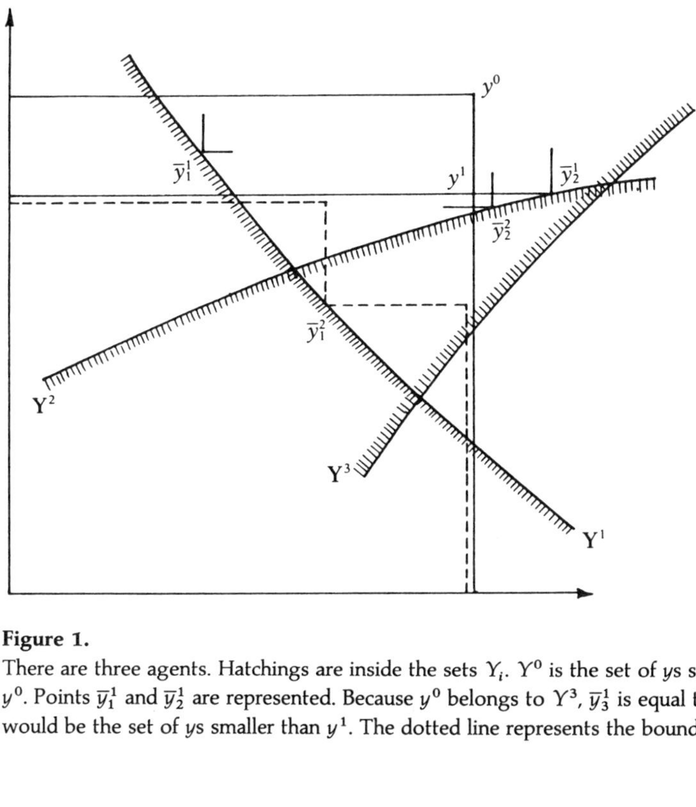

Figure 1.
There are three agents. Hatchings are inside the sets Y_i. Y^0 is the set of ys smaller than y^0. Points $\overline{y}_1^1$ and $\overline{y}_2^1$ are represented. Because y^0 belongs to Y^3, $\overline{y}_3^1$ is equal to y^0. Y^1 would be the set of ys smaller than y^1. The dotted line represents the boundary of Y^2.

union of rectangles (see Lemma 1 below). This approximation becomes finer and finer around the optimum (if it is on the frontier of Y), and stays coarse away from the optimum. This coarseness away from the optimum is a consequence of the fact that $u(y^s)$ is always greater than $u(y^*)$ (because y^* belongs to Y^s, for all s). Hence, if for all y in an approximating rectangle we have $u(y) < u(y^*)$, this rectangle will in general not be subdivided as the procedure progresses.

The procedure is well defined; indeed, at every stage, (a) the agents can answer the question of the centers (b) the set Y^s is not empty, and (c) the center can solve problem P_1^s. The proof of point a relies on assumption G2 and is left to the reader. Point b is obvious by formula (2). Point c is a direct consequence of assumption G3 and of the following lemma, whose proof can be found in Appendix I.

Lemma 1. For all s, there exist a finite family $\mathscr{V}^s$ of rectangles in $\Re^m$ such that Y^s is equal to $\bigcup_{V \in \mathscr{V}^s} V$.

Convergence

We prove that the procedure will locate a global solution of problem P1, by showing that y^s converges to a solution of P1.

We prove this in three steps. First, we have the following lemma:

Lemma 2. The sequence $\{y^s\}$ has at least one limit point.

Proof. By (2), the solution y^* belongs to Y^s for all s. Hence, $u(y^s)$ is greater than or equal to $u(y^*)$. Because y^s belongs to Y^0, the lemma is proved by assumption G6.

Let $\bar{y}$ be any limit point of $\{y^s\}$. Before showing that $\bar{y}$ is a solution of P1, we must impose a further restriction on the choices of $\bar{y}_i^s$ by the agents. Let C_i be a closed cone in $\Re^m$ such that, for any $y \in C_i$ different from 0, we have $0 <_i y$. Agent i can only announce a $\bar{y}_i^s$ such that $y^s - y_i^s$ belongs to C_i. This hypothesis generalizes a similar hypothesis made in ([6]), and guarantees that no component of $y^s - \bar{y}_i^s$ converges to zero faster than the others. In figure 1, it is easy to see that if the answer of agent 1 at iteration 1 is too close to the vertical line through y^1, it carries little information. Our hypothesis guarantees that the answers will not carry less and less information as the procedure progresses.

Lemma 3. For all i, $\overline{y}$ belongs to Y_i.

The proof is similar to that of proposition 1 of [6]. The changes of notation required to carry it over to the present framework are presented in Appendix II.

We can then show the final result of this section:

Theorem 1. $\overline{y}$ is a solution of P1.

Proof. We know that $\overline{y}$ belongs to $\bigcap_{i \in N} Y_i$, and therefore that $u(y^*)$ is greater than or equal to $u(\overline{y})$. For all s we have $u(y^s) \geqslant u(y^*)$. Hence, by assumption G4, and taking limits along a subsequence of $\{y^s\}$ converging to $\overline{y}$, we have

$$u(\overline{y}) = u(\text{limit}\, y^s) \geqslant \liminf u(y^s) \geqslant u(y^*).$$

Hence, $u(y)$ is equal to $u(y^*)$, and the result is proved.

Of course, if the center has a priori, before the planning process has even started, more knowledge about the sets Y_i then we assume, questions and answers can be simplified. For instance, it might know that, for some i, in order to test whether y belongs to Y_i it is sufficient to test whether a truncated vector $(y_{i_1}, y_{i_2}, \ldots, y_{i_p})$ belongs to Y_i' where $\{i_1, i_2, \ldots, i_p\}$ is a subset of M that he knows and Y_i' a subset of $\Re^p$ that he does not know. This is the case, for instance, in production planning without externalities, as in [6].

Even with these simplifications, the amount of information that the center must store in its memory grows without bounds as the procedure progresses. This is unavoidable. Casmiglia ([3]) has shown that it is impossible to build planning procedures that use finite messages and memories if one requires that they find the global optimum for a large enough class of technologies that include some with nondecreasing returns to scale (see also [7] and [21]). I fear, but I am not sure, that, for the procedure presented in this section, the quantity of information increases exponentially with the number of iterations.

There are also some difficulties associated with the fact that the center does not know a feasible decision vector y before the procedure has converged. Note, however, that for each $\overline{y}_i^s$ the set $\{y | y \leqslant_i \overline{y}_i^s\} \cap Y^0$ is a subset Y_i^s of Y_i. For s large enough the set $\bigcap_{i \in N}\{\bigcup_{t \leqslant s} Y_i^t\}$ should not be empty, and the center can choose the best plan in this set with a knowledge of an upper bound on the loss of utility due to truncation of the procedure.

III. Local Procedure

Assumptions

In this section we present a local procedure that solves problem P2 when the functions f_i and u are differentiable. The following five assumptions replace assumptions G1–G4 in this case:

Assumption L1. For all $i \in N$, f_i is continuously differentiable.

Assumption L2. For all $i \in N$, there exists a set $M_i \subset M$ such that f_i is monotonically increasing in each of the variables y_h, $h \in M_i$, and monotonically decreasing in each of the variables y_h, $h \notin M_i$.

In some of the cases where f_i does not satisfy either assumptions L1 or assumption L2, it will be possible to find p functions $f_{i_1}, f_{i_2}, \ldots, f_{i_p}$ satisfying L1 and L2 such that $f_i(y) \leqslant 0$ if and only if $f_{i_l}(y) \leqslant 0$ for all l in $\{1, \ldots, p\}$.

Assumption L3. The center knows how to solve the problem $\max_{y \in X} u(y)$ for any set X defined by linear inequalities.

Assumption L4. u is continuously differentiable.

We assume that before the planning process starts, the center knows $y^0 \in \mathfrak{R}^m$ such that $f_i(y^0) \leqslant 0$ for all i.

Assumption L5. The set of y in $\mathfrak{R}^m$ such that $f_i(y) \leqslant 0$ for all i and $u(y) \geqslant u(y^0)$ is compact.

Definition of a Critical Point

As we have discussed in the introduction, the local procedure only converges to a critical point of the problem. (Although I have not checked this explicitly, I believe that Hori's analysis ([15]) carries over to our setup and that the convergence will "nearly always" be to a local optimum. Indeed, because the procedure is monotonic, it will converge to a local minimum only in very exceptional cases, and if inflection points are isolated from each other, it should nearly never converge to one of them.)

As in [9] we will find it convenient to work with a definition of critical points that is slightly different from the usual one. It can be proved that these definitions are equivalent by the use of the theorems of the alternative (see [20], chapter 2).

Before presenting this definition, we must define the norm we shall use. For any $z \in \mathfrak{R}^m$, we write $\|z\| = \max_{h \in M} |z_h|$. The ball of center z and radius $a \geqslant 0$ will be called $B(z, a)$. It is the set of all $z' \in \mathfrak{R}^m$ such that $|z'_h - z_h| \leqslant a$ for all $h \in M$.

Definition 1. For $y \in Y$, let $P(y, 0)$ be the following problem:

$$\max_{r \in \mathfrak{R}^m} \nabla u(y) \cdot r$$

$$\text{subject to} \begin{cases} \nabla f_i(y) \cdot r \leqslant 0 & \text{for all } i \text{ such that } f_i(y) = 0 \\ \|r\| \leqslant 1. \end{cases}$$

If the maximum of this problem, $\gamma(y, 0)$, is equal to zero, then y is a critical point.

Note that $\gamma(y, 0)$ is always positive. The constraint $\|r\| \leqslant 1$ is imposed to ensure that $\gamma(y, 0)$ is finite for all y.

Approximating the Problem $P(y, 0)$

Because we want to use a discrete, rather than a continuous procedure, we must build a discrete approximation to the problem $P(y, 0)$.

Let $\tilde{Y}_i$ be the set of points in $\mathfrak{R}^m$ such that $f_i(y) = 0$ (this definition is consistent with that of section II). For all $y \in Y_i$, if $B(y, a) \cap \tilde{Y}_i$ is not empty, let $c_i(y, a)$ be the maximum (which could be infinite) of the reals c such that $\nabla f_i(y) \cdot (z - y) \leqslant ac$ and $z \in B(y, a)$ imply $z \in Y_i$. By assumption L2 such a $c_i(y, a)$ exists. The interested reader can easily build a graphic example which will show that $c_i(y, a)$ can be negative, by choosing a concave function f_i and a point y close enough or on $\tilde{Y}_i$.

For any $y \in Y$ and any $a > 0$, $Q(y, a)$ is the following problem:

$$\max_{\rho \in \mathfrak{R}^m} [u(y + \rho) - u(y)]$$

$$\text{subject to} \begin{cases} \nabla f_i(y) \cdot \rho \leqslant ac_i(y, a) & \text{if } B(y, a) \cap \tilde{Y}_i \neq \emptyset. \\ \|\rho\| \leqslant a \end{cases}$$

$Q(y, a)$ is an approximation of P2 around y. Note that $y + \rho$ belongs to Y for any feasible ρ. Let ρ^* be a solution to problem of $Q(y, a)$, and $\delta(y, a)$ the quantity $u(y + \rho^*) - u(y)$. Then, $\delta(y, a)$ is the greatest increase in utility that can be generated in the local approximation to the set Y built from the answers of the agents.

The following lemma is proved in Appendix III.

Lemma 4. Let $\{y^t\}$ be a sequence in Y converging to $y \in Y$, and let $\{a^t\}$ be a sequence of strictly positive real numbers converging to $a = 0$, then we have $\liminf \delta(y^t, a^t)/a^t \geqslant \gamma(y, 0)$.

The Procedure

At the outset, the center knows a feasible y^0, its first approximation of the optimal solution. It also chooses an arbitrary initial pitch a^0. At stage s, the center proposes to the agents a feasible vector y^s that belongs to Y and therefore to all the Y_is, and a pitch a^s which will decrease as the procedure advances. Agent i ($i = 1, \ldots, n$) then tells the planning board whether $B(y^s, a) \cap \tilde{Y}_i$ is empty and, if it is not, provides the planning board with $\nabla f_i(y^s)$ and $c_i(y^s, a^s)$; the definitions presented above show that by doing so agent i announces to the center a subset of $\mathfrak{R}^m$ entirely contained in Y_i and close enough to y^s. Then the center computes $\delta(y^s, a^s)$, that is, the greatest increase in utility that it can obtain if it is constrained by the local approximations to the sets Y_i communicated by the agents. Then, for some arbitrary constant $w > 0$, which indicates the minimal acceptable speed of increase in utility:

- If $\delta(y^s, a^s)$ is greater than or equal to $\omega(a^s)^2$, it chooses $a^s + 1 = a^s$ and $y^{s+1} = y^s + \rho^s$ for some ρ^s solution of $Q(y^s, a^s)$.
- if $\delta(y^s, a^s)$ is strictly smaller than $\omega(a^s)^2$, it chooses $a^{s+1} = a^s/2$ and $y^{s+1} = y^s$.

Figure 2 provides a graphic interpretation. In that figure, $B(y^s, a) \cap \tilde{Y}_3$ is empty. The linear constraints $\nabla f_1(y^s)\nabla\rho \leqslant ac_1(y^s, a)$ and $\nabla f_2(y^s)\cdot\rho \leqslant ac_2(y^s, a)$ are represented. They are, in a loose sense, parallel to the constraints $f_1(y) \leqslant 0$ and $f_2(y) \leqslant 0$. The size of the step a^s provides a limit to the speed of adjustment of the procedure, so that it does not overstep the domain where the local approximation is valid. Over time, y^s moves in the direction of the gradient of u, closer and closer to the binding constraints.

It is easy to show that the procedure is well defined, monotonic, and that y^s belongs to Y for all s. The proofs of lemma 5 and theorem 2 below can be found in [9], with a minor change of notation (changing $\overline{y}, \overline{y}', \overline{y}^s$ into y, y', and y^s, respectively). These proofs owe a lot to the work of Henry and Zylbergerg ([14]).

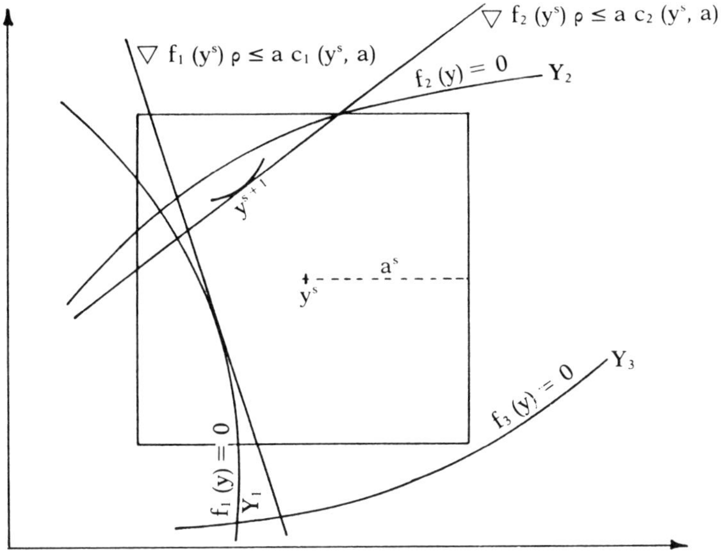

Figure 2.

Lemma 5. The sequence $\{a^s\}$ converges to zero.

Theorem 2. The sequence $\{y^s\}$ has at least one limit point. Every limit point of $\{y^s\}$ is a critical point.

IV. Conclusion

In the conclusion of [18], Malinvaud wonders:

If now we pause to consider the extent to which the procedures described above are similar to those adopted today in various countries, there is an important difference which we cannot fail to notice. In the three procedures we examined, the prospective indices supplied to firms related exclusively to the prices of the different goods. In practice, production targets are fixed by the planning bureau for industries or firms. These targets play an important part not merely in defining the plan, but also during the process of preparing it.

The study presented here proposes two procedures where production quotas play an essential role, and therefore come somewhat closer to the practice to which Malinvaud was making reference. The use of quotas allows us to plan economies where returns to scale are not necessarily decreasing. The contribution of this article is to prove that, if we neglect incentives considerations, practically all economies can be planned in this way, whatever the degree of complexity of the production sets or of the preferences of the agents.

Appendix I

In order to prove Lemma 1, we need three preliminary lemmas.

Lemma A1. Let S_1 and S_2 be families of sets. Then

$$\bigcup_{A \in S_1} A \sim \bigcup_{B \in S_2} B = \bigcup_{A \in S_1} \left\{ \bigcap_{B \in S_2} \{A \sim B\} \right\}$$

Proof.

$$x \in \left\{ \bigcup_{A \in S_1} A \right\} \sim \left\{ \bigcup_{B \in S_2} B \right\}$$

$$\Leftrightarrow \{\exists A \in S_1 \text{ such that } x \in A\} \text{ and } \{\forall B \in S_2, x \notin B\}$$

$$\Leftrightarrow \exists A \in S_1 \text{ such that } x \in \bigcap_{B \in S_2} \{A \sim B\}$$

$$\Leftrightarrow x \in \bigcup_{A \in S_1} \left\{ \bigcap_{B \in S_2} \{A \sim B\} \right\}.$$

Lemma A2. If $V = \overline{w, x}$ is a rectangle and P is a subset of M, then for any $z \in \mathfrak{R}^m$ the set $V \sim \{y | z <_p y\}$ is either a union of rectangles or the empty set.

Proof. Let P' be the set of $h \in M$ such that we have $h \in P$ and $z_h \leqslant x_h$. Let Q' be the set of $h \in M$ such that $h \in P$ and $z_h \geqslant w_h$. If P' and Q' are empty $V \sim \{y | y <_p z\}$ is empty. If not, for each $h \in Q'$, let $w^h = (w_1, w_2, \ldots, w_{h-1}, z_h, \ldots, w_m)$, and for each $h \in P'$ let $x^h = (x_1, x_2, \ldots, x_{h-1}, z_h, \ldots, x_m)$. Then, it is easy to check that $V \sim \{y | y <_p z\}$ is the set $\{\bigcup_{h \in P'} \overline{w, x^h}\} \cup \{\bigcup_{h \in Q'} \overline{w^h, x}\}$.

Lemma A3. If $\mathscr{V}$ and $\mathscr{W}$ are families of rectangles $\{\bigcup_{V \in \mathscr{V}} V\} \cap \{\bigcap_{W \in \mathscr{W}} W\}$ is either a union of rectangles or the empty set.

Proof. $(\bigcup_{V \in \mathscr{V}} V) \cap (\bigcup_{W \in \mathscr{W}} W) = \bigcup_{V \times W \in \mathscr{V} \times \mathscr{W}} (V \cap W)$. It is therefore enough to prove that if V and W are rectangles their intersection is either a rectangle or the empty set. Let $V = \overline{w, x}$ and $W = \overline{w', x'}$. The vector y

belongs to $V \cap W$ if and only if $\max(w_h, w'_h) \leqslant y_h \leqslant \min(x_h, x'_h)$ for all $h \in M$. Hence, if there exists an h such that $\max(w_h, w'_h)$ is strictly greater than $\min(x_h, x'_h)$, $V \cap W$ is empty and the result is proved. If not, $V \cap W = \overline{w'', x''}$ where w''_h is equal to $\max(w_h, w'_h)$ and x''_h is equal to $\min(x_h, x'_h)$ for all h.

Proof of Lemma 1. The proof is by induction. The result is clearly true for $s = 0$. We assume that it is true for $s \geqslant 0$ and show that it is true for $s + 1$.

We have $Y^{s+1} = Y^s \sim \{\bigcup_{i \in N^s} \{y | \overline{y}_i^s <_i y\}\}$. By Lemma A1, Y^{s+1} is equal to

$$\bigcup_{V \in \mathscr{Y}^s} \left\{ \bigcap_{i \in N^s} \{V \sim \{y | \overline{y}_i^s <_i y\}\} \right\}.$$

By Lemmas A2 and A3 this set is either empty or a union of rectangles, and we know that it is not empty as y^* belongs to Y^{s+1}.

Appendix II

Proof of Lemma 2. The proof of Proposition 1 in [6] carries over with the following changes in notation: k becomes i, $\overline{q}_k$ becomes $\overline{y}$, y_s^k becomes y^s, q_k^s becomes $\overline{y}_i^s$, W_k becomes $W_i = \mathring{Y}/\mathring{Y}_i$, $\mathfrak{R}^{n+}$ becomes $R_i^{n+} = \{y \in R^n | 0 \leqslant_i y\}$, Y_k^s becomes Y^s.

Appendix III

Let $P(y, a)$ be the following problem:

$$\max_{r \in \mathfrak{R}^m} [u(y + ar) - u(y)]$$

$$\text{subject to} \begin{cases} \nabla f_i(y) \cdot r \leqslant c_i(y, a) & \text{if } B(y, a) \cap \tilde{Y}_i \neq \emptyset. \\ \|r\| \leqslant 1 \end{cases}$$

Clearly, if ρ^* is a solution to $Q(y, a)$, ρ^*/a is a solution of $P(y, a)$ and, if r^* is a solution of $P(y, a)$, ar^* is a solution of $Q(y, a)$. Let $\gamma(y, a) = [u(y + ar^*) - u(y)]/a$. We have $\delta(y, a) = a\gamma(y, a)$. It is more convenient to use $P(y, a)$ than $Q(y, a)$ for proving Lemma 4.

Before proceeding, it is convenient to rewrite the problems $P(y, a)$ and $P(y, 0)$ in a symmetric way. First, if $f_i(y_i) = 0$, let $c_i(y, 0) = 0$. Then, for $a \geqslant 0$ if $f_i(y_i) \leqslant 0$ and $B(y, a) \cap \tilde{Y}_i$ is empty, let $c_i(y, a) = \sum_h |\partial f_i(y)/\partial y_h|$ (then $\|r\| \leqslant 1$ implies $\nabla f_i(y) \cdot r \leqslant c_i(y, a)$). Finally, define $m(y, a, r)$ as

$(u(y + ar) - u(y))/a$ if $a > 0$ and $\nabla u(y) \cdot r$ if $a = 0$. Then, for $a \geqslant 0$, $P(y, a)$ can be written as

$$\max_{r \in \Re m} m(y, a, r)$$

$$\text{subject to} \begin{cases} \nabla f_i(y) \cdot r \leqslant c_i(y, a) & \text{for all } i \\ \|r\| \leqslant 1 \end{cases}$$

We can then prove the following.

Lemma C1. Let $\{y^t\}$ be a sequence in Y_i converging to $y \in Y_i$, and let $\{a^t\}$ be a sequence of strictly positive real numbers converging to $a = 0$; then $\liminf c_i(y^t, a^t) \geqslant c_i(y, 0)$.

Proof. The proof of Lemma 1 of [9] carries over if the subscript i is dropped from y_i^t and y_i.

Lemma C2. Let $\{y^t\}$ be a sequence in Y converging to $y \in Y$, and let $\{a^t\}$ be a sequence of strictly positive real numbers converging to $a = 0$; then $m(y^t, a^t, r)$ converges to $m(y, 0, r)$ for all $r \in \Re^m$.

Proof. See the proof of lemma 2 in [9].

Proof of Lemma 4. (This proof is similar, but somewhat shorter, than the proof of lemma 3 in [9].)

Let us choose any r^* feasible for $P(y, 0)$ and satisfying $\nabla u(y) \cdot r^* = \gamma(y, 0)$. Choose also an arbitrary α, $0 < \alpha < 1$ and let $r' = \alpha r^*$. We first show that for t large enough r' if feasible for $P(y^t, a^t)$.

First, it is clear that $\|r'\|$ is smaller than one.

Second, by continuity of ∇f_i we have

$$\begin{aligned} \lim \nabla f_i(y^t) \cdot r' &= \alpha \lim_{t \to \infty} \nabla f_i(y^t) \cdot r^* \\ &= \alpha \nabla f_i(y) \cdot r^* \\ &\leqslant \alpha c_i(y, 0) \\ &\leqslant \alpha \liminf_{t \to \infty} c_i(y^t, a^t) \qquad \text{(by lemma C1).} \end{aligned}$$

Hence there exists a T such that $t > T$ implies $\nabla f_i(y^t) \cdot r' \leqslant c_i(y^t, a^t)$.

For $t > T$, r' is a feasible solution of $P(y^t, a^t)$. Therefore $m(y^t, a^t, r')$ is smaller than $\gamma(y^t, a^t)$ for all t, and we have

$$\begin{aligned}\liminf \gamma(y^t, a^t) &\geqslant \lim m(y^t, a^t, r') \\ &= m(y, 0, r') \qquad \text{(by Lemma C2)} \\ &= \alpha m(y, 0, r^*) \\ &= \alpha\gamma(y, 0).\end{aligned}$$

Because this is true for any $\alpha < 1$, however close to 1, Lemma 4 is proved.

References

[1] Aoki, M., "Two Planning Processes for an Economy with Production Externalities," *International Economic Review* 12(1971), 403–413.

[2] Arrow, K. J. and L. Hurwicz, "Decentralization and Computation in Resource-Allocation." In Pfouts, R. (ed.), *Essays in Economics and Econometrics in Honour of Harold Hotelling*, University of North Carolina Press, Chapel Hill, N.C., 1960.

[3] Casalmaglia, X., "Decentralized Resource Allocation and Increasing Returns," *Journal of Economic Theory* 14(1977), 263–283.

[4] Champsaur, P., "Neutrality of Planning Procedures in an Economy with Public Goods," *Review of Economic Studies* 43(1976), 293–299.

[5] Champsaur, P., J. Drèze and C. Henry, "Stability Theorems with Economic Applications," *Econometrica* 45(1977), 273–294.

[6] Crémer, J., "A Quantity-Quantity Algorithm for Planning Under Increasing Returns to Scale," *Econometrica* 45(1977), 1339–1348.

[7] Crémer, J., "A Comment on 'Decentralized Planning and Increasing Returns'," *Journal of Economic Theory* 19(1978), 217–221.

[8] Crémer, J., *Planning Under Non-Decreasing Returns to Scale*, unpublished Ph.D. dissertation, M.I.T., 1978.

[9] Crémer, J., "The Discrete Heal Algorithm with Intermediate Goods," *Review of Economic Studies* 50(1983), 383–391.

[10] Davis, O. A. and M. Whinston, "On Externalities, Information and the Government Assisted Invisible Hand," *Economica* 33(1966), 303–318.

[11] Drèze, J. and D. de la Vallée-Poussin, "A Tâtonnement Process for Public Goods," *Review of Economic Studies* 38(1971), 133–150.

[12] Heal, G. M., "Planning without Prices," *Review of Economic Studies* 36(1969), 347–362.

[13] Heal, G. M., *The Theory of Economic Planning*, North Holland, Amsterdam, 1973.

[14] Henry C. and A. Zylberberg, "Planning Algorithms to Deal with Increasing Returns," *Review of Economic Studies* 45(1978), 67–78.

[15] Hori, H., "The Structure of Equilibrium Points of Heal's Process," *Review of Economic Studies* 38(1971), 457–467.

[16] Laffont, J. J. and P. Saint-Pierre, "Planning with Externalities," *International Economic Review* 20(1979), 617–634.

[17] Lange, O., "On the Economic Theory of Socialism," *Review of Economic Studies* 4(1936–37). Reprinted in Lippincott, B. (ed.), *On the Economic Theory of Socialism,* McGraw Hill, 1964.

[18] Malinvaud, E., "Decentralized Procedures for Planning," in Bacharah, M. O. L. and E. Malinvaud (eds.), *Activity Analysis in the Theory of Growth and Planning,* Macmillan, London, 1967, 170–208.

[19] Malinvaud, E., "Prices for Individual Consumption, Quantity Indicators for Collective Consumptions," *Review of Economic Studies* 39(1972), 385–405.

[20] Mangasarian, O., *Nonlinear Programming,* McGraw-Hill, New York, 1969.

[21] Nayak, J., "An Informationally Efficient Process for Economies with Production Non-Convexities," chapter 7 of *The Informational Efficiency of Resource Allocation Processes,* Ph.D. Dissertation, University of Cambridge, U.K., 1982.

[22] Weitzman, M. L., "Iterative Multi-Level Planning with Production Targets," *Econometrica* 38(1970), 50–65.

[23] Weitzman, M., "Review of 'The Theory of Economic Planning' by G. M. Heal," *Journal of Economic Literature* 12(1974), 499–500.

3 Stability, Expectations, and Predetermined Variables

Jean-Michel Grandmont and Guy Laroque

Stability of a long-run equilibrium, and convergence to self-fulfilling expectations, depend in a complex manner on the interaction between the "fundamental" dynamics of the economy, and the learning processes of the traders. One may hope to get a better understanding of the issue by stylizing these two objects, and by studying how their interaction determines in particular the relationships that may exist between stability in the dynamics with learning, perfect foresight stability, or local determinateness of a long-run equilibrium.

Part of this program, in a deterministic framework, was implemented in a previous paper (Grandmont and Laroque 1986), in the simple case where the fundamental dynamics can be described by a one-dimensional difference equation (for related results, see also Fuchs and Laroque 1976 and Tillmann 1983; for an analysis of the stability of a stationary "sunspot" equilibrium in a similar context, see Woodford 1986b). The aim of the present work is to make progress in the general (deterministic) case in which the state variable is multidimensional, and when there are some lags in the system.

We identify in this context a relatively large set of circumstances under which stability of a stationary state in the dynamics with learning implies its unstability in the perfect foresight dynamics. The study of the specific case in which the state variable is a real number, with only a one-period lag, which involves a perfect foresight dynamics of dimension two, leads to even more definite conclusions: a stationary state that is asymptotically stable in the dynamics with learning is a saddle point in the perfect foresight dynamics (and is thus locally determinate), provided that traders do not make forecasting errors along trajectories that have period two. Conditions sufficient to ensure the converse are also given.

1. Dynamics with Learning and Perfect Foresight Stability

Let us suppose that time is discrete, and that the state of the economy can be described at any date by a vector x in some open subset X of R^m. In a deterministic framework, a temporary equilibrium state depends at each date t on the past states $x_{t-1}, \ldots, x_{t-J}$, with $J \geqslant 0$, and on the forecasts made by the traders at that date, concerning future periods,[1] i.e., ${}_tx^e_{t+1}, \ldots, {}_tx^e_{t+H}$, with $H \geqslant 1$. The precise way in which these variables determine x_t depends upon the "fundamental" characteristics of the traders (tastes, endowments, technologies, demographic structure), the institutional framework (competitive or noncompetitive markets, etc.), and the government's policies. We assume that these "structural" characteristics of the economy are constant (or at least that the laws of their motion are independent of time) and summarize them by the *temporary equilibrium map* $T: X^{J+H+1} \to R^m$. The relation that links the current temporary equilibrium state to past states and current forecasts takes then the form

$$T(x_t, x_{t-1}, \ldots, x_{t-J}, {}_tx^e_{t+1}, \ldots, {}_tx^e_{t+H}) = 0. \tag{1.1}$$

Our analysis is local, that is near a *stationary state*, i.e., a vector $\bar{x}$ of X such that $T(\bar{x}, \ldots, \bar{x}) = 0$. We assume that T is continuously differentiable, and denote A_{-j} (resp. A_h) the matrix of partial derivatives of T with respect to x_{t-J} (resp. ${}_tx^e_{t+h}$), evaluated at $(\bar{x}, \ldots, \bar{x})$. The matrices A_0 and A_H are assumed to be invertible (the last assumption can be somewhat relaxed, see Remark 1.2).

To specify consistently the dynamics of this economy, we need to describe how a temporary equilibrium at any date t is obtained, given any past history. To this end, it is *necessary* to spell out how forecasts are made at every date as a function of the traders' information at that date, and whether expectations are required to be correct or not. We assume that the traders' information at t is $(x_t, x_{t-1}, \ldots)$, and summarize the traders' way of processing that information by the time-independent *expectations functions* $\psi_h: X^L \to X$

$${}_tx^e_{t+h} = \psi_h(x_{t-1}, \ldots, x_{t-L}), \qquad h = 1, \ldots, H. \tag{1.2}$$

Whatever *a priori* information the traders may have on the "structural" characteristics of the economy is implicitly embodied in the forecasting rule (1.2). One may think of the memory length L as very large, with observations in the far distant past, as well as the current one, having a negligible influence on current forecasts (for an extension to the case where the current state does influence forecasts, see Remark 1.1). We assume each ψ_h

continuously differentiable, and denote C_{hj} the matrix of partial derivatives of ψ_h with respect to x_{t-j}, evaluated at $(\bar{x}, \ldots, \bar{x})$.

The formulation (1.2) is compatible with the requirement that forecasts be correct (see footnote 4 below). It actually covers, more generally, a large class of learning processes, in which, for instance, traders try to discover the value of a "structural" parameter, etc.[2]

Given the forecasting rules, a temporary equilibrium state at date t satisfies, given past history, the relation obtained by plugging (1.2) into (1.1),

$$W(x_t, x_{t-1}, \ldots, x_{t-M}) = 0, \tag{1.3}$$

in which M is the largest lag in the system, i.e., the maximum of J and L. By construction, $W: X^{M+1} \rightarrow R^m$ is continuously differentiable. We shall make assumptions ensuring $\psi_h(\bar{x}, \ldots, \bar{x}) = \bar{x}$ for all h. In that case $W(\bar{x}, \ldots, \bar{x}) = 0$, and the matrix of partial derivatives of W with respect to x_t, evaluated at $(\bar{x}, \ldots, \bar{x})$, is equal to A_0, which is invertible. From the implicit function theorem, (1.3) can then be solved uniquely in x_t near the stationary sequence $(\bar{x}, \ldots, \bar{x})$. Specifically, there are open neighborhoods U of $(\bar{x}, \ldots, \bar{x})$ in X^M and V of $\bar{x}$ in X, and a continuously differentiable map $W_{\text{loc}}: U \rightarrow V$ such that $(x_t, \ldots, x_{t-H})$ verifies (1.3), with $(x_{t-1}, \ldots, x_{t-M})$ in U and x_t in V if and only if

$$x_t = W_{\text{loc}}(x_{t-1}, \ldots, x_{t-M}). \tag{1.4}$$

The local temporary equilibrium dynamics are then well defined near the stationary state, and described by the local delayed difference equation (1.4). We shall be concerned in assessing the implications of the asymptotic stability of $\bar{x}$ in these local dynamics. If we denote $P_W(\lambda) = 0$ the characteristic equation associated to (1.4) at the stationary state, and assume that there is no characteristic root of modulus one, the stationary state $\bar{x}$ is asymptotically stable in the local temporary equilibrium dynamics corresponding to the expectations functions (ψ_h) if and only if every characteristic root satisfies $|\lambda| < 1$.[3]

We are especially interested in relating the above stability property with the stability, or unstability, of the stationary state when traders do not make forecasting errors. An *intertemporal equilibrium* with perfect foresight is defined, given the predetermined variables $(x_{-1}, \ldots, x_{-J})$, as a sequence of states (x_t) and of expectations $({}_t x_{t+1}^e, \ldots, {}_t x_{t+H}^e)$ for $t = 0, \ldots, \infty$, such that (1.1) is satisfied and forecasts are correct at all dates, i.e.

$${}_t x_{t+h}^e = x_{t+h}, \qquad \text{for } h = 1, \ldots, H \text{ and all } t \geqslant 0. \tag{1.5}$$

A sequence of states corresponds to such an intertemporal equilibrium if and only if it satisfies for all $t \geqslant 0$

$$T(x_t, \ldots, x_{t-J}, x_{t+1}, \ldots, x_{t+H}) = 0. \tag{1.6}$$

Since $T(\overline{x}, \ldots, \overline{x}) = 0$ and A_H is invertible, (1.6) defines consistently a local *perfect foresight dynamics* near the stationary state $\overline{x}$. Indeed, again from the implicit function theorem, (1.6) can be solved in x_{t+H} near the stationary state, to yield a local difference equation of the form

$$x_{t+H} = F_{\text{loc}}(x_{t+H-1}, \ldots, x_t, \ldots, x_{t-J}) \tag{1.7}$$

in which the continuously differentiable map F_{loc} is defined on an appropriate neighborhood of the constant sequence $(\overline{x}, \ldots, \overline{x})$ in X^{H+J}. Asymptotic stability of the stationary state in these local perfect foresight dynamics can then be assessed by looking at the characteristic equation $P_F(\lambda) = 0$ associated with (1.7) at the stationary state. If there is no characteristic root of modulus one, the stationary state $\overline{x}$ is asymptotically stable in the local perfect foresight dynamics if and only if every root of $P_F(\lambda) = 0$ satisfies $|\lambda| < 1$.[4]

Assuming perfect foresight along any possible sequence of temporary equilibria generated by (1.3), or (1.4) amounts to postulating that each trader knows beforehand the structural characteristics of the economy, i.e., the map T, or F_{loc}. Typically, however, such information is not directly available. In particular, traders know that the economy may converge to a stationary state, or more generally to a periodic orbit, without knowing precisely where these orbits may lie. In such a situation they will try to extract from past data such possible regularities, and will extrapolate them. The expectations functions (1.2) are said to *detect period k* if for any sequence $(x_{t-1}, \ldots, x_{t-L})$ in X that has period k, i.e., such that $x_{t-j} = x_{t-j-k}$ for all relevant j, then for every $h = 1, \ldots, H$,

$$\psi_h(x_{t-1}, \ldots, x_{t-L}) = x_{t+h-nk}$$

for all n such that $1 \leqslant nk - h \leqslant L$. Of course, this definition, to be consistent, requires L to be large enough, in fact greater than k. If the forecasting rules detect period k, they detect also any period that divides k.

Forecasting the future by extrapolating the past amounts in a sense to reversing the direction of time. One should expect accordingly that in such circumstances, asymptotic stability of the stationary state in the (local) temporary equilibrium dynamics (1.4) implies instability in the local perfect foresight dynamics (1.7). The following result displays a set of conditions under which the phenomenon occurs.

Proposition 1.1. Assume that the expectations functions detect period 2 and that $\det(A_0) \neq 0$, $\det(A_H) \neq 0$. Then $\det(A_0)P_W(1) = \det(A_H)P_F(1)$; $\det(A_0)(-1)^{mM}P_W(-1) = \det(A_H)(-1)^{mJ}P_F(-1)$. This implies

(1) if mH is odd, $P_W(1) > 0$ and $(-1)^{mM}P_W(-1) > 0$ is equivalent to

$$P_F(1) < 0 < (-1)^{m(J+H)}P_F(-1),$$

if $\det(A_0)$ and $\det(A_H)$ have opposite signs,[5] and otherwise to

$$(-1)^{m(J+H)}P_F(-1) < 0 < P_F(1).$$

(2) if mH is even, $P_W(1) > 0$ and $(-1)^{mM}P_W(-1) > 0$ is equivalent to

$$P_F(1) < 0, \ (-1)^{m(J+H)}P_F(-1) < 0,$$

if $\det(A_0)$ and $\det(A_H)$ have opposite signs, and otherwise to

$$P_F(1) > 0, \ (-1)^{m(J+H)}P_F(-1) > 0.$$

Corollary 1.2. Assume that the expectations functions detect period 2, that $\det(A_0) \neq 0$, $\det(A_H) \neq 0$, and that all roots of the characteristic equation $P_W(\lambda) = 0$ associated to the local temporary equilibrium dynamics (1.4) at the stationary state are such that $|\lambda| < 1$. Then

(1) if mH is odd, the equation $P_F(\lambda) = 0$ has a real root $\lambda > 1$ if $\det(A_0)$ and $\det(A_H)$ have opposite signs, a real root $\lambda < -1$ otherwise,

(2) if mH is even, and if $\det(A_0)$ and $\det(A_H)$ have opposite signs, the equation $P_F(\lambda) = 0$ has two real roots $\lambda_1 > 1$ and $\lambda_2 < -1$.

Proof. $P_W(\lambda) = 0$ is the characteristic equation of the Jacobian matrix of the map W_{loc}^* defined in footnote 3, evaluated at $(\bar{x}, \ldots, \bar{x})$. This Jacobian matrix is of the form

$$DW^* = \begin{bmatrix} DW_1 & \cdots & DW_M \\ I_m & 0 & \\ & \ddots \quad \ddots & \\ & I_m & 0 \end{bmatrix},$$

where $DW_j = -A_0^{-1}[A_{-j} + \sum_{h=1}^{H} A_h C_{hj}]$ is the matrix of partial derivatives of W_{loc} with respect to x_{t-j}, evaluated at the constant sequence $(\bar{x}, \ldots, \bar{x})$ (with the convention $A_{-j} = 0$ if $j > J$ and $C_{hj} = 0$ if $j > L$), and I_m is the m-dimensional unit matrix.

Hence, finding an eigenvalue and an eigenvector of DW^* amounts to looking for a complex number λ and a complex m-dimensional vector $v \neq 0$ such that

$$\lambda^M v = \sum_1^M \lambda^{M-j} DW_j v.$$

The characteristic equation of DW^* is therefore

$$P_W(\lambda) = \det\left(\lambda^M I_m - \sum_1^M \lambda^{M-j} DW_j\right) = 0,$$

which yields, in view of the expression of DW_j,

$$\det(A_0) P_W(\lambda) = \det\left(\sum_{j=0}^{J} A_{-j}\lambda^{M-j} + \sum_{h=1}^{H} A_h \sum_{j=1}^{L} C_{hj}\lambda^{M-j}\right). \tag{1.8}$$

The same procedure applied to F_{loc} in (1.7) leads to

$$\det(A_H) P_F(\lambda) = \det\left(\sum_{j=0}^{J} A_{-j}\lambda^{J-j} + \sum_{h=1}^{H} A_h \lambda^{J+h}\right). \tag{1.9}$$

Examination of (1.8) and (1.9) shows that any comparison of the stability properties of the stationary state in the local temporary equilibrium dynamics and the local perfect foresight dynamics should involve the behavior of the m-dimensional matrices

$$\Gamma_h(\lambda) = \sum_{j=1}^{L} C_{hj}\lambda^{-j}$$

for $|\lambda| = 1$. The following result, which is partly a generalization of Lemma 3.1 of Grandmont and Laroque 1986, provides some information on this issue.

Lemma. Assume that the expectations functions (1.2) detect period k. Then $\Gamma_h(\lambda) = \lambda^h I_m$ for every $\lambda = e^{2\pi i d/k}$, $d = 1, \ldots, k$ and $h = 1, \ldots, H$.

To prove the lemma, consider an arbitrary sequence $z = (z_1, \ldots, z_L)$ with z_j in R^m, that has period k. With the notation $\bar{y} = (\bar{x}, \ldots, \bar{x})$, $\bar{y} + \alpha z$ is in X^L if the real α is small enough. We get then for all h

$$\psi_h(\bar{y} + \alpha z) - \psi_h(\bar{y}) = \alpha z_{nk-h} \tag{1.10}$$

for all n such that $1 \leqslant nk - h \leqslant L$. Applying the mean value theorem to the pth component of the left member of (1.10), considered as a function of α, shows the existence of $\bar{\alpha}_{hp}$ in $[0, \alpha]$ such that

$$\psi_{hp}(\bar{y} + \alpha z) - \psi_{hp}(\bar{y}) = \alpha \sum_j \sum_q \frac{\partial \psi_{hp}}{\partial x_{jq}}(\bar{y} + \bar{\alpha}_{hp} z) z_{jq} \tag{1.11}$$

in which ψ_{hp}, x_{jq}, z_{jq} are the pth and qth components of the vectors ψ_h, x_h, and z_j, respectively. Comparing (1.10) and (1.11), and letting α go to 0 leads to

$$\sum_{j=1}^{L} C_{hj} z_j = z_{nk-h} \tag{1.12}$$

for all n such that $1 \leqslant nk - h \leqslant L$.

The linear condition (1.12) is of course also valid if each z_j is a complex m-dimensional vector. We may thus apply it to periodic sequences with $z_j = \lambda^{-j} z$, where $\lambda = e^{2\pi i d/k}$ for some $d = 1, \ldots, k$, and z is an arbitrary complex m-dimensional vector. This yields

$$\left(\sum_{j=1}^{L} C_{hj} \lambda^{-j} \right) z = \lambda^h z.$$

Since z is arbitrary, this implies

$$\sum_{j=1}^{L} C_{hj} \lambda^{-j} = \lambda^h I_m,$$

as claimed.

This completes the proof of the lemma. Now, if the expectations functions detect period 2, we get

$$\sum_{j=1}^{L} C_{hj} = I_m$$

and

$$\sum_{j=1}^{L} (-1)^h C_{hj} = (-1)^h I_m.$$

Plugging these conditions into (1.8) implies immediately

$$\det(A_0) P_W(1) = \det(A_H) P_F(1);$$

$$\det(A_0)(-1)^{mM} P_W(-1) = \det(A_H)(-1)^{mJ} P_F(-1), \tag{1.13}$$

which is the first part of the proposition. Statements (1) and (2) are then immediate consequences of (1.13).

To prove the corollary, notice that $P_W(\lambda)$ and $P_F(\lambda)$ are polynomials of degrees mM and $m(J + H)$, respectively, the coefficient of the term of highest degree being 1. If $P_W(1) < 0$, or $P_F(1) < 0$, the equation $P_W(\lambda) = 0$, or $P_F(\lambda) = 0$, has a real root $\lambda > 1$. Symmetrically, if $(-1)^{mM} P_W(-1) < 0$, or $(-1)^{m(J+H)} P_F(-1) < 0$, the equation $P_W(\lambda) = 0$, or $P_F(\lambda) = 0$, has a real root $\lambda < -1$. Thus, if all roots of $P_W(\lambda) = 0$ satisfy $|\lambda| < 1$, one must have $P_W(1) > 0$ and $(-1)^{mM} P_W(-1) > 0$, and the corollary follows from (1) and (2) of the Proposition. Q.E.D.

Remark 1.1. The foregoing results extend easily to the case where the expectations functions depend upon the current state x_t. This introduces new matrices C_{h0}, which stand for the matrices of partial derivatives of ψ_h with respect to x_t, evaluated at $(\bar{x}, \ldots, \bar{x})$. The assumption "$A_0$ is invertible" must be replaced by "$A_0 + \sum_{h=1}^{H} A_h C_{h0}$ is invertible" in order to be able to define the local temporary equilibrium dynamics (1.4). The proposition, and its corollary, are valid once $\det(A_0)$ is replaced everywhere by

$$\det\left(A_0 + \sum_{h=1}^{H} A_h C_{h0}\right).$$

Remark 1.2. The assumption $\det(A_0) \neq 0$, or, more generally, $\det(A_0 + \sum_{h=1}^{H} A_h C_{h0}) \neq 0$, is a "generic" condition ensuring that local temporary equilibrium dynamics can be defined near the stationary state. The status of the condition $\det(A_H) \neq 0$ is much different. That assumption was made here to ensure most conveniently that (1) forecasts do influence the current temporary equilibrium state, and that (2) local perfect foresight dynamics are well defined. The condition may not be satisfied in some economic models, however. For instance, the traders' current actions may depend upon their forecasts of some, but not all, state variables in the future. In that case, none of the matrices A_h for $h = 1, \ldots, H$ may be of full rank. Nevertheless, it is easy to deal with such a situation, through a slight adaptation of the argument of the text.

We have here to "disaggregate" the state variable, i.e., $x = (x_1, \ldots, x_n)$, where each vector x_i has dimension $m_i \geqslant 1$, with $\Sigma_i m_i = m$. We assume that for each i, the forecasts ${}_t x^e_{i,t+h}$ made at t concerning the value of the variables x_i in the future period $t + h$ have a possible influence on the current state x_t, for $h = 1, \ldots, h_i$, where $h_i \geqslant 0$, while the forecasts ${}_t x^e_{i,t+h}$ for periods beyond $t + h_i$, i.e., for $h > h_i$, are irrelevant (the case $h_i = 0$ means that the variables x_i need not be forecasted by the traders to determine their current actions). We suppose, without loss of generality, $h_1 = H \geqslant 1$ (this can be taken as the definition of H).

We may still summarize the workings of the economy by equation (1.1), with the understanding that the temporary equilibrium map T does not actually depend upon ${}_t x^e_{i,t+h}$ whenever $h > h_i$. If we also disaggregate each matrix $A_k = (A_k^1, \ldots, A_k^n)$ for $k = -J, \ldots, +H$, with A_k^i being the $m \times m_i$ matrix composed of the columns of A_k corresponding to the variables x_i, this means $A_h^i = 0$ for $h > h_i$. We shall assume that the matrix $(A_{h_1}^1, \ldots, A_{h_n}^n)$ is invertible, which implies in particular that A_h^i has indeed rank m_i whenever $h = h_i$. Note that to arrive at such a formulation, we may have to make a change of variable of the form $x \to f(x)$, where f is a diffeomorphism.

Forecasts are given by the expectations functions

$$ {}_t x_{i,t+h}^e = \psi_{ih}(x_{t-1}, \ldots, x_{t-L}), \qquad i = 1, \ldots, n;\ h = 1, \ldots, h_i. \tag{1.14} $$

Expectations functions need not be defined for $h > h_i$, since the corresponding forecasts are irrelevant. The associated local temporary equilibrium dynamics are obtained as in the text by plugging (1.14) in (1.1), and by solving the resulting equation (1.3) in x_t, near the stationary state, which is always possible under the "generic" condition $\det(A_0) \neq 0$. We let $P_W(\lambda)$ be the corresponding characteristic polynomial; as before, its degree is mM.

Intertemporal equilibria are sequences of states that satisfy (1.6) for all t. We can no longer obtain a local perfect foresight dynamics by solving this equation in x_{t+H} near the stationary state, since the rank of A_H may be less than m. On the other hand, the variables with the largest time indices that appear in (1.6) are $(x_{1,t+h_1}, x_{2,t+h_2}, \ldots, x_{n,t+h_n})$. If we denote by y_{t+H} this m-dimensional vector (remember that $h_1 = H$), and more generally $y_{t+H-j} = (x_{1,t+h_1-j}, \ldots, x_{n,t+h_n-j})$, we see that (1.6) defines actually a relation of the form

$$ F(y_{t-J}, \ldots, y_t, \ldots, y_{t+H}) = 0. \tag{1.15} $$

Let B_{H-j} be the matrix of partial derivatives of F with respect to y_{t+H-j}, for $j = 0, \ldots, J + H$, evaluated at $(\bar{x}, \ldots, \bar{x})$. By construction, we have $B_{H-j} = (A_{h_1-j}^1, \ldots, A_{h_n-j}^n)$, with the convention that $A_k^i = 0$ when $k < -J$. Here, the "generic" assumption ensuring that forecasts do influence the current state, and that the local perfect foresight dynamics are well defined, is that B_H is invertible. In such a case, (1.15) can be solved in y_{t+H} near the stationary state, to yield a local perfect foresight difference equation of the form

$$ y_{t+H} = F_{\text{loc}}(y_{t+H-1}, \ldots, y_{t-J}). \tag{1.16} $$

We let as before $P_F(\lambda)$ be the characteristic polynomial of this equation, at the stationary state; by construction, its degree is $m(H + J)$.

With these notations, the generalization of the results of the text to the case at hand becomes as follows.

Corollary 1.3. Assume that the expectations functions (1.14) detect period 2, and that the matrices A_0 and B_H are invertible. Then

$$\det(A_0)P_W(1) = \det(B_H)P_F(1),$$

$$\det(A_0)(-1)^{mM}P_W(-1) = \det(B_H)(-1)^{m(J+H)-\Sigma_i h_i m_i}P_F(-1).$$

Then, the comparison made in Proposition 1.1 between the signs of $P_W(1)$, and $P_F(1)$, those of $(-1)^{mM}P_W(-1)$ and $(-1)^{m(H+J)}P_F(-1)$, as well as the statements of Corollary 1.2, are all valid provided one replaces everywhere A_H by B_H, and the sentences "if mH is odd (or even)" by "if $\Sigma_i m_i h_i$ is odd (or even)."

Proof. Notice first that we may add to (1.14) artificial expectations functions ${}_t x^e_{i,t+h} = \psi_{ih}(x_{t-1}, \ldots, x_{t-L})$ for $h > h_i$, and thus consider "augmented" expectations functions ${}_t x^e_{t+h} = \psi_h(x_{t-1}, \ldots, x_{t-L})$ as in (1.2), without changing the local temporary equilibrium dynamics. If we denote by C_{hj}, as in the text, the matrix of partial derivatives of the (augmented) expectations function ψ_h with respect to x_{t-j}, evaluated at $(\bar{x}, \ldots, \bar{x})$, we see that

$$\det(A_0)P_W(\lambda) = Q_W(\lambda) \tag{1.17}$$

where $Q_W(\lambda)$ is the right-hand member of (1.8): in that expression, the elements of the rows of C_{hj} corresponding to the artificial forecasting rules are in fact multiplied by elements of A_h that are equal to 0.

On the other hand, it is not difficult to verify that

$$\det(B_H)P_F(\lambda) = \lambda^{mH-\Sigma_i m_i h_i}Q_F(\lambda), \tag{1.18}$$

where $Q_F(\lambda)$ is the right-hand member of (1.9). Indeed, with the disaggregated notation $A_h = (A_h^1, \ldots, A_h^n)$, we have

$$Q_F(\lambda) = \det\left(\sum_{j=0}^{H+J} \lambda^{H+J-j}A^1_{H-j}, \ldots, \sum_{j=0}^{H+J} \lambda^{H+J-j}A^n_{H-j}\right). \tag{1.19}$$

The characteristic polynomial $P_F(\lambda)$ is given by

$$\det(B_H)P_F(\lambda) = \det\left(\sum_{j=0}^{H+J} \lambda^{H+J-j}B_{H-j}\right),$$

where $B_{H-j} = (A^1_{h_1-j}, \ldots, A^n_{h_n-j})$ is the matrix of partial derivatives of F with respect to y_{t+H-j}, evaluated at $(\bar{x}, \ldots, \bar{x})$, with the convention $A^i_h = 0$ when $h < -J$. Thus,

$$\det(B_H)P_F(\lambda) = \det\left(\sum_{j=0}^{H+J} \lambda^{H+J-j}A^1_{h_1-j}, \ldots, \sum_{j=0}^{H+J} \lambda^{H+J-j}A^n_{h_n-j}\right). \tag{1.20}$$

Comparing (1.20) and (1.19), and remembering that $A_h^i = 0$ when $h > h_i$ yields (1.18).

The final step of the proof is to notice that

$$Q_W(1) = Q_F(1) \qquad \text{and} \qquad (-1)^{mM} Q_W(-1) = (-1)^{mJ} Q_F(-1), \quad (1.21)$$

when the expectations functions (1.14) detect period 2. To establish this fact, it suffices to remark that the result stated in the Lemma, in the proof of Proposition 1.1, is valid for every row p of the matrix $\sum_{j=1}^{L} C_{hj}\lambda^{-j}$ corresponding to the pth component ψ_{hp} of the expectation function, provided that ψ_{hp} detects period k, independently of the behavior of the other components. Thus, we may apply the Lemma to the components ψ_{ih} corresponding to the variables x_i such that $h \leqslant h_i$, and this yields (1.21).

Putting together (1.17), (1.18), and (1.21) leads to the two equalities of Corollary 1.3. The other statements are straightforward consequences of these equalities. Q.E.D.

One can of course combine the results of this remark with Remark 1.1 to cover the case where the expectations functions depend upon the current state.

2. An Example

We consider now the simple case where the state variable at each date is a real number ($m = 1$), the traders plan one period ahead ($H = 1$), and where there is only a one-period lag in the system ($J = 1$). This situation arises, for instance, in simple versions of the overlapping generations model with productive investment with no substitution between capital and labor (Reichlin 1986; Woodford 1984), or in infinite horizon models with cash in advance constraints (Woodford 1986a). In such a case, the local perfect foresight dynamics (1.7) has dimension two ($H + J = 2$), and mH is odd. It follows then from the Proposition that if the traders' expectations function detects period 2, and if all roots of the equation $P_W(\lambda) = 0$ are such that $|\lambda| < 1$, the stationary state is indeed a saddle point (and, thus, generally locally determinate) in the local perfect foresight dynamics. We shall derive these facts most simply in this specific case. We shall also give sufficient conditions for the converse result to be true.

In this context, the temporary equilibrium map takes R^3 into R, and the relation between current and past states and the current forecast is of the form

$$T(x_t, x_{t-1}, {}_t x_{t+1}^e) = 0. \qquad (2.1)$$

We denote by $a_0 \neq 0$, a_1, $b \neq 0$, the partial derivatives of T with respect to x_t, x_{t-1}, ${}_t x_{t+1}^e$, respectively, evaluated at the stationary state $(\bar{x}, \bar{x}, \bar{x})$. The local perfect foresight dynamics are obtained by solving $T(x_t, x_{t-1}, x_{t+1}) = 0$ in x_{t+1} near the stationary state. The corresponding characteristic equation is

$$P_F(\lambda) \equiv \lambda^2 + b^{-1} a_0 \lambda + b^{-1} a_1 = 0. \tag{2.2}$$

Whether or not the modulus of the roots of this equation have modulus less than one is most easily assessed by employing the parameters $\sigma = -b^{-1} a_0 \neq 0$ and $\Delta = b^{-1} a_1$, which represent the sum of the two roots and their product, respectively. In the plane (σ, Δ), the line (AC) of equation $1 + \Delta = \sigma$ describes the locus of all configurations of these parameters for which there is one root equal to 1 (see figure 1). One root is equal to -1 when (σ, Δ) belongs to the line (AB) of equation $1 + \Delta = -\sigma$. On the segment $[BC]$ of equation $\Delta = 1$, $|\sigma| \leqslant 2$, the two roots are complex conjugate of modulus 1. The two roots of (2.2) satisfy $|\lambda| < 1$ if and only if (σ, Δ) belongs to the interior of the triangle ABC. The stationary state is a *saddle point* in the local perfect foresight dynamics when (2.2) has two real roots λ_1, λ_2, with $|\lambda_1| > 1 > |\lambda_2|$. This occurs if and only if (σ, Δ) belongs to the interior of the shaded area in figure 1, which is represented by the inequality

$$|\sigma| > |1 + \Delta|, \qquad \text{or} \qquad |a_0| > |a_1 + b|. \tag{2.3}$$

We turn now to the analysis of temporary equilibrium dynamics. In this context, the traders' forecasting rules reduce to a single real-valued function

$${}_t x_{t+1}^e = \psi(x_{t-1}, \ldots, x_{t-L}). \tag{2.4}$$

We denote by c_j the partial derivative of ψ with respect to x_{t-j}, evaluated at $(\bar{x}, \ldots, \bar{x})$. We assume that ψ detects period 2, in which case, from Grandmont and Laroque (1986, Lemma 3.1), or the lemma in section 1,

$$\sum_j c_j = 1 \qquad \text{and} \qquad \sum_j (-1)^j c_j = -1. \tag{2.5}$$

The temporary equilibrium dynamics are implicitly defined by the relation one gets by putting (2.4) in (2.1), i.e.,

$$T(x_t, x_{t-1}, \psi(x_{t-1}, \ldots, x_{t-L})) = 0. \tag{2.6}$$

The local temporary equilibrium dynamics are obtained by solving (2.6) in x_t near the stationary state. The corresponding characteristic equation is

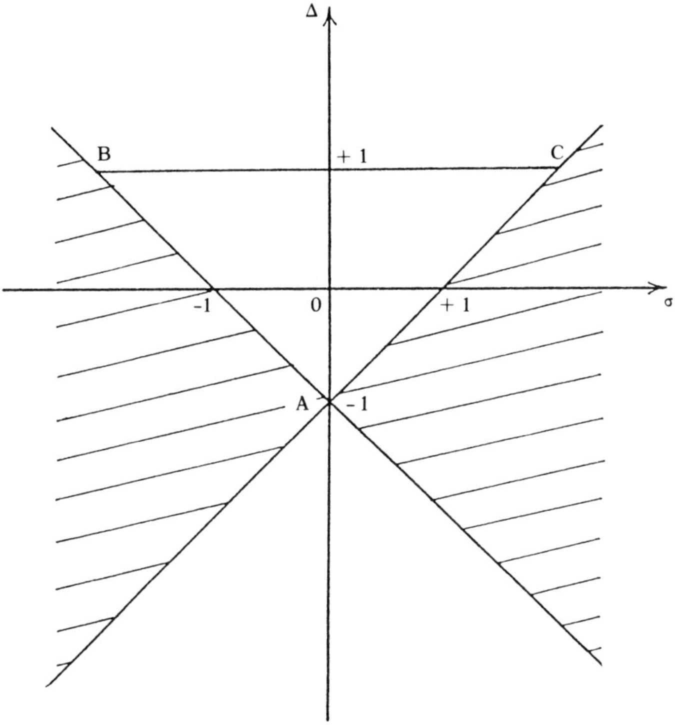

Figure 1.

$$P_W(\lambda) \equiv \lambda^L + a_0^{-1} a_1 \lambda^{L-1} + a_0^{-1} b \sum_{j=1}^{L} c_j \lambda^{L-j} = 0$$

which can be reformulated by using the parameters σ, Δ introduced earlier:

$$P_W(\lambda) \equiv \lambda^L - \sigma^{-1} \Delta \lambda^{L-1} - \sigma^{-1} \sum_{j=1}^{L} c_j \lambda^{L-j} = 0. \tag{2.7}$$

It is now readily verified that if the expectations function detects period 2, then the stationary state is a saddle point in the local perfect foresight dynamics if and only if

$$P_W(1) > 0 \quad \text{and} \quad (-1)^L P_W(-1) > 0. \tag{2.8}$$

Indeed, in view of (2.5),

$$P_W(1) = 1 - \sigma^{-1}(1 + \Delta) \tag{2.9}$$

$$(-1)^L P_W(-1) = 1 + \sigma^{-1}(1 + \Delta) \tag{2.10}$$

and, therefore, (2.8) is equivalent to $|\sigma| > |1 + \Delta|$. The result implies that if ψ detects period 2, and if all roots of $P_W(\lambda) = 0$ are such that $|\lambda| < 1$, then the stationary state is a saddle point in the local perfect foresight dynamics.[6]

The converse does hold if expectations are *myopic*, i.e., ${}_tx^e_{t+1} = x_{t-1}$, or, more generally, if $c_1 = 1$ and $c_j = 0$ for $j = 2, \ldots, L$. For then

$$P_W(\lambda) = \lambda^{L-1}(\lambda - \sigma^{-1}(1 + \Delta))$$

and thus all roots of $P_W(\lambda) = 0$ satisfy $|\lambda| < 1$ if and only if $|\sigma| > |1 + \Delta|$. But beyond that specific case, one should not expect in general a saddle point to be stable in the local temporary equilibrium dynamics, as the following example shows.

Let $L = 3$. Then if the expectation function detects period 2, $c_2 = 0$ and $c_1 + c_3 = 1$. We already know what happens when $c_1 = 1$, so we shall assume $c_1 \neq 1$, or equivalently $c_3 \neq 0$. The temporary equilibrium characteristic equation reduces to

$$P_W(\lambda) = \lambda^3 - \sigma^{-1}(\Delta + c_1)\lambda^2 - \sigma^{-1}c_3 = 0. \tag{2.11}$$

To study this equation, we look at the configurations (σ, Δ) such that (2.11) has a root of modulus 1, given the coefficients c_1, c_3. We already know that the equation has a root equal to 1 (resp. -1), if and only if (σ, Δ) belongs to the line (AC), of equation $1 + \Delta = \sigma$ (resp. (AB), of equation $1 + \Delta = -\sigma$), see (2.9) and (2.10). It remains to see when (2.11) has a pair of complex conjugate roots of modulus 1, or equivalently, two roots λ_1, λ_2 such that $\lambda_1\lambda_2 = 1$ and $|\lambda_1 + \lambda_2| \leqslant 2$. Since the characteristic polynomial can be written $(\lambda - \lambda_1)(\lambda - \lambda_2)(\lambda - \lambda_3)$, where λ_3 is the third root, one verifies easily by identifying the coefficients of this expression with those of $P_W(\lambda)$ that such a situation arises if and only if

$$1 + \Delta = 2c_3 - c_3^{-1}\sigma^2 \qquad \text{and} \qquad |\sigma| \leqslant 2|c_3|. \tag{2.12}$$

The locus of all configurations (σ, Δ) satisfying these relations for given coefficients (c_1, c_3) is a parabolic arc $DEFG$ that is represented in figure 2a for $c_1 > 1$ in figure 2b for $c_1 < 1$.

To conclude, it suffices to remark that given the coefficients c_j, and the parameter Δ, all roots of (2.11) tend to 0 when $|\sigma|$ goes to $+\infty$. Thus, for any (σ, Δ) in the shaded areas in figure 2, all roots of (2.11) are such that $|\lambda| < 1$. By contrast, (2.11) has two roots of modulus greater than 1 in the interior of the regions ADE or AFG. These regions coalesce to the origin if and only if $c_1 = 1$.

One cannot hope, accordingly, to find a subset, say S, of the area defined by the inequality $|\sigma| > |1 + \Delta|$ such that for every (σ, Δ) in S, the stationary state is stable in the temporary equilibrium dynamics for *any* expectation function that detects period 2: in the example, any point of that area belongs to the region ADE or AFG if $|c_3|$ is large enough. One may hope, however, to identify a subset S that leads to a stable temporary equilibrium dynamics for a given restricted *subclass* of expectations functions. In the example, for instance, every (σ, Δ) in the set defined by $|\sigma| > |1 + \Delta|$, $|\sigma|^2 > |1 - \Delta|$, leads to a stable temporary equilibrium dynamics for all expectations functions that detect period 2 and satisfy $c_1 \geqslant 0$, $c_3 \geqslant 0$: this follows from the fact that the equation of the parabolic arc $DEFG$ corresponding to $c_3 = 1$ is $\sigma^2 = 1 - \Delta$, $|\sigma| \leqslant 2$.

In the general case, where L is arbitrary, the answer to this question hinges upon the behavior of the expression $\gamma(\lambda) = \sum_j c_j \lambda^{-j}$ for $|\lambda| = 1$.

Lemma. Assume that the expectations function detects period 1, and that the parameters $\sigma = -b^{-1}a_0$, $\Delta = b^{-1}a_1$ satisfy $|\sigma| > \beta$, where β is the maximum of $|\Delta + \lambda\gamma(\lambda)|$ when $|\lambda| = 1$. Then all characteristic roots of the local temporary equilibrium dynamics at the stationary state satisfy $|\lambda| < 1$.

Proof. Assume that (σ, Δ) and $(c_1, \ldots, c_L)$ are such that (2.11) has a root $|\lambda| \geqslant 1$. Since all roots of (2.11) tend to 0 when σ goes to $+\infty$, there exists $r \geqslant 1$ such the characteristic equation (2.11) corresponding to $\sigma' = r\sigma$, with Δ and the c_j unchanged, has a root λ_0 of modulus 1. Dividing by λ_0^{L-1} both members of (2.11) when $\lambda = \lambda_0$ yields

$$\lambda_0 \sigma' = \Delta + \lambda_0 \sum_j c_j \lambda_0^{-j}.$$

Hence

$$|\sigma| \leqslant |\sigma'| = |\Delta + \lambda_0 \gamma(\lambda_0)| \leqslant \beta.$$

Thus, $|\sigma| > \beta$ implies that all roots of (2.11) satisfy $|\lambda| < 1$. Q.E.D.

The assumption that ψ detects period 1 is there to ensure that $\psi(\bar{x}, \ldots, \bar{x}) = \bar{x}$. In that case, the condition $|\sigma| > \beta$ leads to a subset of the region defined by $|\sigma| > |1 + \Delta|$. Indeed $\gamma(1) = 1$ and thus $\beta \geqslant |1 + \Delta|$. This subset contains always the set defined by $|\sigma| > |\Delta| + \alpha$, where α is the maximum of $|\gamma(\lambda)|$ for $|\lambda| = 1$. This follows from the fact that for $|\lambda| = 1$

$$|\Delta + \lambda\gamma(\lambda)| \leqslant |\Delta| + |\gamma(\lambda)| \leqslant |\Delta| + \alpha,$$

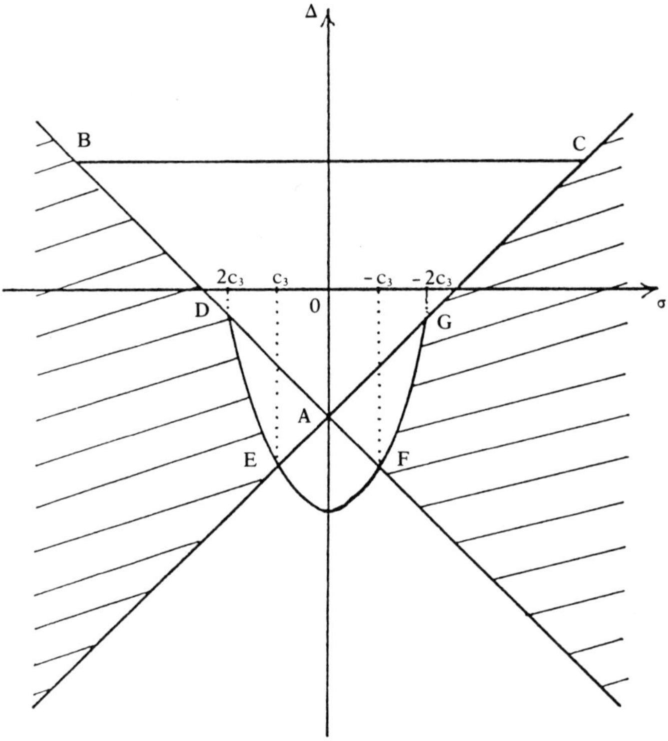

Figure 2a.
$c_3 = 1 - c_1 < 0.$

and thus $\beta \leqslant |\Delta| + \alpha$. Since $\gamma(1) = 1$, we know that $\alpha \geqslant 1$. If $\alpha = 1$, we are sure that the stationary state is stable in the local temporary equilibrium dynamics if $|\sigma| > |\Delta| + 1$, which corresponds to the shaded area in figure 3a. The case $\alpha = 1$ occurs in particular if $c_j \geqslant 0$ for all j.[7] As a matter of fact, it is possible to refine a little the sufficient stability condition in that case. If $c_j \geqslant 0$ for all j, then we have for $|\lambda| = 1$,

$$|\Delta + \lambda\gamma(\lambda)| = \left|\Delta + c_1 + \sum_{2}^{L} c_j \lambda^{-j+1}\right|$$

$$\leqslant |\Delta + c_1| + (1 - c_1)$$

and thus $\beta \leqslant |\Delta + c_1| + (1 - c_1)$. Thus, if ψ detects period 1 and $c_j \geqslant 0$ for all j, the stationary state is stable in the local temporary equilibrium dynamics if $|\sigma| > |\Delta + c_1| + (1 - c_1)$, which corresponds to the shaded area in figure 3b.

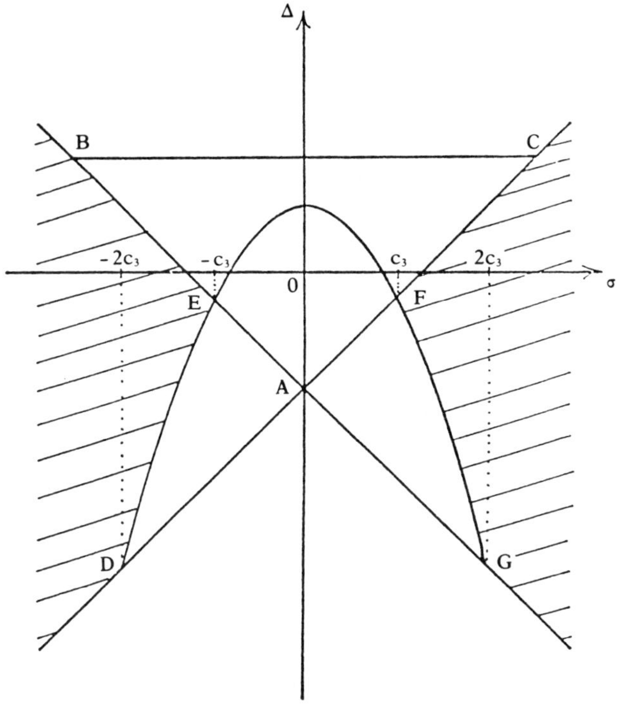

Figure 2b.
$c_3 = 1 - c_1 > 0.$

Remark 2.1. The following example, where the state variable is two dimensional and where the local perfect foresight dynamics have dimension two, can also be analyzed with the methods of this section. This case arises in simple versions of the overlapping generations model with productive investment, when there is substitution between capital and labor (Farmer 1986; Jullien 1986; Tirole 1985).

The state variable is $x_t = (p_t, k_t)$; we may interpret p_t as a price and k_t as the stock of capital at the end of the period. The temporary equilibrium relation is of the form

$$T(k_{t-1}, p_t, k_t, {}_tp^e_{t+1}) = 0, \tag{2.13}$$

with T taking values in R^2, and $T(\overline{k}, \overline{p}, \overline{k}, \overline{p}) = 0$. This example is a particular case of the specification considered in Remark 1.2, with $\Sigma_i m_i h_i = 1$. Although $m(J + H) = 4$ here, (2.13) leads actually to a local perfect foresight dynamics of dimension 2, in which (p_{t+1}, k_t) is function (p_t, k_{t-1}),

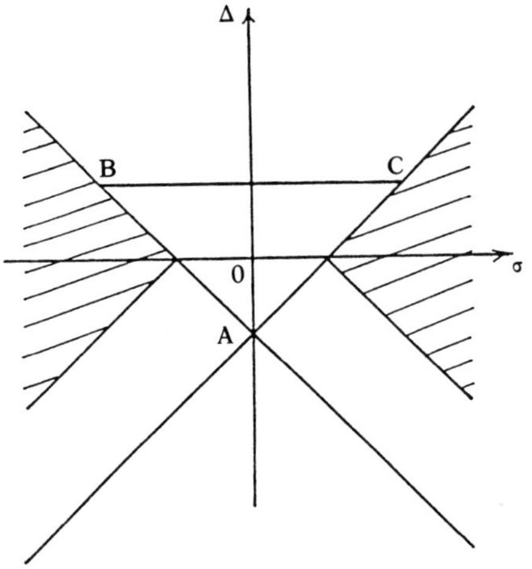

Figure 3a.

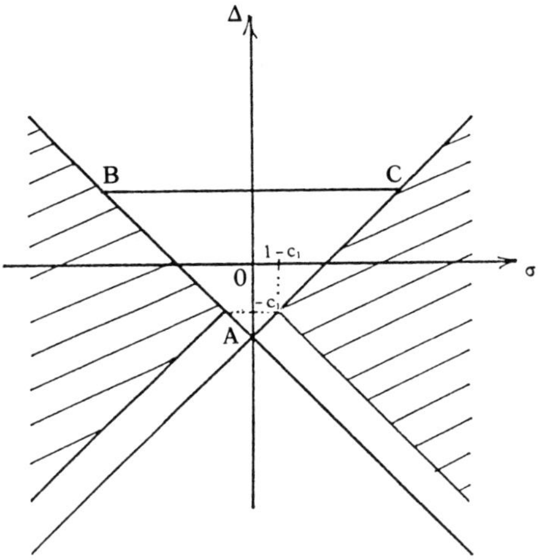

Figure 3b.

since the temporary equilibrium map does not depend on p_{t-1}. The analysis of Remark 1.2 shows then that if the expectations function detects period 2, and if all roots of $P_W(\lambda) = 0$ are such that $|\lambda| < 1$, then the stationary state is a saddle point in the local perfect foresight dynamics, and is thus generally locally determinate.

These facts can be verified directly. Let A_{-1}^k, A_0^p, A_0^k, A_1^p be the 2×1 matrices of partial derivatives of (the two components of) the temporary equilibrium map T with respect to k_{t-1}, p_t, k_t, and ${}_tp_{t+1}^e$, respectively, evaluated at the stationary state. If the matrix (A_1^p, A_0^k) is invertible, the equation $T(k_{t-1}, p_t, k_t, p_{t+1}) = 0$ can be solved in (p_{t+1}, k_t) near the stationary state $(\overline{p}, \overline{k})$. This leads to the two-dimensional local perfect foresight difference equation

$$\begin{pmatrix} p_{t+1} \\ k_t \end{pmatrix} = F_{\text{loc}} \begin{pmatrix} p_t \\ k_{t-1} \end{pmatrix}. \tag{2.14}$$

Then $P_F(\lambda)$ is the characteristic polynomial of the Jacobian matrix of F_{loc} evaluated at the stationary state, that is, of the matrix

$$-(A_1^p, A_0^k)^{-1}(A_0^p, A_{-1}^k) = \begin{pmatrix} \alpha & \beta \\ \gamma & \delta \end{pmatrix}.$$

The perfect foresight characteristic equation reduces then to

$$P_F(\lambda) \equiv \lambda^2 - \sigma\lambda + \Delta = 0, \tag{2.15}$$

where $\sigma = \alpha + \delta$ and $\Delta = \alpha\delta - \beta\gamma$ are, as usual, the sum and the product of the two roots of (2.15). As in the text, the stationary state is a saddle point in the local perfect foresight dynamics if and only if $|\sigma| > |1 + \Delta|$.

The temporary equilibrium dynamics are obtained by plugging the expectations function

$${}_tp_{t+1}^e = \psi(p_{t-1}, k_{t-1}, \ldots, p_{t-L}, k_{t-L}) \tag{2.16}$$

into (2.13). We note c_j and d_j the partial derivatives of ψ with respect to p_{t-j} and k_{t-j}, evaluated at the stationary state. If ψ detects period 2, we have

$$\sum_j c_j = 1, \quad \sum_j (-1)^j c_j = -1, \qquad \sum_j d_j = 0, \quad \sum_j (-1)^j d_j = 0. \tag{2.17}$$

A local temporary equilibrium dynamics can be defined when the matrix (A_0^p, A_0^k) is invertible. It can be verified that this condition is equivalent to $\alpha \neq 0$ whenever (A_1^p, A_0^k) is itself invertible, and that the corresponding characteristic equation is given by

$$P_W(\lambda) \equiv \lambda^{2L} - \alpha^{-1}\Delta\lambda^{2L-1} - \alpha^{-1}\lambda^L\left(\sum_j c_j\lambda^{L-j} + \gamma\sum_j d_j\lambda^{L-j}\right)$$
$$+ \alpha^{-1}\delta\lambda^{L-1}\sum_j c_j\lambda^{L-j} = 0. \tag{2.18}$$

It follows from (2.18) that, if the expectations function detects period 2, then

$$P_W(1) = \alpha^{-1}[\sigma - (1 + \Delta)], \quad P_W(-1) = \alpha^{-1}(\sigma + 1 + \Delta),$$

and thus, that if all roots of (2.18) are such that $|\lambda| < 1$, then $|\sigma| > |1 + \Delta|$. This result is valid even if we allow ψ to depend on the current state.

The reader will verify that the converse also holds in the particular case $c_1 = 1$, $c_2 = \ldots = c_L = 0$ and $d_j = 0$ for all j. More generally, sufficient conditions ensuring that all roots of (2.18) satisfy $|\lambda| < 1$ can be found as in the text; they involve, as in the Lemma, the behavior of the expressions $\Sigma_j c_j\lambda^{-j}$ and $\Sigma_j d_j\lambda^{-j}$ for $|\lambda| = 1$. The details are left to the reader.

Acknowledgments

This work has been supported by a grant from the National Science Foundation at the Institute for Mathematical Studies in the Social Sciences, Stanford University, Stanford, California.

Notes

1. We adopt here, to save notations, the "aggregate" viewpoint in which all traders make the same forecast at each date. To be general, we should have distinguished the forecasts made at t by each trader i, that is ${}_tx^e_{i,t+h}$. The reader will easily verify that our results are still valid in this more general formulation.

2. The case in which forecasts made in previous periods influence current expectations, and thus the sort of "error learning" behavior that was extensively studied in a temporary competitive equilibrium framework by Fuchs (see, e.g., Fuchs 1979), can be handled with the methods of this paper by modifying only slightly the conceptual apparatus (the state of the economy has to be defined as x_t *and* the forecasts made at t, i.e., ${}_tx^e_{t+1}, \ldots, {}_tx^e_{t+H}$), and leads to qualitatively similar results.

3. More rigorously, let W^*_{loc} be the map that associates to every $(x_{t-1}, \ldots, x_{t-M})$ in U the vector $(x_t, \ldots, x_{t-M+1})$ with x_t given by (1.4). Then $P_W(\lambda)$ is the characteristic polynomial of the Jacobian matrix of W^*_{loc}, evaluated at the fixed point $(\bar{x}, \ldots, \bar{x})$.

4. The concept of an intertemporal equilibrium is inherently static, since there, all states and forecasts for $t \geqslant 0$ are brought into equilibrium *simultaneously*. A related

point is that in (1.5), forecasts are determined at t by the *future* equilibrium states, whereas these are not part of the traders' information at that date.

It is possible nevertheless to "implement" intertemporal equilibria as dynamic sequences of temporary equilibria, by restricting appropriately the expectations functions in (1.2). For instance, let us focus on the immediate vicinity of the stationary state $\bar{x}$, and assume that the traders know the map T or at least F_{loc}. They can then use (1.7) to form expectations. Specifically, let $L = H + J$ and look at the (local) trajectory generated by (1.7) for t, $t + 1$, ..., from the initial conditions $(x_{t-1}, \ldots, x_{t-L})$, i.e., $x_t = F_{\text{loc}}(x_{t-1}, \ldots, x_{t-L})$, $x_{t+1} = F_{\text{loc}}(x_t, x_{t-1}, \ldots, x_{t-L+1})$, and so on. Such x_{t+h} are well defined for all $0 \leqslant h \leqslant \tau$ for any given τ, and functions of the initial conditions, i.e., $\psi_h(x_{t-1}, \ldots, x_{t-L})$, provided that these initial conditions are close enough to the stationary state. Using these functions as (local) forecasting rules $\psi_1, \ldots, \psi_H$ in (1.2) yields sequences of temporary equilibria, near the stationary state, along which there are no forecasting errors. (This discussion of the relations between temporary equilibrium and perfect foresight dynamics is adapted from the introduction to Grandmont 1987b, where only the simple case $m = 1$, $H = 1$, $J = 0$ was considered.)

5. The determinant of a matrix is equal to the product of its eigenvalues, counting multiplicities. Thus $\det(A_0)$ and $\det(A_H)$ have opposite signs if and only if one of these matrices has an even number of negative real eigenvalues (again counting multiplicities), whereas this number is odd for the other matrix. Note that the matrix of partial derivatives of F_{loc} with respect to x_t, evaluated at $(\bar{x}, \ldots, \bar{x})$ is equal to $-A_H^{-1}A_0$. The condition of the text is satisfied if and only if this matrix has an even number of negative real eigenvalues, i.e., is orientation preserving.

6. The reader will verify that these results are valid even if ψ depends upon the current state, as one should expect from Remark 1.1.

7. In the case $\Delta = 0$, i.e., when the predetermined variable x_{t-1} has no influence locally at the stationary state, these results reduce to those of theorem 5.1 of Grandmont and Laroque 1986.

References

Farmer, R. E. A. (1986), "Deficits and Cycles," *Journal of Economic Theory* 40, 77–88.

Fuchs, G. (1979), "Is Error Learning Behaviour Stabilizing?" *Journal of Economic Theory* 20, 300–317. Reprinted in Grandmont 1987.

Fuchs, G. and G. Laroque (1976), "Dynamics of Temporary Equilibria and Expectations," *Econometrica* 44, 1157–1178. Reprinted in Grandmont 1987.

Grandmont, J. M. (ed.) (1987), *Temporary Equilibrium. Selected Readings*, Academic Press.

Grandmont, J. M. and G. Laroque (1986), "Stability of Cycles and Expectations," *Journal of Economic Theory* 40, 138–151.

Jullien, B. (1986), "Competitive Business Cycles in an Overlapping Generations Economy with Productive Investment," mimeo, Harvard University.

Reichlin, P. (1986), "Equilibrium Cycles in an Overlapping Generations Economy with Production," *Journal of Economic Theory* 40, 89–102.

Tillmann, G. (1983), "Stability in a Simple Pure Consumption Loan Model," *Journal of Economic Theory* 30, 315–329. Reprinted in Grandmont 1987.

Tirole, J. (1985), "Asset Bubbles and Overlapping Generations," *Econometrica* 53, 1071–1100. Reprinted with corrections in *Econometrica* 53, 1499–1528.

Woodford, M. (1984), "Indeterminacy of Equilibrium in the Overlapping Generations Model: A Survey," mimeo, Columbia University.

Woodford, M. (1986a), "Stationary Sunspot Equilibria in a Finance Constrained Economy," *Journal of Economic Theory* 40, 128–137.

Woodford, M. (1986b), "Learning to Believe in Sunspots," mimeo, University of Chicago.

4 Notes on Sunspot Equilibria in Finite Horizon Models

Roger Guesnerie and
Jean-Jacques Laffont

1. Introduction

With his characterization of an efficient accumulation of capital in an infinite horizon general equilibrium model, Edmond Malinvaud (1953) has made an essential contribution to our understanding of the intertemporal economic equilibrium. The advances of normative theory, among which Malinvaud's paper is one of the most brilliant, called for complementary developments in the positive theory of intertemporal equilibrium. A central role was given by these developments to the role of economic agents' expectations. This paper is an attempt to synthesize and extend our knowledge of this role in a *finite* horizon general equilibrium model.

The rational expectations hypothesis has been the object of an often confused debate. It remains that its central role in modern economic theory makes necessary a study of general equilibrium with rational expectations as thorough as the study of economies with a complete system of Arrow-Debreu markets.

One of the first questions raised by the rational expectations hypothesis can be formulated as follows: To what extent does this hypothesis enable us to extend the Walrasian ideas on intertemporal equilibrium? Rational expectations have often been viewed as a substitute for an intertemporal invisible hand, which leads to constructions preserving most normative properties of Walrasian equilibria. It is true that there are intimate connections between the equilibria à la Walras-Arrow-Debreu-Malinvaud and some rational expectations equilibria. For example, it is well known that in finite horizon economies there is a (possibly generic) one-to-one relationship between the Radner (1972) equilibria of prices, plans, and price expectations and the Arrow-Debreu equilibria as long as the market structure is rich enough.[1] It is also known that this relationship ceases to be valid in infinite horizon models. Slowly the idea has emerged, that, even in finite horizon models, a garbling of expectations by what Cass and Shell have called *extrinsic uncertainty* could lead to rational expectations equilibria quite different from the intertemporal Arrow-Debreu equilibria. Can this garbling by what has also been called *sunspots* effectively occur? Cass and Shell (1983a, b) have given in a two-period horizon model—but their arguments apply to any finite horizon model—conditions that imply that "sunspots do not matter."

Their theorem, that we will review in section 2, requires a number of restrictive conditions to restore the identification of rational expectations general equilibria with Arrow-Debreu equilibria. In view of the difficulties met to relax these assumptions, it has been conjectured that robust sunspot equilibria should exist in any (sufficiently large) class of models in which some conditions of the "ineffectivity theorem" are violated. Cass and Shell (1983a, b) see in this conjecture a "Pholk" theorem that has already received a number of illustrations.

The proof of the Cass and Shell theorem suggests classifying the assumptions it requires into four categories:

(a) The agents have strictly concave von Neumann-Morgenstern (VNM) utility functions.

(b) Sunspots lead to the creation of markets contingent to the values taken by the sunspots. These markets are complete in the usual sense of the word and enable agents to buy insurance against sunspots.

(c) The existing markets (not inclusive of the markets contingent on sunspots) are themselves complete.

(d) In the absence of sunspots, the intertemporal equilibria are Pareto-efficient.

We will exclude from our present analysis the infinite horizon models,[2] and the imperfect competition models,[3] which can lead to a violation of condition d. We can then note that the current results on the existence of sunspot equilibria in finite horizon models illustrate a violation of condition b. By assuming that the markets contingent on sunspots are open but that some agents are excluded from these markets (because they belong to a generation born later than the date at which these markets are active), Cass and Shell (1983a) have stressed "participation constraints," which falsify condition b. They have provided robust examples of participation constraints in that context, which are the basis for a more general theory of participation constraints (Balasko 1987; Balasko, Cass, and Shell 1988). The approach that we follow in this paper goes beyond an exclusive attention to participation constraints.

First, we provide in section 2 an example of an economy in which a violation of condition a leads to sunspot equilibria. This example, although elementary, fills a gap of the literature.

Next, we consider an economy with two periods in which asset markets may be incomplete in the absence of sunspots. When these assets can be made contingent on sunspots—we then define *-Radner equilibrium—then only condition c is violated, if initial markets were actually incomplete. When insurance markets on sunspots cannot be organized—we then define *-extended Radner equilibrium then only condition b is violated (but here it is an interdiction and not a participation constraint) if initial asset markets were complete or both conditions b and c are violated if the initial asset markets were incomplete. In each of these cases we prove the existence of sunspot equilibria. Our proofs are not very general because they rely on a two-period model with two commodities, two states for *intrinsic* uncertainty and two states for extrinsic uncertainty. However, they go beyond the simple construction of robust examples. They rest on the use of the Poincaré-Hopf theorem, which has already been shown to be useful in this literature by Azariadis and Guesnerie (1982) for infinite-horizon models.[4] Further research will determine the generality of our results.

Finally, after proving the existence of sunspot equilibria in new contexts, we discuss their normative properties with an example. This limited analysis gives results similar to those already obtained in the second-best literature.

Finally, let us stress the exploratory character of our work. We put forward a number of points requiring more systematic studies that we hope to stimulate.

2. Sunspots Do Not Matter: Back to the Ineffectivity Theory

We consider an exchange economy with L commodities and I consumers. Consumer i, $i = 1, \ldots, I$, has a continuous strictly increasing von Neumann-Morgenstern utility function defined on his consumption set R_+^L. Consumer i owns initial resources $w^i \in R_+^L$, $i = 1, \ldots, I$.

At date 0 markets are set up. At date 1, a sunspot, that is to say a random variable $\tilde{\theta}$, takes its value in a finite set $H = \{\theta_1, \ldots, \theta_K\}$ with (common knowledge) associated probabilities $\{\pi_1, \ldots, \pi_K\}$. The value taken by the sunspot is observed by all agents.

This timing of events is worth commenting upon. If sunspots were observed before the opening of markets, they could not have an effect on the agents' behavior. These agents take prices parametrically and their demand functions are not affected by their expectations of sunspot values.

However, sunspots could already serve, in a case of multiple static equilibria, of conventional selection mechanism among equilibria. We will come back to this role later on.

With our present timing, opening of markets, then sunspots, the existence of sunspots creates the opportunity of opening markets contingent on sunspots.

We say that we have a *complete market system* if, at date 0, L markets—one for each physical commodity—are opened.

We say that we have a **-complete market system* (sun complete) if, at date 0, $L \times K$ markets are opened, i.e., markets contingent on sunspots are organized for each physical commodity.

Let us define the equilibria emerging in each market system.

A competitive equilibrium of the complete market system is a price-vector $\overline{p} \in R_+^L$ and an allocation, $(\overline{x}^1, \ldots, \overline{x}^I) \in R_+^{LI}$, such that

$$(\alpha) \quad \overline{x}^i \in \underset{x^1}{\operatorname{argmax}} \{u^i(x^i) \colon \overline{p}x^i \leqslant \overline{p} \cdot w^i\},$$

$$(\beta) \quad \sum_i x^i = \sum_i \overline{w}^i,$$

where $i = 1, \ldots, I$.

A *competitive equilibrium of the *-complete market system* is a vector of prices contingent on sunspots, $\overline{p}(\cdot) \colon H \to R_+^L$, and a contingent allocation, $(\overline{x}^1(\cdot), \ldots, \overline{x}^I(\cdot) \colon H \to R_+^{LI})$, such that

$$(\alpha) \quad \overline{x}^i(\cdot) \in \underset{x^i(\cdot)}{\operatorname{argmax}} \left\{\sum_k \pi_k u^i(\mathrm{x}^i(\theta_k)) \colon \sum_k \overline{p}(\theta_k) x^i(\theta_k) \leqslant \sum_k \overline{p}(\theta_k) w^i\right\},$$

$$(\beta) \quad \sum_i \overline{x}^i(\theta_k) = \sum_i w^i,$$

where $i = 1, \ldots, I$ and $k = 1, \ldots, K$.

Finally, a contingent allocation $(\overline{x}^1(\cdot), \ldots, \overline{x}^I(\cdot))$ is said to be *ex ante Pareto optimal* iff there does not exist $(\tilde{\mathrm{x}}^1(\cdot), \ldots, \tilde{\mathrm{x}}^I(\cdot)) \colon H \to R_+^{LI}$ such that

$$(\alpha) \quad \sum_k \pi_k u^i(\tilde{x}^i(\theta_k)) > \sum_k \pi_k u^i(\overline{x}^i(\theta_k)),$$

$$(\beta) \quad \sum_i \tilde{x}^i(\theta_k) \leqslant \sum_i w^i,$$

where $i = 1, \ldots, I$ and $k = 1, \ldots, K$.

Is it possible that the creation of markets contingent on sunspots alters the competitive equilibria of a complete market system? Cass and Shell (1983a,b)[5] have shown that, under some conditions, the answer is negative. This ineffectivity theorem takes here the following form.

Proposition 1. (Cass and Shell). If the VNM utility functions of consumers are strictly concave, any competitive equilibrium of the *-complete market system coincides with a competitive equilibrium of the complete market system.

Proof. Consider a competitive equilibrium of the *-complete market system, $\bar{p}(\theta), \bar{x}^1(\theta), \ldots, \bar{x}^I(\theta), \theta \in H$, which "depends effectively" on θ. From the first welfare theorem extended to uncertainty (Debreu 1956), the contingent allocation, $(\bar{x}^1(\cdot), \ldots, \bar{x}^I(\cdot))$, is *ex ante* Pareto optimal.

For any $\theta \in H$, we have

$$\sum_i \bar{x}^i(\theta) = \sum_i w^i. \tag{1}$$

Consider the expected allocation defined by

$$Ex^i = \sum_k \pi_k \bar{x}^i(\theta_k), \quad i = 1, \ldots, I. \tag{2}$$

From (1) we know that the noncontingent allocation, $Ex^1, \ldots, Ex^I$ is feasible. From the Jensen inequality we have

$$u^i(Ex^i) \geqslant \sum_k \pi_k u^i(\bar{x}^i(\theta_k)), \quad i = 1, \ldots, I. \tag{3}$$

The inequality is strict for at least one agent i, since for at least one i,

$$\bar{x}^i(\theta_k) \neq \bar{x}^i(\theta_{k'})$$

for two values $\theta_k, \theta_{k'}$. The *ex ante* Pareto optimality of $(\bar{x}^1(\cdot), \ldots, \bar{x}^I(\cdot))$ is therefore contradicted. (Remember that preferences are monotonic.) The competitive equilibrium of the *-complete market system is then nonstochastic. It is left to the reader to check that it then coincides with a competitive equilibrium of the complete market system. QED

Let us come back to the four ingredients of the reasoning already underlined in the introduction.

The Pareto superiority of the noncontingent allocation on the stochastic allocation rests on the *strict* risk aversion of agents (point a).[6]

The Pareto optimality of the stochastic allocation requires that markets be *-complete (see Debreu 1956). Initial markets must therefore be complete (point c) as well as markets contingent on sunspots (point b).

The Pareto optimality of the stochastic allocation is ensured in finite horizon models only when agents behave competitively (point d).

In the next section we consider the relaxation of the strict concavity assumption (point a).

3. Sunspot Equilibria in the Absence of Risk Aversion

Relaxing the strict concavity of the VNM utility functions can indeed lead to the existence of sunspot equilibria. More precisely, we can state:

Proposition 2. There exist economies in which the consumers' VNM utility functions are not strictly concave and such that:

(i) There exists a competitive equilibrium of the *-complete market system that is not a competitive equilibrium of the complete market system.

(ii) The stochastic equilibrium of the *-complete system is unique and strictly dominates in the Pareto sense the (unique) deterministic equilibrium of the complete system.

Proof. We construct a robust example in which the proposition holds. Consider an economy with two consumers and one commodity. There exists a sunspot

$$\theta_1, \theta_2; \pi_1, \pi_2 (= 1 - \pi_1).$$

Consumer 1 is risk-neutral and consumer 2 has the VNM utility function represented by figure 1. Marginal utility is monotonic in intervals between inflexion points of the graph.

Consumer 2's initial resource w^2 is such that

$$\pi_1 \bar{x}_1^2 + \pi_2 \bar{x}_2^2 = w^2 \quad (\pi_1 > 0, \pi_2 > 0) \tag{4}$$

Let us show then that the price system (π_1, π_2) of the *-complete market system supports a competitive equilibrium that Pareto dominates the initial allocation (which is a trivial competitive equilibrium for any price vector).

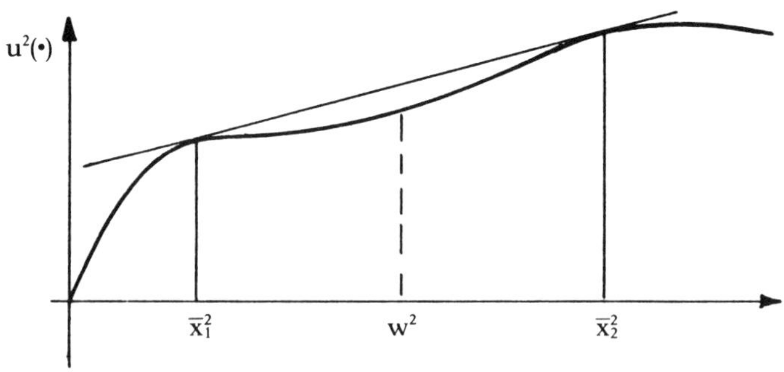

Figure 1.

Faced with the price vector (π_1, π_2), consumer 1 is indifferent between all bundles (x_1^1, x_2^1) such that

$$\pi_1 x_1^1 + \pi_2 x_2^1 = w^1 \tag{5}$$

which are compatible with his budget constraint.

We now show that the allocation $(\bar{x}_1^1, \bar{x}_2^1)$, $(\bar{x}_1^2, \bar{x}_2^2)$ defined by

$$\bar{x}_1^1 + \bar{x}_1^2 = w^1 + w^2; \bar{x}_2^1 + \bar{x}_2^2 = w^1 + w^2 \tag{6}$$

is a competitive equilibrium of the *-complete market system. Indeed,

(i) the bundle $(\bar{x}_1^1, \bar{x}_2^1)$ belongs to the budget set of agent 1 (combine (4) and (6) to get (5)) and maximizes (weakly) his utility function in this set.

(ii) the bundle $(\bar{x}_1^2, \bar{x}_2^2)$ maximizes agent 2's utility function under his budget constraint (4). We first note that the first-order conditions of this maximization are satisfied (and imply the equality of marginal utilities at $\bar{x}_1^2$ and $\bar{x}_2^2$). Then, we verify that these conditions cannot be verified elsewhere. Indeed, every pair (x, y) satisfying the budget constraint must be such that either $x < \bar{x}_1^2$ and $y > \bar{x}_2^2$ or $w^2 > x > \bar{x}_1^2$ and $w^2 < y < \bar{x}_2^2$. In each of these cases, it is not possible to have the equality of marginal utilities. Finally, we observe that this (unique) equilibrium Pareto dominates the initial allocation. QED

In the general model with strictly concave preferences, the possibility of insurance against sunspots annihilates their effects. On the contrary, in the absence of risk aversion the prior uncertainty wished by some agents can effectively emerge in a (stochastic) equilibrium of the *-system. Such is the general message behind Proposition 2. Note, however, that the possibility of constructing an example such as in Proposition 2 does not follow from the three obvious observations that we can make on an economy with non-strictly-concave VNM utility functions.

(α) There exists generally, in the class of random allocations, allocations that are Pareto-superior to allocations independent of the extrinsic uncertainty.

(β) An equilibrium of the *-complete market system, *if it exists*, is Pareto-optimal in the class of random allocations generated by extrinsic uncertainty.

(γ) An equilibrium of the *-system dominates in the Pareto sense the initial allocation generating this equilibrium (even if this initial allocation is the equilibrium of the complete system) as soon as it is different from it.

Proposition 2 illustrates these remarks but does not follow from them. In particular it illustrates observation γ, which we might wish to extend.

We would have to find general conditions ensuring the *existence* of an equilibrium in the *-complete system different from the equilibrium of the complete system taken as defining initial resources.

Let us conclude this section with a few additional remarks:

(i) The reader will verify easily that the example presented here and valid for a one-commodity simplistic economy can be transposed in an exchange economy with L goods. For example, for $L = 2$, assume that the above preferences are preferences along the diagonal of R^2 and that the preferences outside the diagonal are symmetric for each agent (with a quasi-concave utility function). Note also that the examples we have constructed have a single (initial) equilibrium and do not correspond to a *randomization* between competitive equilibria.

(ii) In appendix 2 we provide an example of sunspot equilibrium that Pareto-dominates the competitive equilibrium of the complete system by relying on a weakening of condition a to only linear (indirect) VNM utility functions and using externalities to upset condition d.

(iii) We have assumed that agents have the same a priori beliefs on the probabilities of sunspots. When these beliefs differ, an additional degree of freedom appears *for* the construction of sunspot equilibria (see also Maskin and Tirole 1985).

(iv) Cass and Polemarchakis (1987) have observed that nonconvexities in production combined with strictly concave VNM utility functions do not generate sunspot equilibria Pareto superior to deterministic equilibria. This point (which does not contradict proposition 2) is intuitive enough, since garbling of production does not provide any gain when preferences are strictly convex. In a private communication, K. Shell has informed us that examples of sunspot equilibria relying on the *nonconvexity of consumption sets* (that we have not considered) exist.

4. Incomplete Market Economies: Model and Concepts

We consider an exchange economy similar to the one in section 2, but with two periods and where, for simplification, consumers do not have initial resources in period 1 or where $u^i(\cdot)$: $R^L_+ \to R$ is the VNM utility function of consumer i in period 2.

Moreover, in period 2, there are S possible states of nature with probabilities $\gamma_1, \ldots, \gamma_S$. They represent intrinsic uncertainty which affects either preferences or initial resources. Still, to simplify, we assume that only initial resources are affected by intrinsic uncertainty. Let w^i_{ls} be consumer i's initial resource in good l in state s, $i = 1, \ldots, I$, $l = 1, \ldots, L$, $s = 1, \ldots, S$.

There exists also a sunspot $\tilde{\theta}$, independent of the intrinsic uncertainty, that can take K values $\theta_1, \ldots, \theta_K$ with probabilities $\pi_1, \ldots, \pi_K$.

A complete market system is here a system of LS Arrow-Debreu markets contingent on the intrinsic uncertainty.

A *-complete market system is a system of KLS markets contingent on the intrinsic and extrinsic uncertainty.

We could define competitive equilibria for both market systems and obtain an extension of Proposition 1. This is left to the reader and, instead, we introduce the possibility of incomplete markets.

We define an asset (real asset in the usual terminology), characterized by the following matrix:

$$a^m = [a_1^m, \ldots, a_S^m] = \begin{bmatrix} a_{11}^m & \cdots & a_{1S}^m \\ a_{L1}^m & \cdots & a_{LS}^m \end{bmatrix},$$

where a_{ls}^m is the quantity (positive or negative) of commodity 1 that the owner of one unit of asset m receives in state s of period 2.

These assets are exchanged in period 1 during which there is no consumption activity. Given that exchanges are sequential, the relevant equilibrium concept is the Radner equilibrium of prices, plans, and price expectations.

A *Radner equilibrium* is a price system $q^* \in R^M$ for assets, a price system $p_s^* \in R_+^L$ for goods in each state s of period 2, a portfolio of assets $z^{*i} \in R^M$ for each consumer, and an allocation $(x^{*1}, \ldots, x^{*I}) \in R^{LI}$ for each state s of period 2 such that

$$\text{(i)} \quad (z^{*i}, x_1^{*i}, \ldots, x_S^{*i}) \in \underset{(z^i, x_1^i, \ldots, x_S^i)}{\operatorname{argmax}} \left\{ \sum_s \gamma_s u^i(x_s^i) \colon \sum_m q_m^* z_m^i \leqslant 0 \right.$$

$$\left. \text{and } p_s^* x_s^i \leqslant p_s^* \left(w_s^i + \sum_m a_s^m z_m^i \right), s = 1, \ldots, S \right\}$$

for $i = 1 \ldots I$,

$$\text{(ii)} \quad \sum_i z^{*i} \leqslant 0,$$

$$\text{(iii)} \quad \sum_i x_s^{*i} = \sum_i w_s^i, \quad s = 1, \ldots, S.$$

We also define a new notion of equilibrium in which asset markets are contingent on extrinsic uncertainty.[7]

A **-Radner equilibrium* is a price system of assets contingent on extrinsic uncertainty, $q^*(\cdot)\colon H \to R_+^M$, a price system of goods contingent on extrinsic uncertainty for each state s (intrinsic uncertainty) of period 2, $p_s^*(\cdot)$: $H \to R_+^L$, $s = 1 \ldots, S$, a portfolio contingent on extrinsic uncertainty for each agent i, $z^{*i}(\cdot)$: $H \to R^M$, $i = 1, \ldots, I$, and a contingent allocation $(x_s^{*1}(\cdot), \ldots, x_s^{*I}(\cdot))$: $H \to R^{IL}$ for each state of nature (intrinsic uncertainty) of period 2, such that

(i) $(z^{*i}(\cdot), x_1^{*i}(\cdot), \ldots, x_S^{*i}(\cdot))$

$$\in \underset{(z^i(\cdot), x_1^i(\cdot) \ldots, x_S^i(\cdot))}{\operatorname{argmax}} \left\{ \sum_s \sum_k \gamma_s \pi_k u^i(x_s^i(\theta_k)) \colon \sum_m \sum_k q_m^*(\theta_k) z_m^i(\theta_k) \leqslant 0 \right.$$

$$\left. p_s^*(\theta_k) x_s^i(\theta_k) \leqslant p_s^*(\theta_k)\,[w_s^i + \sum_m a_s^m z_m^i(\theta_k)]\, \forall s, \forall k \right\}$$

for $i = 1, \ldots, I$,

(ii) $\sum_i z^{*i}(\theta_k) \leqslant 0 \ \forall k$,

(iii) $\sum_i x_s^{*i}(\theta_k) = \sum_i w^i \ \forall k, \forall s$.

In the Radner equilibrium, the first period is characterized by the exchange of assets, which determine, once the state of nature is revealed in period 2, the initial resources that agents have on the spot markets which then open. In the *-Radner equilibrium, the asset markets of period 1 are themselves markets contingent on sunspots. The realized values of both sunspots and intrinsic uncertainty determine the agents' initial resources in period 2. Of course, the introduction of transactions contingent on sunspots is problematic—even somewhat paradoxical in a world of incomplete markets. Verifiability (in the sense of contract theory) of the values taken by sunspots is of course essential.[8] When this verifiability condition is not met, or for any other reason making the opening of these contingent markets impossible, the description of equilibrium requires an intermediary concept. This notion of equilibrium allows expectations and consequently second period's realizations to depend on sunspots. But, as in a Radner equilibrium, it excludes asset markets contingent on sunspots.

An **-extended Radner equilibrium* is a price system of assets, $q^* \in R^M$, a price system of goods contingent on sunspots in each state s of period 2, $p^*(\cdot)$: $H \to R_+^L$, $s = 1, \ldots, S$, a portfolio of assets for each agent, $z^{*i} \in R^M$, $i = 1, \ldots, I$, a contingent allocation $(x_s^{*1}(\cdot), \ldots, x_s^{*I}(\cdot)$: $H \to R^{IL}$, for each state of nature s of period 2, such that

(i) $(z^{*i}, x_1^{*i}(\cdot), \ldots, x_S^{*i}(\cdot)) \in \underset{(z^i, x_1^i(\cdot)\ldots, x_S^i(\cdot))}{\operatorname{argmax}} \left\{\sum_{sk} \gamma_s \pi_k u^i(x_s^i(\theta_k)):\right.$

$$\left.\sum_m q_m^* z_m^i \leqslant 0,\ p_s^*(\theta_k) x_s^i(\theta_k) \leqslant p_s^*(\theta_k)\left(w_s^i + \sum_m a_s^m z_m^i\right) \forall k, \forall s\right\}$$

for $i = 1, \ldots, I$,

(ii) $\sum_i z^{*i} \leqslant 0$,

(iii) $\sum_i x_s^{*i}(\theta_k) = \sum_i w_s^i\ Vk.$

Some clarification among these concepts is obtained from the following lemma.

Lemma. If the VNM utility functions are strictly concave,

(1) a Radner equilibrium is a degenerated *-Radner equilibrium;

(2) a Radner equilibrium is a degenerated *-extended Radner equilibrium.

Proof. (1) Start from a Radner equilibrium $(q^*, (p_s^*), (z^{*i}), (x_s^{*i}))$ and let us show that $q_m^*(\theta_k) = \pi_k q_m^*$, $p_s^*(\theta_k) = p_s^*$, $z^{*i}(\theta_k) = z^{*i}$, $x_s^{*i}(\theta_k) = x_s^{*i}$. Vi, s, k is a *-Radner equilibrium. Note first that, since the initial consumption plans satisfy the Radner budget constraints, the new consumption plans satisfy the *-Radner budget constraints. Next we observe that if, for the price candidates for a *-Radner equilibrium, consumer i can obtain a (extrinsic) random consumption $x_s^i(\theta_k)$ (satisfying his budget constraint), he can also obtain the consumption vector $\sum_k \pi_k x_s^i(\theta_k)$ independent of extrinsic uncertainty. Since the consumer has strict risk aversion he will choose the nonrandom consumption. Therefore he will choose (x_s^{*i}), z^{*i}.

(2) Start also from a Radner equilibrium $(q^*, (p_s^*), (z^{*i}), (x_s^{*i}))$ and let us show that q_m^*, $p_s^*(\theta_k) = p_s^*$, z^{*i}, $x_s^{*i}(\theta_k) = x_s^{*i}$, Vi, s, k, is a *-extended Radner equilibrium. We verify as above that the new allocation satisfies the appropriate budget constraints. Since the second period budget constraints are independent of θ_k for the given prices, a risk-averse consumer will choose a consumption vector x_s^i independent of θ_k and therefore he chooses x_s^{*i}. QED

This lemma will provide the basis for the method of proof in the next section.

We are now equipped to formulate precisely the main questions raised in the introduction:

- When does there exist nondegenerated *-Radner equilibria and *-extended Radner equilibria?
- What can we say, from the normative point of view, about the three types of equilibria we have defined?

5. Existence of Nondegenerated *-Radner Equilibria

Note first that the equilibrium allocations obtained in the spot markets of period 2 are *ex post* Pareto-optimal (since all good markets are open and behavior is competitive). If this were not the case, there would be a reason why the garbling of the period 2 allocation might have beneficial effects. Also, if the VNM utility functions were not strictly concave, the creation of markets conditional on sunspots might be beneficial, just as in proposition 2.

With enough assets ($M \geqslant S$), Radner equilibria are not only *ex post* Pareto-optimal, but also generically *ex ante* Pareto-optimal (see Kreps 1982; Magill and Shafer 1986; Geanakoplos and Polemarchakis 1986). This result suggests that a *-Radner equilibrium is also generically optimal and therefore coincides generically with a Radner equilibrium. However, there is a pitfall in this reasoning.

The genericity argument (see Magill and Shafer 1986 for a clear exposition) rests on the genericity of the "regularity" of the assets' matrix of returns. But by construction, in a *-complete market system, these matrices of returns are *not* regular. Therefore, proposition 1 cannot be extended generically to *-Radner equilibria. Nevertheless, we can state:

Proposition 3. If the VNM utility functions are strictly concave, a *-Radner equilibrium is either not *ex ante* Pareto-optimal or coincides with a Radner equilibrium.

Proof. as proposition 1.

Thus, the opening of markets contingent on sunspots may have the potentiality of leading to equilibria that are not generically Pareto-optimal contrary to the initial Radner equilibria that are generically Pareto-optimal (see section 7).

Next, we consider the case of truly incomplete markets ($M < S$).

Proposition 4. If the number of assets is insufficient ($M < S$), there exist economies with nondegenerated *-Radner equilibria.

Proof. We consider a simplified version of the two-period exchange economy defined in section 4. There are two states of intrinsic uncertainty and two states of extrinsic uncertainty; there are two goods and good 1 is defined as the numeraire in each state s. Initial endowments of both goods are strictly positive in each state s for all consumers; the two values of the sunspot have equal probability ($\pi_1 = \pi_2 = \frac{1}{2}$); there is a single asset, which corresponds to the noncontingent delivery of one unit of the numeraire in period 2; agents have strictly concave utility functions.

Let us denote $x^i(p_s, R^i)$ the (unique) solution of the program

$$\text{Max } \{u^i(x_s^i) | p_s x_s^i \leqslant R^i\}.$$

In this particular model the unique asset is not exchanged in a Radner equilibrium. Then, a Radner equilibrium is a system of spot prices in period 2, $(\overline{p}_s)$,[9] such that

$$\sum_i x^i(\overline{p}_s, \overline{p}_s \cdot w_s^i) - \sum_i w_s^i = 0 \qquad \forall s \tag{7}$$

Consider now the maximization program of an agent in a *-complete market system. We have

$$\text{Max} \sum_{s,k} \gamma_s \pi_k u^i(x_{sk}^i) z_1^i + q z_2^i \leqslant 0,$$

$$p_{sk} x_{sk}^i \leqslant p_{sk} w_s^i + z_k^i,$$

where $k = 1, 2$ and $s = 1, 2$.

We use in this proof more compact notation: $x_{sk}^i \equiv x_s^i(\theta_k)$; $p_{sk} \equiv p_s(\theta_k)$; $z_k^i = z^i(\theta_k)$; the relative price of the asset conditional on θ_2 is denoted q.

Let $z_k^i(q, (p_{sk}))$, $(x^i(p_{sk} p_{sk} w_s^i + z_k^i))$ be the (unique) solution of the above program.

A *-Radner equilibrium is a system of asset prices and spot prices, $\tilde{q}$, $(\tilde{p}_{sk})$, such that

$$\sum_i z_k^i(\tilde{q}, (\tilde{p}_{sk})) = 0, \tag{8}$$

$$\sum_i (x^i(\tilde{p}_{sk}, \tilde{p}_{sk} w_s^i + z_k^i(\tilde{q}, (\tilde{p}_{sk}))) - w_s^i) = 0, \tag{9}$$

where $s = 1, \ldots, S$.

The proof has now three steps.[10]

Step 1. We prove that $\tilde{q} = 1$, $\tilde{p}_{sk} = \overline{p}_s$, $k = 1, 2$, $\tilde{x}^i_{sk} = \overline{x}^i_s$ is a *-Radner equilibrium.

This follows from Lemma 1 or directly from the fact that asset markets with $\tilde{q} = 1$ enable consumers to achieve only random (in k) consumption vectors with mean $\overline{x}^i_s$, an operation that is not desirable because of risk aversion. Therefore, $\overline{z}^i_1 = \overline{z}^i_2 = 0$.

Step 2. We compute the determinant of the Jacobian associated with equations (8) and (9) at the degenerated *-Radner equilibrium $(1, (\overline{p}_s), (\overline{x}_s))$.

Rewrite (8) and (9) by keeping in (8) only the market equilibrium condition for the asset contingent on θ_2 and in (9) the equilibrium conditions for good 2. Before doing so, denote $z^i = z^i_2$ so that $z^i_1 = -z^i$. (Note here that at the initial equilibrium since $z^i_1 + z^i_2 = 0$ from the budget constraint, and $\overline{z}^i = 0$ and $(\partial z^i_1/\partial u) + (\partial z^i_2/\partial u) = 0$ for any variable u, in particular for $u = q$.) Let us also identify $\tilde{p}_{sk}$, w^i_s and x^i_s with their second components (unless they appear in an inner product). With a slight abuse of notation we get

$$\sum_i z^i(\tilde{q}, (\tilde{p}_{sk})) = 0, \tag{8'}$$

$$\sum_i x^i(\tilde{p}_{sk}, \tilde{p}_{sk} w^i_s + z^i(\tilde{q}, (\tilde{p}_{sk}))) - w^i_s = 0,^{11} \tag{9'}$$

where $s = 1, 2$.

Then, define (with the same conventions)

$$A^s_u \overset{\text{def}}{=} \sum_i \frac{\partial x^i}{\partial R}(\overline{p}_s, \overline{p}_s w^i_s) \frac{\partial z^i}{\partial u}(1, \overline{p}_s),$$

$$Z_{sk} \overset{\text{def}}{=} \sum_i \frac{\partial x^i}{\partial p_{sk}}(\overline{p}_s, \overline{p}_s w^i_s) + \sum_i \frac{\partial x^i}{\partial R}(\overline{p}_s, \overline{p}_s w^i_s) w^i_s,$$

$$\alpha_u \overset{\text{def}}{=} \sum_i \frac{\partial z^i}{\partial u}(1, \overline{p}_s).$$

The determinant of the (5×5) Jacobian matrix of the (independent) (8′) and (9′) system is

$$\Delta = \begin{vmatrix} \alpha_q & \alpha_{p_{11}} & \alpha_{p_{12}} & \alpha_{p_{21}} & \alpha_{p_{22}} \\ -A^1_q & Z_{11} - A^1_{p_{11}} & -A^1_{p_{12}} & -A^1_{p_{21}} & -A^1_{p_{22}} \\ A^1_q & A^1_{p_{11}} & Z_{12} + A^1_{p_{12}} & A^1_{p_{12}} & A^1_{p_{22}} \\ -A^2_q & -A^2_{p_{11}} & -A^2_{p_{12}} & Z_{21} - A^2_{p_{21}} & -A^2_{p_{22}} \\ A^2_q & A^2_{p_{11}} & A^2_{p_{12}} & A^2_{p_{21}} & Z_{22} + A^2_{p_{22}} \end{vmatrix}$$

The determinant is not modified if we add the third line to the second line, and also the fifth line to the fourth line. Moreover, the symmetry assumption for the sunspots implies $\alpha_{p_{s1}} = \alpha_{p_{s2}}$, $Z_{s1} = Z_{s2}$, and $A^s_{s1} = A^s_{s2}$, where $s = 1, 2$. We subtract the third column from the second and also the fifth column from the fourth. Finally, we obtain

$$\Delta = \begin{vmatrix} \alpha_q & 0 & \alpha_{p_{12}} & 0 & \alpha_{p_{22}} \\ 0 & 0 & Z_{12} & 0 & 0 \\ A^1_q & -Z_{12} & Z_{12} + A^1_{p_{12}} & 0 & A^1_{p_{22}} \\ 0 & 0 & 0 & 0 & Z_{22} \\ A^2_q & 0 & A^2_{p_{12}} & -Z_{22} & Z_{22} + A^2_{p_{22}} \end{vmatrix}$$

$$= (-1)^8 \alpha_q (Z_{12})^2 (Z_{22})^2.$$

Since income in each state of nature is normal (in view of the expected utility hypothesis), $\alpha_q < 0$; therefore, $\Delta < 0$, independent of the Radner equilibrium considered.

Step 3. The vector field on R^5_+ defined by (8′) and (9′) points inward. The Poincaré-Hopf degree is then $(-1)^5 = -1$. For each Radner equilibrium the degree is -1.

Therefore if we have n Radner equilibria there must be $(n - 1)$ nondegenerated *-Radner equilibrium. We have then shown the following: *If the economy has several Radner equilibria, then it has truly stochastic *-Radner equilibria.* But here the existence of several Radner equilibria follows from the existence of multiple spot equilibria in one state of nature at least (see appendix 2 for an example). This concludes the proof since many economies have this property. QED

Existence of *-Extended Radner Equilibria

Consider first the relationship between *-Radner equilibria and *-extended Radner equilibria. In both cases, spot prices in period 2 are perfectly correlated with sunspots. But in a *-equilibrium an agent has the ability to vary his wealth with sunspots, but cannot do so in a *-extended equilibrium. This suggests that in a *-extended equilibrium, sunspots play essentially the role of a selection mechanism among equilibria. We make this intuition more precise in the next Proposition.

Let ξ be the set of economies e in which the competitive equilibrium of period 2 is unique for all endowments that can be generated by the first-period assets. We then obtain the following proposition:

Proposition 5. For any $e \in \xi$, the *-extended Radner equilibria coincide with Radner equilibria.

Proof. Since sunspots do not affect the behaviors in the second (and last) period, for any endowments in period 2, there are unique equilibrium spot prices. Since the prices of assets and therefore transactions on assets are independent of sunspots in a *-extended Radner equilibrium, the endowments are independent of sunspots in each state s of period 2. Therefore, the prices $(p_s^*(\theta))$ coincide for all θ and, consequently, they coincide with the second period prices (p_s^*) of a Radner equilibrium. QED

Consider now the more general case where, for the same endowments in period 2, multiple equilibria may exist. Even if we restrict our attention to strictly concave VNM utility functions, we obtain the following proposition.

Proposition 6. If an economy of the type considered in proposition 4 has multiple Radner equilibria, i.e., here multiple second-period spot equilibria in at least one state of nature, it has at least one nondegenerated *-extended Radner equilibrium.

Proof. Since the (unique) asset market remains inactive, the equations defining an *-extended Radner equilibrium are

$$\sum_i (x^i(\tilde{p}_{sk}, \tilde{p}_{sk} w_s^i) - w_s^i) = 0, \qquad s = 1, 2.$$

If the economy has two Radner equilibria, $(\overline{p}_s)$ and $(\overline{\overline{p}}_s)$, with $\overline{p}_s \neq \overline{\overline{p}}_s$ for at least one s, then $\tilde{p}_{s1} = \overline{p}_s$, $\tilde{p}_{s2} = \overline{\overline{p}}_s$ produces an *-extended Radner equilibrium. This equilibrium is nothing else than a selection among Radner equilibria achieved through the help of sunspots. QED

7. Normative Comparisons

A first remark follows from proposition 4: In the economy considered in that proposition, a Radner equilibrium may dominate a *-Radner equilibrium from the point of view of a given usual welfare function. The economy may be constructed in such a way that at least one of the initial Radner equilibria is Pareto-efficient. The nondegenerated *-Radner equilibria that appear in this proposition are inferior for a social-welfare function that is maximized at that Pareto-optimal Radner equilibrium.

The next proposition affirms that the normative comparison between these two types of equilibria is ambiguous, even from the point of view of the Paretian criterion.

Proposition 7. In an economy of the type considered in Proposition 4, a Radner equilibrium may Pareto-dominate a *-extended Radner equilibrium and reciprocally.

Proof. See appendix 2 for an example.

However, when the number of assets is sufficient, nondegenerated *-extended Radner equilibria have less desirable normative properties than Radner equilibria.

Proposition 8. If the VNM utility functions are strictly concave, Radner equilibria are generically Pareto-optimal, but the nondegenerated *-extended Radner equilibria are not Pareto-optimal.

Proof. Obvious from proposition 3.

Note, finally, that in the absence of assets, *-extended Radner equilibria and *-Radner equilibria coincide. It follows that appendix 2 provides, formally, examples where the Pareto comparison between Radner equilibria and *-Radner equilibria is ambiguous. We conjecture that this ambiguous comparison subsists in any economy with incomplete markets in the following sense: For any number $M(<S)$ of given assets, there exist open sets of economies in which a Radner equilibrium dominates (resp. is dominated by) in the Pareto sense a *-Radner equilibrium. The same conclusion is likely if we substitute *-extended Radner equilibria instead of *-Radner equilibria.

Appendix 1

Consider an exchange economy with two consumers and two commodities. Consumer 1 has initial resources (1, 0) and preferences represented by the VNM utility function $x_1^{\alpha 1} x_2^{\alpha 2} (\alpha_1 + \alpha_2 = 1)$. Consumer 2 has initial resources (0, 1) and a VNM utility function $z_1^{\beta_1} z_2^{\beta_2} (\beta_1 + \beta_2 = 1)$. In the complete market system there exists in this Cobb-Douglas economy a unique equilibrium characterized by the price of good 2 (good 1 is the numeraire),

$$p = \frac{\alpha_2}{\alpha_1 + \alpha_2} \frac{\beta_1 + \beta_2}{\beta_1},$$

with associated utility levels

$$U^1 = \left(\frac{\alpha_1}{\alpha_1 + \alpha_2}\right)^{\alpha_1}\left(\frac{\beta_1}{\beta_1 + \beta_2}\right)^{\alpha_2}; U^2 = \left(\frac{\beta_2}{\beta_1 + \beta_2}\right)^{\beta_2}\left(\frac{\alpha_2}{\alpha_1 + \alpha_2}\right)^{\beta_1}.$$

Consider now a two-state sunspot with probabilities π and $1 - \pi$, and let $1, p, q_1, q_2$ be the price system with

$p =$ the price of good 2 in state 1,

$q_1 =$ the price of good 1 in state 2,

$q_2 =$ the price of good 2 in state 2.

With obvious notations, the behavior of consumer 1 is defined by the program

$$\max_{(x_{11}, x_{21}, x_{12}, x_{22})} \{\pi x_{11}^{\alpha_1} x_{21}^{\alpha_2} + (1 - \pi) x_{12}^{\alpha_1} x_{22}^{\alpha_2}\}$$

$$\text{S. T. } x_{11} + p x_{21} + q_1 x_{12} + q_2 x_{22} = 1 + q_1.$$

Maximization with respect to x_{11}, x_{21} on the one hand, and x_{12}, x_{22} on the other hand, implies

$$x_{21} = \frac{\alpha_2}{\alpha_1}\frac{x_{11}}{p}; \qquad x_{22} = \frac{\alpha_2}{\alpha_1}\frac{q_1}{q_2} x_{12}.$$

Substituting in the objective function the optimization problem reduces to

$$\max_{(x_{11}; x_{21})} \left\{\pi\left(\frac{\alpha_2}{\alpha_1 p}\right)^{\alpha_2} x_{11} + (1 - \pi)\left(\frac{\alpha_2}{\alpha_1}\frac{q_1}{q_2}\right)^{\alpha_2} x_{12}\right\}$$

$$\text{S. T. } \frac{\alpha_1 + \alpha_2}{\alpha_1} x_{11} + \frac{\alpha_1 + \alpha_2}{\alpha_1} q_1 x_{12} = 1 + q_1.$$

Similarly, we obtain for consumer 2

$$z_{21} = \frac{\beta_2}{\beta_1}\frac{z_{11}}{p}, \quad z_{22} = \frac{\beta_2}{\beta_1}\frac{q_1}{q_2} z_{12},$$

and

$$\max_{(z_{11}, z_{12})} \left\{\pi\left(\frac{\beta_2}{\beta_1 p}\right)^{\beta_2} z_{11} + (1 - \pi)\left(\frac{\beta_2 q_1}{\beta_1 q_2}\right)^{\beta_2} z_{12}\right\}$$

$$\text{S. T. } \frac{\beta_1 + \beta_2}{\beta_1} z_{11} + \frac{\beta_1 + \beta_2}{\beta_1} q_1 z_{12} = p + q_2.$$

Let us look for an equilibrium with $z_{11} = 0$, $z_{21} = 0$, $x_{12} = 0$ and $x_{22} = 0$. We need

$$\pi\left(\frac{\beta_2}{\beta_1}\frac{1}{p}\right)^{\beta_2} < (1-\pi)\left(\frac{\beta_2}{\beta_1}\frac{q_1}{q_2}\right)^{\beta_2} \tag{A.1}$$

and

$$\pi\left(\frac{\alpha_2}{\alpha_1}\frac{1}{p}\right)^{\alpha_2} > (1-\pi)\left(\frac{\alpha_2}{\alpha_1}\frac{q_1}{q_2}\right)^{\alpha_2}. \tag{A.2}$$

Then, $x_{11} = x_{21} = z_{12} = z_{22} = 1$; hence, $p = \alpha_2/\alpha_1$ and $q_2/q_1 = \beta_2/\beta_1$. It remains to find q_1, which leads to incomes compatible with these choices, namely

$$\frac{\alpha_1 + \alpha_2}{\alpha_1} = 1 + q_1 \rightarrow q_1 = \frac{\alpha_2}{\alpha_1}.$$

For $\beta_1 = 0.1$, $\alpha_1 = 0.7$ and $\pi = \frac{1}{2}$, (A.1) and (A.2) are verified. We get $U_1 = 0.390$, $U_2 = 0.805$ in the competitive equilibrium and $U_1 = 0.5$, $U_2 = 0.5$ in the sunspot equilibrium. Let us add a negative externality created only by the consumption of agent 1 in good 2. The external effect decreases the utility of each consumer by $\gamma\psi(x_2)$ with $\psi(\cdot)$ defined by

$$\begin{aligned}\psi(x) &= \frac{x}{0.3}\cdot\bar{\psi} \qquad &\text{for } x \in [0, 0.3]\\ &= \bar{\psi} &\text{for } x \geqslant 0.3.\end{aligned}$$

The loss of utility in the sunspot equilibrium is $\gamma\psi(1)$ in state 1 and $\gamma\psi(0) = 0$ in state 2, i.e., $\frac{1}{2}\gamma\bar{\psi}$.

In the competitive equilibrium without sunspots, the loss of utility is $\gamma\psi(0.3) = \gamma\bar{\psi}$. For γ large enough the (relatively) positive effect of the externality in the sunspot equilibrium dominates the initial negative impact of sunspots on consumer 2.

Appendix 2

Consider a reinterpretation of Hart's (1975) example with two consumers, two states of nature, and separable VNM utility functions:

$$u^i(x_1^i, x_2^i) = v^i(x_1^i) + \beta^i w^i(x_2^i)$$

and initial resources, $w_1^i > 0$, $1 = 1, 2$, $i = 1, 2$. There are only spot markets in state 2. Denote by p_1 (resp. p_2) the price of good 2 in state 1 (resp. 2).

Consumer i solves

$$\text{Max}\ \{v^i(x_{11}^i, x_{21}^i) + \beta^i w^i(x_{12}^i, x_{22}^i)\}$$

$$\text{S. T.}\ x_{11}^i + p_1 x_{21}^i \leqslant w_{11}^i + p_1 w_{21}^i, \quad x_{12}^i + p_2 x_{22}^i \leqslant w_{12}^i + p_2 w_{22}^i.$$

Since there is no possibility of transferring wealth across states of nature, the Radner equilibrium is simply the combination of a spot equilibrium in each state. Suppose that there are two equilibria at least in each state (see figure 2). We have four Radner equilibria: (A, C), (A, D), (B, C), and (B, D).

Compare (A, D) and (B, C). Agent 1 is better off in state 1 in (B, C) than in (A, D) and less well off in state 2. On the contrary, agent 2 is better off in state 2 in (B, C) than in (A, D) and less well off in state 1.

Therefore, if we choose β^1 small enough and β^2 large enough, then (B, C) dominates (A, D) in the Pareto sense.

Consider now a two-state sunspot with probabilities $(\pi, 1 - \pi)$ and with the nondegenerated *-extended Radner equilibria constructed as follows:

A^* composed of A, with expectations of C if state 1 of the sunspot occurs (i.e., with probability π) and expectations of D if state 2 of the sunspot occurs (i.e., with probability $(1 - \pi)$), is such an equilibrium.

B^* is composed of B and the same expectations as in A^*.

Suppose that β^1 and β^2 are taken such that (B, C) Pareto-dominates (A, D) and is itself a Pareto optimum. Then, symbolically,

$$u^1(B^*) = v^1(B) + \beta^1[\pi w^1(C) + (1 - \pi)w^1(D)] > u^1(B, C)$$

and

$$u^2(B^*) = v^1(B) + \beta^2[\pi w^1(C) + (1 - \pi)w^1(D)] < u^2(B, C).$$

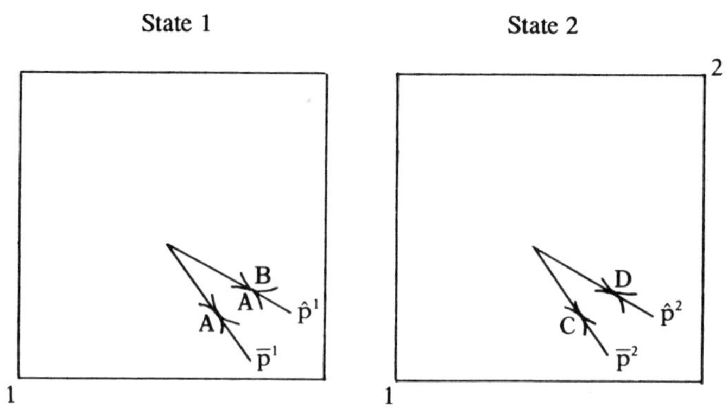

Figure 2.

We can say that B^* is not a Pareto optimum. Otherwise we could consider the nonrandom allocation $\pi C + (1 - \pi)D$ in state 2, and the allocation $(B, \pi C + (1 - \pi)D)$ in state 2 and the allocation $(B, \pi C + (1 - \pi)D)$ would be better as soon as the $w^i(\cdot)$ were strictly concave—a contradiction.

From above, if π is large enough, then

$$u^1(B^*) > u^1(A, D),$$

$$u^2(B^*) > u^2(A, D),$$

which shows the first part of the proposition. Now A^*, with π small enough, is a *-Radner equilibrium dominated by the Radner equilibrium BC. This completes the proof of proposition 8.

Notes

1. See Arrow 1953 for the first formalization of this idea, Guesnerie and Jaffray 1974 for a first fairly general formulation, Kreps 1982 for a synthetic evaluation of its impact on the theory of financial markets, and Duffie 1987a, Magill and Shafer 1986, and Duffie and Shafer 1985 for its most recent developments.

2. In addition to the references provided in note 4 see Azariadis 1981, Grandmont 1985, 1987, and Peck 1987.

3. See Peck and Shell 1987.

4. See Spear 1984, Azariadis and Guesnerie 1986, Guesnerie 1986, Woodford 1986, and Chiappori and Guesnerie 1987.

5. See Balasko 1984 for an extension of this result to cases where the expected utility hypothesis is relaxed.

6. If risk aversion is weak it can only be shown that, for any equilibrium of the *-complete system, there exists an equilibrium of the complete system that yields the same expected utility for each agent.

7. An alternative would be to create contingent (on extrinsic uncertainty) markets for the numeraire. The two methods turn out to be equivalent in the economy we consider in the next section.

8. The interpretation of sunspots as "animal spirits," as in Azariadis and Guesnerie 1986, cannot be reconciled with this observability hypothesis.

9. In the sequel we identify the two-dimensional vector $\overline{p}_s$, which has its first component equal to one, to its second component.

10. The proof rests on the Poincaré-Hopf theorem, as in Azariadis and Guesnerie 1986.

11. Remember that now x^i is one-dimensional.

References

Arrow, K. (1953), "Le rôle des valeurs boursières dans la repartition la meilleure des risques," Paris, *Cahiers du Seminaire d'Econometrie*, CNRS.

Azariadis, C. (1981), "Self-fulfilling prophecies," *Journal of Economic Theory* 25, 380–396.

Azariadis, C. and R. Guesnerie (1982), "Prophéties créatrices et persistance des theories," *Revue Economique* 33, 787–806.

Azariadis, C. and R. Guesnerie (1986), "Sunspots and cycles," *Review of Economic Studies* 53, 725–737.

Balasko, Y. (1984), "Extrinsic uncertainty revisited," *Journal of Economic Theory*.

Balasko, Y. (1987), "Equivariant equilibrium theory," mimeo, Université de Genève.

Balasko, Y., Cass, D. and K. Shell (1988), "Market participation and sunspot equilibria," mimeo.

Cass, D. and H. Polemarchakis (1987).

Cass, D. and K. Shell (1983a), "Les taches solaires ont elles de l'importance," *Cahiers du Seminaire d'Econometrie* 24, 93–127.

Cass, D. and K. Shell (1983b), "Do sunspots matter," *Journal of Political Economy* 91, 193–227.

Chiappori, P. A. and R. Guesnerie (1987), "Stationary sunspot equilibria of order k," mimeo, EHESS, to appear in *Proceedings of the Conference on Economic Complexity*, Cambridge University Press.

Debreu, G. (1956), *Theory of Value*, New Haven, Yale University Press.

Duffie, D. (1987a), "Stochastic equilibria: Existence, spanning number and the no expected gains from trade hypothesis," *Econometrica* 54, 1161–1184.

Duffie, D. (1987b), "Stochastic equilibria with incomplete financial markets," *Journal of Economic Theory* 41, 405–416.

Duffie, D. and W. Shafer (1985), "Equilibrium in incomplete markets I: A basic model of generic existence," *Journal of Mathematical Economics* 14, 285–300.

Geanakoplos, J. and H. Polemarchakis (1986), "Existence, regularity and constrained suboptimality of competitive allocations when the asset market is incomplete," Ch. 3 in *Essays in Honor of K. Arrow*, Vol. III, W. Heller, R. Starr, and D. Starrett (eds.), Cambridge University Press.

Grandmont, J. M. (1985), "On endogenous competitive business cycles," *Econometrica* 55, 995–1047.

Grandmont, J. M. (1987), "Local bifurcations and stationary sunspots," mimeo CEPREMAP.

Guesnerie, R. (1986), "Stationary sunspot equilibria in n. commodity world," *Journal of Economic Theory* 40, 103–127.

Guesnerie, R. and Y. Jaffray (1974), "Optimality of equilibria of plans, prices and price expectations," in *Allocation under Uncertainty: Equilibrium and Optimality*, ed. J. H. Dreze, New York, J. Wiley and Sons.

Hart, O. (1975), "On the optimality of equilibrium when the market structure is incomplete," *Journal of Economic Theory* 11, 418–443.

Kreps, D. (1979), "Three essays on capital markets," Technical Report 298, IMSSS, Stanford University.

Kreps, D. (1982), "Multiperiod securities and the efficient allocation of risk: A comment on the Black-Scholes option pricing model," *The Economics of Uncertainty and Information*, University of Chicago Press.

Magill, M. and W. Shafer (1986), "Equilibrium and efficiency in a canonical asset market model," Ecole Polytechnique Discussion Paper, A2930586.

Malinvaud, E. (1953), "Capital accumulation and efficient allocation of resources," *Econometrica* 21, 233–266.

Maskin, E. and J. Tirole (1985), "Correlated equilibria and sunspots: A note," *Journal of Economic Theory*.

Peck, J. (1981), "On the existence of sunspot equilibria in an overlapping generation model," *Journal of Economic Theory*.

Radner, R. (1972), "Existence of equilibrium of plans, prices and price expectations," *Econometrica* 40, 289–303.

Shell, K. (1977), "Monnaie et allocation intertemporelle," Paris, mimeo, *Seminaire d' Econometrie*.

Spear, S. (1984), "Sufficient conditions for the existence of sunspot equilibria," *Journal of Economic Theory* 34, 360–370.

Woodford, M. (1986), "Learning to believe in sunspots," mimeo.

5

Intertemporal Efficiency, Intergenerational Transfers, and Asset Pricing: An Introduction

Jean Tirole

1. Motivation

The question of efficiency in infinite-horizon economies was pioneered by Malinvaud (1953). Malinvaud found a sufficient condition for an intertemporal path to be "consumption efficient." This question is important for at least two reasons.

First, an infinite-horizon competitive equilibrium need not be efficient if there are infinitely many agents.[1] It is easy to construct overlapping generations models in which successive redistributions from the young generations to the old generations (or a reduction in capital accumulation) make all generations better off. Samuelson (1958) and Diamond (1965) offer examples of economies without and with capital accumulation that are intertemporally inefficient.[2]

Second, there exist centralized and decentralized ways of affecting the intertemporal efficiency of dynamic paths in such economies. Centralized ways include national debt and social security. Asset bubbles (the "excess of asset prices over their real value") are decentralized solutions. One important issue is to what extent productive savings are crowded out by debt, social security, bubbles, and the like.[3]

In an economy with a representative infinitely-lived consumer, for instance,[4] any issuing of public debt today will later on be financed through taxes, say, levied on the same consumer. The consumer then ought to save the exact amount of the income currently redistributed to her in order to meet future tax liabilities. Thus, the crowding-out of productive savings by debt is totally offset by an increase in savings. In other words, debt is neutral (Ricardo's neutrality theorem). As for asset bubbles, we will see that these cannot exist in such a setup. So again, no crowding out occurs.

When generations overlap, the debt issued now will be repaid by future generations: it thus redistributes income among generations and affects intertemporal capital accumulation and consumption. Similarly, assets can be priced above their real value without facing the "hot potato problem": each generation can realize its capital gain on an asset without another generation getting stuck with this asset (the fact that the asset is overvalued means that the asset must circulate forever; otherwise the last acquirer would lose money).

These remarks suggest that there exists a deep connection between intertemporal efficiency, intertemporal redistribution programs, and asset pricing. The purpose of this paper is to sketch this connection.

2. Intertemporal Efficiency

By efficiency is usually meant Pareto efficiency: no consumer can be made better off without another consumer being made worse off. We will start with a weaker (or necessary) notion of efficiency, that in a sense captures the intertemporal aspect of Pareto efficiency: "consumption efficiency."

Consumption efficiency is a partial characterization, and we do not need to specify the environment; *a priori* the economy can have infinitely-lived traders or overlapping generations. There is one good, which can be used as consumption or capital. The capital accumulation equation is given by

$$k_{t+1} = f(k_t) - c_t, \tag{1}$$

where k_t denotes capital and c_t consumption. Production takes one period. Capital fully depreciates after one period. Suppose for the moment that there is no population growth, no technological progress, etc. And make the following assumption:

$$f(0) = 0;\ f' > 0;\ f'' < -a < 0;\ 0 \leqslant f'(\infty) < 1 < f'(\mathbf{k}) < \infty, \tag{A}$$

where $\mathbf{k}$ is some minimum admissible level of capital (possibly zero); consumption must be non-negative and capital levels must exceed the minimum value of capital.

Definition. A path $\{k_t, c_t\}_{t=0}^{+\infty}$ is consumption inefficient if there exists another path $\{\tilde{k}_t, \tilde{c}_t\}_{t=0}^{+\infty}$ satisfying (1) such that for all t $\tilde{c}_t \geqslant c_t$ (with at least one strict inequality).

Note that "consumption inefficiency" is somewhat of a misnomer. A better term would be "production inefficiency," because the criterion refers to the possibility that the productive system could produce more of each (time-contingent) good. Nevertheless, we adhere to the standard terminology in the rest of the paper.

Define

$$\prod_t \equiv \prod_{s=1}^{t} f'(k_s). \tag{2}$$

Note that in a competitive economy, $f'(k_s) = 1 + r_s$, where r_s is the rate of interest, so that $\prod_t$ is the inverse of the discount factor between 0 and t.

We now give a necessary condition for a path to be consumption inefficient. (This condition was progressively developed in the 1960s and the early 1970s. It is mainly due to Phelps and Koopmans. Theorem 1 and its proof follow Cass 1972):

Theorem 1. For an inefficient path, $\lim_{t\to\infty} \prod_t = 0$.

To obtain some intuition about Proposition 1, suppose one starts from a steady state with $f'(k) = 1 + r > 1$ (so that $\prod_t \to \infty$). Increasing consumption at date 0 by ε leads to a reduction in k_1 equal to ε. Therefore, production decreases by approximately $\varepsilon(1 + r)$ at date 1. If consumption is not reduced (say is kept constant) at date 1, date 1 investment decreases by $\varepsilon(1 + r)$ and production is reduced by approximately $\varepsilon(1 + r)^2$ at date 2. By induction, the reduction in production grows exponentially if $r > 0$: it is at least equal to $\varepsilon(1 + r)^t$ at date t [it actually exceeds this number from the concavity of $f(\cdot)$]. At some point, some decrease in consumption must be allowed as production cannot be negative. This "shows" that long-run positive interest rates are a sign of consumption efficiency in this economy. Theorem 1 is a bit more precise, and states that $\prod_t$ must actually go to zero in order to have consumption inefficiency.

Proof. (a) The first stage of the proof consists in showing that $\prod_t$ is bounded above. If $\{k_t, c_t\}$ is inefficient, it is dominated by a feasible path $\{\tilde{k}_t, \tilde{c}_t\}$. Intuitively, there should be less capital accumulation in the dominating path:

$$k_{t+1} - \tilde{k}_{t+1} \equiv \varepsilon_{t+1} = \tilde{c}_t - c_t + f(k_t) - f(\tilde{k}_t).$$

But, $\tilde{c}_t \geqslant c_t$. Furthermore, $k_t - \tilde{k}_t \equiv \varepsilon_t \geqslant 0$ by induction. Since f is concave, we get

$$\varepsilon_{t+1} \geqslant f'(k_t)\varepsilon_t.$$

Note also that from some time t_0 on, ε_t is strictly positive (otherwise the

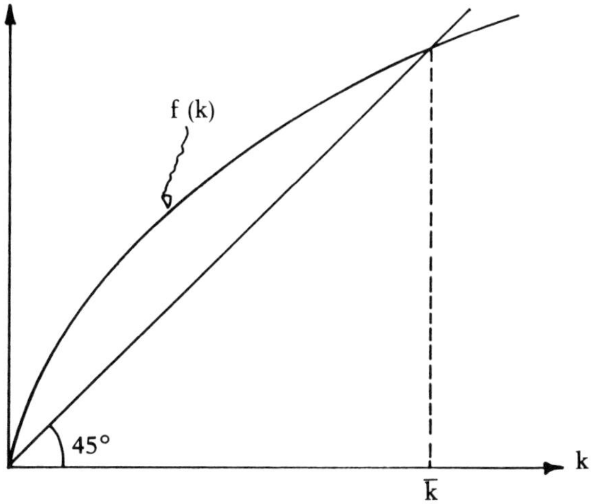

Figure 1.

two paths $\{k_t, c_t\}$ and $\{\tilde{k}_t, \tilde{c}_t\}$ would coincide). So

$$\varepsilon_{t+1} \geqslant f'(k_t)\varepsilon_t \geqslant \cdots \geqslant f'(k_t)\ldots f'(k_{t_0})\varepsilon_{t_0} = \frac{\prod_t}{\prod_{t_0-1}}\varepsilon_{t_0}.$$

From (A), we know that k_{t+1} is bounded above by $\bar{k}$, when $f(\bar{k}) = \bar{k}$ (see figure 1). So ε_t and, thus, $\prod_t$ are bounded above.

(b) Now consider a consumption path such that $\tilde{\tilde{k}}_t = k_t - \eta \prod_{t-1}$, for η small and positive. Consumption must satisfy

$$\begin{aligned} \tilde{\tilde{c}}_t - c_t &\equiv [f(\tilde{\tilde{k}}_t) - \tilde{\tilde{k}}_{t+1}] - [f(k_t) - k_{t+1}] \\ &= \eta\prod_t + f(\tilde{\tilde{k}}_t) - f(k_t) \\ &\leqslant \eta\prod_t - f'(k_t)(k_t - \tilde{\tilde{k}}_t) = 0 \end{aligned}$$

(using the concavity of f). So, the new path $(\tilde{\tilde{k}}_t, \tilde{\tilde{c}}_t)$ is dominated by the path (k_t, c_t), and thus is inefficient. Lastly,

$$\frac{\tilde{\tilde{\prod}}_t}{\prod_t} = \prod_{s=1}^{t} \frac{f'(\tilde{\tilde{k}}_s)}{f'(k_s)} \geqslant \prod_{s=1}^{t} \left(1 + \frac{a\eta\prod_{s-1}}{f'(k_s)}\right),$$

where use is made of the fact that the curvature of f is bounded away from zero.

Imagine that $\prod_{s-1}$ does not converge to zero. Since $f'(k_s)$ is bounded above (by $f'(\mathbf{k})$) as well as $\prod_t$ (as we just saw), $\tilde{\tilde{\prod}}_t$ goes to infinity as t goes to infinity. But the path $\{\tilde{\tilde{k}}_t, \tilde{\tilde{c}}_t\}$ itself is inefficient; so $\tilde{\tilde{\prod}}_t$ must be bounded above, a contradiction. QED

Remark. Malinvaud (1953) had shown in a different context that if the present discounted value of capital $\{k_t/\prod_t\}$ converges to zero, the path is consumption-efficient.

One may wonder whether the converse of Theorem 1 is true. It is not. The condition that is equivalent to consumption-inefficiency is slightly stronger. Indeed, we have:

Theorem 2. (Cass 1972). The path is consumption inefficient if and only if

$$\sum_{t=1}^{\infty} \prod_t < +\infty$$

(i.e., $\prod_t$ goes to zero "sufficiently fast").

Remark. For a discussion of the importance of the assumption of minimum curvature of the production function, see Cass's original paper.

Application. The Golden Rule for this economy is obtained when the steady-state level of capital k^* maximizes steady-state consumption max $\{f(k) - k\}$ or $f'(k^*) = 1$. (Since this economy does not grow, the Golden Rule rate of interest is equal to zero.)

Now consider a feasible path $\{k_t, c_t\}$ that satisfies $k_t \geqslant k^* + \varepsilon$ *for all* $t \geqslant t_0$ (where $\varepsilon > 0$). Theorem 2 tells us that this path is *consumption-inefficient*: $f'(k_t) \leqslant \theta < 1$ for $t \geqslant t_0$ (where $\theta \equiv f'(k^* + \varepsilon)$), which implies that

$$\prod_t \leqslant \prod_{t_0} \theta^{t-t_0} \rightarrow \sum_t \prod_t \leqslant \sum_0^{t_0-1} \prod_t + \frac{\prod_{t_0}}{1-\theta} < +\infty.$$

In particular, if the rate of interest converges to a rate of interest under the Golden Rule rate (here, zero), the path is inefficient. A Pareto improvement can then be made by reducing capital accumulation (i.e., raising the rate of interest). Conversely, if the rate of interest converges to a strictly positive value, the path is consumption-efficient.

Depreciation, Population Growth, etc.

The previous criterion assumes that capital depreciates entirely, that the economy does not grow, etc. Some variants can easily be incorporated into the model. Imagine, for instance, that population grows at rate n and that capital depreciates at rate δ. So

$$K_{t+1} = F(K_t, L_t) + (1 - \delta)K_t - C_t,$$

$$L_{t+1} = (1 + n)L_t.$$

Let $L_0 \equiv 1$. F now denotes the *net* production (a fraction $(1 - \delta)$ of capital remains for next period's production). Assume that F exhibits constant returns to scale, and let $k_t = K_t/L_t$ denote capital per capita. Then

$$k_{t+1} = f(k_t) - c_t,$$

where $c_t = C_t/(1 + n)^{t+1}$ is consumption per capita (up to the multiplicative factor $1/(1 + n)$) and where

$$f(k_t) \equiv \frac{F(k_t, 1) + (1 - \delta)k_t}{1 + n}.$$

Next, in a competitive economy, $F_K + 1 - \delta = 1 + r_t$. So we are back to the basic model, except that

$$\prod_t = \prod_{s=1}^{t} \left(\frac{1 + r_s}{1 + n}\right). \tag{3}$$

In this economy the Golden Rule rate of interest is n. A steady state (or a path converging to it) with $r < n$ is inefficient (efficient if $r > n$).

3. Link between Asset Pricing and the Consumption Efficiency Criterion

To simplify, consider a riskless asset that yields a real dividend d_t at period t. This asset is infinitely lived; the dividend can be realized without destroying the asset (see below for examples of assets that satisfy the first condition, but not the second). For instance, the asset can be a stock. Or it can be land; the dividend is then the real rent per period on the land (net value of crop if agricultural land). Or it can be a painting; the corresponding dividend is the consumption value associated with enjoying the painting. An intrinsically useless asset (paper asset) is such that the dividend is zero.

In a certain, perfect-foresight world, any asset will be priced by arbitrage. If r_t denotes the riskless real rate of interest, and if p_t denotes the asset price,

$$r_{t+1}p_t = (p_{t+1} - p_t) + d_{t+1}, \tag{4}$$

or

interest = capital gain + dividend,

assuming, by convention, that the dividend at $(t + 1)$ accrues to holders of the asset between t and $(t + 1)$. By induction, we obtain

$$p_t = \frac{p_{t+1} + d_{t+1}}{1 + r_{t+1}} = \frac{\left(\dfrac{p_{t+2} + d_{t+2}}{1 + r_{t+2}}\right) + d_{t+1}}{1 + r_{t+1}} = \cdots$$

$$= \sum_{s=1}^{T} \frac{d_{t+s}}{(1 + r_{t+1})\cdots(1 + r_{t+s})} + \frac{p_{t+T+1}}{(1 + r_{t+1})\cdots(1 + r_{t+T+1})}, \tag{5}$$

or

$$p_t = F_t + B_t,$$

where

$$F_t \equiv \sum_{s=1}^{\infty} \frac{d_{t+s}}{(1 + r_{t+1})\cdots(1 + r_{t+s})} = \lim_{T\to+\infty} \sum_{s=1}^{T} \frac{d_{t+s}}{(1 + r_{t+1})\cdots(1 + r_{t+s})}$$

and

$$B_t \equiv \lim_{T\to+\infty} \frac{p_{t+T+1}}{(1 + r_{t+1})\cdots(1 + r_{t+T+1})}.$$

Note that, from equation (5), B_t is well defined if F_t is well defined (i.e., if the series of discounted dividends is summable).

F_t, the *market fundamental* of the asset, is equal to the present discounted value of dividends. It, in a sense, represents the real value of the asset. Conduct the following thought experiment: Suppose there exists an infinitely lived agent (or family with strong bequest motives), and ask the following question at date t: "Assume that reselling this asset is prohibited, how much are you willing to pay for the asset?" The answer clearly is F_t.

B_t is the difference between the market price and the market fundamental of the asset and is called a *bubble*. B_t is a measure of speculation. Indeed, if traders were prevented from reselling the asset from time $(t + 1)$ on, a bubble at time t could not exist. Thus, only the prospect of capital gains can give rise to a bubble. The bubble on an asset is defined by its initial value B_0 and the sequence of real rates of interest.

Can a bubble be negative? The answer is no, if the asset can be freely disposed of. Because $p_{t+T+1} \geqslant 0$, taking the limit of (5) as T goes to infinity shows that the market fundamental is a lower bound on the valuation of an asset.

Another crucial property of a bubble that stems from its definition is that it grows at a rate equal to the rate of interest:

$$B_{t+1} = (1 + r_{t+1})B_t.$$

Remark. Take the case of a firm with a sequence of net profits P_t. The accounting equation for this firm is

$$P_t + (D_t - D_{t-1}) = d_t + r_t D_{t-1},$$

where D_t denotes the firm's debt and d_t the dividend distributed to shareholders. Assume that

$$\lim_{t\to\infty} \frac{D_t}{(1 + r_1)\cdots(1 + r_t)} = 0,$$

so that asymptotically the firm is neither a creditor nor a debtor. Then it is easy to see that the market fundamental of the firm is equal to the present discounted value of profits:

$$\sum_{s=1}^{\infty} \frac{P_{t+s}}{(1 + r_{t+1})\cdots(1 + r_{t+s})} = \sum_{s=1}^{\infty} \frac{d_{t+s}}{(1 + r_{t+1})\cdots(1 + r_{t+s})} = F_t.$$

Let us now uncover the simple link between asset valuation and consumption efficiency. First, notice that if the economy does not grow ($n = 0$):

$$B_t = \prod\nolimits_t B_0. \tag{6}$$

So if we are in a nongrowing economy, *consumption inefficiency implies that any bubble must in the long run vanish.* The path is then "asymptotically bubbleless." *Conversely,* assume that for some asset the price does not converge to the market fundamental as time goes to infinity. Then the *"asymptotically bubbly" economy is consumption-efficient.* In other words, asymptotic bubbles are a signal of intertemporal efficiency.

If population grows at rate n, then $\prod_t$ is given by (3). So

$$B_t = \prod\nolimits_t (1 + n)^t B_0,$$

or

$$b_t = \prod\nolimits_t b_0, \tag{7}$$

where $b_t \equiv B_t/(1+n)^t$ is the bubble per capita. (Note that $L_0 = 1 \to b_0 = B_0$.) Exactly the same conclusions hold, except that an "asymptotically bubbly" path is now defined as a path in which the bubble *per capita* does not converge to zero.

In section 4, we will investigate the circumstances under which asset bubbles can exist. Before doing so, let us derive the connection between Cass's Theorem 2 and the valuation of a *rent* like land. Assuming that an asset distributes a constant dividend $d_t = R$ per period, the market fundamental of this asset is equal to

$$F_0 = \sum_{s=1}^{\infty} \frac{R}{(1+r_1)\cdots(1+r_s)},$$

or

$$F_0 = R\left(\sum_{s=1}^{\infty} \frac{1}{\prod_s}\right), \tag{8}$$

if the economy does not grow.

So if the economy does not grow, the existence of an asset that guarantees a fixed real return (or more generally, whose dividend is bounded away from zero) implies consumption efficiency: Imagine that $\sum_{s=1}^{\infty} \prod_s < +\infty$ (the path is consumption-inefficient). Then

$$F_0\left(\sum_{s=1}^{\infty} \prod_s\right) = R\left(\sum_{s=1}^{\infty} \frac{1}{\prod_s}\right)\left(\sum_{s=1}^{\infty} \prod_s\right) = +\infty;$$

thus, the market fundamental and, hence, the asset price must be infinite, which is impossible (at least if some of the rent is not under state ownership).

Note that if population grows at rate n, the dividend of the rent "must" also grow at rate n (or higher) to ensure consumption efficiency, i.e., $d_t = R(1+n)^t$. It is then easy to see that, if such a rent exists, bubbles cannot exist:

$$\sum_{s=1}^{\infty} \frac{R(1+n)^s}{(1+r_1)\cdots(1+r_s)} < \infty \to \sum_{s=1}^{\infty} \frac{RB_0}{b_t} < \infty,$$

where $b_t \equiv B_t/(1+n)^t$ denotes the bubble on an asset per capita. So b_t must go to infinity; this is impossible, as it would violate wealth constraints (for instance, in an overlapping generations economy, the young generations could not afford to buy such an asset from the old generation).

Remark. The previous argument showed that if there exists an asset, the dividend of which grows at the rate of growth of the economy, bubbles cannot exist. This does not mean that if the total amount of dividends in the economy grows as quickly as the economy, bubbles cannot exist. The point is that dividends can also grow because new rents are created. If these rents are not capitalized in advance (think of new paintings, new patents or monopoly situations, and so forth), they do not crowd out other assets the way they do when they are traded from time zero on. Consider, for instance, an overlapping generations economy in which population grows at rate n, and in which each generation is born with 1 unit of rent. Each unit gives a dividend of 1 forever. The market fundamental of *existing* rents at date t is

$$F_t = [1 + (1 + n) + \cdots + (1 + n)^t] \sum_{s=1}^{\infty} \left(\frac{1}{(1 + r_{t+1}) \cdots (1 + r_{t+s})} \right).$$

Thus, F_t finite simply implies that the *total* bubble on an asset must go to infinity, but this does not imply that the bubble *per capita* goes to infinity; so we do not get nonexistence of bubbles if rents are not capitalized in advance. On the other hand, the dividend per capita associated with current rents converges to a strictly positive number:

$$\frac{1 + (1 + n) + \cdots + (1 + n)^t}{(1 + n)^t} \to \frac{1 + n}{n}.$$

We just suggested that the presence of rents in the economy may prevent asset bubbles, although they certainly need not. We now turn to the influence of the arrival of new traders on the possibility of bubbles.

4. Existence of Asset Bubbles

We saw that there is a strong connection between asset valuation and intertemporal efficiency. Therefore, it should not be surprising that the possibility of asset bubbles depends on the efficiency of the competitive equilibrium. This section explores to what extent this is so. Let us consider successively the two polar formulations of the intertemporal economy: finite number of infinitely-lived traders and overlapping generations.

Infinitely-Lived Agents

Assume that there exist n infinitely-lived traders. Consider an asset that distributes real dividends d_t and is traded at price $p_t (t = 1, \ldots, \infty)$. Dividends at time t are distributed to the traders who hold the asset from time $(t-1)$ to time t. Assume for simplicity that there is no uncertainty in the economy and that traders have perfect foresight. The asset is valued by arbitrage with capital (or real bonds); let r_t denote the real rate of interest. The price of this asset must obey

$$p_t = \sum_{\tau \geqslant 1} \frac{d_{t+\tau}}{(1+r_{t+1})\cdots(1+r_{t+\tau})} + B_t = F_t + B_t,$$

where B_t is a bubble ($B_{t+1} = (1+r_{t+1})B_t$).

Theorem (Tirole 1982). In a perfect-foresight equilibrium, $B_t = 0$ for all t.

Proof. Let s_t^i denote trader i's share of the asset at time t. Obviously, $\sum_i s_t^i = 1$ for all t. Starting with holding s_0^i, each trader i designs an intertemporal strategy of asset holdings. The present discounted value of this strategy from time t on (which we assume to be different from $+\infty$, otherwise, the trader would have an infinite wealth[5]) is given by

$$V_t^i = \sum_{\tau \geqslant 1} \left(\frac{d_{t+\tau} s_{t+\tau-1}^i + p_{t+\tau}(s_{t+\tau-1}^i - s_{t+\tau}^i)}{(1+r_{t+1})\cdots(1+r_{t+\tau})} \right) \equiv \sum_{\tau \geqslant 1} a_{t+\tau}^i.$$

Assume that V_t^i is well defined. $(d_{t+\tau} s_{t+\tau-1}^i)$ denotes the dividend received by trader i at time $(t+\tau)$. $p_{t+\tau}(s_{t+\tau-1}^i - s_{t+\tau}^i)$ represents the gain (loss) from selling (buying) the asset at date $(t+\tau)$.

Notice that trader i can always at time t sell her shares of the asset and leave the market. Hence,

$$V_t^i \geqslant p_t s_{t-1}^i.$$

Adding up over all agents, we get

$$\sum_{i=1}^{n} V_t^i \geqslant p_t.$$

Let us now show that the sum of all the V_t^i equals the market fundamental of the asset. Let us first recall Fubini's Theorem.

Fubini's Theorem.[6] Consider a sequence of numbers $a_t^i (t = 1, \ldots, \infty)$.

(i) If i goes from 1 to n and if $|\sum_{t=1}^{\infty} a_t^i| < \infty$ for all i, then

$$\sum_{i=1}^{n} \sum_{t=1}^{\infty} a_t^i = \sum_{t=1}^{\infty} \sum_{i=1}^{n} a_t^i.$$

(One can switch the summation signs.)

(ii) If i goes from 1 to ∞, and if $\sum_{i=1}^{\infty} \sum_{t=1}^{\infty} |a_t^i| < \infty$, then

$$\sum_{i=1}^{\infty} \sum_{t=1}^{\infty} a_t^i = \sum_{t=1}^{\infty} \sum_{i=1}^{\infty} a_t^i.$$

We will make use only of part i of the theorem for the moment. It implies that

$$\sum_{i=1}^{n} V_t^i = \sum_{\tau \geqslant t+1} \frac{d_\tau \left(\sum_{i=1}^{n} s_{\tau-1}^i \right) + p_\tau \left(\sum_{i=1}^{n} s_{\tau-1}^i - \sum_{i=1}^{n} s_\tau^i \right)}{(1 + r_{t+1}) \cdots (1 + r_\tau)} = F_t.$$

Thus, we get $F_t \geqslant p_t$. Since a bubble cannot be negative (see section 3), $B_t = 0$. QED

Intuition
The trading "game" between the n traders is basically a zero-sum game. What is gained by some traders is lost by the others. If the market for the asset did not exist and each trader i started with a share s_0^i, then trader i's valuation would be $\{s_0^i F_1\}$ at date 1. If the market exists and there is a bubble on the asset, trader i's valuation strictly exceeds $\{s_0^i F_1\}$, as she could sell the asset and leave the market. So, for some other trader j at least, trader j's valuation is less than the real value of initial asset holding $\{s_0^j F_1\}$. This trader would then be better off by not trading (or at least by refusing to buy).

Remark 1. The point is that in an equilibrium with a finite number of traders, it is not possible for everyone to find a buyer and avoid getting stuck with a "hot potato." This suggests that we should consider economies with an infinite number of traders if we want to avoid the hot potato problem. In an overlapping generations framework, this problem does not arise, since each generation can leave the market and at the same time, no generation gets stuck with the asset.

Remark 2. The previous reasoning is very general. We dealt with a perfect foresight equilibrium (no uncertainty). When uncertainty exists (about the level of dividend, or even about the level of the bubble), the same proof holds, using the more general concept of rational expectations equilibrium. One may also allow asymmetric information among the traders, or trading constraints such as short-sales constraints (see Tirole 1982).

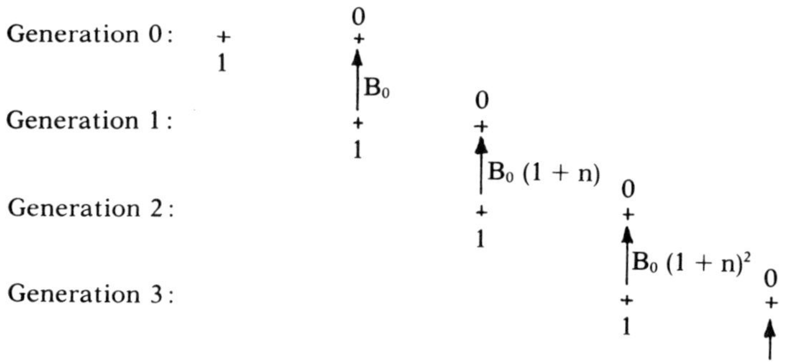

Figure 2.

Overlapping Generations

We just saw that bubbles cannot exist if the number of traders is finite. The picture is different for overlapping generations economies. Let us first show why the previous nonexistence proof does not go through anymore. A crucial step in the proof was switching summation signs. When both the number of traders and the number of periods are infinite, one can switch the summation signs if the condition in Fubini's Theorem, part ii holds. However, it need not hold. Consider the following simple "Samuelson economy," depicted in figure 2.

Each generation lives for two periods: a generation t consumer lives at t and $(t + 1)$. There is a unique, nonstorable good. A consumer has endowment 1 when young and 0 when old. The utility function is $U(c^y) + \delta U(c^o)$, where c^y and c^o are consumptions when young and old. δ is the discount factor. U is concave. The utility of each generation in the absence of intergenerational transfers is $\{U(1) + \delta U(0)\}$.

Population grows at rate n. The population at time t is $L_t = (1 + n)^t$. Define B_0 by the following equation:

$$U'(1 - B_0) = \delta(1 + n)U'(B_0(1 + n)). \tag{9}$$

B_0 is well defined if $U'(1) < \delta U'(0)$, which we will assume. We also assume that B_0 is unique (see below). B_0 denotes the optimal savings by young consumers if they could have access to a fictitious capital market with interest rate n.

Now imagine that generation 0 creates a paper asset and sells it to the new generation 1 at price B_0. A paper asset is an asset that does not yield dividends; in other words, it is a pure bubble. Assume that generation 1 sells the paper asset when old to generation 2 at price $B_0(1 + n)$, i.e., the rate of interest on the asset for generation 1 is n. Then each member of generation 2 pays B_0(because generation 2's population is $(1 + n)$ times that of 1). And so on, forever. The bubble per capita remains constant at B_0; and the rate of interest is equal to the rate of growth of the economy.

This clearly is an equilibrium. Two things are worth noticing:

1. The new equilibrium is better for all the generations than the old (bubbleless) one.
2. The paper asset has a positive value. So a bubble does exist.

Let us now go back to the nonexistence proof to see where it fails. Note that for generation i

$$\begin{aligned} a_t^i &= -B_0 \quad \text{for } t = i \\ &= +B_0 \quad \text{for } t = i + 1 \\ &= 0 \qquad \text{otherwise,} \end{aligned}$$

where we use the facts that for the paper asset

$$d_t = 0$$

and

$$p_t = (1 + r_1)\cdots(1 + r_t)B_0 \quad (= (1 + n)^t B_0)$$

and that for generation i

$$s_{i-1}^i = 0, \quad s_i^i = 1, \quad s_{i+1}^i = 0.$$

Hence,

$$\sum_{i=1}^{\infty} \sum_{t=1}^{\infty} |a_t^i| = +\infty,$$

so that we cannot apply Fubini's Theorem.

We have shown that (1) the nonexistence proof does not carry over to the infinite number of traders case and bubbles can indeed exist in such economies and (2) the bubbleless competitive economy is Pareto-inefficient.

Remark. The reader may be puzzled by the fact that the bubbleless economy is *not* consumption-inefficient: Because there is no production, aggregate per-period consumption is equal to 1 in all consumption programs. There are two ways of attacking the problem. One consists in introducing a production technology that satisfies assumption (A) and for which the bubbleless competitive equilibrium approximates the autarkic equilibrium of the above exchange economy. That is, one can introduce a neoclassical production function satisfying (A) with $\mathbf{k} = 0$ and such that

$$f'(0) = \frac{U'(1)}{\delta U'(0)} + \varepsilon,$$

where ε is positive and small. Then in the new bubbleless economy, the young generation invests a little bit (i.e., an amount k such that $f'(k) = U'(1-k)/\delta U'(f(k))$). One can then apply Cass's criterion. Note that this production technology is not used in the bubbly equilibrium (in which the rate of interest is n) as long as ε is small and n is non-negative. The other route consists in deriving Cass's criterion for exchange economy: see Balasko and Shell 1980, Proposition 5.6.[7] (The analogy of assumption A in the case of an exchange economy is a minimum-curvature assumption on the utility function. To see the need for this assumption, consider a linear utility $V(c^y, c^o) = c^y + c^o$ and the previous autarkic equilibrium $\{c^y = 1, c^o = 0\}$. Suppose that $n = 0$ The implicit rate of interest is equal to 0, so that $\sum_{t=0}^{\infty} \prod_t = \sum_{t=0}^{\infty} 1 = +\infty$; however, the autarkic equilibrium is Pareto-inefficient, as generation 2 could give x in (0, 1] to generation 1 and receive x from generation 3, and so forth.)

How general is the existence-of-bubbles result? Roughly speaking, bubbles may be ruled out on two grounds:

(a) Traders in the asset market are in finite number, and therefore play a "zero-sum" game.

(b) The price of the asset inflates too quickly so that the asset at some point of time cannot find traders with sufficient wealth to buy it.

Since we ruled out (a) in this section, let us investigate the "wealth constraint." In our overlapping-generations framework, (b) takes the following form: Young generations may not have enough wealth to buy the asset from the old generation.

A bubble must grow at the rate of interest, so that, normalized to the size of the economy (in per capita terms, say), it grows at the rate of interest minus the rate of growth of the economy. This suggests that, if the long-term rate of interest (r, say) exceeds the long-run rate of growth of the economy (n, say), the young generations at some point will not be able to buy the asset. So an equilibrium with a bubble cannot exist. But there is no reason why r should, in the long run, exceed n. Indeed, consider the simple

Samuelson economy described above. Without a paper asset, the long-run rate of interest (and short-run as well) is

$$1 + r = \frac{U'(1)}{\delta U'(0)} < 1 + n,$$

by assumption. Now introduce a "small" bubble at date zero (a paper asset with a small real price). Let b_0 denote the initial level of the bubble ($0 < b_0 < B_0$). The first-period rate of interest must satisfy

$$1 + r_1 = \frac{U'(1 - b_0)}{\delta U'(b_0(1 + r_1))};$$

r_1 is close to r if b_0 is small. The bubble *per capita* at date 1 is then

$$b_1 = \frac{1 + r_1}{1 + n} b_0.$$

The second-period rate of interest is then given by

$$1 + r_2 = \frac{U'(1 - b_1)}{\delta U'(b_1(1 + r_2))},$$

and

$$b_2 = \frac{1 + r_2}{1 + n} b_1.$$

And so on. The dynamic path is then determined by the initial bubble.

If b_0 is small, b_t will be small as well and will actually converge to zero (asymptotically bubbleless economy): If the rate of interest converges to r, then b_t converges to 0 "exponentially." Conversely, if b_t converges to 0, the economy behaves asymptotically like the bubbleless economy, and so the rate of interest converges to r.

It is easy to show the following result: For any initial bubble $b_0 \in [0, B_0)$, where B_0 is defined by equation 9, the path is asymptotically bubbleless. For initial bubble B_0, one obtains the steady-state/Golden rule/asymptotically bubbly path described above. Bubbles above B_0 cannot exist as they run into wealth constraints. (They become bigger than the young generation's endowment.) This type of result is proved, for instance, in Gale 1973 (see also Balasko and Shell 1981).

What happens if the rate of interest for the bubbleless economy exceeds n? Assume that a bubble exists—then, *a fortiori*, the rate of interest exceeds n. (A lower first-period consumption and a higher second-period one raise time preference.) So the bubble per capita must grow exponentially, which is impossible.

Thus, the *flavor* of the results is that bubbles can exist if and only if the bubbleless path is intertemporally inefficient. This proposition actually is not true as stated; counterexamples to it can be found—some regularity conditions are needed.

Remark. We have implicitly assumed that the equation

$$1 + r_{t+1} = \frac{U'(1 - b_t)}{\delta U'(b_t(1 + r_{t+1}))}$$

defines a unique rate of interest r_{t+1}. This is clearly the case if savings do not decrease with the rate of interest (check that the condition is that the relative degree of "risk aversion" $\{-[U''b_t(1 + r_{t+1})/U']\}$ in the second period is less than 1). If savings do decrease with the rate of interest, then a given level of initial bubble may correspond to different equilibrium paths. If savings decrease sufficiently fast with the rate of interest over some range, new types of equilibria (cycles, sunspot equilibria) can appear; see Gale 1973, Grandmont 1985, and Azariadis and Guesnerie 1986.

What about economies with production? It is clear that the analysis is not going to be modified much. One can think of the Samuelson model as being an extreme case with totally inefficient production, i.e., in which capital accumulation yields no output. In the first part of his paper on overlapping generations and public debt, Diamond (1965) shows how to incorporate a constant returns to scale production technology into the Samuelson model, and demonstrates that there is no presumption that r should exceed n in the long run.

If r is indeed lower than n, there is still space for a bubble in the economy, provided that it is not too big: a bubble crowds out capital (productive savings) and, therefore, raises the marginal productivity of capital (i.e., the real rate of interest); it must be the case that the rate of interest is not raised "too much" (i.e., does not strictly exceed n in the long run). See Tirole 1985 and Weil 1987a.

What about economies with rents? As shown in section 3, whether the existence of assets that distribute real dividends each period even in the absence of capital accumulation forces the rate of interest to exceed the rate of growth depends on the nature of rents. We refer to section 3 for a discussion. So, for instance, a rent, the dividend of which grows at the rate of growth of the economy, crowds out bubbles completely; this is roughly because the rate of interest must exceed the rate of growth in order for this rent to have a finite price. If, however, the number of rents, rather than their dividend, grows at the rate of growth of the economy, bubbles need not be crowded out. For a more complete treatment of bubbles in economies with rents, see Tirole 1985.

5. Public Debt and Social Security

An important issue in dynamic macroeconomic theory is the effect of government redistribution programs such as the issuance of public debt or social security programs. In this section we will stress the analogy between such programs and asset bubbles.

Assume first that the economy is composed of a finite number of infinitely-lived traders. Can public debt in such an economy have real effects? The answer is yes, if the debt is financed through taxes and consumers are heterogeneous. Taxes may then redistribute wealth between consumers and change the equilibrium. More "interesting" is the case of homogeneous consumers. The Ricardo Neutrality Theorem then asserts that public debt has no effect on the dynamic equilibrium. Imagine, for instance, that debt at time t, d_t, takes the form of one-period bonds (to be repaid at $t + 1$), and consider an increase of debt to $\{d_t + \delta d_t\}$. The proceeds are redistributed to the consumers through a decrease in taxes $\{\delta \tau_t = -\delta d_t\}$. Assume first that this increase in debt is a one-shot phenomenon, i.e., that it is not rolled over at $(t + 1)$. Then $\delta \tau_{t+1} = (1 + r_{t+1})\delta d_t$. Now the consumer's intertemporal wealth is not affected:

$$\delta \tau_{t+1} + \frac{1}{1 + r_{t+1}} \delta \tau_{t+1} = 0,$$

assuming that intertemporal prices are unchanged. So consumption in each period has not changed. This means that the tax proceeds δd_t at time t are completely saved, and thus offset the decrease in savings in alternative assets associated with the substitution toward debt. The set of competitive equilibria is unaffected by the change in fiscal policy.

If the debt were rolled over at date $t + 1$, a similar reasoning would obtain, and therefore debt would again be neutral. (As we shall see, debt cannot always be rolled over forever.)

Consider now an overlapping-generations economy. Intuitively, a debt issued now and redistributed to the old generation, say, redistributes wealth between generations, contrary to the case of a finite number of traders; current debt will not be repaid later by those who currently benefit from it. So neutrality in general will not hold. Diamond (1965) showed how public debt affects the intertemporal path.

Can public debt be rolled over forever? The answer is that this depends again on the relative magnitudes of the rate of interest and the rate of growth of the economy. Consider first the simple Samuelson model constructed in section 4. Ignoring bubbles, let us assume that the government issues an amount of debt (one-period bonds) d at date 0, where d is given by

$$1 + n = \frac{U'(1 - d)}{\delta U'(d(1 + n))}$$

(in other words, $d = B_0$). Next, assume that the government pays the interest and principal on date-0 bonds at date 1 by rolling over the debt. If the rate of interest turns out to be n, the amount of debt per capita remains constant and equal to n. And so on. The definition of d guarantees that the young generations are willing to hold an amount of one-period bonds equal to d in per capita terms, if these bonds yield a real rate of interest of n. So the debt can be rolled over forever, and thus is never repaid. Note the strong analogy with an asymptotically bubbly path. This analogy makes sense as bubbles and debt are alternative ways of redistributing intertemporal wealth toward the old generations.

If the rate of interest already exceeds n before the introduction of public debt, the government is not able to roll the debt over forever. Indeed, the government debt crowds out other forms of savings (for instance, capital) and raises the real rate of interest along the intertemporal path. So a rolled-over public debt must grow faster than the rate of growth rate of growth of the economy. This at some point of time violates wealth constraints (the young generations will not be able to buy the one-period bonds). Such reasoning can be found, for instance, in Sargent and Wallace 1981.

Let us now look at public debt as a bubble. Technically speaking, one-period bonds do not include a bubble, as they are priced at their market fundamental. (*More generally, any finite horizon asset must be priced at its market fundamental*: in the last period of the asset's life, traders do not want to pay more than the last period dividend; working backward immediately shows that a bubble cannot exist on an asset that stops being traded in finite time.) Public debt acts as a bubble when it is rolled over because, like a bubble, it is never repaid. It is therefore not surprising that the results are similar; to some extent a bubble is the decentralized equivalent of public debt. There are, however, some differences between them. For example, when the rate of interest exceeds the rate of growth of the economy, an asymptotically debtless path can exist while even asymptotically disappearing bubbles cannot exist. Also the government cannot easily control bubbles. For a further discussion of the link between debt and bubbles, see O'Connell and Zeldes 1986.

Remark 1. If public debt were subject to a 100% reserve requirement (the government invests the debt proceeds in capital, say), then debt would clearly be neutral. No redistribution would occur, and the government would be a simple veil or financial intermediary (see Wallace 1981 and Chamley and Polemarchakis 1984).

Remark 2. Social security on a "pay as you go" system much resembles public debt. "Pay as you go" means roughly that the wealth redistributed to the old generation has not been financed through savings of this generation, but is financed through taxes on the young generation. Similar results thus obtain (non-neutrality, etc). If social security is "fully funded" (the equivalent of debt with a 100% reserve requirement), the redistribution to the old generation now results from forced savings by the same generation when it was young: Taxes are levied by the government on young consumers that are put into interest-bearing assets and redistributed to the same consumers when they are old. So again, the government is a veil and neutrality is obtained: any amount of forced savings is exactly offset by an equivalent amount of voluntary dissavings.

Bequests

Bubbles and debt redistribute wealth toward the current generation. Bequests do the reverse.

Barro (1974) has argued that an economy in which bequests are operative behaves like an economy with infinitely-lived traders.[8] Consider the following simple model (this section is inspired by Weil 1987):

The model is an overlapping-generations model. Each generation lives for two periods, but cares about the welfare of the next generation (their children). Each member of the t generation has $(1 + n)$ children, who form the $(t + 1)$ generation. The utility function of a member of the generation born at t is

$$V_t = U(c_t^y) + \delta U(c_t^o) + \gamma V_{t+1}^*,$$

where c_t^y and c_t^o are consumptions when young and old, δ and γ are the intertemporal and interpersonal discount factors (δ and γ are less than 1), and V_{t+1}^* is the maximum of the utility of a generation-($t+1$) agent.

Let us only consider a steady state, to simplify the analysis. Each consumer earns w in the first period of her life (w can be thought of as a wage), and 0 in the second period; in the first period she also receives h units of good from her parents. She saves $(s_1 + s_2)$, where s_1 is savings for her own consumption when old and s_2 is savings for bequests. Let r denote the rate of interest (the marginal productivity of capital). Then consumption when old equals $\{s_1(1+r)\}$ and bequests per member of the next generation are equal to

$$\left\{\frac{s_2(1+r)}{(1+n)}\right\}.$$

Thus, the consumer maximizes

$$V_t^* = \max_{\{s_1, s_2\}} \left\{ U(w + h - s_1 - s_2) + \delta U(s_1(1+r)) + \gamma V_{t+1}^*\left(w + \frac{s_2(1+r)}{1+n}\right)\right\}.$$

Assuming an interior solution (in particular, bequests are operative), the first-order conditions are

$$\frac{\partial U}{\partial c_t^y} = \delta(1+r)\frac{\partial U}{\partial c_t^o} = \gamma \frac{\partial V_{t+1}^*}{\partial I_{t+1}} \frac{(1+r)}{1+n},$$

where I_{t+1} is generation $(t+1)$'s income. From the envelope theorem,

$$\frac{\partial V_{t+1}^*}{\partial I_{t+1}} = \frac{\partial U}{\partial c_{t+1}^y}.$$

In a steady state,

$$\frac{s_2(1+r)}{1+n} = h.$$

Thus, using the first-order conditions,

$$\gamma \frac{1+r}{1+n} = 1.$$

Since γ must be less than 1 (otherwise, V_t is unbounded), r must exceed n. So a *necessary condition for bequests to be operative is that the rate of interest exceeds the rate of growth.* The smaller the interpersonal discount factor, the bigger the difference between the rate of interest and the rate of growth.

This result, due to Weil, shows that the condition for bequests to be operative is stringent. It is also fairly appealing. It somewhat confirms the view of bequests as reverse bubbles. The analogy between bequests and reverse bubbles should nevertheless not be carried out too far. First, consumption efficiency is not sufficient for the existence of bequests. Second, bequests come from individual decisions. Bubbles require a "social consensus" on the choice of the assets that carry them (and public debt by definition requires government intervention).

If bequests are operative, the set of first-order conditions for the successive generations can be shown to be associated with the optimization of a *single infinite-horizon* fictitious program, which confirms Barro's view of successive generations with bequest motives as a single family (see Weil 1987b).

In a Barro economy, public debt is neutral (and cannot be rolled over) and bubbles cannot exist.

Remark 1. The fact that there exist "families with infinite horizon" (i.e., such that bequests are operative for each generation) is not sufficient for these conclusions about debt and bubbles. If new "families" appear over time, debt non-neutrality and bubbles cannot be ruled out, in spite of the existence of "agents" optimizing over the infinite horizon (see Weil 1987c). Consider, for instance, the case of bubbles. The arrival of new participants in the asset markets destroys the "zero-sum-game argument" against bubbles. One then must make sure that the economy grows sufficiently fast so that bubbles are not ruled out by wealth constraints.

Remark 2. To close the model, one can introduce a neo-classical production function, which relates savings (investment), wage, and interest rate.

Exhaustible Resources, Bubbles, and Inefficiency

Bubbles crowd out productive savings, but they need not introduce inefficiency. Indeed, we saw that the Cass criterion implies that an asymptotically bubbly path (i.e., a path in which the bubble does not become small relative to the economy) is consumption-efficient. Bubbles can allow an otherwise inefficient economy to reach efficiency by preventing capital overaccumulation.

This is the nice side of bubbles. However, bubbles can introduce a new type of inefficiency if their supports (assets) are not the "right" supports. Consider as benchmarks a painting or a rare stamp. If their market value exceeds the enjoyment (consumption value) associated with the assets, i.e., if there exist bubbles, their consumption values are not affected; in other words, the bubbles on these assets could be transferred to other assets (e.g., paper assets) without modifying the dynamic path of the economy. This property does not hold for all assets as shown by the following metaphor.

Schmooland is an overlapping-generations economy in which the rate of interest does not exceed the rate of growth. The produced good is called a schmoo. It is well known that produced schmoos are white. However, by a fluke firms at date zero produce a few black schmoos. Everyone agrees that this productive miracle will never occur again. Also it turns out that black and white schmoos are perfect substitutes in the consumers' utility function, and that, moreover, black schmoos are costlessly storable. At date zero everyone thinks that due to their scarcity the black schmoos should be priced above the white schmoos. The excess of their price over to one is low enough that a perfect foresight equilibrium prevails. In such an equilibrium the black schmoos are never consumed if interest rates are positive because their price in terms of white schmoos always exceeds one.

It is clear that such an equilibrium is inefficient. Imagine that the old generation at date zero issues pieces of paper with the same value as that of black schmoos, and consumes the black schmoos. The rest of the path is unchanged and the old generation is better off. This phenomenon is nothing but the well-known problem of potential inefficiency of private extraction of a nonrenewable resource (see, e.g., Dasgupta and Heal 1979, chapter 8). In this alternative formulation, oil (our black schmoos) is not exhausted in the long run because the owners of oil fields are concerned with future capital gains (bubbles on black schmoos).

The nonexhaustion of the market fundamental of an asset is a potential source of inefficiency, if bubbles affect those assets the consumption of which destroys the store of value aspect.

Let us mention that another source of inefficiency may be linked with the presence of bubbles. A bubbly asset must be costly to create. The cost may be infinite; this is the case of assets that, for historical or physical reasons, cannot be reproduced. If the cost of creating the asset is positive but finite (think of gold), a higher price for the asset encourages more creation (extraction). This may be inefficient, as the price conveys the "wrong signal" about the social dividends associated with the assets. Society would then be better off if the bubble affected an already existing asset instead.

Acknowledgments

This is a revised version of "Lecture Notes on Efficiency, Debt, Bubbles, Rents, Bequests and the Like" written in the spring of 1985 for the core course on capital and uncertainty at MIT. The author is grateful to Olivier Blanchard, Peter Diamond, Robert Gertner, and Roger Guesnerie for helpful comments and to the National Science Foundation for financial support.

Notes

1. The usual theorem on optimality of competitive equilibria holds if traders are in finite number and infinitely lived; the fact that the commodity space is not finite in an infinite-horizon economy does not matter—see Debreu 1954 on valuation equilibria.

2. Allais (1947) was the first to study the efficiency implications of overlapping generations. See Malinvaud 1986 for an assessment of his contribution.

3. See Blanchard and Fischer 1989 for a more complete description of some of the issues developed here.

4. The result can be extended somewhat.

5. Bewley's work on economies with a finite number of agents and an infinite-dimensional commodity space basically shows that if traders are impatient (discount the future), Debreu's (1954) linear functional (which is used to define valuations and obtain the two welfare theorems) can be written as a price system; that is, incomes and expenditures can be written as an infinite sum of products of (discounted) prices and quantities. (If the traders are not impatient, the linear functional $v(x)$ that represents the valuation of an infinite-dimensional bundle of goods $c = (c_1, \ldots, c_t, \ldots)$ in a competitive equilibrium need not have a scalar product representation $v(c) = \sum_{t=0}^{\infty} p_t c_t$. See chapter 7 of Stokey et al. 1986 for a good introduction to the issue.) Malinvaud (1953, 1961) shows that an infinite sequence of discounted prices p_t can be associated with a consumption efficient economy (with either a finite number of infinitely-lived traders or overlapping generations); these prices should be used to compare the efficient program with other feasible programs which are identical after some *finite* horizon T. That is, the efficient program $c \equiv \{c_t\}_{t=0}^{\infty}$ has up to T the highest value among all feasible programs $\tilde{c} \equiv \{\tilde{c}_t\}_{t=0}^{\infty}$ which are identical to it after T:

$$\sum_{t=0}^{T} p_t c_t \geqslant \sum_{t=0}^{T} p_t \tilde{c}_t.$$

6. See, e.g., Rudin 1964, Th. 8.3, p. 161.

7. For extensions of the Cass criterion to stochastic economies, see Abel et al. 1989 and Zilcha 1987. Zilcha shows that a consumption program is inefficient if and only if the rate at which the future value of a unit of capital available at date 0 goes to zero "fast" (in the sense of Theorem 2), on a set of positive measure in the space of states of nature.

8. With heterogeneous families, operative bequests do not guarantee neutrality if, for instance, the present discounted value of streams of a family associated with changes in the national debt is not equal to zero (an aggregate zero present discounted value does not imply individual zero present discounted values). The point is that changes in taxes associated with changes in debt may have redistributive effects. A case in which these redistributive effects do not exist and the Ricardian equivalence theorem holds is when all market participants (current and future) are linked by active resource transfers (Bernheim and Bagwell 1988). That is, if my granddaughter marries your grandson, operative transfers will flow not only between generations, but also between families, so that, in a sense, we all form a big family (see Bernheim and Bagwell for a critique of this conclusion).

References

Abel, A., G. Mankiw, L. Summers, and R. Zeckhauser (1989) "Assessing Dynamic Efficiency." *Review of Economic Studies* 56: 1–20.

Allais, M. (1947) *Economie et Intéret* (two volumes). Paris: Imprimerie Nationale.

Azariadis, C. and R. Guesnerie (1986) "Sunspots and Cycles." *Review of Economic Studies* 53: 725–738.

Balasko, Y. and K. Shell (1980) "The Overlapping Generations Model, I: The Case of Pure Exchange without Money." *Journal of Economic Theory* 23: 281–306.

Balasko, Y. and K. Shell (1981) "The Overlapping Generations Model, II: The Case of Pure Exchange with Money." *Journal of Economic Theory* 24: 112–142.

Barro, R. (1974) "Are Government Bonds Net Wealth?" *Journal of Political Economy* 82: 1095–1117.

Bernheim, D. and K. Bagwell (1988) "Is Everything Neutral?" *Journal of Political Economy* 96: 308–338.

Bewley, T. (1972) "Existence of Equilibria in Economies with Infinitely Many Commodities." *Journal of Economic Theory* 4: 514–540.

Blanchard, O. and S. Fischer (1989) *Lectures in Macroeconomics.* MIT Press.

Cass, D. (1972) "On Capital Overaccumulation in the Aggregative, Neoclassical Model of Economic Growth: A Complete Characterization." *Journal of Economic Theory* 4: 200–223.

Chamley, C. and H. Polemarchakis (1984) "Assets, General Equilibrium and the Neutrality of Money." *Review of Economic Studies* 51: 129–138.

Dasgupta, P., and G. Heal (1979) *Economic Theory and Exhaustible Resources.* Cambridge University Press.

Debreu, G. (1954) "Valuation Equilibrium and Pareto Optimum." *Proceedings of the National Academy of Sciences* 40: 588–592.

Diamond, P. (1965) "National Debt in a Neoclassical Growth Model." *American Economic Review* 55: 1126–1150.

Gale, D. (1973) "Pure Exchange Equilibrium of Dynamic Economic Models." *Journal of Economic Theory* 6: 12–36.

Grandmont, J.-M. (1985) "On Endogenous Competitive Business Cycles." *Econometrica* 53: 995–1046.

Malinvaud, E. (1953) "Capital Accumulation and Efficient Allocation of Resources." *Econometrica* 21: 223–268.

Malinvaud, E. (1961) "The Analogy between Atemporal and Intertemporal Theories of Resource Allocation." *Review of Economic Studies,* 28: 143–160.

Malinvaud, E. (1986) "The Overlapping Generations Model in 1947." *Journal of Economic Literature* 25: 103–105.

O'Connell, S. and S. Zeldes (1988) "Rational Ponzi Games." *International Economic Review* 29: 431–450.

Rudin, W. (1964) *Principles of Mathematical Analysis.* McGraw-Hill.

Sargent, T. and N. Wallace (1981) "Some Unpleasant Monetarist Arithmetics." *Federal Reserve Bank of Minneapolis Quarterly Review* 5: 1–17.

Samuelson, P. (1958) "An Exact Consumption-Loan Model of Interest with or without the Social Contrivance of Money." *Journal of Political Economy* 66: 467–482.

Stokey, N., R. Lucas, and E. Prescott (1986) *Recursive Methods in Economic Dynamics.* Forthcoming.

Tirole, J. (1982) "On the Possibility of Speculation under Rational Expectations." *Econometrica* 50: 1163–1181.

Tirole, J. (1985) "Asset Bubbles and Overlapping Generations." *Econometrica* 53: 1163–1181 (reprint: pp. 1499–1528).

Wallace, N. (1980) "The Overlapping Generations Model of Fiat Money." In *Models of Monetary Economics,* ed. J. Kareken and N. Wallace. Federal Reserve Bank of Minneapolis.

Wallace, N. (1981) "A Modigliani-Miller Theorem for Open-Market Operations." *American Economic Review* 71: 267–274.

Weil, P. (1987a) "Confidence and the Real Value of Money in an Overlapping Generations Economy." *Quarterly Journal of Economics* 102: 1–22.

Weil, P. (1987b) "'Love thy Children': Reflections on the Barro Debt Neutrality Theorem." *Journal of Monetary Economics* 19: 377–391.

Weil, P. (1987c) "Overlapping Families of Infinitely Lived Agents." Mimeo, Harvard University.

Zilcha, I. (1987) "Dynamic Efficiency in Overlapping Generations Models with Stochastic Production." Mimeo, Tel-Aviv University.

II Industrial Organization

6 Rules of Thumb for Optimal Tolls

Alain Bernard

Implementation of second-best models for setting optimal tolls or optimal taxes comes up against a major difficulty, which is the knowledge of all relevant price elasticities. As was pointed to by Guesnerie (1975, 1979a, 1979b) in the case of general formalisms, but as also appears in more specific ones (Boiteux 1956; Baumol and Bradford 1970; Dixit 1970; Diamond and Mirrlees 1971; Atkinson and Stiglitz 1972), even the direction of price changes—or the sign of taxes—is not obvious. They depend heavily on some cross-elasticities whose value is generally unknown.

As has now been acknowledged in several areas of economics (e.g., aggregate demand, capital theory, fixed-price equilibria), and as has long been taught to us by E. Malinvaud, the possibility of getting more precise results without failing in peculiar cases requires us to specify, at least broadly, models.

A Specific Framework . . .

Some situations, mainly encountered in transportation, have a common specific framework, which can be dubbed the "two-markets-two-modes" problem. Two modes (rail, road), or more generally two firms, each produce two goods (passenger or freight transport) and are competing in each of the related markets. If some constraint prevails on one (or both) of the modes or markets, preventing implementation of marginal-cost pricing, tolls are to be set for the other (or both of the) mode(s) or good(s), according to a second-best approach. There is some reason to wonder whether, at the price of some simplifying but "reasonable" assumptions, "reasonable" and easy-to-implement results—i.e., "rules of thumb"—can be derived.

. . . But One that Applies to Many Problems

In transportation, a lot of problems can be put within this framework, including the following two, which will later be taken as examples: (i) the Boiteux problem of setting optimal tolls when the two modes, exhibiting economies of scale or fixed costs, are constrained to budgetary equilibrium; (ii) the pricing of peak hours (relative to off-peak hours) in public urban transport when there is no peak-hours toll in private-car use (though the marginal social cost is higher).

But of course, this framework is to be found in other sectors' problems: for instance, energy with competition between products and different groups of consumers (households, industry). A general study is then of a broader scope.

The paper has two parts. The first presents this general structure, which is mainly embedded in the specification of a five-commodities utility function (the considered four commodities plus the current good of the economy, which represents all other goods and which serves as numeraire). The second part applies this framework to the two above-mentioned transport problems.

Representing Utility and Demand with a "Two Markets–Two Modes" Sector

General Specification of Utility Function

Let us suppose that the two goods are final goods, which are supposed to be those appearing as arguments in a utility function; we will show afterward how to cope with intermediate goods.

Only Final Goods

The first idea—or assumption—is that the substitutability in each market is relatively high, significantly higher than with other goods. Basically, there is a relationship between the two related commodities (two modalities of the same "good"), which is independent of other commodities. Each "good" (consumer theorists would say each "consumption function") is an aggregate of the two related modalities, and this can be represented by a utility function of the form

$$U = U(F_1, F_2, C_5),$$

where

F_1 = good 1 (e.g., passenger transport),

F_2 = good 2 (freight),

C_5 = current good,

with

$F_1 = F_1(C_1, C_2)$,

$F_2 = F_2(C_3, C_4)$.

C_1, C_2 (resp. C_3, C_4) represent the two modalities (e.g., rail, road) of good 1 (resp. good 2). In other words, the utility function is separable in C_1 and C_2, and in C_3 and C_4.

The second assumption is homogeneity (of degree 1 without loss of generality) of U, which implies homogeneity of degree 1 for F_1 and F_2.[1] This is a generally accepted assumption for consumer demand theory at the aggregate level.

The third assumption—also frequently made in consumer demand theory—is symmetry between goods or functions, meaning that elasticity of substitution between F_1 and C_5 is the same as that between F_2 and C_5. A relevant specification is then the generalized CES utility function, of the form

$$U = [\gamma F_1^{-\mu} + \gamma' F_2^{-\mu} + (1 - \gamma - \gamma')C_5^{-\mu}]^{-1/\mu}, \tag{1}$$

implying constant elasticities of substitution, which is not a liability since we are to consider small price variations.

The last aspect to specify is functions F_1 and F_2. The important point to stress is the degree of substitutability between modalities of each good. This also can be represented by a CES specification, with

$$F_1 = [\delta_1 C_1^{-\mu_1} + (1 - \delta_1)C_2^{-\mu_1}]^{-1/\mu_1},$$

$$F_2 = [\delta_2 C_3^{-\mu_2} + (1 - \delta_2)C_4^{-\mu_2}]^{-1/\mu_2}.$$

Intermediate Goods

Taking into account intermediate goods, such as freight transport, would normally require specifying all the productive aspects of the economy. To cope with this difficulty, we can assume that, apart from final good 1, there is another final good (the current good of the economy) whose production incorporates intermediate good 2:

$C_5 = f(F_2, C_5')$,

where C_5' is the "net" current good (the value added to the production of current good by factors other than F_2).

This "net" current good, in which production costs of other commodities (C_1 to C_4) can be measured,[2] is then the relevant numeraire.

As previously, the important point is elasticity of substitution between F_2 and C_5', so that we can retain

$$C_5 = [\delta' F_2^{-\mu'} + (1 - \delta')C_5'^{-\mu'}]^{-1/\mu'}$$

and we get the "three-level" CES utility function (dropping the prime in C_5'):

$$U = [\gamma F_1^{-\mu} + (1 - \gamma)Z^{-\mu}]^{-1/\mu}, \tag{2}$$

with

$$Z = [\delta F_2^{-\mu'} + (1 - \delta)C_5^{-\mu'}]^{-1/\mu'},$$

$$F_1 = [\delta_1 C_1^{-\mu_1} + (1 - \delta_1)C_2^{-\mu_1}]^{-1/\mu_1},$$

$$F_2 = [\delta_2 C_3^{-\mu_2} + (1 - \delta_2)C_4^{-\mu_2}]^{-1/\mu_2}$$

and

$s = \dfrac{1}{1 + \mu}$ elasticity of substitution between F_1 and aggregate (F_2, C_5)

$s' = \dfrac{1}{1 + \mu'}$ elasticity of substitution between F_2 and C_5

$s_1 = \dfrac{1}{1 + \mu_1}$ elasticity of substitution in market 1

$s_2 = \dfrac{1}{1 + \mu_2}$ elasticity of substitution in market 2.

We can note that specification (1) is a special case ($s = s'$) of specification (2). With this general specification, allowing for various substitutability relationships between goods and between commodities in each market, it becomes possible to cope with second-best analysis.

Finally, let us remember that this is a convenient and stylized representation of the utility function, but that all the results are unchanged with any three-level homothetic-separable specification with proper definitions of elasticities s, s', s_1, and s_2.

Determination of Matrix of Price Elasticities

Let us consider a situation where prices of commodities ($p_1, p_2, p_3, p_4, p_5 = 1$) and income ($R$) are given.

As the utility function is strictly quasi-concave, demands (C_1 to C_5) are uniquely determined and the situation can be characterized by the shares of each commodity:

$$\alpha_i = \frac{p_i C_i}{R} = \frac{p_i C_i}{\sum_i p_i C_i},$$

with

$$\sum_i \alpha_i = 1.$$

As the matrix of compensated derivatives of demand is symmetrical, the matrix of (compensated) elasticities e_{ij} is such that

$$\frac{e_{ij}}{\alpha_j} = \frac{e_{ji}}{\alpha_i}$$

and we also have the relations

$$\sum_j e_{ij} = 0 \quad \forall i.$$

Thus the number of degrees of liberty is 10 and we need 10 relations to determine completely the matrix. Generalizing a method used in the case of a two-level CES function (Bernard 1988), we will consider price changes giving easy-to-calculate changes in demand.

First consider a change of price p_1 (all other prices being held constant). We know that

$$d \log \frac{C_2}{C_1} = s_1 d \log p_1,$$

$$d \log \frac{C_i}{C_j} = 0 \quad i, j \in (3, 4, 5).$$

Then

$$e_{21} - e_{11} = s_1,$$

$$e_{31} = e_{41} = e_{51}.$$

Similarly, from a variation of p_2,

$e_{12} - e_{22} = s_1,$

$e_{32} = e_{42} = e_{52}.$

From the same relative variation of prices p_3 and p_4, we obtain

$e_{43} - e_{33} = s_2,$

$e_{34} - e_{44} = s_2,$

$e_{13} = e_{23},$

$e_{14} = e_{24}.$

Let us now consider a variation of price p_5. Variations of C_1 and C_2 are proportional; so are variations of C_3 and C_4. Then

$e_{15} = e_{25},$

$e_{35} = e_{45}.$

Moreover, we can verify that

$$d \log \frac{C_3}{C_5} = s' d \log p_5.$$

Then

$e_{35} = e_{55} + s',$

$e_{45} = e_{55} + s'.$

Let us finally consider proportional changes of p_3, p_4, and p_5. Changes of C_3, C_4, and C_5 are proportional; so are changes of C_1 and C_2, and we can verify that

$$d \log \frac{C_1}{C_5} = s d \log p_3.$$

We can then write

$e_{13} + e_{14} + e_{15} - e_{53} - e_{54} - e_{55} = s,$

or, equivalently,

$e_{11} + e_{12} - e_{51} - e_{52} = -s.$

We now have (even redundantly) enough relations to determine the matrix e_{ij}; the result is as follows:

$$
\begin{bmatrix}
\dfrac{-\alpha_2 s_1 - \alpha_1(1-\alpha_1-\alpha_2)s}{\alpha_1+\alpha_2} & \dfrac{\alpha_2 s_1 - \alpha_2(1-\alpha_1-\alpha_2)s}{\alpha_1+\alpha_2} & \alpha_3 s & \alpha_4 s & \alpha_5 s \\[2ex]
\dfrac{\alpha_1 s_1 - \alpha_1(1-\alpha_1-\alpha_2)s}{\alpha_1+\alpha_2} & \dfrac{-\alpha_1 s_1 - \alpha_2(1-\alpha_1-\alpha_2)s}{\alpha_1+\alpha_2} & \alpha_3 s & \alpha_4 s & \alpha_5 s \\[2ex]
\alpha_1 s & \alpha_2 s & e_{33} & e_{34} & \dfrac{\alpha_5 s' - \alpha_5(\alpha_1+\alpha_2)s}{1-\alpha_1-\alpha_2} \\[2ex]
\alpha_1 s & \alpha_2 s & e_{43} & e_{44} & \dfrac{\alpha_5 s' - \alpha_5(\alpha_1+\alpha_2)s}{1-\alpha_1-\alpha_2} \\[2ex]
\alpha_1 s & \alpha_2 s & \dfrac{\alpha_3 s' - \alpha_3(\alpha_1+\alpha_2)s}{1-\alpha_1-\alpha_2} & \dfrac{\alpha_4 s' - \alpha_4(\alpha_1+\alpha_2)s}{1-\alpha_1-\alpha_2} & \dfrac{-(\alpha_3+\alpha_4)s' - \alpha_5(\alpha_1+\alpha_2)s}{1-\alpha_1-\alpha_2}
\end{bmatrix}
$$

with

$$e_{33} = \frac{-\alpha_4(1-\alpha_1-\alpha_2)s_2 - \alpha_3\alpha_5 s' - \alpha_3(\alpha_1+\alpha_2)(\alpha_3+\alpha_4)s}{(\alpha_3+\alpha_4)(1-\alpha_1-\alpha_2)},$$

$$e_{34} = \frac{\alpha_4(1-\alpha_1-\alpha_2)s_2 - \alpha_4\alpha_5 s' - \alpha_4(\alpha_1+\alpha_2)(\alpha_3+\alpha_4)s}{(\alpha_3+\alpha_4)(1-\alpha_1-\alpha_2)},$$

$$e_{43} = \frac{\alpha_3}{\alpha_4} e_{34},$$

$$e_{44} = \frac{-\alpha_3(1-\alpha_1-\alpha_2)s_2 - \alpha_4\alpha_5 s' - \alpha_4(\alpha_1+\alpha_2)(\alpha_2+\alpha_4)s}{(\alpha_3+\alpha_4)(1-\alpha_1-\alpha_2)}.$$

Just a few words to indicate how s, s', s_1, and s_2 can be determined in a given real situation:

s_1 and s_2 are elasticities of substitution in markets 1 and 2: they can emerge from econometric analysis of the relative shares when relative prices vary across time.

s and s' are related to the price elasticities of demand of aggregate goods 1 and 2. We get (assuming proportional variations of p_1 and p_2) a non-compensated elasticity for good 1:

$$\varepsilon_1 = -[(1-\alpha_1-\alpha_2)s + (\alpha_1+\alpha_2)]$$

and (assuming proportional variations of p_3 and p_4):

$$\varepsilon_2 = -\left[\frac{\alpha_5 s' + (\alpha_1+\alpha_2)(\alpha_3+\alpha_4)s}{1-\alpha_1-\alpha_2} + \alpha_3 + \alpha_4\right].$$

Thus, for instance, with

$\alpha_1 + \alpha_2 = 0.15,$

$\alpha_3 + \alpha_4 = 0.15,$

$\varepsilon_1 = -0.5,$

$\varepsilon_2 = -0.3,$

we obtain

$s = 0.412,$

$s' = 0.169.$

Application to Pricing in the Transport Sector

Optimal Tolls with Budget Constraints[3]

We consider two modes (rail, road) servicing passenger and freight transport with fixed costs (resp. D_1, D_2) and, above, constant marginal costs (m_1, m_2, m_3, m_4). Taking into account budgetary constraints (one for each mode), the model can be written, with indirect utility function,

Max $V(p_1, p_2, p_3, p_4, R)$

subject to the following constraints:

$$(\mu) \quad m_1 C_1 + m_2 C_2 + m_3 C_3 + m_4 C_4 + C_5 \leqslant W_0$$

$$(\beta) \quad -(p_1 - m_1)C_1 - (p_3 - m_3)C_3 = -D_1 \quad [\text{eventually} \leqslant -D_1]$$

$$(\beta') \quad -(p_2 - m_2)C_2 - (p_4 - m_4)C_4 = -D_2 \quad [\text{eventually} \leqslant -D_2].$$

The first relation represents the frontier of the production set of the economy, the following two the budget constraints of the two modes.

μ is of course positive; so are β and β' if inequalities ($\leqslant$) hold. If strict equalities hold, it can happen, as we will see later, that even though D_1 and D_2 are positive one of the β will be negative. Anyway, we will say that mode 1 is more constrained than mode 2 if $\beta > \beta'$, i.e., if the constraint on mode 1 bites more than the constraint on mode 2. This normally, but not necessarily, results from the fact that fixed costs are proportionally higher.

Optimality conditions can be written (setting $m_5 = p_5 = 1$) as follows:

$$(p_1) \quad -\lambda C_1$$

$$= \mu \sum_{i=1}^{5} m_i \frac{\partial C_i}{\partial p_i} - \beta\left[(p_1 - m_1)\frac{\partial C_1}{\partial p_1} + (p_3 - m_3)\frac{\partial C_3}{\partial p_1} + C_1\right]$$

$$-\beta'\left[(p_2 - m_2)\frac{\partial C_2}{\partial p_1} + (p_4 - m_4)\frac{\partial C_4}{\partial p_1}\right],$$

with λ = marginal utility of income (and similarly for p_2, p_3, p_4)

$$(R) \quad \lambda = \mu \sum_{i=1}^{5} m_i \frac{\partial C_i}{\partial R} - \beta\left[(p_1 - m_1)\frac{\partial C_1}{\partial R} + (p_3 - m_3)\frac{\partial C_3}{\partial R}\right]$$

$$- \beta'\left[(p_2 - m_2)\frac{\partial C_2}{\partial R} + (p_4 - m_4)\frac{\partial C_4}{\partial R}\right].$$

Multiplying (R) by C_1 and summing member to member with (p_1), and taking into account the relation $\sum_{i=1}^{5} p_i(\partial C_i/\partial R) = 1$, we get (assuming, without loss of generality $\mu = 1$)

$$(1 + \beta)\frac{p_1 - m_1}{p_1}e_{11} + (1 + \beta')\frac{p_2 - m_2}{p_2}e_{12} + (1 + \beta)\frac{p_3 - m_3}{p_3}e_{13} + (1 + \beta')\frac{p_4 - m_4}{p_4}e_{14} = -\beta$$

and similarly for p_2, p_3, p_4. We then get a linear system of four equations determining optimal tolls $\tau_i = (p_i - m_i)/p_i$ ($i = 1$ to 4). We will, to restore symmetry, consider tolls inflated by shadow prices:

$$\tau'_1 = (1 + \beta)\tau_1,$$

$$\tau'_2 = (1 + \beta')\tau_2,$$

$$\tau'_3 = (1 + \beta)\tau_3,$$

$$\tau'_4 = (1 + \beta')\tau_4,$$

which are not far from tolls τ_i when β and β' are small.

The resolution is then as follows. The system writes

$$(p_1) \quad \tau'_1 e_{11} + \tau'_2 e_{12} + \tau'_3 e_{13} + \tau'_4 e_{14} = -\beta,$$

$$(p_2) \quad \tau'_1 e_{21} + \tau'_2 e_{22} + \tau'_3 e_{23} + \tau'_4 e_{24} = -\beta',$$

$$(p_3) \quad \tau'_1 e_{31} + \tau'_2 e_{32} + \tau'_3 e_{33} + \tau'_4 e_{34} = -\beta,$$

$$(P_4) \quad \tau'_1 e_{41} + \tau'_2 e_{42} + \tau'_3 e_{43} + \tau'_4 e_{44} = -\beta'.$$

Let us set

$$\tau_P = \frac{\alpha_1 \tau'_1 + \alpha_2 \tau'_2}{\alpha_1 + \alpha_2},$$

$$\tau'_P = \tau'_1 - \tau'_2,$$

where

τ_P = average toll for passenger transport and

τ'_P = differential toll between rail and road.

Similarly, for freight,

$$\tau_F = \frac{\alpha_3 \tau_3' + \alpha_4 \tau_4'}{\alpha_3 + \alpha_4},$$

$$\tau_F' = \tau_3' - \tau_4'.$$

Equations (p_1) and (p_2) can be written

$$-(1 - \alpha_1 - \alpha_2) s \tau_P - \frac{\alpha_2}{\alpha_1 + \alpha_2} s_1 \tau_P' + (\alpha_3 + \alpha_4) s \tau_F = -\beta,$$

$$-(1 - \alpha_1 - \alpha_2) s \tau_P + \frac{\alpha_1}{\alpha_1 + \alpha_2} s_1 \tau_P' + (\alpha_3 + \alpha_4) s \tau_F = -\beta',$$

from which we get

$$\tau_P' = \frac{\beta - \beta'}{s_1} \tag{3}$$

and

$$(1 - \alpha_1 - \alpha_2) s \tau_P - (\alpha_3 + \alpha_4) s \tau_F = \frac{\alpha_1 \beta + \alpha_2 \beta'}{\alpha_1 + \alpha_2}. \tag{4}$$

Similarly, from equations (p_3) and (p_4),

$$\tau_F' = \frac{\beta - \beta'}{s_2} \tag{5}$$

and

$$-(\alpha_1 + \alpha_2) s \tau_P + \frac{\alpha_5 s' + (\alpha_1 + \alpha_2)(\alpha_3 + \alpha_4) s}{1 - \alpha_1 - \alpha_2} \tau_F = \frac{\alpha_3 \beta + \alpha_4 \beta'}{\alpha_3 + \alpha_4}, \tag{6}$$

and from (4) and (6)

$$\tau_P - \tau_F \left[1 + \frac{\alpha_5 (s' - s)}{(1 - \alpha_1 - \alpha_2) s} \right] = \frac{(\alpha_1 \alpha_4 - \alpha_2 \alpha_3)(\beta - \beta')}{(\alpha_1 + \alpha_2)(\alpha_3 + \alpha_4) s}. \tag{7}$$

Interpretation of (3) and (5) is straightforward. Formula (7) shows that the respective values of τ_P and τ_F depend on both $(s' - s)$ and $(\beta - \beta')$. Suppose first $\beta \sim \beta'$, i.e., that the two modes are equally constrained (or, equivalently, that there is a single constraint for both of them): then $s - s'$ becomes smaller as $(\tau_F - \tau_P)/\tau_F$ becomes smaller.

Suppose now $s \sim s'$: then $\tau_P - \tau_F > 0$ if either $\beta > \beta'$ and $(\alpha_1/\alpha_3) > (\alpha_2/\alpha_4)$ or $\beta < \beta'$ and $(\alpha_1/\alpha_3) < (\alpha_2/\alpha_4)$.

Thus, we get the following general rules of taxation (which are approximate since they concern "inflated" tolls and not exact tolls).

First rule. Toll differentials between modes are of the same sign in the two markets, and inversely proportional to elasticities of substitution.

Second rule. Ceteris paribus, the average toll is smaller for the good that is the more substitutable to other consumer goods.

Third rule. Ceteris paribus, the average toll is larger for the good whose share is proportionally higher in the more constrained mode.

These three rules give the direction in which tolls are to be set. Together with the break-even conditions [constraints (β) and (β') of the model], they allow an approximate implementation of optimal tolls. This of course needs some knowledge of elasticities of substitution s, s', s_1, and s_2.

One straightforward consequence of these rules is what happens when there is a single constraint for the two modes (and then, necessarily, transfer payments from one mode to the other), i.e., when $\beta = \beta'$.

Then

$$\tau_1 = \tau_2,$$

$$\tau_3 = \tau_4,$$

and

$$\tau_P = \tau_F \qquad \text{if } s = s'.$$

Proportional taxation holds in each market, and between the two goods if $s = s'$. This result can be compared to conditions given in the literature for special cases (Andersen 1972) or more general situations (Baumol and Bradford 1970; Dixit 1970; Atkinson and Stiglitz 1972; Sandmo 1974, 1987).

The Complete Solution

Resolution of (4) and (6) gives τ_P and τ_F, which, in turn, together with τ'_P on the one hand and τ'_F on the other hand, give τ'_1, τ'_2, τ'_3, and τ'_4 and consequently τ_1, τ_2, τ_3, and τ_4 in relation to β and β'.

In the special case where $s = s'$, we get

$$\tau_1 = \frac{1}{(1+\beta)(\alpha_1+\alpha_2)}\left[\left(\frac{\alpha_1 - e}{\alpha_5 s} + \frac{\alpha_2}{s_1}\right)\beta + \left(\frac{\alpha_2 + e}{\alpha_5 s} - \frac{\alpha_2}{s_1}\right)\beta'\right]$$

$$\tau_2 = \frac{1}{(1+\beta')(\alpha_1+\alpha_2)}\left[\left(\frac{\alpha_1 - e}{\alpha_5 s} - \frac{\alpha_1}{s_1}\right)\beta + \left(\frac{\alpha_2 + e}{\alpha_5 s} + \frac{\alpha_1}{s_1}\right)\beta'\right]$$

with $e = \alpha_1\alpha_4 - \alpha_2\alpha_3$ (and similarly for τ_3 and τ_4).

Taking into account budgetary constraints, which can be written

$$\alpha_1\tau_1 + \alpha_3\tau_3 = \frac{D_1}{R},$$

$$\alpha_2\tau_2 + \alpha_4\tau_4 = \frac{D_2}{R},$$

with

$$R = \sum_i p_i C_i,$$

determines completely tolls and shadow prices β and β'.

Two additional remarks can be made:

- In the case of isoelasticity ($s = s' = s_1 = s_2$) we can verify that $\tau_1 = \tau_3$ (and $\tau_2 = \tau_4$): there is proportional taxation, not in each market as previously, but for each mode.
- It can happen, if fixed costs are proportionally much higher in one mode than in the other, and if s and s' are small comparatively to s_1 and s_2, that the resolution gives, for instance, $\beta' < 0$. The solution corresponding to nonstrict budgetary constraints is obtained by making $\beta' = 0$. Optimal taxation paradoxically involves a surplus for this mode, though it exhibits economies of scale. This can be explained by overcompetitiveness of this mode that would arise from a much lower average rate of tolling than in the other modes.

For instance, with the following values

$\alpha_1 = 5\%$ $\quad\alpha_2 = 10\%$ $\quad\alpha_3 = 2.5\%$ $\quad\alpha_4 = 12.5\%$

$s = s' = 0.3;$ $\quad s_1 = 1;$ $\quad s_2 = 1;$ $\quad \frac{D_1}{R} = 1\%;$ $\quad \frac{D_2}{R} = 1\%$

we obtain in the case of strict constraints

$\beta = 8.4\%$ $\quad\beta' = -0.86\%$

$\tau_1 = 14.4\%;$ $\quad\tau_2 = 6.4\%;$ $\quad\tau_3 = 11.1\%;$ $\quad\tau_4 = 2.8\%$

and in the case of nonstrict constraints

$\beta = 7.1\%$ $\beta' = 0$

$\tau_1 = 14.2\%;$ $\tau_2 = 8.1\%;$ $\tau_3 = 11.6\%;$ $\tau_4 = 5.3\%.$

Public Urban Transport Pricing

Suppose that car use (i.e., road use) is priced (through taxes on fuel) the same at peak and off-peak hours, though marginal social costs are very different; how should peak and off-peak public transport be priced?

The related second-best model can be written

Max $V(p_1, p_2, p_3, p_4, R)$

subject to the constraints

(μ) $m_1 C_1 + m_2 C_2 + m_3 C_3 + m_4 C_4 + C_5 = W_0$

(β) $p_1 = p_3$

where

C_1 = peak car use,

C_2 = peak public transport,

C_3 = off-peak car use,

C_4 = off-peak public transport,

C_5 = current consumption good (and numeraire).

The writing of optimality conditions using the same technique that previously led to the linear system for optimal tolls gives

$$\sum_{i=1}^{4} \frac{p_i - m_i}{p_i} e_{1i} = \frac{\beta}{C_1},$$

$$\sum_{i=1}^{4} \frac{p_i - m_i}{p_i} e_{2i} = 0,$$

$$\sum_{i=1}^{4} \frac{p_i - m_i}{p_i} e_{3i} = -\frac{\beta}{C_3},$$

$$\sum_{i=1}^{4} \frac{p_i - m_i}{p_i} e_{4i} = 0.$$

Solving in the case $s = s'$ gives

$$\tau_1 = -\frac{\beta}{(\alpha_1 + \alpha_2)C_1}\left(\frac{\alpha_1}{s} + \frac{\alpha_2}{s_1}\right),$$

$$\tau_2 = -\frac{\beta\alpha_1}{(\alpha_1 + \alpha_2)C_1}\left(\frac{1}{s} - \frac{1}{s_1}\right),$$

$$\tau_3 = \frac{\beta}{(\alpha_3 + \alpha_4)C_3}\left(\frac{\alpha_3}{s} + \frac{\alpha_4}{s_2}\right),$$

$$\tau_4 = \frac{\beta\alpha_3}{(\alpha_3 + \alpha_4)C_3}\left(\frac{1}{s} - \frac{1}{s_2}\right),$$

β being determined by the condition $p_1 = p_3$, which gives

$$\frac{1}{m_3} - \frac{1}{m_1} = \beta\left[\frac{1}{(\alpha_1 + \alpha_2)m_1 C_1}\left(\frac{\alpha_1}{s} + \frac{\alpha_2}{s}\right) + \frac{1}{(\alpha_3 + \alpha_4)m_3 C_3}\left(\frac{\alpha_3}{s} + \frac{\alpha_4}{s_2}\right)\right].$$

Since $m_1 > m_3$, $\beta > 0$ and τ_2 is negative (as is τ_1) and τ_4 is positive (as is τ_3) under the condition that $s_1 > s$ and $s_2 > s$. This is a reasonable assumption, and there is some sense to price below marginal cost at peak hours and above marginal cost at off-peak hours if it is the same for private transport.

However, the difference is smaller (since $\tau_1 - \tau_2 < 0$ and $\tau_3 - \tau_4 > 0$). It can happen, and some transport economists argue, that elasticity of substitution in peak periods is small (users being captive). Then τ_2 can be small, even positive. Peak-hours public transport should then be priced at or even above marginal cost.

Conclusion

Second-best models rarely give even qualitative rules for pricing or tax (real or shadow) setting in the different actual situations that can be encountered. It has been shown that retaining a minimal set of assumptions—thus leaving large degrees of freedom—allows much more precise results, even computable ones, with relatively limited information.

Some assumptions, for instance homogeneity, could be dropped,[4] but at a price that may be fairly high in terms of simplicity and implementability. This, of course, has to be considered if there is good reason to think that one is far from verifying the related assumption, which actually is very seldom obvious.

Finally, it would be interesting to see if the method used in this paper is also able to produce manageable and easy-to-interpret results in the case of second-best analysis within disequilibrium models such as the ones developed by Guesnerie (1981), Dreze (1985), and Fourgeaud et al. (1986).

Acknowledgments

This paper generalizes results that were obtained—by numerical computation—in an economic study made for the Ministry of Transportation while I was in the Ministry of Finance (see Laval et al. 1978). I am indebted to the two referees for checking errors and making helpful comments.

Notes

1. Thus, the utility function is homothetic-separable, and so is the related cost function (see Blackorby et al. 1978).

2. At least in terms of "opportunity cost," i.e., the loss of production of C_5' for an increase of production of one of the C_i ($i = 1$ to 4).

3. The formalization is not identical to Boiteux's, as we consider real—and not shadow—tolls (see Bernard 1972 and 1976). Boiteux's model would not apply anyway, since elasticities of supply are infinite when marginal costs are constant.

4. For instance, using Stone's demand function.

References

Andersen, P. S. (1972) "The Optimum Tax Structure in a Three Good One Consumer Economy." *Swedish Journal of Economics* 185–200.

Atkinson, A. B. and J. E. Stiglitz (1972) "The Structure of Indirect Taxation and Economic Efficiency." *Journal of Public Economics* 1: 97–119.

Baumol, W. J. and D. F. Bradford (1970) "Optimal Departures from Marginal Cost Pricing." *American Economic Review* 60: 265–283.

Bernard, A. (1972) "Fiscalité Optimale et Calcul Economique Public." Mimeo, Commissariat Général du Plan.

Bernard, A. (1976) "Optimal Taxation and Public Production with Budget Constraints," in *The Economics of Public Services*, M. Feldstein and R. Inman, eds. Macmillan.

Bernard, A. (1988) "Measuring and Representing Substitutability." Mimeo, Commissariat à l'Energie Atomique, Paris.

Blackorby, C., Primont, D., and R. Russel (1978) *Duality, Separability and Functional Structure: Theory and Economic Applications.* North-Holland.

Boiteux, M. (1956) "Sur la Gestion des Monopoles Publics Astreints à l'Equilibre Budgétaire." *Econometrica* 24: 22–40.

Diamond, P. A. and J. A. Mirrlees (1971) "Optimal Taxation and Public Production." *American Economic Review* 61: 8–27 and 261–278.

Dixit, A. K. (1970) "On the Optimal Structure of Commodity Taxes." *American Economic Review* LX, 295–301.

Dreze, J. H. (1985) "Second Best Analysis with Markets in Disequilibrium." *European Economic Review* 29(3): 263–301.

Fourgeaud, C., Lenclud, B. and P. Picard (1986) "Shadow Prices and Public Policies in a Disequilibrium Model of an Open Economy." *European Economic Review* 30: 991–1012.

Guesnerie, R. (1975) "Production of the Public Sector and Taxation in a Simple Second Best Model." *Journal of Economic Theory* 10: 127–156.

Guesnerie, R. (1979a) "General Statements on Second Best Pareto Optimality." *Journal of Mathematical Economics* 6: 169–194.

Guesnerie, R. (1979b) "Second Best Pricing Rules in the Boiteux Tradition." Mimeo, Cepremap No. 7920.

Guesnerie, R. (1981) "Analyse microéconomique normative du modèle Keynesien élémentaire." Mimeo, Cepremap, Paris.

Laval, D. et al. (1978) "Tarification de l'Usage des Infrastructures de Transport." Rapport du groupe de travail interministériel créé par décision du Premier Ministre du 23 Mars 1972.

Sandmo, A. (1974) "A Note on the Structure of Optimal Taxation." *American Economic Review* 64: 701–706.

Sandmo, A. (1987) "Reinterpretation of Elasticity Formulae in Optimum Tax Theory." *Economica* 32(2): 215–230.

7 Price Competition and Multiproduct Firms

Paul Champsaur and
Jean-Charles Rochet

1. Introduction

The literature on product differentiation offers two very different explanations of how the characteristics and the variety of products are determined. In the first case each firm is identified with a single product, that is, a point in the set of potential characteristics or quality scale. Then the product variety is governed by the entry and exit process. In particular, under free entry, it is explained by the maximum number of firms that can survive. Well-known contributions along this line have been made by Spence (1976), by Dixit and Stiglitz (1977), and, more recently, by Shaked and Sutton (1982). On the contrary, in the other branch of the literature, a firm is not limited to a single product and offers a range of qualities. Following Mussa and Rosen (1978), attention has been focused on the analysis of a monopolistic situation (Philips and Schuler 1981; Gabszewicz et al. 1986; Maskin and Riley 1984). Then a wide quality range enables the monopolist to discriminate among customers with different tastes.

Of course, the difference between these two approaches might be justified to some extent by different assumptions concerning the cost structure. For example, a rather high fixed cost attached to the production of any new quality would discourage a firm from offering many qualities. However, it seems difficult to justify why, if many single-product firms can survive as in Spence (1976) or Dixit and Stiglitz (1977), multiproduct firms should be discarded.

Broadly stated, the question we seek to address is: How will firms choose their product lines in an oligopolistic situation if there is no *a priori* constraint on the scope of their quality ranges? More precisely, we study a duopoly situation, and we model the interactions between the two firms as a two-stage noncooperative game where firms choose their quality ranges during the first stage and decide upon their prices during the second stage with full knowledge of irreversible quality decisions.

This line of research was initiated in a preceding paper (Champsaur and Rochet 1987) under the assumption that firms' fixed costs are independant of their quality ranges, an assumption always made in the aforementioned literature on monopoly. Following a well-established tradition going back to Hotelling (1929), we supposed that, when firms choose their quality ranges, they expect that (Bertrand) price competition prevails afterward—or, more precisely, that the prices emerging from the subsequent price game will constitute a Nash equilibrium of that game. A detailed study of the price-game equilibrium allowed us to show that the quality decisions of each firm are more influenced by the Chamberlinian incentive to differentiate its products from those of its rivals than by the gains resulting from the possibility of discrimination. As a consequence, the latter is severely limited for both firms at a full equilibrium of the two-stage game. We were led to conjecture that, after all, the single-product-per-firm assumption yields a good approximation of the market operation under the following two conditions:

- The cost structure is fully additive.
- Price competition prevails once quality decisions have been made.

The main objective of the present paper is to confirm the above conjecture. For that, we need a characterization of the equilibrium quality decisions, a task we were able to carry out only in a rather specific setup borrowed from Mussa and Rosen (1978). As a by-product, we are able to make welfare comparisons between market structures—monopoly and duopoly—that could not before be compared validly. The comparison is not trivial, because consumers are offered in one case (monopoly) too many products at rather high prices and in the other case (duopoly) too few products at moderate prices.

Our analysis brings to light the strong connection between two assumptions: (Bertrand) price competition and single-product firms. It is clear that if firms do not expect price competition to follow, they will make their quality decisions in a very different way. This point has been emphasized by Dixit (1979); however, Dixit keeps the single-product-per-firm assumption. Now the main consequence of a less competitive pricing is precisely to induce wider and, very likely, overlapping quality ranges. That would be the case if, for example, quality decisions were implemented through irreversible capacity investments so as to yield a Cournot outcome (see Kreps and Scheinkman 1983). Then the relationship between the market structure and the product variety is much more complex and its study remains to be done.

The economic model and the monopolistic situation are presented in section 2. Then the full equilibrium of the two-stage game is characterized in two steps (sections 3 and 4). Section 5 is devoted to welfare comparisons. Mathematical proofs are gathered in the Appendix.

2. The Model

We describe a market for a commodity that can be produced in a number of different varieties; its characteristics are supposed to be perfectly distinguishable by consumers. The attributes of a particular variety can be subsumed in a one-dimensional index q, where $q \geqslant 0$. We focus here on the *commercial* rather than the technological (increasing returns, economies of scale) reasons that may lead a firm to enlarge or to restrict the line of products it offers for sale. Thus, we adopt the neutral assumption that production costs are additive: the unit cost of producing variety q is supposed to be independent of the produced quantity of that or any other quality; it is denoted by $c(q)$.

The commodity is treated as a divisible good at an aggregate level and as an indivisible good from the consumers' viewpoint. Each consumer chooses a quality q among those offered and purchases one unit of that quality at a price p. This choice is made in accord with preferences on pairs (q, p) represented by a quasi-linear utility function:

$$u(\theta, q) - p,$$

where θ is a one-dimensional *non-negative* parameter characterizing the consumers' taste. In such a context, efficiency is obtained when the price of each variety is equal to its unit production cost. Consumer θ then chooses variety $q_c(\theta)$, which maximizes the surplus $u(\theta, q) - c(q)$. As our objective is simply to study a sensible example as completely as possible, we shall adopt the drastic simplification that this surplus is a quadratic function of θ and q, so that $q_c(\theta)$ is a linear function of θ. More precisely, we assume that

$$u(\theta, q) - c(q) = \theta q - \tfrac{1}{2}q^2 \tag{2.1}$$

and therefore

$$q_c(\theta) = \theta. \tag{2.2}$$

Parameter θ can then be interpreted as the index of the quality that would be chosen in an efficient system of resource allocation.

Such a specification can be interpreted in several ways. Vertical differentiation as formalized by Mussa and Rosen (1978) provides us with a first interpretation: $u(\theta, q) = \theta q$, a higher value of the q index indicating a higher quality for everyone. The unit production cost is a strictly convex (quadratic) function of q: $c(q) = \frac{1}{2}q^2$. Another interpretation comes from models of spatial differentiation. Producers and consumers are located along a line; parameters θ and q represent their respective locations. The unit cost of production is independent of these locations: $c(q) = a$, $\forall q$. When buying one unit of the commodity from a producer located in q, a consumer located in θ incurs a (quadratic) transportation cost equal to $\frac{1}{2}(\theta - q)^2$ in addition to the price charged by the producer. We then have

$$u(\theta, q) = \theta q - \tfrac{1}{2}q^2 - \tfrac{1}{2}\theta^2.$$

Since adding an arbitrary function of θ to $u(\theta, q)$ does not modify the corresponding preferences over couples (q, p), both of these interpretations lead to the same surplus and the same efficient allocation, $q_c(\theta)$. For the sake of a less abstract presentation, we shall stick to a vocabulary adapted to the interpretation in terms of vertical differentiation ($u(\theta, q) = \theta q$ and $c(q) = \frac{1}{2}q^2$), although the only thing that matters for our purposes[1] is the surplus $u(\theta, q) - c(q)$.

The action of a firm consists of two elements: a range of qualities it plans to offer for sale (that is, a subset Q of $\mathbb{R}^+$) and a price schedule (i.e., a mapping $\mathbf{p}$ from Q to $\mathbb{R}$, $\mathbf{p}(q)$ being the price charged for one unit of quality q commodity). If forced to buy from that firm, consumer θ will choose a quality $q(\theta)$ that maximizes $u(\theta, q) - \mathbf{p}(q)$. It is not restrictive to assume that firms consider only couples $(Q, \mathbf{p})$ such that the above maximization program has at least one solution for every θ. By definition, we have

$$V(\theta) = \underset{q \in Q}{\text{Max}}\, [u(\theta, q) - \mathbf{p}(q)],$$
$$\mathbf{q}(\theta) \in \underset{q \in Q}{\text{argmax}}\, [u(\theta, q) - \mathbf{p}(q)]. \tag{2.3}$$

$V(\theta)$ is an indirect utility function which is convex as a supremum of linear functions. Hence, $\mathbf{q}(\theta)$ and $V(\theta)$ are nondecreasing functions and we have, for every θ,

$$V(\theta) = V(0) + \int_0^\theta \mathbf{q}(s)\, ds. \tag{2.4}$$

In other words, an increasing function $\mathbf{q}\colon \mathbb{R}_+ \to Q$ and a level of indirect utility $V(0)$ constitute an equivalent representation of a price schedule $\mathbf{p}$, since the latter is unambiguously defined by

$$\mathbf{p}(q) = u(\theta, q) - V(0) - \int_0^{\theta} \mathbf{q}(s)\, ds, \tag{2.5}$$

where θ is such that $q(\theta) = q$. This representation will prove more convenient for the analysis of the firm behavior.

We shall assume that the distribution of consumer characteristics is continuous and is known to all firms. More precisely, parameter θ is uniformly distributed on an interval $[\underline{\theta}, \overline{\theta}]$, $\underline{\theta} < \overline{\theta}$, with a density $f = 1/(\overline{\theta} - \underline{\theta})$ and a distribution function F given by

$$F(\theta) = \int_{\underline{\theta}}^{\theta} f(s)\, ds = f(\theta - \underline{\theta}),$$

where $F(\theta) = 0$ if $\theta < \underline{\theta}$ and $F(\theta) = 1$ if $\theta > \overline{\theta}$.

Before examining the case of a duopoly, it is useful to recall briefly the analysis of a monopolistic situation made by Mussa and Rosen (1978). A monopoly is limited in the prices it can set by the ability a consumer has to refuse to buy if he considers prices to be too high. There exist several ways of modeling consumer behavior in this respect. The approach followed by Mussa and Rosen (1978), which we use here, consists in assuming that any consumer is able to turn to a substitute product (an "outside good" according to the terminology of Salop 1979), equivalent to a commodity with very low[2] quality q_0 and a given price, p_0. Let $\Delta V(\theta)$ be the utility gain of consumer θ, when buying from the monopoly, rather than the outside good:

$$\Delta(\theta) = V(\theta) - [u(\theta, q_0) - p_0]. \tag{2.6}$$

By definition consumer θ will be one of the monopoly's customers if $\Delta V(\theta)$ is positive. Moreover, provided that $q_0 < \mathbf{q}(\underline{\theta})$, $\Delta V(\theta)$ is an increasing function of θ, for every $\theta \geqslant \underline{\theta}$. This will always be the case, because *we assume from now on that* $q_0 = 0$. Therefore, there exists a unique value $\hat{\theta}$ belonging to $[\underline{\theta}, \overline{\theta}]$ such that

$$\hat{\theta} = \underline{\theta} \quad \text{if } \Delta V(\theta) > 0 \text{ on }]\underline{\theta}, \overline{\theta}[,$$

$$\theta = \overline{\theta} \quad \text{if } \Delta V(\theta) < 0 \text{ on }]\underline{\theta}, \overline{\theta}[\ \ldots,$$

and

$$\Delta V(\hat{\theta}) = 0 \text{ otherwise.}$$

Interval $[\hat{\theta}, \overline{\theta}]$ represents the set of monopoly's customers, whereas consumers belonging to $[\underline{\theta}, \hat{\theta}]$ prefer buying the "outside quality" $q_0 = 0$ at price p_0. The monopoly's profit is then given by

$$B = \int_{\hat{\theta}}^{\overline{\theta}} [p(\mathbf{q}(\theta)) - c(\mathbf{q}(\theta))] f \, d\theta.$$

Using (2.5) and (2.6), and integrating by parts, we get

$$B = \int_{\hat{\theta}}^{\overline{\theta}} [p_0 - u(\hat{\theta}, q_0) + \phi(\theta, \mathbf{q}(\theta))] f \, d\theta - [1 - F(\hat{\theta})] \Delta V(\hat{\theta}),$$

where

$$\phi(\theta, q) = u(\theta, q) - c(q) - \frac{1 - F(\theta)}{f} q = \left(\theta - \frac{1 - F(\theta)}{f}\right) q - \tfrac{1}{2} q^2.$$

Notice that $[1 - F(\hat{\theta})] \Delta V(\hat{\theta}) = 0$ except possibly for $\hat{\theta} = \underline{\theta}$, i.e., in the case where the whole market is served by the monopoly. But in the latter case, it is clearly optimal for the monopoly to set

$$\Delta V(\underline{\theta}) = 0. \tag{2.7}$$

The next step consists in maximizing B with respect to $\mathbf{q}$. The maximum is reached for $\mathbf{q}(\theta)$ such that

$$\mathbf{q}(\theta) \in \arg \operatorname*{Max}_{q \in \mathbb{R}_+} \phi(\theta, q)$$

provided we obtain a nondecreasing function of θ. This is the case here. Moreover, we assume that $\overline{\theta} \leqslant 2\underline{\theta}$, which ensures a *complete segmentation* of the market by the monopoly: consumers with different characteristics buy different qualities. Indeed, the optimal selling strategy $q_M(\theta)$ for the monopoly is

$$q_M(\theta) = \arg \operatorname*{Max}_{q \in \mathbb{R}_+} \phi(\theta, q) = \theta - \frac{1 - F(\theta)}{f} = 2\theta - \overline{\theta}, \qquad \text{for } \underline{\theta} \leqslant \theta \leqslant \overline{\theta}$$

which is an increasing function of θ.

It remains to check when it is in the monopolist's interest to serve all the market. From the expression of B we obtain

$$\frac{\partial B}{\partial \hat{\theta}} = -[p_0 + \phi(\hat{\theta}, q_M(\hat{\theta}))].$$

That is,

$$\frac{\partial B}{\partial \hat{\theta}} = -[p_0 + \tfrac{1}{2} q_M^2(\hat{\theta})].$$

It is therefore in the monopoly's interest to serve all of the market as soon as p_0 is high enough:

$$p_0 > -\tfrac{1}{2}q_M^2(\underline{\theta}) = -\tfrac{1}{2}(2\underline{\theta} - \overline{\theta})^2. \tag{2.8}$$

We assume from now on that this condition is satisfied (it is enough to assume $p_0 = 0$).

The maximum profit B_M the monopoly can obtain is then

$$B_M = \int_{\underline{\theta}}^{\overline{\theta}} [p_0 + \phi(\theta, q_M(\theta))] f \, d\theta,$$

or

$$B_M = p_0 + \tfrac{1}{6}[\overline{\theta}^2 - 2\underline{\theta}\,\overline{\theta} + 4\underline{\theta}^2]. \tag{2.9}$$

Let us finally point out that, as q_M is continuous, the quality range sold by the monopoly is an interval.

$$Q_M = [q_M(\underline{\theta}), q_M(\overline{\theta})] = [2\underline{\theta} - \overline{\theta}, \overline{\theta}].$$

This interval Q_M is greater than the interval of qualities that are bought in the efficient situation ($Q_c = [q_c(\underline{\theta}), q_c(\overline{\theta})] = [\underline{\theta}, \overline{\theta}]$).

3. A First Analysis of the Duopoly

There are now two firms indexed by i, where $i = 1, 2$. Firm i has to set a pair $(Q_i, \mathbf{p}_i)$, where Q_i is a quality range and $\mathbf{p}_i$ is a price schedule. Interactions between the two firms are formalized through a two-stage noncooperative game. Following a well-established tradition, we shall assume that prices can be easily and quickly changed by a firm, but that all modifications of its quality range are far more lengthy and costly. Thus, when a firm chooses its price schedule $\mathbf{p}_i$, it takes all product lines, including its own, as given. Thus, we can associate to every pair of ranges (Q_1, Q_2) a (second-stage) price game denoted by $G(Q_1, Q_2)$, in which the strategy of firm i consists in its price schedule $\mathbf{p}_i$.

It is well known that the set of Nash equilibria of such two-stage games is typically very large. Therefore it is now customary to retain the subset of perfect equilibria. A perfect equilibrium is a Nash equilibrium of the two-stage game $((Q_1, \mathbf{p}_1), (Q_2, \mathbf{p}_2))$ such that the couple of price schedules (p_1, p_2) constitutes a Nash equilibrium of the second-stage game, $G(Q_1, Q_2)$. In order to characterize the perfect equilibria of the two-stage game we must first study the Nash equilibria of all price games $G(Q_1, Q_2)$. Unfortunately, the complete determination of such price equilibria for arbitrary (Q_1, Q_2) is intractable. This makes a complete characterization of the set of perfect equilibria out of reach. Hence, our objective in this paper is more limited: it is to prove the existence of "sensible" perfect equilibria, to characterize them, and then to put forward a set of reasons making it likely that other perfect equilibria do not exist.

In a first step to this approach, it is convenient to study a game in which each firm i is forced to offer a quality range Q_i that is an interval. This section is dedicated to the analysis of the properties of this game. Although simplified by this restrictive assumption, these properties will clarify matters when we will come back to the unrestricted game.

We shall assume that the whole market is served in the sense that every consumer prefers to buy from one of the two firms rather than buying quality $q_0 = 0$ at price p_0. This means that p_0 is sufficiently high, a condition that will be checked only *a posteriori*.

We are now in a position to apply results obtained in a more general framework (Champsaur and Rochet 1987).

First, there always exists a Nash equilibrium in the price game $G(Q_1, Q_2)$. At such an equilibrium, if a quality q bought by a consumer is offered by both firms ($q \in Q_1 \cap Q_2$), we have $\mathbf{p}_1(q) = \mathbf{p}_2(q) = c(q)$. This is the well-known Bertrand effect. As a consequence, a situation in which each firm offers all possible qualities ($Q_1 = Q_2 = \mathbb{R}_+$) and where prices are down to unit costs is obviously a perfect equilibrium of the two-stage game. We exclude such trivial equilibria by restricting ourselves from now on to equilibria such that each firm makes a (strictly) *positive profit*. This can be justified by the usual assumption of the existence of a fixed entry cost.

Second, at a perfect equilibrium (where each firm makes a positive profit) quality ranges chosen by competing firms cannot overlap. It means that one firm—say firm 1—specializes in lower qualities: $Q_1 = [q_1^-, q_1]$, $0 \leqslant q_1^- \leqslant q_1$, whereas the other specializes in higher qualities: $Q_2 = [q_2, q_2^+]$, $q_2 \leqslant q_2^+$ with $q_1 \leqslant q_2$.

Third, for the existence of a Nash equilibrium of the price game yielding a positive profit to firm 1 (respectively firm 2), it is necessary that

$$q_2 > 2\underline{\theta} - \overline{\theta} \qquad \text{(respectively } q_1 < 2\overline{\theta} - \underline{\theta}\text{).} \tag{3.1}$$

Under these conditions, the price game $G(Q_1, Q_2)$ possesses a unique Nash equilibrium, whose corresponding profit levels are denoted by $B_1(Q_1, Q_2)$ and $B_2(Q_1, Q_2)$. These have now to be interpreted as the profit functions of the first-stage game (quality game). Quality ranges corresponding to a perfect equilibrium necessarily constitute a Nash equilibrium of this quality game.

Finally, the profit levels that are obtained at the equilibrium of the game $G(Q_1, Q_2)$ can be decomposed in the following way:

$$B_1(Q_1, Q_2) = B_1(\{q_1\}, \{q_2\}) + B_1(Q_1, \{q_1\}),$$

$$B_2(Q_1, Q_2) = B_2(\{q_1\}, \{q_2\}) + B_2(\{q_2\}, Q_2).$$

$B_i(\{q_1\}, \{q_2\})$ is the profit level that would be reached by firm i, in the price game where each firm i would offer a unique quality, q_i. We call it the "pure differentiation profit" and denote it by $b_i(q_1, q_2)$. Indeed, market shares and prices of limit qualities q_1 and q_2 are the same at the respective Nash equilibria of price games $G(Q_1, Q_2)$ and $G(\{q_1\}, \{q_2\})$.

$B_1(Q_1, \{q_1\})$ (respectively $B_2(\{q_2\}, Q_2)$) is the profit level that would be reached by firm 1 (respectively 2) in the price game where firm 2 (respectively firm 1) would offer a single quality, equal to the highest (respectively lowest) quality supplied by firm 1. We call it "pure discrimination profit." It is clear that q_1^- and q_2^+ do not influence the differentiation profit. On the other hand, $B_1(Q_1, \{q_1\})$ (respectively $B_2(\{q_2\}, Q_2)$ is a nonincreasing (respectively nondecreasing) function of q_1^- (resp. q_2^+). Therefore, when looking for an equilibrium of the quality game, we might as well take $q_1^- = 0$ and $q_2^+ = +\infty$. Let $d_1(q_1)$ and $d_2(q_2)$ denote the corresponding pure discrimination profits. Their expressions can be computed easily (see the appendix for details):

$$d_1(q_1) = 0 \quad \text{if } q_1 < \underline{\theta},$$

$$d_1(q_1) = \frac{f}{12}(q_1 - \underline{\theta})^3 \quad \text{if } \underline{\theta} \leqslant q_1 \leqslant 2\bar{\theta} - \underline{\theta}; \tag{3.2}$$

$$d_2(q_2) = 0 \quad \text{if } q_2 > \bar{\theta},$$

$$d_2(q_2) = \frac{f}{12}(\bar{\theta} - q_2)^3 \quad \text{if } 2\underline{\theta} - \bar{\theta} \leqslant q_2 \leqslant \bar{\theta}. \tag{3.3}$$

Cases where $q_1 > 2\theta - \bar{\theta}$ or $q_2 < 2\underline{\theta} - \bar{\theta}$, respectively, can be ignored, because they contradict condition (3.1), the latter being necessary for each firm to obtain a positive profit.

The search for an equilibrium of the quality game is now simplified, since the strategy of firm i reduces to a unique parameter, the limit quality q_i. We are now in a position to state the main result of this section (its proof is to be found in the appendix):

Proposition 1. Provided that p_0 is high enough, the quality game admits a unique Nash equilibrium. Equilibrium values of limit qualities are equal to

$$q_1^* = \underline{\theta} - \tfrac{1}{4}(\overline{\theta} - \underline{\theta}) \qquad \text{and} \qquad q_2^* = \overline{\theta} + \tfrac{1}{4}(\overline{\theta} - \underline{\theta}).$$

At the corresponding equilibrium of the price game, the prices charged for these qualities are

$$p_1^* = C(q_1^*) + (q_2^* - q_1^*)\frac{(\overline{\theta} - \underline{\theta})}{2},$$

$$p_2^* = C(q_2^*) + (q_2^* - q_1^*)\frac{(\overline{\theta} - \underline{\theta})}{2}. \qquad ■$$

Let, immediately, $q_1^* < \underline{\theta}$ and $q_2^* > \overline{\theta}$. Hence $d_1(q_1^*) = 0$ and $d_2(q_2^*) = 0$, which means that firm 1 (resp. 2) sells only the highest quality, q_1^* (resp. the lowest, q_2^*) of its product line. The differentiation effort of each firm is such that there is not enough space left for profitable segmentation of its customers. Of course, other (nonuniform) distributions of consumers' characteristics could allow, at equilibrium, for some kind of segmentation to appear at either end of the characrteristics scale. Proposition 1 is, however, a striking illustration of the power of the Chamberlinian incentive to differentiate oneself from competitors.

We have to be precise about what we mean by "provided that p_0 is high enough" in the statement of proposition 1. This condition ensures that each firm need not be concerned with the existence of the "outside" quality q_0. This is the case when consumer $\underline{\theta}$ prefers buying from firm 1:

$$u(\underline{\theta}, q_0) - p_0 < u(\underline{\theta}, q_1^*) - p_1^*$$

or (3.4)

$$p_0 > \tfrac{1}{32}(9\underline{\theta}^2 + 25\overline{\theta}^2 - 50\underline{\theta}\overline{\theta}).$$

In particular, if quantity $q_0 = 0$ is sold at its cost ($p_0 = 0$), inequality (3.4) is satisfied as soon as $\overline{\theta} < \tfrac{9}{5}\underline{\theta}$. If this latter inequality is not satisfied, but $p_0 = 0$, it is still possible to prove the existence of a unique perfect equilibrium, the characteristics of which (notably, no segmentation among customers of the same firm) are similar to that of the equilibrium described in proposition 1.

We gave a rigorous proof that any pair

$$Q_1 = [q_1^-, q_1^*],\ Q_2 = [q_2^*, q_2^+]$$

constitutes a Nash equilibrium of the quality game where every firm is forced to offer an interval. In particular, the pair $(\{q_1^*\}, \{q_2^*\})$ for which each firm supplies a single quality constitutes such an equilibrium, every other equilibrium being essentially equivalent to it.

4. Equilibrium without Restriction on Quality Ranges

The search for a perfect equilibrium in the preceding section was eased by the *a priori* restriction on the set of possible strategies that firms are obliged to offer an interval of qualities. It is true that, as noticed in the case of a monopolistic situation—easily generalized to an oligopolistic situation in this regard—it is never in the interest of a firm to maintain a gap in its product line, at least as long as this gap does not contain qualities offered by competing firms. This argument, however, does not allow us to neglect the fact that it may be in a firm's interest to offer qualities that are either higher or lower to intermediate ones offered by another firm. Nevertheless, such a situation of "entangled product lines" was ruled out by assumption. We now abandon this restriction, i.e., we come back to the *general game* in which firms have no restriction on their quality ranges. It is therefore likely that the set of perfect equilibria is altered. However, as we will prove in the remainder of this section, the equilibrium obtained in the preceding section is also an equilibrium of this unrestricted game.

Let us first examine the two product lines $\{[0, q_1^*], [q_2^*, +\infty]\}$ that constitute a Nash equilibrium of the constrained quality game. Consider the decision of firm 1. It is clear that it is not in the interest of the latter to offer qualities belonging to the product line of firm 2: $[q_2^*, +\infty[$. In fact, firm 1 cannot hope to make profits on such qualities, since attracting customers on these qualities implies selling them at their cost, and the induced increase in competition could only lower the equilibrium price of quality q_1^*. Since it is in its interest to restrict itself to qualities belonging to interval $[0, q_1^*]$ only, firm 1 does not incur any loss by offering a convex range. A similar argument holds for firm 2. The line of reasoning can be developed rigorously (cf. Champsaur and Rochet 1987, proposition 6).

Therefore, there exists a perfect equilibrium for the general-case two-stage game such that firm 1 (resp. 2) offers the range $[0, q_1^*]$ (resp. $[q_2^*, +\infty[$).

In such an equilibrium, each firm offers qualities that are not bought by any consumer. These qualities play, nevertheless, a potential strategic role. That is, firm 1 supplies qualities $[0, q_1^*[$ which do not yield anything directly, but deter firm 2 from offering them. In fact it appears that, at least in the particular setup adopted in this paper, such a deterrent is not necessary: knowing that firm 1 offers q_1^*, it is never in the interest of firm 2 to offer qualities that are inferior to q_1^*. This is summarized in the next proposition, the proof of which is to be found in the appendix.

Proposition 2. The pair $\{(q_1^*, p_1^*), (q_1^*, p_1^*)\}$ where each firm offers a single quality, *is a perfect equilibrium of the unrestricted two-stage game.*

This proposition is likely to be easily generalized to an oligopolistic situation, with an arbitrary number of firms. It provides a (partial) justification of the approach initiated by Chamberlin, identifying each firm with a unique quality.

Although satisfactory, because it provides a "natural" perfect equilibrium of the unrestricted two-stage game, proposition 2 does not preclude the existence of other perfect equilibria with entangled ranges. Our opinion is that the existence of such equilibria is rather unlikely in the particular setup that we have adopted; we were, however, unable to prove this conjecture. The objective of the last part of this section is to put forward some elements that should improve the understanding of this problem.

Let us suppose now that a firm offers a product line that is not convex. This product line is then the union of several separated connected components. But, in a perfect equilibrium, these corrected components are necessarily isolated from one another, in the sense that between two of them, there must be a group of qualities offered by a competing firm. This comes from the fact, already mentioned, that it is never in a firm's interest to maintain a gap in its product line if it is not forced to do so by competitors.

Furthermore, a firm does not incur any loss by taking away from its product line a connected component of qualities that does not attract any customer. That is, maintaining such a component in its product line, in as much as its presence influences prices of other qualities, can only lower equilibrium prices of these qualities. It is therefore not restrictive to consider only situations where *each connected component attracts a positive market share* at equilibrium.

Hence, since the function $\mathbf{q}: [\underline{\theta}, \overline{\theta}] \to \mathbb{R}_+$, which describes consumers' choices, is nondecreasing, customers of some connected component are necessarily *isolated* from customers of any other connected component belonging to the same product line.

These remarks have an important consequence. At any price equilibrium, a small variation of the price schedule restricted to a connected component —the prices charged for all other qualities remaining fixed at their equilibrium level—does not modify the firm's profit coming from the other connected components of its range. So the Nash equilibria of the duopolistic price game are identical to the Nash equilibria of the oligopolistic price game, where each connected component represents the entire product line of an independent firm. In other words, if a company sets up subsidiaries for each connected component in its line, its total profit is the same if each subsidiary chooses its own price schedule independently. For the study of the price game, we come back to a situation similar to the one studied in the preceding section: each firm's range consists in an interval which does not overlap intervals offered by other firms. However, the number of firms is, of course, no longer limited to two. We will not therefore take many chances by postulating that the main lesson of the beginning of this section remains valid: by reducing each convex component of its range to a single quality, a firm increases its profit through increased differentiation by more than it loses from reducing its segmentation possibilities. We have thus brought our initial problem back to a more convenient formulation, since the range of each of the two firms is composed of isolated qualities. From results concerning an oligopolistic situation where each firm offers a unique quality (see Champsaur and Rochet 1988), one deduces the existence of a unique Nash equilibrium for the price game. Therefore, we are in principle able to define and calculate gain functions for the quality game. Unfortunately, we were unable to solve the quality game, because the best response of a firm typically is a solution of a nonprogram. We nevertheless conjecture that there does not exist a Nash equilibrium of the quality game, such that the total number of qualities offered by the two firms together is greater than two. The next proposition, proved in the appendix, is one step toward such a conjecture.

Proposition 3. There does not exist an equilibrium of the quality game, in which a firm offers one quality and the other one offers two qualities.

We must emphasize that the formulation of propositions 2 and 3 are highly dependent upon the very specific assumptions that have been made. In particular proposition 3 would no longer be valid if the distribution of characteristics of the buyers differed markedly from a uniform distribution. However, propositions 2 and 3 illustrate a fundamental phenomenon: if firms expect price competition to prevail, they are led, in the choice of their products' characteristics, to prefer a strong differentiation at the expense of their segmentation ability.

5. Welfare Comparisons and Concluding Remarks

Our setup has the advantage of allowing a welfare comparison between monopolistic and oligopolistic situations. However, in comparing different market structures, we must in principle take into account the fixed costs. Once the market structure is fixed as in the preceding sections, it is legitimate to forget about them as far as they are independent of the quality decisions taken by a firm.

Indeed, the duopoly equilibrium described in Proposition 2 would not, *a posteriori*, be affected in the least by fixed costs increasing with the number of qualities or the width of the quality range offered by a firm, an assumption often made in the literature on product differentiation. Fixed costs of this kind would even reinforce the incentive for a firm to shrink its quality range to just a single quality. On the contrary, our analysis of the monopolistic situation, borrowed from Mussa and Rosen (1978), stands only if fixed costs are strictly independent of the quality ranges, which means they are pure entry costs. In the rest of this section we shall stick to this independence assumption.

Of course the magnitude of the entry cost influences the welfare comparison between different market structures. On the other hand, for such a comparison to be meaningful, this magnitude has to be compatible with minimal stability properties of the structures that are considered. More precisely, the entry cost has to be low enough for the survival of firms that are supposed to be active, and high enough to deter the entry of additional firms. Without a formal explanation of entry decisions, which is beyond the scope of this paper, this is a rather vague statement. Nevertheless a brief discussion of the quesiton will provide us with some references.

The cheapest way to introduce entry decisions in our setup is to make them part of the game's first stage. In other words, entry decisions would be taken simultaneously with quality decisions by potential firms that are identical *ex ante*. Then a potential firm has a rather pessimistic evaluation of its entry reward since it expects price competition to prevail in the second stage of the game. Thus, a monopolistic situation is stable even for an arbitrarily small but positive entry cost. The monopolist deters the entry of other firms simply by offering a large enough quality range. Looking back at inequalities (3.1), we see that such a quality range would have to be strictly larger than the range of qualities actually sold by a monopolist (at least for a low entry cost). The incumbent firm has to keep in its quality range unsold qualities because of their strategic role, a phenomenon very similar to overinvestment to deter the entry of rivals (a "top dog" strategy according to the taxonomy proposed by Fudenberg and Tirole (1984)).

Let us now examine the stability of the duopoly equilibrium described by proposition 1. Given the quality decisions q_1^* and q_2^* of the incumbent firms, the best quality decision that a potential firm can make, if it decides to enter, is clearly to occupy the market center, that is to offer a quality equal to $(q_1^* + q_2^*)/2 = (\overline{\theta} + \underline{\theta})/2$. Then, computations similar to the ones given in the appendix for the proof of Proposition 3 give, at the equilibrium of the price game, an expected profit level B_E equal to

$$B_E = (\tfrac{7}{12})^2 \times \tfrac{3}{8}(\overline{\theta} - \underline{\theta})^2. \tag{5.1}$$

This profit level should be interpreted as the minimum entry cost such that our duopoly equilibrium is also a Nash equilibrium of the more complex game with endogenous entry decisions.

Let us now turn to the welfare comparison. It is rather straightforward because of our partial equilibrium setup. It is based on a welfare index W, which is the sum of two terms: the integral S of the surplus of individual consumers over the population and the sum B of the profits earned by active firms.

We begin with the monopolistic situation with the notations of section II, the surplus of consumer θ (equation 2.6) is equal to

$$\Delta V(\theta) = V(\theta) - [u(\theta, q_0) - p_0].$$

Therefore we have

$$S = \int_{\underline{\theta}}^{\overline{\theta}} \Delta V(\theta) f \, d\theta.$$

Under monopoly we have

$$\frac{d}{d\theta}[\Delta V(\theta)] = q_M(\theta) - q_0 = 2\theta - \overline{\theta}$$

and

$$\Delta V(\underline{\theta}) = 0.$$

Then, integrating by parts, the aggregate surplus S_M under monopoly is equal to

$$S_M = \int_{\underline{\theta}}^{\overline{\theta}} [q_M(\theta) - q_0][1 - F(\theta)] \, d\theta,$$

and

$$S_M = \tfrac{1}{6}(\overline{\theta} - \underline{\theta})(4\underline{\theta} - \overline{\theta}).$$

Taking into account the fixed entry cost e and equation 2.9, we get the monopolistic gross profit

$$B_M = \tfrac{1}{6}(\bar{\theta}^2 - 2\underline{\theta}\bar{\theta} + 4\underline{\theta}^2) + p_0.$$

The welfare index is equal to

$$W_M = S_M + B_M - e = \tfrac{1}{2}\underline{\theta}\bar{\theta} + p_0 - e. \tag{5.2}$$

We proceed to the duopoly equilibrium. The computation of the whole benefit B_D earned at equilibrium by the two firms gives

$$B_D = \tfrac{3}{4}(\bar{\theta} - \underline{\theta})^2 - 2e.$$

The consumers' surplus is given by

$$\Delta V(\theta) = \theta q_1^* - p_1^* - (\theta q_0 - p_0), \text{ if } \theta \leqslant \tfrac{1}{2}(\underline{\theta} + \bar{\theta})$$

$$\Delta V(\theta) = \theta q_2^* - p_2^* - (\theta q_0 - p_0), \text{ if } \tfrac{1}{2}(\underline{\theta} + \bar{\theta}) \leqslant \theta.$$

Therefore the total consumer surplus S_D is equal to

$$S_D = p_0 - \tfrac{1}{2}(p_1^* + p_2^*) + \frac{(\bar{\theta} + 3\underline{\theta})}{8} q_1^* + \frac{(3\bar{\theta} + \underline{\theta})}{8} q_2^*,$$

or

$$S_D = \tfrac{1}{32}(62\underline{\theta}\bar{\theta} - 23\underline{\theta}^2 - 23\bar{\theta}^2) + p_0,$$

and the welfare index is equal to

$$W_D = B_D + S_D = \tfrac{1}{32}(\underline{\theta}^2 + \bar{\theta}^2 + 14\underline{\theta}\bar{\theta}) + p_0 - 2e. \tag{5.3}$$

The comparison between (5.2) and (5.3) yields

$$W_D - W_M = \tfrac{1}{32}(\theta - \theta)^2 - e.$$

Let us suppose first that e is small. Then the duopoly equilibrium is always preferable to the monopolistic situation. Of course, in that case, the duopoly equilibrium is no longer an adequate concept since it leaves enough room for a profitable entry ($e \leqslant \tfrac{1}{32}(\bar{\theta} - \underline{\theta})^2 \leqslant B_E$, with B_E defined by equation 5.1). However, it is extremely likely that the conclusion against the monopolistic situation would be strengthened if the entry threat was properly taken into account. Thus, under duopoly, consumers face a poor choice between two qualities that do not even belong to the efficient quality range whereas the monopolist displays a rich variety of products, richer than the efficient one. Why is the former situation still preferable? The reason is that quality choices are less distorted than under monopoly. Indeed, the choice between the two qualities q_1^* and q_2^* is the same under duopoly as if these two qualities were sold at their marginal cost.

On the contrary if e is large enough to suppress the entry threat ($\frac{1}{2}B_D > e > B_E$) the monopoly situation is preferable. Then our duopoly equilibrium corresponds to the Chamberlinian monopolistic competition equilibrium. As a consequence, this equilibrium does not enjoy in our setup the kind of second-best superiority that it possesses in another context (see Spence 1976; Dixit and Stiglitz 1977). However, we prefer not to insist on this point because it is mainly due to different assumptions concerning fixed costs. In the latter formalization the sum of the fixed costs is determined only by the product variety, whereas we made it a function of the number of active firms.

6. Appendix: Mathematical Proofs

Computing Segmentation Profits

Let us start with firm 2. At the unique equilibrium of the price game $G(\{q_2\}, [q_2, +\infty[)$, the price of quality q_2 is equal to its cost $c(q_2)$. Therefore, the segmentation profit d_2 $(q_2,$ is obtained by maximizing B_2 with respect to the price schedule $\mathbf{p}_2 = [q_2, +\infty[\to \mathbb{R}$ under the constraint that $\mathbf{p}(q_2) = c(q_2)$. Since it is equivalent for firm 2 not to sell quality 2 or to sell it at its cost, we have

$$d_2(q_2) = \underset{\mathbf{p}_2}{\text{Max}} \int_{\underline{\theta}}^{\overline{\theta}} [\mathbf{p}_2(\mathbf{q}_2(\theta)) - (c(\mathbf{q}_2(\theta))]f\,d$$

under the constraints $\mathbf{p}_2(q_2) = c(q_2)$ and

$$\mathbf{q}_2(\theta) \in \underset{q \in [q_2, +\infty}{\text{argmax}} \{\theta q - \mathbf{p}_2(q)\}.$$

This program is similar to the one corresponding to the monopoly case. It is convenient to substitute $\mathbf{q}_2$ and $V(\underline{\theta})$ for $\mathbf{p}_2$ as decision variables. These new variables have to satisfy the following constraints:

$\mathbf{q}_2$ is nondecreasing and $V(\underline{\theta}) \geqslant \underline{\theta} q_2 - c(q_2)$.

Consequently,

$$d_2(q_2) = \underset{\mathbf{q}_2, V(\underline{\theta})}{\text{Max}} \left[\int_{\underline{\theta}}^{\overline{\theta}} \Phi(\theta, q_2(\theta)) f\,d\theta - V(\underline{\theta}) \right].$$

The maximum is obtained for

$V(\underline{\theta}) = \underline{\theta} q_2 - c(q_2)$ and $\mathbf{q}_2(\theta) = \text{Max}\{q_M(\theta), q_2\}$,

which yields formula 3.2. ■

The computation of $d_1(q_1)$ obeys the same logic. The maximization can be made with respect to $\mathbf{q}_1$ and $V(\bar{\theta})$ under similar constraints:

q_1 is nondecreasing and $V(\bar{\theta}) \geqslant \bar{\theta} q_1 - c(q_1)$.

Consequently,

$$d_1(q_1) = \operatorname*{Max}_{\mathbf{q}_1, V(\bar{\theta})} \left[\int_{\underline{\theta}}^{\bar{\theta}} \psi(\theta, \mathbf{q}_1(\theta)) f \, d\theta - V(\bar{\theta}) \right]$$

with

$$\psi(\theta, q) = u(\theta, q) - c(q) + \frac{F(\theta)}{f} q = (2\theta - \underline{\theta}) q - \tfrac{1}{2} q^2.$$

The maximum is obtained for

$$V(\bar{\theta}) = \bar{\theta} q_1 - c(q_1)$$

and

$$\mathbf{q}_1(\theta) = \operatorname*{Max}_{q \in [0, q_1]} \psi(\theta, q)$$

or

$$\mathbf{q}_1(\theta) = \operatorname{Min}\{q_{\mathrm{m}}(\theta), q_1\}$$

with

$$q_{\mathrm{m}}(\theta) = \theta + \frac{F(\theta)}{f} = 2\theta - \underline{\theta},$$

and formula 3.3 follows. ■

Proof of Proposition 1. From Champsaur and Rochet 1987 we take the characteristics of the price equilibrium, when each firm i offers a single quality q_i:

$$p_1 = c(q_1) + \tfrac{1}{6}(q_2 - q_1)(2\bar{\theta} - 4\underline{\theta} + q_1 + q_2),$$

$$p_2 = c(q_2) + \tfrac{1}{6}(q_2 - q_1)(4\bar{\theta} - 2\underline{\theta} - q_1 - q_2).$$

Then we have

$$b_1(q_1, q_2) = \frac{f}{36}(q_2 - q_1)(2\bar{\theta} - 4\underline{\theta} + q_1 + q_2)^2,$$

$$b_2(q_1, q_2) = \frac{f}{36}(q_2 - q_1)(4\bar{\theta} - 2\underline{\theta} - q_1 - q_2)^2.$$

Firm 1 (resp. 2) wants to maximize its profit $b_1(q_1, q_2) + d_1(q_1)$ (resp. $b_2(q_1, q_2) + d_2(q_2)$), where $d_1(q_1)$ (resp. $d_2(q_2)$) is given by equation 3.2 (resp. (3.3)).

Let us assume that there exists a Nash equilibrium of the quality game, such that at least for one of the firms—for instance firm 1—the chosen quality belongs to the open interval $]\underline{\theta}, \overline{\theta}[$. We then have

$$\underline{\theta} < q_1 < q_2.$$

The derivative of the profits $b_1 + d_1$ of firm 1 with respect to q_1 is then equal to

$$\frac{f}{36}(2\overline{\theta} - 4\underline{\theta} + q_1 + q_2)(q_2 - 3q_1 - 2\overline{\theta} + 4\underline{\theta}) + \frac{f}{4}(q_1 - \underline{\theta})^2$$

$$= \frac{f}{36}[6(q_1 - \underline{\theta})^2 - 2(q_1 - \underline{\theta})(q_2 + 4\overline{\theta} - 5\underline{\theta}) + (q_2 - \underline{\theta})^2 - 4(\overline{\theta} - \underline{\theta})^2].$$

This is a quadratic function of $(q_1 - \underline{\theta})$. Therefore, there are two solutions to the first-order condition of the maximization of firm 1's profit. The smaller of these solutions defines the best response of firm 1. If $q_2 < \overline{\theta} + (\overline{\theta} - \underline{\theta})$, this solution is such that $q_1 \leqslant \underline{\theta}$ and a contradiction appears. If, on the contrary, $q_2 > \overline{\theta} + (\overline{\theta} - \underline{\theta}) \geqslant \overline{\theta}$, the profit of firm 2 is simply equal to $b_2(q_1, q_2)$. First- and second-order conditions for the maximization of b_2 yield

$$q_2 = \tfrac{1}{3}(q_1 + 4\overline{\theta} - 2\underline{\theta}). \tag{6.1}$$

Since $q_1 < \overline{\theta}$, we have $q_2 < \overline{\theta} + \frac{2}{3}(\overline{\theta} - \underline{\theta})$ and another contradiction appears.

Thus, the only possible Nash equilibrium of the quality game is such that $q_1 \leqslant \underline{\theta} < \overline{\theta} \leqslant q_2$. Equation 6.1 then defines the best response of firm 2. Similarly, the best response of firm 1 is given by

$$q_1 = \tfrac{1}{3}(q_2 + 4\underline{\theta} - 2\overline{\theta}).$$

The combination of these two equations yields the proposed result. ■

Proof of Proposition 2. The situation of the two firms being symmetric, it suffices to study the best response of firm 1 in the quality game, when firm 2 offers the unique quality $q_2^* = \overline{\theta} + \frac{1}{4}(\overline{\theta} - \underline{\theta})$. The optimal product line of firm 1 is the union of at most two intervals. Suppose then that firm 1 controls two subsidiary companies: a high-range subsidiary selling qualities higher than q_2, and a low-range subsidiary selling qualities lower than q_2^*. By the same arguments used in the proof of proposition 1 it is never in the interest of the high-range subsidiary to discriminate among its customers: therefore it sells a unique quality $q_3 > q_2^*$. Denote by q_1 the highest quality offered by the low-range subsidiary. Equilibrium prices of the three qualities $q_1 < q_2^* < q_3$ are the same as if the low-range subsidiary offered a single quality q_1 and if the two subsidiaries of firm 1 were independent.

Let us now compute the price equilibrium. Denote by p_i the price of quality q_i ($i = 1, 2, 3$). Let θ_1 (resp. θ_2) be the characteristic of the consumer that is indifferent between qualities q_1 and q_2^* (resp. q_2^* and q_3). We have

$$\theta_1 = \frac{p_2 - p_1}{q_2^* - q_1} \quad \text{or} \quad \theta_2 = \frac{p_3 - p_2}{q_3 - q_2^*}.$$

Profit levels obtained by each subsidiary are, respectively,

$$B_1 = f(\theta_1 - \underline{\theta})(p_1 - C(q_1)),$$

$$B_2 = f(\theta_2 - \theta_1)(p_2 - C(q_2^*)),$$

$$B_3 = f(\bar{\theta} - \theta_2)(p_3 - C(q_3)).$$

We can use the characterization of price equilibria obtained in Champsaur and Rochet 1988 in the case where n firms offer a single quality each. For the case we consider, where each quality attracts a positive market share, we have

$$p_1 = c(q_1) + (\theta_1 - \underline{\theta})(q_2^* - q_1), \tag{6.2}$$

$$p_2 = c(q_2) + (\theta_2 - \theta_1)\frac{(q_3 - q_2^*)(q_2^* - q_1)}{(q_3 - q_1)}, \tag{6.3}$$

$$p_3 = c(q_3) + (\bar{\theta} - \theta_2)(q_3 - q_2^*), \tag{6.4}$$

$$\theta_1 - \underline{\theta} = -\frac{\underline{\theta}}{2} + \frac{q_1 + q_2^*}{4} + \frac{(q_3 - q_2^*)}{12} + \frac{(q_3 - q_2^*)(\bar{\theta} - \underline{\theta})}{6(q_3 - q_1)}, \tag{6.5}$$

$$\theta_2 - \theta_1 = \frac{(\bar{\theta} - \underline{\theta})}{3} + \frac{(q_3 - q_1)}{6}, \tag{6.6}$$

$$\bar{\theta} - \theta_2 = \frac{\bar{\theta}}{2} - \frac{q_2^* + q_3}{4} + \frac{(q_2^* - q_1)}{12} + \frac{(q_2^* - q_1)(\bar{\theta} - \underline{\theta})}{6(q_3 - q_1)}. \tag{6.7}$$

The profit earned by the higher-quality subsidiary is equal to

$$B_3 = f(q_3 - q_2^*)(\theta - \theta_2)^2.$$

The profit earned by the lower quality subsidiary is equal to sum of the differentiation profits,

$$B_1 = f(q_2^* - q_1)(\theta_1 - \underline{\theta})^2,$$

and the (possible) discrimination profits $d_1(q_1)$, defined by (3.2).

We still have to prove that, even with coordination of qualities' choice for its subsidiaries, firm 1 earns a total profit that is necessarily less than what it could earn by offering the single quality q_1^*. More precisely, we have:

Lemma 1. If each subsidiary has a positive market share ($\theta_1 - \underline{\theta} > 0$ and $\overline{\theta} - \theta_2 > 0$, we have

$$q_1(q_1) + B_1 + B_3 < b_1(q_1^*, q_2^*) = \tfrac{3}{8}(\overline{\theta} - \underline{\theta})^2. \qquad ■$$

Proof of Lemma 1. Assume first that $q_1 > \overline{\theta}$. Then

$$d_1(q_1) \leqslant d_1(q_2^*) = \frac{f}{12}(q_2^* - \underline{\theta})^3$$

or

$$d_1(q_1) \leqslant \tfrac{1}{12}(\tfrac{5}{4})^3(\overline{\theta} - \underline{\theta})^2.$$

Thanks to equation 6.6, we know that

$$(\theta_1 - \underline{\theta}) \leqslant \tfrac{2}{3}(\overline{\theta} - \underline{\theta}).$$

Consequently,

$$B_1 = f(q_2^* - q_1)(\theta_1 - \underline{\theta})^2 \leqslant \frac{(\overline{\theta} - \underline{\theta})}{4}\left[\frac{2(\overline{\theta} - \underline{\theta})}{3}\right]$$

or

$$B_1 \leqslant \tfrac{1}{9}(\overline{\theta} - \underline{\theta})^2.$$

Furthermore, it is clear that

$$B_3 = f(q_3 - q_2^*)(\overline{\theta} - \theta_2)^2 \leqslant b_2(q_2^*, q_3)$$

or

$$\max_{q_3 \geqslant q_2^*} b_2(q_2^*, q_3) = \tfrac{1}{72}(\overline{\theta} - \underline{\theta})^2,$$

and the desired result is obtained. ■

We still have to examine the other possible case, where $q_1 \leqslant \bar{\theta}$. We then have

$$d_1(q_1) < d_1(\bar{\theta}) = \tfrac{1}{12}(\bar{\theta} - \underline{\theta})^2.$$

Furthermore,

$$B_1 + B_3 = f(q_2^* - q_1)(\theta_1 - \underline{\theta})^2 + f(q_3 - q_2^*)(\bar{\theta} - \underline{\theta}_2)^2$$

and

$$B_1 + B_3 \leqslant f(q_3 - q_1)[\theta_1 - \underline{\theta} + \bar{\theta} - \theta_2]^2.$$

But equation 6.6 yields

$$\theta_2 - \theta_1 = \frac{(\bar{\theta} - \underline{\theta})}{3} + \frac{(q_3 - q_1)}{6}.$$

Consequently,

$$B_1 + B_3 < f(q_3 - q_1)\left[\frac{2(\bar{\theta} - \underline{\theta})}{3} - \frac{(q_3 - q_1)}{}\right]$$

or

$$B_1 + B_3 < \tfrac{1}{3}(\tfrac{8}{9})^2(\bar{\theta} - \underline{\theta})^2,$$

and the desired result is obtained.

Proof of Proposition 3. Since ranges are entangled, we must prove that there does not exist a Nash equilibrium of the quality game, in which a firm (firm 1) offers extreme qualities q_1 and q_3, whereas the other intermediate firm (firm 2) offers a single quality q_2 (with $q_1 < q_2 < q_3$), these three qualities attracting a positive market share.

We will use the notations defined in the beginning of the proof of proposition 2 (with q_2 instead of q_2^*). Characterization of the price equilibrium given by equations 6.2–6.7 of course remains valid. It allows us to calculate the profit functions of the quality game.

Let us first examine the best response of the intermediate firm. Its market share (cf. equation 6.6) does not depend on quality q_2. Therefore maximization of its profits comes down to maximizing its markup $p_2 - C(q_2)$ with respect to q_2. Given equation 6.3, the best response therefore is

$$q_2 = \frac{q_1 + q_3}{2}. \tag{6.8}$$

Let us consider now the other firm. Its best response results from the maximization of $B_1 + B_3$ with respect to q_1 and q_3. We have

$$B_1 = f(q_2 - q_1)(\theta_1 - \underline{\theta})^2 \text{ and } B_3 = f(q_3 - q_2)(\bar{\theta} - \theta_2)^2. \tag{6.9}$$

Computing derivatives of $B_1 + B_3$ with respect to q_1 and q_3, with obvious notations, we get

$$\frac{1}{f}\frac{\partial B_1}{\partial q_1} = -(\theta_1 - \underline{\theta})^2 + 2(\theta_1 - \underline{\theta})(q_2 - q_1)\frac{\partial \theta_1}{\partial q_1},$$

$$\frac{1}{f}\frac{\partial B_3}{\partial q_1} = -2(q_3 - q_2)(\bar{\theta} - \theta)\frac{\partial \theta_2}{\partial q_1},$$

with

$$\frac{\partial \theta_1}{\partial q_1} = \frac{1}{4} + \frac{(q_3 - q_2)}{6(q_3 - q_1)^2}(\bar{\theta} - \underline{\theta})$$

and

$$\frac{\partial \theta_2}{\partial q_1} = \frac{1}{12} + \frac{(q_3 - q_2)}{6(q_3 - q_1)^2}(\bar{\theta} - \underline{\theta}).$$

Similarly,

$$\frac{1}{f}\frac{\partial B_3}{\partial q_3} = (\bar{\theta} - \theta_2)^2 - 2(\bar{\theta} - \theta_2)(q_3 - q_2)\frac{\partial \theta_2}{\partial q_3},$$

$$\frac{1}{f}\frac{\partial B_1}{\partial q_3} = 2(q_2 - q_1)(\theta_1 - \underline{\theta})\frac{\partial \theta_1}{\partial q_3},$$

with

$$\frac{\partial \theta_2}{\partial q_3} = \frac{1}{4} + \frac{(q_2 - q_1)}{6(q_3 - q_1)^2}(\bar{\theta} - \underline{\theta})$$

and

$$\frac{\partial \theta_1}{q_3} = \frac{1}{12} + \frac{(q_2 - q_1)}{6(q_3 - q_1)^2}(\bar{\theta} - \underline{\theta}).$$

For the couple (q_1, q_3) to constitute the best response, the following first-order conditions have to be satisfied:

$$\frac{\partial}{\partial q_1}(B_1 + B_3) = 0 \text{ and } \frac{\partial}{\partial q_3}(B_1 + B_3) = 0.$$

It is in particular necessary that

$$A = \frac{1}{f}\left[\frac{\partial}{\partial q_1}(B_1 + B_3) + \frac{\partial}{\partial q_3}(B_1 + B_3)\right] = 0.$$

Let us compute A when equation 6.8, which defines the best response of the intermediate firm, is satisfied. We adapt our notations by introducing the variable $d = q_2 - q_1 = q_3 - q_2$. We have then

$$\frac{\partial \theta_1}{\partial q_1} = \frac{\partial \theta_2}{\partial q_3} = \frac{1}{4} + \frac{(\bar{\theta} - \underline{\theta})}{24d}$$

and

$$\frac{\partial \theta_1}{\partial q_3} = \frac{\partial \theta_2}{\partial q_1} = \frac{1}{12} + \frac{(\bar{\theta} - \underline{\theta})}{24d}.$$

Consequently,

$$A = (\bar{\theta} - \theta_2)^2 - (\theta_1 - \underline{\theta})^2 + 2d\left[\frac{1}{12} + \frac{(\bar{\theta} - \underline{\theta})}{24d}\right](\theta_1 - \underline{\theta} - \bar{\theta} + \theta_2)$$

$$+ 2d\left[\frac{1}{4} + \frac{(\bar{\theta} - \underline{\theta})}{24d}\right](\theta_1 - \bar{\theta} + \theta_2),$$

where $A = (\bar{\theta} - \theta_2)^2 - (\theta_1 - \underline{\theta})^2 + \frac{1}{6}(\theta_1 + \theta_2 - \underline{\theta} - \bar{\theta})(4d + \bar{\theta} - \underline{\theta})$. Taking into account equations 6.5–6.7, we obtain

$$A = \left[\frac{(\bar{\theta} - \underline{\theta})}{2} - d\right]\left[\frac{(\bar{\theta} - \underline{\theta})}{2} - q_2\right].$$

There are two possibilities for $A = 0$. Starting with the first,

$$d = \frac{(\bar{\theta} - \underline{\theta})}{2},$$

we then have that

$$\frac{\partial(B_1 + B_3)}{q_3} = \frac{f}{12}[3(\bar{\theta} - q_2)^2 - 3(\bar{\theta} - q_2)(\bar{\theta} - \underline{\theta}) + (\bar{\theta} - \underline{\theta})^2]$$

is always positive. It rules out this first case. Let us examine the second case:

$$q_2 = \frac{\underline{\theta} + \bar{\theta}}{2},$$

In this case, the intermediate firm is located exactly in the center of the market. The profit of the outer firm is then equal to

$$B_1 + B_3 = \frac{fd}{18}(2\bar{\theta} - 2\underline{\theta} - d)^2.$$

It is maximum for $d = \frac{2}{3}(\bar{\theta} - \underline{\theta})$ and then yields the following amount:

$$\frac{16(\bar{\theta} - \underline{\theta})^2}{243} = \frac{16}{27}\frac{(\bar{\theta} - \underline{\theta})^2}{9}.$$

The outer firm, however, has to compare this profit level with that obtained by offering a single quality, say q_1. By definition, the latter is equal to

$$b_1(q_1, q_2) \qquad \text{with} \qquad q_2 = \frac{\bar{\theta} + \underline{\theta}}{2}.$$

We know that

$$b_1(q_1, q_2) = \frac{f(q_2 - q_1)}{36}(2\bar{\theta} - 4\underline{\theta} + q_1 + q_2)^2.$$

Maximizing b_1 with respect to q_1 yields

$$q_1 = \tfrac{1}{3}(q_2 - 2\bar{\theta} + 4\underline{\theta}),$$

where, as $q_2 = (\bar{\theta} + \underline{\theta})/2$,

$$q_1 = \underline{\theta} - \tfrac{1}{2}(\bar{\theta} - \underline{\theta}).$$

In this way, the outer firm would obtain

$$b_1\left(\underline{\theta} - \tfrac{1}{2}(\bar{\theta} - \underline{\theta}), \frac{\underline{\theta} + \bar{\theta}}{2}\right) = \frac{(\bar{\theta} - \underline{\theta})^2}{9},$$

i.e., a profit level greater than the one resulting from offering two qualities that are symmetric with respect to q_2. ■

Notes

1. Distinction between vertical and horizontal differentiation could be of importance through individual rationality constraints. These constraints result from the possibility to consumers not to buy anything from existing firms.

2. See Champsaur and Rochet 1986 for the analysis of a polar situation, where the substitute is similar to a high-quality good. Such a hypothesis would not modify our main results applying to the duopolistic situation.

References

Champsaur, P. and J.-C. Rochet (1986) "Concurrence par les prix et variétés des produits." *Annales d'Economie et de Statistique* 1: 153–173.

Champsaur, P. and J.-C. Rochet (1987) "Multiproduct duopolists" (revised version of CORE Discussion paper No. 8515). *Econometrica* 57(3): 533–557.

Champsaur, P. and J.-C. Rochet (1988) Existence of a Price Equilibrium in a Differentiated Industry. Document de travail INSEE No. 8801.

Dixit, A. K. and J. E. Stiglitz (1977) "Monopolistic competition and optimum product diversity." *American Economic Review* 67(3): 297–308.

Fudenberg, G. and J. Tirole (1984) "The fat-cat effect and the lean and hungry look." *American Economic Review* 74(2): 361–366.

Gabszewicz, J., A. Shaked, J. Sutton and J. F. Thisse (1986) "Segmenting the market: The monopolist's optimal product mix." *Journal of Economic Theory* 39(2): 273–289.

Gal-Or, E. (1983) "Quality and quantity competition." *Bell Journal of Economics* 14(2): 590–600.

Hotelling, N. (1929) "Stability in competition." *Economic Journal* 39: 41–57.

Kreps, D. M. and J. A. Scheinkman (1983) "Quantity precommitment and Bertrand competition yield Cournot outcomes." *Bell Journal of Economics* 14(2): 326–337.

Maskin, E. and J. Riley (1984) "Monopoly with incomplete information." *Rand Journal of Economics* 15(2): 171–196.

Mussa, M. and S. Rosen (1978) "Monopoly and product quality." *Journal of Economic Theory* 18: 301–317.

Philips, M. and R. E. Schuler (1981) Product Selection and Price Discrimination. CORE Discussion Paper No. 8126, Université Catholique de Louvain, Belgique.

Salop, S. (1979) "Monopolistic competition with outside goods." *Bell Journal of Economics* 10: 141–156.

Selten, R. (1975) "Re-examination of the perfectness concept for equilibrium points in extensive games." *International Journal of Game Theory* 4: 25–55.

Shaked, A. and J. Sutton (1982) "Relaxing price competition through product differentiation." *Review of Economic Studies* 49: 3–13.

Spence, A. M. (1976) "Product selection, fixed costs and monopolistic competition." *Review of Economic Studies* 43: 217–235.

8

Network Externality: Its Impact on Growth and Pricing of the Telephone Service

N. Curien and M. Gensollen

This paper aims at proposing an integrated microeconomic modelization: first, the main features of telephone demand are discussed; then, by making simple assumptions about production conditions, the characteristics of a network growing toward its social optimum can be derived.

In section 1, the individual consumption preferences are defined by specifying the weight of the telephone service relative to other commodities and by introducing the willingness to pay for joining the network and making use of it. In section 2, the individual decision to join the network is examined and it is shown that the expectations of future usage do indeed influence that decision. The telephone demand is in fact a joint demand for two bound services: optional usage, which is made possible by access to the network, on the one hand, and actual usage, i.e., making calls, on the other hand. The aggregate demand for access is then analyzed in section 3 and the equilibrium in size of the telephone network, at given prices of access and usage, is discussed in section 4.

Section 5 is devoted to the study of the social utility of the network; the latter is greater than the maximum revenues that can be recovered from charges for access, which gives rise to a network externality. This externality can be internalized, at least partially, by asking present subscribers to make a financial contribution to the future growth of the network. However, to design inciting pricing contracts with a rental component proves difficult. In section 6, the social utility of the network is compared with the cost of its construction and maintenance; the social surplus and then the social optimum are derived. If production costs are low enough, the telephone service is socially desired and the whole or part of the population is connected at the optimum point; nevertheless, the operator of the network generally suffers a loss at this point, so that he should look for a second-best optimum, bringing in a null or positive profit. As will be discussed in section 7, such an equilibrium is characterized by a cross-subsidy from traffic toward access and by a rationing of the network size relative to the first-best optimum.

The present paper is both a unitary presentation and an extension of two kinds of analyses that are usually treated separately in the economic literature applied to telecommunications: modelizations of the telephone demand on the one hand (see Artle and Averous 1973; Rohlfs 1974; Von Rabenau and Stahl 1973; Taylor 1980; Curien and Gensollen 1987) and studies of the optimal telephone pricing on the other (see Hazlewood 1950; Littlechild 1970, 1975; Gravelle 1972; Pyatt 1972; Squire 1973; Turvey 1974). Unlike the former authors, who have only described the demand for pure access, i.e., the demand for optional usage of the network, we shall here explicitly take into account actual usage. Similarly, whereas the authors concerned with pricing issues have directly considered a network in equilibrium without deriving the latter from an accurate microeconomic analysis of demand, we propose to carry out just such an analysis here and to consider the path toward equilibrium.

The presentation is deliberately rapid; the reader interested in detailed proofs and complementary explanations concerning sections 1 to 4 could usefully refer to prior publications: Curien 1986 and especially Curien 1987. However, the argument in sections 5 to 7 concerning network externality and its partial internalization is original, as far as we know. Finally, the conclusion of the paper summarizes our main results and places them within the context of the general literature on pricing.

1. The Individual Preferences

It is assumed that the individual preferences may be represented by the following utility function:

$$u = u(c, \delta \cdot q, \delta \cdot p), \tag{1.1}$$

in which c is the budget devoted to non-telephone consumption, δ is a binary variable indicating the decision to join the network ($\delta = 1$ if the individual decides to subscribe, $\delta = 0$ otherwise), q is telephone usage, and p is the rate of penetration of the telephone service. More accurately, p is the number of main telephone stations in relation to the size of the population. Variables c and q are aggregates over time of future nontelephone and telephone consumption, respectively; these aggregates are discounted at the date of access decision. As a result, $u(c, q, p)$ is the utility of using q of the telephone and consuming c of other commodities when connected to a network of size p, while $u(r, 0, 0)$ is the utility of devoting all future incomes r to non-telephone consumption. Besides the usual requirements of continuity, monotonicity, and quasi-concavity, we shall make two further assumptions on the utility function, which are specific to our present study of the telephone service.

The first assumption is that non-telephone goods take priority over the telephone service: in the absence of telephone access, utility increases strictly with respect to general consumption, whereas the telephone does not provide any utility in the absence of general consumption, i.e.,

$$\begin{aligned} &\forall c > 0\colon u(c, 0, 0) > u(0, 0, 0) \\ &\forall q, p \geqslant 0\colon u(0, q, p) \equiv u(0, 0, 0). \end{aligned} \tag{1.2}$$

In a sense, the second assumption attenuates the first one by stating that connection to the network and the consequent telephone usage give better access to information on the markets of the other goods, so that the marginal utility u_C of consuming those goods is increased at a given level of utility. Considering an individual who is exactly indifferent to the two situations of access and nonaccess to the network, the assumption takes the following analytical form:

$$u(c, q, p) = u(r, 0, 0) \Rightarrow u_c(c, q, p) \geqslant u_C(r, 0, 0), \tag{1.3}$$

in which r is the discounted aggregate of the individual's future flows of income. The assumption 1.3 will prove essential later on in the model, to show that individual demand for access appears in descending order of income.

As well as through utility, individual preferences can be described through willingness to pay. By definition, the willingness to pay for the telephone service, i.e., $w(r, q, p)$, is the amount of money that an individual with a given income r is ready to spend without loss in utility, when he joins a network of size p and makes use q of it. Like r and q, the willingness to pay w is an intertemporal aggregate, discounted at the date of access decision; it is defined by the following identity:

$$u(r - w(r, q, p), q, p) \equiv u(r, 0, 0). \tag{1.4}$$

Using the above assumptions, it is easily shown that the willingness to pay for the telephone service increases with respect to income r (as a consequence of assumption 1.3), to size p of the available network, and to level q of the telephone usage:

$$w_r \geqslant 0, \quad w_q \geqslant 0, \quad w_p \geqslant 0. \tag{1.5}$$

2. The Access Decision

The individual's program of utility maximization is as follows:

$$\text{Max}[u(c, \delta \cdot q, \delta \cdot p) | c, \delta, q: c + \delta(a + bq) = r], \tag{2.1}$$

in which a is the price of access, b is the price of usage, and p is the penetration rate as it is observed or expected by the individual when making his choice. It can then be shown that the individual demand for access is $\delta = 1$ (rather than $\delta = 0$) if

$$s(r, a, b, p) \equiv \text{Max}[w(r, q, p) - a - bq | q \geqslant 0] \geqslant 0,^{1} \tag{2.2}$$

in which $s(r, a, b, p)$ is interpreted as the largest surplus $w - a - bq$ that the individual can derive from the telephone service, by optimizing the level q of his usage. Thus, according to (2.2), an individual requests access if and only if there exists at least one level of usage that provides him with a positive surplus (utility being kept constant during the connection).[2]

Usage does actually play a role in the decision of access only if the price b of usage is not too high. If $h(r, b, p)$ solves for q program (2.2), then using the convexity of preferences ($w_{q^2} \leqslant 0$), we derive

$$h(r, b, p) \equiv 0 \qquad \text{if } b \geqslant \bar{b}(r, p) \equiv w_q(r, 0, p). \tag{2.3}$$

Thus, when price b exceeds the marginal willingness to pay $\bar{b}(r, p)$ for the first units of traffic (i.e., for starting telephone usage), then the usage that maximizes surplus is null and the surplus is restricted to a pure access one, i.e., $w(r, 0, p) - a$; in this case, the access decision is made exclusively by considering the desirability of receiving and being potentially able to place phone calls.

In the case where $b < \bar{b}(r, p)$, usage $h(r, b, p)$ is positive; the maximum surplus is then greater than the pure surplus of access $w(r, 0, p) - a$ and, from the first-order condition of program (2.2), i.e., $w_q = b$, we derive the following relations:

$$s_b(r, 0, b, p) \equiv -h(r, b, p) \tag{2.4}$$

and

$$s(r, a, b, p) \equiv v(r, b, p) - a, \tag{2.5}$$

in which

$$v(r, b, p) \equiv w(r, 0, p) + \int_b^{\bar{b}(r, p)} h(r, b', p)db' \tag{2.6}$$

is the willingness to pay for optional usage, i.e., $w(r, 0, p)$, increased by the surplus actually gained from traffic (integral term); $v(r, b, p)$ is interpreted as the overall "value" brought to the individual by his joining the network: indeed, according to (2.2) and (2.5), the access decision is made by comparing the value v with the entry fee a.

Our conclusion that the price of usage, and not only the price of access, influences the individual decision to enter the network is a characteristic property of the two-part tariffs, the fixed part of which is an access charge. However, the present application of this conclusion to the telephone service generalizes the results of Artle and Averous (1973) and Von Rabenau and Stahl (1973), as they are surveyed in Curien and Gensollen (1987): ignoring usage and its price, the former authors made demand for access a function solely of the connection charge. Moreover, our present analysis supports the classical specification in econometric models for the telephone demand, in which the price of the unit pulse of traffic is consistently introduced as an explanatory variable (see, for instance, Cozanet and Gensollen 1987).

3. The Aggregate Demand for Access

Prices and level of supply (a, b, p) being given, surplus $s(r, a, b, p)$ is an increasing function with respect to income, as one can easily see from the first-order condition of program 2.2, and from the first inequality in 1.5:

$$s_r(r, a, b, p) \equiv w_r(r, h(r, b, p), p) \geqslant 0. \tag{3.1}$$

If the surplus is positive for a given individual, it is then *a fortiori* positive for any individual with a greater income, so that the decisions to join the network are made in descending order of income.

The last applicant, or marginal applicant, has an exactly null surplus $(s = v - a = 0)$; then, for any strictly positive rate of penetration p, the following identity defines a threshold income $r^s(a, b, p)$, above which access is decided:

$$a \equiv v(r^s(a, b, p), b, p). \tag{3.2}$$

The network value v increases with respect to r and p and decreases with respect to b, from (2.6); then, from (3.2), the threshold income r^s increases with respect to both prices of access and usage and decreases with respect to the size of the available network:

$$r^s_a \geqslant 0, \qquad r^s_b \geqslant 0, \qquad r^s_p \leqslant 0. \tag{3.3}$$

The aggregate demand for access to the telephone service, i.e., the ratio of the number of applicants to the size of the population, is the fraction of individuals whose income exceeds the threshold, i.e.,

$$d(a, b, p) \equiv F[r^s(a, b, p)], \tag{3.4}$$

in which $F(\cdot)$ is the integral and descending distribution function of incomes throughout the population; $F(\cdot)$ is assumed to be stationary over time, decreasing, and such that

$$F(0) = 1; \; F(r_M) = 0, \tag{3.5}$$

where r_M is the income of the wealthiest individual. We then derive from (3.3) and (3.4) that the aggregate demand for access is a decreasing function of both prices of access and usage and an increasing function of the supplied network:

$$d_a \leqslant 0, \qquad d_b \leqslant 0, \qquad d_p \geqslant 0. \tag{3.6}$$

If the threshold income for access decision, i.e., $r^s(a, b, p)$, is greater than the income r_M of the wealthiest individual, then the aggregate demand for access is null, prices a and b seeming too high to all individuals or size p of the network too low. Thus, at given prices and in order to generate a strictly positive demand for access, the penetration rate must reach a bottom size $p_m(a, b)$, which solves for p equation $r^s(a, b, p) = r_M$ or $v(r_M, b, p) = a$; $p_m(a, b)$ increases with respect to both prices a and b.

When, at given prices, the network size grows above the bottom level of supply $p_m(a, b)$, then the demand increases and the income of the marginal applicant decreases. However, the rate of demand cannot exceed a top value $d_M(a, b)$, which is less than unity: when the network spreads, the threshold income $r^s(a, b, p)$, which decreases with respect to p, tends toward the value $r^s(a, b, 1)$ which is greater than the access charge a; nevertheless, the associated top level of demand, i.e.,

$$d_M(a, b) \equiv F[r^s(a, b, 1)] \leqslant 1,$$

can be raised by the network operator by lowering the price of access and the price of usage; the top level $d_M(a, b)$ is strictly below unity unless the access charge is null (since the poorest individual in the population, whose income is assumed to be null, cannot pay for his access) (figure 1).

4. The Size Equilibrium of the Network

The network operator connects the individuals in order of applications, i.e., in descending order of income. At given prices (a, b), the network is in

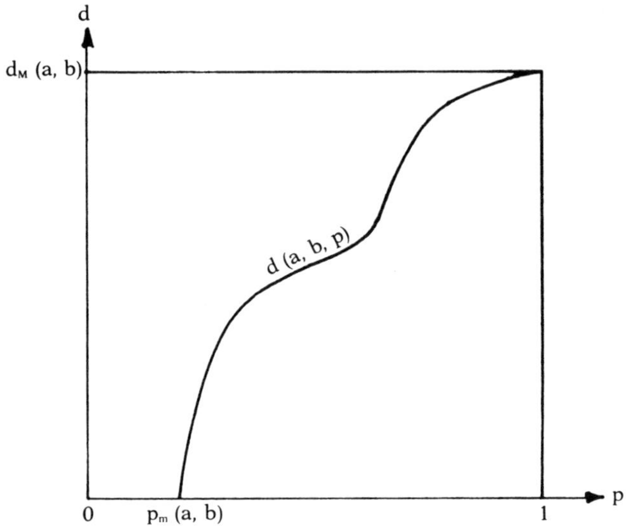

Figure 1.
The aggregate demand for access.

equilibrium if the number of applicants is equal to that of connected individuals, i.e., if

$$d(a, b, p) = p. \tag{4.1}$$

Equation 4.1 clearly reveals a first equilibrium, i.e., $p = 0$, since a zero supply generates a zero demand ($d(a, b, 0) = 0$). This equilibrium is stable, as the supply must reach a strictly positive level $p_m(a, b)$ before any demand appears.

For any strictly positive penetration rate p, equation 4.1 is, from equation 3.4, equivalent to

$$r^s(a, b, p) = F^{-1}(p). \tag{4.2}$$

Equation 4.2 states that the last connected individual with income $F^{-1}(p)$, is also the last applicant with income $r^s(a, b, p)$. Given equation 3.2, the equilibrium condition 4.2 can be rewritten as

$$a = v(F^{-1}(p), b, p), \tag{4.3}$$

in which $v(F^{-1}(p), b, p)$ is the value to the marginal subscriber of his joining the network. If this value is precisely equal to the access charge (according to equation 4.3), then the marginal subscriber has a zero surplus and coincides with the last applicant, so that the network of size p is in equilibrium.

Solving for p equation 4.3 yields the network equilibria other than zero; let us now discuss the existence and the number of such equilibria. The value of the network to the last subscriber is such that

$$v(r_M, b, 0) = v(0, b, 1) = 0. \tag{4.4}$$

The reason is that when the penetration of the service is zero, not even the wealthiest individual is interested in a nonexistent network; similarly, when the whole population is connected, the marginal subscriber, whose income is conventionally assumed to be null, has no money to spare for his access to the network. Given equation 4.4, the continuous function $v(F^{-1}(p), b, p)$ reaches a positive maximum within the interval [0, 1], i.e.,

$$a_M(b) = \text{Max}[v(F^{-1}(p), b, p) | 0 < p < 1]. \tag{4.5}$$

The maximum $a_M(b)$ increases as the price of usage b decreases.

If the access charge a is raised over $a_M(b)$, equation 4.3 has no solution and no network equilibrium is possible, apart from zero. When a nonzero equilibrium exists ($a < a_M(b)$), there is an even number of strictly positive equilibrium sizes for the network: half are stable and half of them unstable, the latter alternating with the former.

The stable (resp. unstable) equilibria are those in the neighborhood of which the network value to the marginal subscriber, i.e., $v(F^{-1}(p), b, p)$, decreases (resp. increases). Stability thus occurs when the marginal subscriber's surplus switches from positive to negative values when crossing the equilibrium point from left to right: equilibrium logically tends to be restored if the marginal subscriber values the network above (resp. below) the price of access, as the number of connections is reduced (resp. expanded).

The greatest stable size of equilibrium, i.e., $p^*(a, b)$, is lower than the top level of demand $d_M(a, b)$; it represents the rate of saturation of the service at given prices. The lowest unstable equilibrium size, i.e., $p_c(a, b)$, is greater than the bottom level of supply $p_m(a, b)$ and may be interpreted as the "critical mass" below which the pump of the telephone diffusion cannot be primed (figure 2).

Let us assume that the demand function $d(a, b, p)$ is smooth enough for the equilibrium equation 4.1 to yield only three solutions: the zero network, the critical mass, and the saturation level of the market. Then, any actual or expected level of supply between the bottom level $p_m(a, b)$ and the critical mass $p_c(a, b)$ is associated with a lower demand level and with a marginal subscriber's willingness to pay below the price of access; therefore, the network will progressively collapse toward the stable size zero.

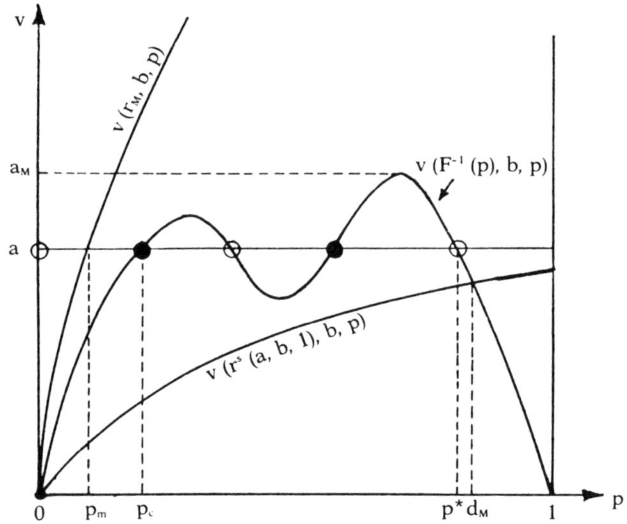

Figure 2.
The multiplicity of network equilibria: o stable; ● unstable.

Similarly, starting from a network larger than the saturation level $p^*(a, b)$, supply will be reduced in order to match the demand and will converge toward the stable equilibrium p^*. Finally, if supply is initially set between the critical mass and the saturation equilibrium, the latter will be reached asymptotically at the end of a "snowballing" process; in the course of this process, supply pulls demand upward, the marginal subscriber's willingness to pay exceeding the price of access at every stage of the growth[3] (see figure 3).

A full modelization of the telephone dynamics requires further assumptions about delays in the formulation of demand and in the reaction of supply. Considering, for instance, that the reduction of the number of orders in hand, i.e., $d(a, b, p) - p$, obeys a Poisson process with parameter k, then the penetration rate $p(t)$ is the solution of the following differential equation:

$$\dot{p}(t) = k \cdot [d(a, b, p(t))] - p(t)]; \qquad p(0) > p_c(a, b). \tag{4.6}$$

Coefficient k has the inverse dimension of duration; it is a measure of the diffusion speed.

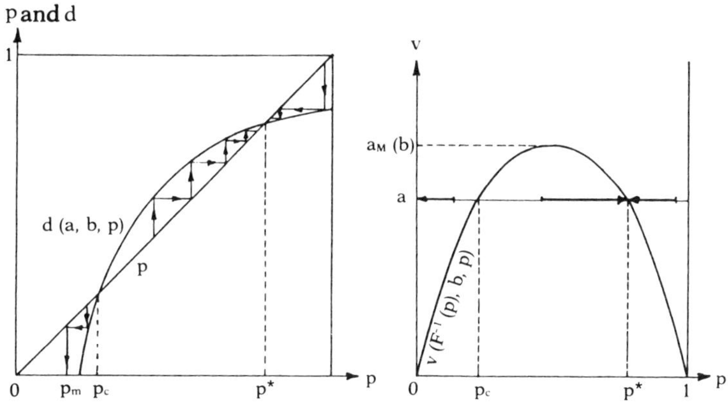

Figure 3.
Dynamic stability of network equilibria.

5. The Social Utility of a Network

Let us consider an individual with income

$$r \geqslant F^{-1}(p) \geqslant r^s(a, b, p),$$

being a member of a network of size p (not necessarily in equilibrium). In order to assess this individual's willingness to pay to join the network and make use of it, let us imagine that he is not yet connected; then, subject to the constraint of keeping the same utility after his connection, he would contemplate adopting usage $h(r, b, p)$, which maximizes his surplus according to (2.2). Were the network operator able to confiscate this surplus in excess of the telephone bill, he could extract the individual's entire willingness to pay for access and for traffic, i.e., $w(r, h(r, b, p), p)$, according to definition 1.4.[4]

The social willingness to pay for access to the network and for using it is the sum, throughout the network of size p, of all the individuals' willingness to pay. Given that the marginal subscriber's income is $r = F^{-1}(x)$ when the size of the network is $x \leqslant p$, this social willingness (or utility) is

$$W(b, p) \equiv \int_0^p w(F^{-1}(x), h(F^{-1}(x), b, p), p)dx. \tag{5.1}$$

It thus depends not only on the penetration rate p but on the price b of usage as well, through the demand of traffic h.

Noting that $w \equiv a + bh + s$, according to definition 2.2 of the surplus, and that $a + s \equiv v$ according to definition 2.5 of the individual value of the network (which excludes the expenditure of usage but includes the linked surplus), then the social utility takes the form

$$W(b,p) \equiv b \cdot H(b,p) + V(b,p), \tag{5.2}$$

in which

$$V(b,p) \equiv \int_0^p v(F^{-1}(x), b, p)dx \tag{5.3}$$

is a measure of the social value of the network, and

$$H(b,p) \equiv \int_0^p h(F^{-1}(x), b, p)dx \tag{5.4}$$

is the aggregate demand for usage. The social utility of the network thus consists in the value of usage, i.e., $b \cdot H$, increased by the value of the network, i.e., V.

The "social value" of a network of size p, i.e., $V(b,p)$, cannot be totally converted into revenues of access. When the network reaches size x, the highest price of access that the marginal subscriber can accept is equal to the value he sets on the network, i.e., $v(F^{-1}(x), b, x)$ (if price a was greater than v, surplus $v - a$ of the marginal subscriber would be negative and he would not be an applicant). The maximum revenues of access are thus

$$R(b,p) \equiv \int_0^p v(F^{-1}(x), b, x)dx. \tag{5.5}$$

The difference between the social value of the network and the revenues of access is by definition the network externality, i.e.,

$$E(b,p) \equiv V(b,p) - R(b,p)$$
$$\equiv \int_0^p [v(F^{-1}(x), b, p) - v(F^{-1}(x), b, x)]dx. \tag{5.6}$$

The source of this externality is the necessary progressiveness in the individual applications and in the construction of the network. There would be no externality if, instead of following the continuous dynamics resulting from equation 4.6, the network instantly reached size p by the collusion of all individuals with income greater than $F^{-1}(p)$. The externality is specific to the growth of a network and is not related to the influence of income on the process of demand: a network externality would still be present in a model without income effect, in which the individuals would be willing to pay the same amount to have access to the service and would therefore be connected by the network operator in an arbitrary order (but not simultaneously); in such a model, the externality associated with a network of size p would be

$$p \cdot v(p) - \int_0^p v(x)dx,$$

$v(x)$ being the value of a network of size x to any individual in the population.

The network externality could theoretically be recovered as a revenue, by altering the initial access contract of every subscriber, so as to charge him for what he gains from the further growth of the network.[5] The pricing system would then consist of three components: the initial access charge, a rental charge tied to the growth of the network, and the price of traffic. An individual connected when the size of the network is x would then owe the rental

$$v(F^{-1}(x), b, p') - v(F^{-1}(x), b, p),$$

for the period during which the network grows from p to p' ($p' > p > x$). Implementing such a pricing system would nevertheless generate a risk of instability; the rental charge being individualized with respect to the date of connection, and the senior subscribers (being wealthier) paying more than the newcomers, adverse selection could occur: if the operator is able to observe the date of connection only, and not the income, some members of the network will be tempted to cancel their subscription and then to recontract in order to benefit from more favorable conditions.

The issue then arises of designing a contract with three terms (access, membership, and usage) that, on the one hand, would provide an incentive, i.e., would deter adverse selection and moral hazard, and, on the other hand, would recover as much as possible of the network externality. Solving this problem would mean extending the theory of incentives in two directions: first, by taking into account externalities among consumers, and second, by introducing intertemporal pricing contracts involving agents' expectations about the future growth of the telephone network. Such an extension is clearly beyond the scope of the present paper, in which we propose to simplify the analysis by considering only the inciting pricing systems in which the instantaneous rental charge is the same for all members inside a network of a given size. Within this class of contracts, the most internalizing rental that can be set is the highest one that the marginal (i.e., least willing) subscriber would agree to pay. The part of the externality which can be recovered through such a rental is then

$$A(b,p) \equiv \int_0^p x v_x(F^{-1}(x), b, x)dx, \tag{5.7}$$

in which $v_x(F^{-1}(x), b, x)$ is the last subscriber's willingness to pay in order for a successor to join the network.

Eventually, the social value of the network, $V(b,p)$, can be broken down in the following way:

$$V(b,p) \equiv R(b,p) + E(b,p) \equiv R(b,p) + A(b,p) + S(b,p), \tag{5.8}$$

in which $R(b,p)$ is the maximum revenue of access, $A(b,p)$ is the maximum amount of rental that can be paid by subscribers, and $S(b,p)$ is the unrecovered part of the externality $E(b,p)$, i.e., the surplus remaining with the consumers if the network operator actually makes revenues $R(b,p)$ and $A(b,p)$.[6]

The variations of the marginal quantities associated with the different terms in identity 5.8 are represented in figure 4. We already know that the marginal revenue of access, i.e., $R_p \equiv v(F^{-1}(p), b, p)$ from equation 5.5, is null at $p = 0$ and $p = 1$, and reaches a maximum in between. One can easily show that the same is true of the marginal recoverable externality, i.e., $A_p \equiv p v_p(F^{-1}(p), b, p)$ from equation 5.7. It will further be assumed that the marginal social value of the network, V_p, which consists of an increas-

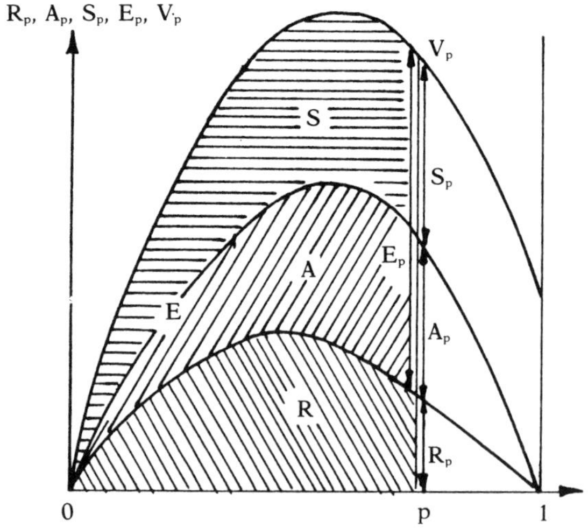

Figure 4.
The network value split in revenue and externality.

ing then decreasing component that is null at $p = 0$ and $p = 1$, i.e., R_p, and of a component that is null at $p = 0$ and strictly positive at $p = 1$, i.e.,

$$E_p \equiv \int_0^p v_p(F^{-1}(x), b, p)dx$$

from equation 5.6, itself increases then decreases in the interval $[0, 1]$. Finally, the integral quantities R, A, S, E, and V are visualized in the figure as the areas bound by the representative curves of the associated marginal variables.

6. The Social Optimum

In order to determine the social optimum, the utility of the network must be compared with the costs of its construction and operation. Assuming that the connection costs are separable from the traffic routing ones and that the returns to scale are constant in both activities, then the cost function is

$$C(b, p) \equiv b_0 H(b, p) + pa_0,^7 \qquad (6.1)$$

in which a_0 and b_0 are the unit costs (both marginal and average) of supplying access and traffic, respectively. More accurately, b_0 is the cost of routing one unit of traffic, and a_0 is the discounted aggregate cost of building and maintaining a telephone line. Although ignoring internal economies of production is somewhat unrealistic in the case of a telecommunications network, this assumption is convenient here, in order to focus attention on the characteristics of consumption only and to analyze their impact on the optimum.

From expressions 5.2 of the social utility and 6.1 of the cost, the social surplus associated with a network of size p is

$$B(b, p) \equiv W(b, p) - C(b, p) \equiv (b - b_0)H(b, p) + V(b, p) - pa_0. \qquad (6.2)$$

It is the sum of the profit made on traffic, i.e., $(b - b_0)H$, and of the value of the network minus the connection cost, i.e., $V - pa_0$. Seeking the social optimum then amounts to determining the values b^* of the price of traffic and p^* of the penetration rate, if any, which yield a positive maximum of the social net benefit B.

For any given size p of the network, the social surplus is maximum when the price b of usage is equal to the related marginal cost, i.e., $b^* = b_0$.[8] Therefore, as far as traffic is concerned, the standard result on marginal cost pricing holds.

However, if an externality due to incoming calls is taken into account, then the social benefit B should be increased by a term $w_0 H$, in which H is the incoming traffic (globally equal to the outgoing traffic) and w_0 is the willingness to pay for receiving one unit of traffic. The optimal price for sending traffic would become $b^* = b_0 - w_0$ (which solves for b the equation $(b + w_0 - b_0)H_b = 0$). The externality of usage, if at all significant, could be easily internalized by splitting the cost b_0 of routing a call between the caller and the callee, the former paying $b_0 - w_0$ and the latter, w_0.

The marginalist pricing rule for traffic and the assumption of constant returns to scale imply that the operator should make no profit on traffic when aiming at the social optimum. From identity (6.2), where b has been substituted for b_0, the social surplus is then restricted to the net value of the network, i.e.,

$$B(b_0, p) \equiv V(b_0, p) - pa_0. \tag{6.3}$$

According to equation 6.3, the maximum of $B(b_0, p)$, if not negative or a corner optimum reached on the boundary at $p = 0$ or $p = 1$, necessarily satisfies the relations

$$V_p(b_0, p) = a_0 \qquad \textit{and} \qquad V(b_0, p)/p \geqslant a_0. \tag{6.4}$$

In order to discuss the variations and the sign of B, it is thus convenient to study the two functions V_p and V/p, i.e., the marginal and average social values of the network, respectively; these functions are plotted in figure 5.

According to the assumption made in section 5, the marginal value V_p reaches a single maximum in the interval $[0, 1]$; this value is null at $p = 0$ and coincides at $p = 1$ with the marginal externality of a network extended to the whole population, i.e., $V_p(b_0, 1) = E_p(b_0, 1)$ (since the last subscriber, with no income, cannot provide any financial contribution toward his connection).

As for the average social value V/p, it is below the marginal value V_p for small p's, since V/p is then close to the individual value of the network to the marginal subscriber, i.e., $v(F^{-1}(p), b, p)$, whereas V_p comprises the same term increased by the willingness to pay of the existing subscribers to attract newcomers, i.e., E_p. We shall assume that, like V_p, V/p reaches a single maximum v_M in the interval $[0, 1]$, i.e., the social utility of the network exhibits decreasing returns to scale when the penetration rate is high; at its maximum, the average value of the network V/p is equal to the marginal value V_p (for $(V/p)' = (V' - V/p)/p$) and it is greater than the latter for any higher penetration rate.

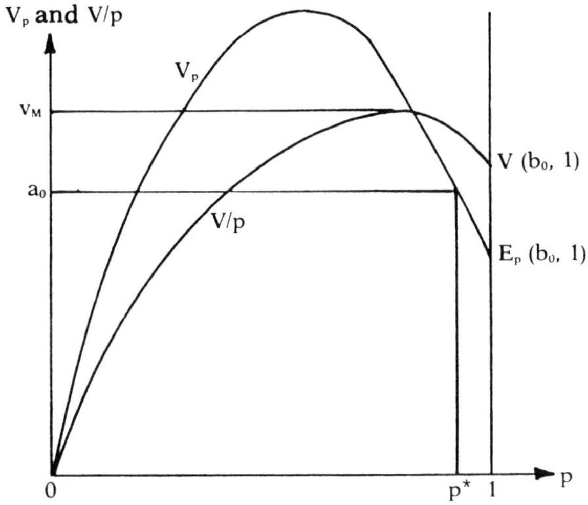

Figure 5.
Marginal and average values of the network.

Three situations may then occur as concerns the optimum (see figure 6).

(i) The cost of a connection is greater than the maximum of the average social value of the network ($a_0 > v_M$), which means that, whatever its size, the telephone network will never be in a position to find the willingness to pay necessary for its construction. Then, the social surplus $B = p(V/p - a_0)$ is negative for all p's and the optimum is reached at the "corner" $p^* = 0$; the telephone service is not desirable (see figure 6a).

(ii) The cost of a connection is lower than the limit v_M of desirability and greater than the marginal externality of a network extended to the whole population ($E_p(b_0, 1) < a_0 < v_M$), which means that connecting the individuals with the lowest resources costs the collectivity more than the benefits it brings. In this case, the social surplus $B = p(V/p - a_0)$ is negative for small p's (as long as $V/p < a_0$), but there exists a range of penetration rates within which this surplus becomes positive, increases as long as $V_p > a_0$, and then decreases. The social optimum is reached at $p^* < 1$, p^* being the greater of the two solutions of equation $V_p(b_0, p) = a_0$; therefore, some individuals do not belong to the network at the optimum (see figure 6b).

(iii) The cost of a connection is lower than the marginal externality of a completed network ($a_0 < E_p(b_0, 1)$), so that even the last connections are socially desired. Then the social surplus is negative as long as $V/p < a_0$, is positive beyond, and maximum at the corner $p^* = 1$: equation $V_p(b_0, p) =$

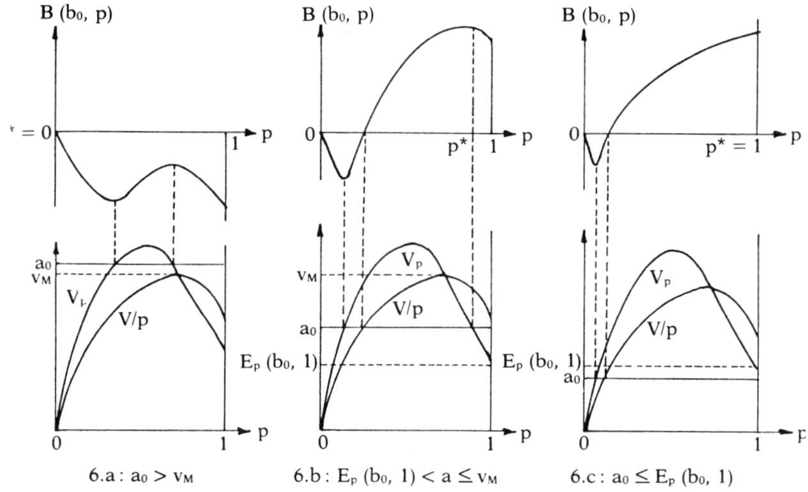

Figure 6.
Variations of the social surplus and social optimum.

a_0 has a single solution related to the negative minimum of B. Thus, in this case, the social optimum is reached when the whole population is connected (see figure 6c).

In cases ii and iii, where the social optimum is reached at a strictly positive penetration rate p^*, we must examine the viability of the associated network, i.e., whether the latter can be built and operated without suffering losses.

We will assume that the operator recovers the maximum revenue $R(b_0, p^*)$ that he can extract from the pricing of access. For any intermediate size p of the network on its path toward the optimum p^*, the price of access is therefore set at the value of the network to the marginal subscriber, i.e., $v(F^{-1}(p), b, p)$. As a result, the network grows in a quasi-static way, being in equilibrium at all times: the number of applicants is always equal to that of connections, according to our analysis in section 4. The optimal size p^* is a particular equilibrium, which can be shown to be stable provided that some regularity assumptions hold.[9]

Were the whole externality $E(b_0, p^*)$ to be recovered through rentals over and above the revenues of access, then the building and operating of the optimal network would be profitable, since the social value $V(b_0, p^*)$ of this network is greater than its cost p^*a_0. However, as discussed above (see section 5), only a part of the externality can be internalized, i.e., $A(b_0, p^*)$, so that the budget balance may be negative.

Even when building and operating the optimal network are globally profitable, the first connections run at a deficit to the operator (since the willingness to pay for a small network is close to zero and less than the production cost a_0). By examining successively cases ii and iii, let us now prove that the same is necessarily true of the last supplied connections.

In case ii, where the optimal penetration rate p^* is strictly lower than unity, the marginal value $V_p(b_0, p^*)$ of the network is, from equation 6.4, equal to the cost a_0 of a connection. Therefore,

$$a_0 = v(F^{-1}(p^*), b_0, p^*) + A_p(b_0, p^*) + S_p(b_0, p^*). \tag{6.5}$$

According to equation 6.5, the last subscriber's willingness to pay for his access, i.e., v, and the willingness which can be extracted from the present subscribers in order to complete the network, i.e., A_p, are not sufficient to recover the related cost, a_0: the reason is the noninternalized residual externality, i.e., s_p. Nevertheless, from a social point of view, the last connection is balanced (since $V_p - a_0 = 0$).

In case iii, where the whole population is connected at the optimum point ($p^* = 1$), the last subscriber, whose income is zero, cannot contribute toward his own access, while the whole network externality is irrecoverable. The right-hand side of equation 6.5 is thus reduced to $S_p(b_0, 1)$ while the equality becomes an inequality (corner optimum), i.e.,

$$a_0 < S_p(b_0, 1) = E_p(b_0, 1). \tag{6.6}$$

As a result, the connection of the poorest individual in the population means a net cost a_0 to the operator; however, from a social point of view, the marginal surplus $B_p(b_0, 1) = S_p(b_0, 1) - a_0$ is non-negative.

7. Traffic as a Means to Break Even

In this last section, we shall concentrate on the situation where the social optimum is not viable and the operator consequently seeks states of the network at which he makes a profit or at least breaks even: this is possible by compensating for losses on access through gains on traffic.

We will thus consider the case where the cost a_0 of a connection is such that the optimal penetration rate p^*, strictly positive, cannot be reached without losses, i.e., from the results of section 6:

$$[R(b_0, p^*) + A(b_0, p^*)]/p^* < a_0 < v_M = \text{Max}[V(b_0, p)/p \mid 0 < p < 1]. \tag{7.1}$$

In addition, we will assume that there exists at least a price b of usage and a penetration rate p warranting a profit to an operator who internalizes the recoverable part $A(b,p)$ of the network externality $E(b,p)$, i.e.,

$$a_0 < \mathrm{Max}[[(b - b_0)H(b,p) + R(b,p) + A(b,p)]/p | b \geqslant 0; \qquad 0 < p < 1]. \tag{7.2}$$

When condition 7.2 holds, the profit function reaches non-negative values and a positive maximum with respect to b and p. As the sum of profits of usage and of access, this function is

$$Pr(b,p) \equiv (b - b_0)H(b,p) + [R(b,p) + A(b,p) - pa_0]; \tag{7.3}$$

i.e., from (5.8) and (6.2),

$$Pr(b,p) \equiv B(b,p) - S(b,p), \tag{7.4}$$

in which it clearly appears that the operator's profit Pr, increased by the consumers' surplus S, is nothing but the social surplus B.

If a regulator compels the network operator to break even and not to exceed a certain amount of profit $z \geqslant 0$, then the second-best optimization program is

$$B_M(z) \equiv \mathrm{Max}[B(b,p) | b,p\colon B(b,p) - S(b,p) = z]. \tag{7.5}$$

The Lagrangian associated with this program assumes the following form:

$$L(b,p) \equiv B(b,p) + k[z - B(b,p) + S(b,p)], \tag{7.6}$$

in which the multiplier k is classically shown to be the derivative of the social surplus with respect to the level of tolerated profit, i.e.,

$$k = B'_M(z). \tag{7.7}$$

When the profit level z varies from zero toward its maximum value, i.e., $z_M = \mathrm{Max}(B - S)$, parameter k takes all negative values between $B'_M(0)$ and $-\infty$.[10] We can then derive from (7.7) that the social surplus $B_M(z)$ is a decreasing and concave function of the profit level z (since $k \leqslant 0$ and $dk/dz \leqslant 0$): when z increases, this is overcompensated by the decrease of consumers' surplus S and the overcompensation itself increases with respect to z.

The first-order conditions of the Lagrangian (7.6) maximization are as follows:

$$B_b = KS_b; \qquad B_p = KS_p, \tag{7.8}$$

in which

$$0 \leqslant K = |k|/(1 + |k|) \leqslant 1. \tag{7.9}$$

The value $K = 0$, i.e., $k = 0$, is associated with the nonviable social optimum, the value $k = |B'_M(0)|/(1 + |B'_M(0)|)$, i.e., $k = B'_M(0)$, with the budget balance, and the value $K = 1$, i.e., $k = -\infty$, with the maximization of profit.

Given the expression (6.2) of the social surplus (and using identity $V_b \equiv -H$), the optimality conditions (7.8) become

$$(b - b_0)H_b = KS_b, \tag{7.10}$$

$$(b - b_0)H_p + V_p - a_0 = KS_p, \tag{7.11}$$

with $S_p \geqslant 0$, and where $S_b \leqslant 0$ is a term whose absolute value rises as incomes are widely distributed over the population and as the sensitivity of traffic to the growth of the network is high.[11]

Equation 7.10 indicates that the price b of usage is set higher than its cost b_0 (for inequalities $K \geqslant 0$, $H_b \leqslant 0$ and $S_b \leqslant 0$ imply $b \geqslant b_0$). The markup is

$$(b - b_0)/b = K(|S_b|/H)/|E|, \tag{7.12}$$

in which

$$E = bH_b/H \tag{7.13}$$

is the price elasticity of the demand for traffic. The overpricing of traffic is therefore all the greater as the profit level is high (influence of K), as incomes are widely distributed (influence of $|S_b|/H$), and as the demand for traffic is price-inelastic (influence of $|E|$). Although over pricing of traffic is consistent with a strictly positive rate of penetration, it can be shown that this rate is lower than at the social optimum, i.e., $p \leqslant p^*$.[12]

As for equation 7.11, using expression 5.8 of V, it can be rewritten as follows:

$$a_0 = R_p + A_p + (b - b_0)H_p + (1 - K)S_p. \tag{7.14}$$

Noting that $K \leqslant 1$ and $S_p \geqslant 0$, equation 7.14 implies that the last connection supplied by the network operator is nonprofitable: the access fee that is paid by the marginal subscriber, i.e., R_p, augmented by the rentals billed to the existing subscribers in order to attract the marginal one, i.e., A_p, and by the net revenues generated from the last subscriber's outgoing and incoming traffic, i.e., $(b - b_0)H_p$, cannot make up for the connection cost a_0, because of the noninternalized part S_p of the externality. However, in the particular case of profit maximization ($K = 1$), the last connection is a finely balanced operation: a nonregulated monopoly stops connecting individuals as soon as the marginal cost exceeds the marginal revenue.

Since the last connections mean losses to the operator (unless profit is maximized) and as the same is necessarily true of the first connections, the globally positive balance is gained during the intermediate stage of the network development. During this phase, the revenues of access and the partial internalization of the network externality are not sufficient to generate a positive result: profits made on traffic are essential to that end.

Finally, whether it be a public utility monopoly subject to a profit constraint ($k = B'_M(0)$), or a private monopoly maximizing its profit ($k = -\infty$), the telecommunications operator cross-subsidizes access by using the revenues derived from traffic during the growth of the network, and this is the very phenomenon that can be observed in most countries, whatever the structure of the telecommunications industry.[13]

Conclusion

In this paper, we have studied the role that the so-called network externality plays in the growth and pricing of the telephone service. Though applied here to the telephone, our results could easily be transposed onto the analysis of any phenomenon involving a "club" effect. In this respect, Artle and Averous (1973) and Von Rabenau and Stahl (1973) had mentioned an analogy between the spread of the telephone and urban development; in the latter case, the club effect is connected with the accessibility to trade and services, which increases in relation to the size of the city center.

In the case of the telephone service, the network externality originates in the interdependence of the individual access decisions: each individual benefits from the presence of others in the network, as they represent a stock of potential interlocutors. In the model presented here, the interdependence was taken into account in a very simple way by introducing the size of the network into the individual utility function. A more accurate modelization should take into consideration not only the number but also the identity of the individuals who are connected to the network; this would recognize the existence of closed groups characterized by propensities of communication that are much greater internally than with the rest of the population. The study of such "communities of interest" (for instance, a firm, its suppliers, and its clients) has been studied by Rohlfs (1974).

However, the telephone service cannot be restricted to pure access to a club; the final aim of users is to place and to receive calls, so that the demand is indeed a joint demand for two bound commodities: the access to the network, i.e., optional usage, and the actual usage. Any given individual values the network up to an amount equal to his willingness to pay for optional usage, increased by the surplus that he may gain from traffic. He applies to be connected when this amount exceeds the price of access; the price of usage is involved in the decision too, since it influences the surplus of usage. This is a particular demonstration, in the case of the telephone service, of a general property of the two-part tariffs in which the fixed component is an access fee and the variable one is a price of usage.

Under the simplifying assumption that individuals differ only through their incomes and not through their tastes, we showed that they apply for the service in descending order of income. The applicants are those whose income exceeds a threshold value, which is all the greater as the prices are high and the size of the available network is small. The telephone network is in equilibrium when all applications are satisfied; in such a state, the price which is billed to the last subscriber for his entry is exactly equal to the value he sets on becoming a member of the network; this value is itself a function of the price of usage. At given prices of access and usage, there typically exist three equilibria: the stable zero equilibrium at which an inexistent supply generates no demand; another stable equilibrium associated with the saturation of the market; and, finally, an intermediate unstable equilibrium, which is the "critical mass" to be reached by the operator in order to avoid the network collapsing toward zero and to make it converge toward saturation, in a snowballing process during which the supply pulls the demand upward. In France, the telephone network grew in this way during the 1970s, when the hitherto rationed supply suddenly provoked an avalanche in demand.

At the individual level, the network externality is due to the impact of the network size on the access decision; at the aggregate level, it means an excess of the social utility of the network over the revenues derived from the charging for access. This surplus can only be internalized by making the users pay for the benefits that they gain from the further growth of the network, after their connection. A simple way to design inciting pricing contracts then consists in requesting the same marginal rental from every subscriber in a network of a given size, equal to the last comer's willingness to pay toward his successor's entry into the network. The nondiscrimination of the rental with respect to the income or to the date of connection implies that a part of the network externality is not recovered by the operator: this is the surplus of consumption that remains with the users.

The social optimum of the network is reached when the marginal utility of the latter balances its cost. Such an optimum is characterized by three parameters: the price of usage, that of access, and the size of the network. Provided that an externality of usage due to incoming calls may be ignored, as being of secondary importance, we first showed that the optimal price of traffic must be equal to the marginal cost of its routing. As for the price of access to the network and membership of the telephone club, it is lower than the related marginal cost at every stage of the growth of the network, because of the noninternalized part of the externality. Finally, as concerns the size of the network, three situations may occur. (i) The connection cost may be so high that the telephone network, whatever its size, cannot find the willingness to pay that is necessary for it to build up and operate; then, the telephone service is not socially desirable and the absence of a network is optimal. (ii) If the connection cost is lower than the limit of desirability, but greater than the population's willingness to pay for subsidizing the entry of the poorest individuals, then the optimal network should exclude some consumers. (iii) If the population is willing to pay in excess of what the last connections cost, then the network will be completed. In the last two cases, the social value of the optimal network is greater than its cost, but the latter may be greater than the sum of the access and the rental fees, leading to operating losses.

When the socially optimal network is nonprofitable, a second-best optimum should be looked for, at which the operator is subject to budget balance or to a maximal level of profit. We showed that such a behavior implies an overpricing of usage that is all the greater as incomes are widely distributed over the population, as demand is price-inelastic, and as the level of profit is high. The profits made on traffic then compensate for the losses suffered on access, according to a cross-subsidization which is universally practiced by the operators of telecommunications networks all over the world.

Finally, our paper fits into the tradition of applying the microeconomic theory to the management and the pricing of regulated monopolies. Long established in the field of electricity (see Boiteux 1949, 1951, 1956, 1960; Houthakker 1951; Feldstein 1972), this tradition is much more recent in the telecommunications industry (see Littlechild 1970, 1975; Rohlfs 1979; Sharkey 1982; Brown and Sibley 1986; Encaoua and Moreaux 1987; Curien 1986, 1987). Relative to the existing literature, three original aspects have been dealt with here. (i) First, a full and integrated microeconomic modelization of the decisions that are made by all the agents involved: the consumers of access and traffic, the network operator, and the regulator. (ii) Then, a systematic analysis of the "club" externality among consumers and of its influence on the evolution of demand and the pricing of a telecommunications service. (iii) Last, a first study of intertemporal pricing contracts involving three parts (access, membership, usage); the inciting character of such contracts in a dynamic context raises some issues that are still to be investigated.

Notes

1. $\delta = 1$ if $u(r, 0, 0) \leqslant \text{Max}[u(c, q, p) | c, q \colon c + bq = r - a]$, i.e., from duality, if $r - a \geqslant \text{Min}[c + bq | c, q \colon u(c, q, p) = u(r, 0, 0)]$, or, from (1.4), if $r - a \geqslant \text{Min}[r - w(r, q, p) + bq | q \geqslant 0]$; hence, (2.2).

2. The Marshallian demand for access therefore depends on the Hicksian demand for usage, which maximizes surplus and conserves utility. The latter demand, i.e., $h(r, b, p)$, solves for q program (2.2). When the income effect is significant, h diverges from the Marshallian demand of usage, i.e., $q = g(r - a, b, p)$, which solves for q program (2.1) when $\delta = 1$; g, which maximizes utility subject to the budget constraint, is the future usage by the subscriber, once connected.

3. A snowballing effect for the telephone demand for access was actually observed in France during the sixth and seventh five-year national plans. The hitherto rationed supply then suddenly developed and a control through prices proved necessary (the connection charge was raised from 500 F to 1100 F in 1975), in order to keep the waiting list of unsatisfied applicants within a tolerable range (see Curien et al. 1981).

4. This concept of individual willingness to pay is "ex-ante," for it considers the situation of a member of the network as the final state of a process where the initially unconnected individual keeps a constant utility. The ex-ante definition is well fitted to our purpose here but it is not the only one; an alternative ex-post definition would evaluate the willingness to pay as the compensation that should be given to a subscriber in order to make him accept his disconnection from the network. Ex-ante and ex-post definitions are different, since they both refer to constant utility transitions and since utility ex-post is greater than utility ex-ante for all members of the network (otherwise the latter would not have applied for the service).

5. For the subscriber of a network of size x who was connected when the size was $y < x$, the gain derived from a further marginal growth is $v_x(F^{-1}(y), b, x)$. Adding up this gain over all the subscribers in the network of size x, and then integrating along the network trajectory between 0 and p, externality $E(b, p)$ is indeed recovered: from (5.7), $\int_0^x v_x(F^{-1}(y), b, x)dy \equiv E_x(b, x)$, hence $\int_0^p [\int_0^x v_x(F^{-1}(y), b, x)dy]dx \equiv E(b, p)$.

6. A simple and illustrative computation can be carried out in the particular case where the individual value of the network is separable with respect to r, b, p and linear with respect to r and p, i.e., $v(r, b, p) \equiv r \cdot f(b) \cdot p$, and where the income distribution is uniform, i.e., $F(r) \equiv 1 - r/r_M$. It turns out that the three terms in (5.8) have similar weights (exactly equal under the assumption made). Therefore,

about one-third of the social value of a network does not generate revenues, so that some socially desirable networks (the social value of which exceeds the cost) cannot be supplied without operating losses.

7. $C(b, p)$ is the "*ex ante*" cost function, i.e., conditional to the Hicksian demand for usage $H(b, p)$; the ex-post demand and cost (i.e., after connection) are greater than their ex-ante equivalents, the individuals substituting general consumption for telephone usage so as to enhance their utility once connected to the network. However, it will be assumed for convenience that the operator makes his decisions (on prices and network size) on the basis of the ex-ante cost and usage.

8. The partial derivative of B with respect to b is $B_b \equiv (b - b_0)H_b + H + V_b$; now, $V_b \equiv \int v_b$ and $v_b \equiv -h$ from (2.6); hence, $(H + V_b) \equiv \int (h + v_b) \equiv 0$, and $B_b \equiv (b - b_0)H_b$; as the latter expression switches from a positive to negative sign when b crosses the value b_0 from left to right $(H_b \leqslant 0)$, B reaches a maximum for $b = b_0$.

9. At $p = p^*$, function $V_p(b_0, p)$ decreases with respect to p. Under assumptions $v_{pr}^2 \geqslant 0$, $v_p^2 \leqslant 0$, $p|v_p^2|/v_p \leqslant 1$, the same is true of the following function of p: $v(F^{-1}(p), b_0, p) \equiv V_p(b_0, p) - \int_0^p v_p(F^{-1}(x), b_0, p)dx$. The decrease of v at point p^* then implies stability, as shown in section 4.

10. (1) $B_M'(0) < 0$, since it is assumed that the maximum surplus $B_M(z)$ is reached to the left of zero, where operations are nonprofitable. (2) When k tends toward minus infinity, maximizing the Lagrangian L amounts to maximizing the profit $B - S$, according to (7.6).

11. From (5.6), (5.7), and (5.8), the surplus $S(b, p)$ assumes the following expression:

$$S(b, p) \equiv E(b, p) - A(b, p)$$

$$\equiv \int_0^p [v(F^{-1}(x), b, p) - v(F^{-1}(x), b, x) - xv_x(F^{-1}(x), b, x)]dx.$$

Hence, derivating with respect to p:

$$S_p(b, p) \equiv \int_0^p v_p(F^{-1}(x), b, p)dx - pv_p(F^{-1}(p), b, p) \geqslant 0;$$

and then, with respect to b:

$$S_b(b, p) = \int_0^p [h(F^{-1}(x), b, x) + xh_x(F^{-1}(x), b, x)]dx - H(b, p)$$

$$S_b(b, p) = -\int_0^p \int_0^y [h_y(F^{-1}(x), b, y) - h_y(F^{-1}(y), b, y)]dxdy \leqslant 0.$$

12. Given that $S_p \geqslant 0$ and $H \equiv -V_b$, equation 7.11 implies $V_p(b, p) - (b - b_0)V_{pb}(b, p) \geqslant a_0$, hence $V_p(b_0, p) \geqslant a_0$ provided that V_p is convex with respect to b ($V_{pb^2} \geqslant 0$ or $H_{pb} \leqslant 0$), i.e., that price b impedes the increase of traffic H with respect to the penetration rate p. Now, $a_0 = V_p(b_0, p^*)$ from (6.4), hence $V_p(b_0, p) \geqslant V_p(b_0, p^*)$, and finally $p \leqslant p^*$, using the above assumed concavity of V with respect to p, i.e., $V_{p^2} \leqslant 0$.

13. Defining, identifying and measuring such cross-subsidies in the telecommunications industry is the subject of a rich literature, both theoretical and empirical. For the United States, see various references mentioned in Brown and Sibley 1986 concerning the theory of cost allocation and the assessment of cross-subsidies that were subject to debate between ATT and its regulator FCC. For France, see de la Brunetière and Curien 1984 for an analysis of the revenue tradeoffs between types of telephone activities and types of subscribers.

References

Artle, A., and Averous, C. (1973) "The Telephone System as a Public Good: Static and Dynamic Aspects." *Bell Journal of Economics and Management Science* 4(1): 89–100.

Boiteux, M. (1949) "La tarification des demandes en pointe." *Revue Générale de l'Electricité* 58: 321–340.

Boiteux, M. (1951) "La tarification au coût marginal et les demandes aléatoires." *Cahiers du Séminaire d'Econométrie* 1: 56–69.

Boiteux, M. (1956) "Sur la gestion des monopoles publics astreints à l'équilibre budgétaire." *Econometrica* 24: 22–40.

Boiteux, M. (1960) "Peak Load Pricing." *Journal of Business* 33: 157–179.

Brown, S. J., and Sibley, D. S. (1986) *The Theory of Public Utility Pricing*. Cambridge University Press.

Cozanet, E., and Gensollen, M. (1987) "Les modèles de prévision de la demande téléphonique en France." *Revue Economique* 38(2): 203–256.

Curien, N., Gensollen, M., and Vilmin, E. (1981) "Prévision de la demande téléphonique: besoins, instruments, procédures." *Bulletin RCB* 44, March.

Curien, N. (1986) "The Telephone Service: Demand Analysis and Optimal Prices," in Jain S. B., ed., *Management and Role of Public Enterprises: Indo-French Experiences*. Chawla Composers, New Dehli.

Curien, N. (1987) "L'accès et l'usage téléphoniques: Modélisation conjointe et tarification optimale." *Revue Economique* 38(2): 375–414.

Curien, N., and Gensollen, M. (1987) "Les théories de la demande de raccordement téléphonique." *Revue Economique* 38(2): 197–202.

de la Brunetière, J., and Curien, N. (1984) "Les transferts de revenus induits par la tarification téléphonique entre catégories d'abonnés et entre types de prestations." *Annales des Télécommunications* 39: 469–485.

Encaoua, D., and Moreaux, M. (1987) "L'analyse théorique des problèmes de tarification et d'allocation des coûts dans les télécommunications." *Revue Economique* 38(2): 375–413.

Feldstein, M. (1972) "Equity and Efficiency in Public Sector Pricing: The Optimal Two Part Tariff." *Quarterly Journal of Economics* 86: 175–187.

Gravelle, H. S. E. (1972) "A Note on Telephone Rentals: Comment." *Applied Economics* 4(2): 235–238.

Hazlewood, A. (1950) "Optimum Pricing as Applied to Telephone Service." *Review of Economic Studies* 18: 67–68. Reprinted with amendments as "Telephone Service" in Turvey R., ed., *Public Enterprise: Selected Readings*. Penguin Books, 1968.

Houthakker, H. S. (1951) "Electricity Tariffs in Theory and Practice." *Economic Journal* 61: 1–25.

Littlechild, S. C. (1970) "A Note on Telephone Rentals." *Applied Economics* 2(2): 73–74.

Littlechild, S. C. (1975) "Two Part Tariffs and Consumption Externalities." *Bell Journal of Economics and Management Science* 6(2): 661–670.

Pyatt, G. (1972) Some Economics of a Public Utility. Centre of Industrial Economic and Business Research, University of Warwick, Coventry, Paper 28.

Von Rabenau, T. B., and Stahl, K. (1973) "Dynamic Aspects of Public Goods: A Further Analysis of the Telephone System," *Bell Journal of Economics and Management Science* 4(2): 515–525.

Rohlfs, J. H. (1974) "A Theory of Interdependent Demand for a Communications Service." *Bell Journal of Economics and Management Science* 5(1): 16–37.

Rohlfs, J. H. (1979) Economically Efficient Bell System Pricing. Bell Laboratories Economics Discussion Paper No. 138.

Sharkey, W. W. (1982) *The Theory of Natural Monopoly*, Cambridge University Press.

Squire, L. (1973) "Some Aspects of Optimal Pricing for Telecommunications." *Bell Journal of Economics and Management Science* 4(2): 515–525.

Taylor, L. D. (1980) *Telecommunications Demand: A Survey and Critique*, Ballinger.

Turvey, R. (1974) Externality Problems in Telephone Pricing. Presented at International Conference in Telecommunications Economics, University of Aston, Birmingham.

9

Efficiency of Market Equilibria with Adverse Selection: The Case of Insurance

Dominique Henriet and Jean-Charles Rochet

I. Introduction

The two "fundamental theorems of welfare economics" constitute a clear, rigorous formulation of the neoclassic view of the government's role in a competitive economy. In particular, they put forward in a clear way, within the set of assumptions adopted, the perfect compatibility between the government's redistributive capacity and the market's efficiencies in allocating resources.

Owing to Arrow's ingenious concept of a "contingent good," i.e., a commodity whose supply is made conditional upon the realization of a random event, it is possible to extend this analysis to an economy under uncertainty.

The best concrete example of a contingent good is probably an insurance contract: paid with certainty, the insurance premium is balanced by an indemnity payoff that is conditioned upon the occurrence of a damage. Unfortunately, the assumption of a complete set of contingent markets, which is compulsory for the analysis described above, is completely unrealistic as far as insurance markets are concerned. Cases where the fundamental insurance mechanism, the Law of Large Numbers, is a good approximation of reality, are also those in which the number of necessary contingent markets increases dramatically (for instance, it is exactly 2^N when N insured agents are subject to a simple 0–1 risk).

Malinvaud's (1971, 1973) works made this difficulty redundant. Malinvaud suggests a model of economic organization that is closer to real insurance markets. This model is based on the concept of an aggregated state of nature; under identical exposition to risk, an aggregate state of nature gives the proportions of people that are in each individual state of nature. For a large population, two cases have to be considered:

(a) the case of purely microeconomic risks when the aggregated state of nature is constant with probability 1;

(b) the case of a macroeconomic risk when several aggregated states of nature have a positive probability.

In an organization à la Malinvaud, only the first kind of risk is truly insurable, whereas macroeconomic risks can be partially reinsurable in some cases. Only a limited number of contingent markets are needed, conditional on aggregated states of nature and individual states. In such an economy, competitive equilibria yield the same result as a sytem of competitive insurance markets. When it is possible to set apart classes of individuals who are homogeneous with respect to risk, an organization à la Malinvaud requires as many insurance markets as there are risk classes. Even in the absence of a complete set of markets, Malinvaud proves that the two fundamental theorems remain valid, insofar as individual risks are sufficiently independent (so that the Law of Large Numbers can apply).

Since the beginning of the 1970s, another stream in the literature concentrates on markets with asymmetric information. Particular attention has been drawn to adverse selection phenomena, notably since Akerlof (1970). Insurance markets also provide an excellent illustration of adverse selection: when the different classes of individuals are not exactly distinguishable *a priori* from one another, the organization à la Malinvaud does not work. Indeed, if insurance companies persist in offering complete coverage at actuarial premia, they won't be able to keep "high-risk consumers" from choosing contracts designed for "good risks," hence a possible deficit for the companies. In this setup several interesting results have been obtained: it is possible for a competitive equilibrium not to exist, and even if it does, it may not constitute a second-best optimum. The chief reason for this inefficiency is the incompatibility of some resource redistribution schemes with second-best optimality. In particular, the best equitable pricing policy (i.e., without cross-subsidies) can be Pareto-dominated. Since the market alone cannot spontaneously generate cross-subsidies, the competitive equilibrium may be dominated. This paper attempts to clarify the relation between equilibria and optima for markets with adverse selection.

After presenting the model of Rothschild, Stiglitz, and Wilson in section II, we obtain the full classification of second-best optima in section III. In particular, we put forward important relations between efficiency, cross-subsidization, and statistical distribution of risks. The different equilibrium concepts are examined in section IV. In section V, we show how some of them can be reinterpreted within a truly dynamic setup. Finally, we suggest in section VI a quantitative regulation mode that enables recovering some analogy with the two fundamental theorems of welfare economics. Mathematical proofs are gathered in an appendix.

II. The Model of Rothschild, Stiglitz, and Wilson

This model gives the simplest possible description of a market with adverse selection. It is, however, rich enough to have given rise to an abundant theoretical literature, since the seminal papers of Rothschild and Stiglitz (1976) and Wilson (1977).[1]

One is interested in a noncompulsory insurance product (e.g., damage insurance of a motor vehicle), directed toward a population of potential policy holders, which is homogeneous regarding observable characteristics[2] (for instance, students under 25 driving a Renault 5 in the Toulouse area). Adverse selection problems come from heterogeneity of this population regarding driving hazards, i.e., existence of "good" and "bad" risks, which are nondiscernible *a priori.* Of course, a partial solution to these problems can be found using technological devices that allow including new observables in the pricing policy: a sealed kilometric counter giving an indication of risk exposition, or a microprocessor recording petrol consumption viewed as a proxy for driving quality, and so on. Such possibilities are nevertheless limited: imperfection of *a priori* pricing[3] remains a fundamental issue for insurance markets, as well as for credit markets. This problem is the basis of the Rothschild-Stiglitz-Wilson model, which we now describe.

A population is made of a large number of economic agents, who are subject to a risk of accident, with a corresponding damage, D. This population is subdivided into N homogeneous risk classes indexed by i, $i = 1, \ldots, N$, characterized by their accident probability p_i. We assume $p_1 > \cdots > p_N$.

Agents are furthermore identical: we denote by R their income and by U their Von Neumann–Morgenstern utility function (assumed to be C^2, strictly increasing and strictly concave).

With no insurance, agent i reaches the expected utility level:

$$v_i^0 = p_i U(R - D) + (1 - p_i) U(R).$$

An insurance policy is described as a pair $z = (q, \Pi)$, where q is compensation and Π is the premium level. The associated expected utility level for agent i is

$$v_i(q, \Pi) = p_i U(R - \Pi + q - p) + (1 - p_i) U(R - \Pi). \tag{1}$$

One always assumes that compensation is positive and that it does not exceed the damage (overinsurance is excluded):

$$0 \leqslant q \leqslant D. \tag{2}$$

Insurance companies possess statistical data on the population of policy holders; they know the proportions of every kind of insured people: $(\lambda_1, \ldots, \lambda_N)$, where $\sum_{i=1}^{n} \lambda_i = 1$. In particular, they know the average incident frequency of the population:

$$p = \sum_{i=1}^{n} \lambda_i p_i. \tag{3}$$

Neglecting operating costs, expected profit is the difference between receipts and the mathematical expectation of liabilities. In particular, if a single contract $(\overline{q}, \overline{\Pi})$ is marketed and bought by the whole population, it is profit making for companies supplying it iff

$$\Pi \geqslant \overline{p\overline{q}}. \tag{4}$$

More generally, if ε represents the (presumably finite) set of contracts simultaneously supplied to the market, each insured individual of type i will choose z_i as solution of

$$V_i(z_i) = \operatorname*{Max}_{z \in \varepsilon} V_i(z). \tag{5}$$

Neglecting possible indifferences,[4] it is legitimate to restrict the analysis to the subset $Z = \{z_1, \ldots, z_N\}$, which satisfies by construction the self-selection constraints

$$\forall i, j \qquad V_i(z_i) \geqslant V_i(z_j).$$

We say that Z is the pricing policy corresponding to the set of contracts ε. Hence the following definition:

Definition 1. An admissible pricing policy Z is an N-set of contracts $\{z_1, \ldots, z_N\}$ such that

$$\forall i, j \qquad V_i(z_i) \geqslant V_i(z_j), \tag{6}$$

$$\sum_{i=1}^{n} \lambda_i(\Pi_i - p_i q_i) \geqslant 0. \tag{7}$$

The constraint 7 is interpreted as the positivity of expected total profit over all of the contracts (if we assume that, in case of indifference between

z_i and z_j, a consumer of type i always chooses z_i). Definition 1 does not imply that z_i are distinct: the special case of a uniform pricing policy $\overline{z} = (\overline{z}, \ldots, \overline{z})$, such that z satisfies (4) is admissible. More generally, definition 1 allows cross-subsidies between different categories of insured agents. Indeed the premium Π_i, paid by insured people of type i, can diverge from actuarial premium $p_i q_i$.

Apart from the fact that implementing such a policy in a competitive market may seem tricky (this point will be discussed later), equity considerations suggest a more restrictive definition:

Definition 2. An equitable pricing policy Z^e is an N-set $\{z_1^e, \ldots, z_N^e\}$ of contracts satisfying

$$\forall i, j \qquad V_i(z_i^e) \geqslant V_i(z_j^e), \tag{6}$$

$$\forall i \qquad \Pi_i^e = p_i q_i^e. \tag{7}$$

We denote by C^λ the set of admissible policies when the risk distribution is $\{\lambda_1, \ldots, \lambda_N\}$ and C_0 the subset of equitable policies, the latter being independent on λ.

Definition 3. An admissible pricing policy Z is a second-best optimum iff there does not exist another admissible policy Z' that Pareto dominates it.

The set of second-best optimal pricing policies is denoted by P^λ. Section III is devoted to the characterization of P^λ.

III. Optimality

We first concentrate on equitable pricing policies.

Proposition 1. There exists a unique equitable policy z that Pareto dominates all equitable policies. It is defined by

$$\forall i \qquad \Pi_i^* = p_i q_i^*, \tag{9}$$

$$q_1^* = D \text{ and } \forall i \geqslant 2, \qquad V_{i-1}(z_{i-1}^*) = V_{i-1}(z_i^*). \tag{10}$$

The so-called "best equitable policy" is obtained by offering complete insurance to agents of type 1 (the worse risks), and increasing deductibles to others; the deductible for type i is just sufficient to prevent people of category $(i-1)$ from choosing a contract devised for category (i). The

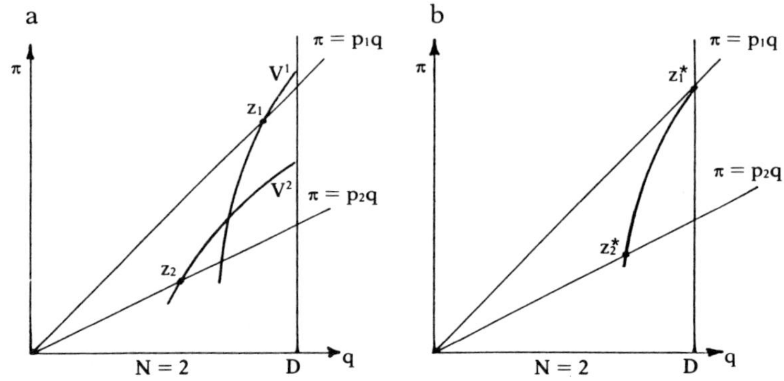

Figure 1.
(a) An example of an equitable pricing policy. (b) The optimal equitable pricing policy.

chain of externalities generated by asymmetric information weighs more heavily on lower-risk agents (figure 1).

These external effects can be considered unnecessarily binding, as suggested by the following (extreme) example. Let us start from a homogeneous situation ($N = 1$) where the equitable optimal contract provides complete actuarial insurance to all agents. Suppose now a very small number of very "bad" risks enters the population. If one wants to stick to equitable pricing policies, the initial population of "good" risks is now forced to accept a high deductible, the social cost of which is disproportionate to earnings. It is then natural to consider implementation of cross-subsidies.

Definition 4. Given the risk distribution λ, an admissible system of cross-subsidies is a vector α such that

$$\langle \lambda, \alpha \rangle = \sum_{i=1}^{N} \lambda_i \alpha_i \leqslant 0. \tag{11}$$

α_i has to be interpreted as the subsidy (or tax if $\alpha_i < 0$) perceived (or paid) by each policy holder of the ith category. Relation (11) ensures that the overall system is not in deficit, given risk distribution λ.

Definition 5. A pricing policy supported by a tax subsidy scheme α is an N-set $\{z_1, \ldots, z_n\}$ satisfying

$$\forall i, j \qquad V_i(z_i) \geqslant V_i(z_j), \tag{6}$$

$$\forall i \qquad \Pi_i^e = p_i q_i - \alpha_i. \tag{12}$$

C_α denotes the set of all policies supported by the tax-subsidy scheme α. For $\alpha = 0$, we come back into the set of equitable policies which we denoted C_0. Furthermore, one obviously gets

$$C^\lambda = U\{C_\alpha, \langle\lambda, \alpha\rangle \leqslant 0\}.$$

A generalization of proposition 1 is easily obtained.

Proposition 2. For any α satisfying (11), there exists a unique policy $Z^*(\alpha) = \{z_1^*(\alpha), \ldots, z_N^*(\alpha)\}$ in C_α that Pareto dominates all elements in C_α. It is implicitly defined by

$$\forall i \qquad \Pi_i^e(\alpha) = p_i q_i^*(\alpha) - \alpha_i \tag{13}$$

and

$$q_1^*(\alpha) = D \qquad \text{and} \qquad \forall i \geqslant 2, \qquad V_{i-1}(z_{i-1}^*(\alpha) = V_{i-1}(z_i^*(\alpha)). \tag{14}$$

$Z^*(\alpha)$ denotes the "best pricing policy supported by α." Again, externalities weigh more heavily on lower risk classes. We are now able to give a characterization of the set P^λ of second-best optima.

Proposition 3. There exists a mapping $\delta\colon \mathbb{R} \to \mathbb{R}^{N-1}$ satisfying the following property:

$$\forall\lambda \in \textstyle\sum_N P^\lambda = \left\{z^*(\alpha), \langle\alpha, \lambda\rangle = 0, \text{ and } \dfrac{\lambda_i}{\lambda_{i+1}} \geqslant \delta_i(\alpha), \; i = 1, 2, \ldots, N-1\right\}.$$

In other words, every admissible optimal policy necessarily belongs to the $Z^*(\alpha)$ category, for a subsidy scheme α satisfying the global constraint (11). However, such a policy $z^*(\alpha)$ is not always second-best Pareto-optimal. For instance, the best equitable policy ($\alpha = 0$) does yield a second-best optimum only if, for two adjacent categories, the relative proportion of higher risks exceeds some thresholds $\delta_i(0)$. For $N = 2$, we obtain a more straightforward characterization:

Proposition 4. There exists an increasing mapping $\alpha^*[0, 1] \to \mathbb{R}$ that satisfies the following property:

$$\forall\lambda \in \textstyle\sum_2 \qquad P^\lambda = \left\{z^*(\alpha), \quad \begin{matrix} \alpha_1\lambda_1 + \alpha_2\lambda_2 = 0 \\ \alpha_1 \geqslant \alpha_1^*(\lambda_1) \end{matrix}\right\}.$$

In particular, $Z^*(0)$ leads to a second-best optimum iff $0 \geqslant \alpha_1^*(\lambda_1)$. Proposition 4 can be interpreted as follows: a necessary and sufficient condition for a pricing policy to lead to a second-best optimum is that it must be the best policy supported by a cross-subvention system, where high risks receive a subsidy, the amount of which is greater than or equal to $\alpha_1^*(\lambda_1)$.

IV. Equilibrium

The concept of competitive equilibrium does not extend easily to markets with asymmetric information, as suggested by the multiplicity of solutions considered in the literature. We shall review most of these different concepts. For the sake of simplicity, we shall restrict the analysis from now on to the case of two risk classes ($N = 2$). We follow some of the Crocker-Snow (1985) presentation. The starting point of Rothschild and Stiglitz is the principle according to which an equilibrium pricing policy must not contain contracts in deficit.

Definition 6. An E1 equilibrium (à la Rothschild-Stiglitz) is a set Z1 of contracts which are not in deficit, such that there exists no contract that would make a positive profit if supplied together with Z1.

Proposition 5 (Rothschild and Stiglitz 1976). The only pricing policy that may correspond to an E1 equilibrium is the best equitable pricing policy $\{z_1^*(0); z_2^*(0)\}$. It corresponds effectively to an E1 equilibrium if $\{z_1^*(0); z_2^*(0)\}$ is not Pareto-dominated by the uniform policy $\{z_2, z_2\}$ defined by

$$V_2(z_2) = \text{Max } V_2(q, pq). \tag{15}$$

It can easily be shown that this property is satisfied (and therefore equilibrium E1 exists) iff the relative proportion of high risks λ_1/λ_2 is greater than some threshold δ_1^{rs} that is less than $\delta_1^*(0)$ as defined in proposition 3.

As a result, not only an E1 equilibrium may not exist (if $\lambda_1/\lambda_2 < \delta_1^{rs}$), but still in the case it does, it can be Pareto-dominated [if $\delta_1^{rs} \leqslant \lambda_1/\lambda_2 \leqslant \delta_1^*(0)$]. However, in the latter case, equilibrium could be unbalanced by a *pair* of contracts forming an admissible pricing policy.

To solve nonexistence problem, Riley (1979) suggested the concept of "reacting" equilibrium, which corresponds to our "best equitable policy" for all values of λ.[5] In order to keep away from the market a company offering a uniform policy (z, z) which can be unanimously preferred to $\{z_1^*(0); z_2^*(0)\}$, Riley suggests that the potential newcomer anticipates possible *reactions* from the established company, in this case the setting up of a contract $\tilde{Z}$ now becoming profitable because of the introduction of the contract (z, z) (figure 2).

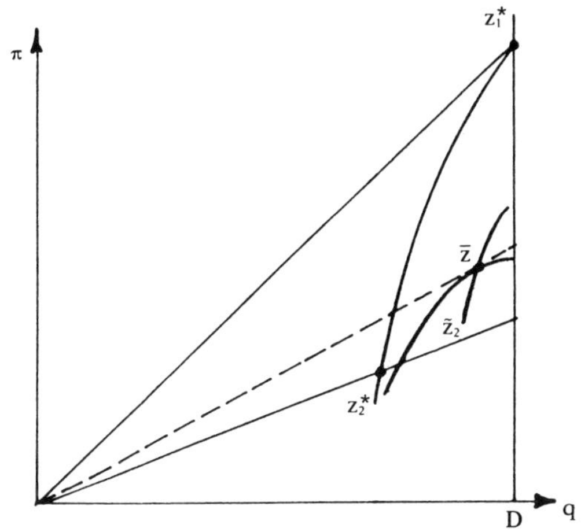

Figure 2.
Reaction $\tilde{z}_2$ to arrival of $\bar{z}$ causes the latter to be in deficit.

Unfortunately, even if it does always exist, the reactive equilibrium is Pareto-dominated as soon as $\lambda_1/\lambda_2 < \delta_1^*(0)$. Wilson (1977) proposes the concept of "anticipating" equilibrium where, contrary to Riley, every potential entrant anticipates eventuality of contracts *withdrawal* by the established company.

Definition 7. An E2 equilibrium (à la Wilson) is a subset Z^2 of contracts not in deficit, such that there doesn't exist a contract which, were it offered jointly with Z^2, would yield a positive profit, after the withdrawal of contracts which became in deficit (if any).

Proposition 6 (Wilson 1977). There always exists an E2 equilibrium. The corresponding pricing policy is unique and is given by

$$\{z_1^*(0); z_2^*(0)\} \qquad \text{if } \lambda_1/\lambda_2 \geqslant \delta_1^{rs},$$

$$\{z_2, z_2\} \qquad \text{if } \lambda_1/\lambda_2 < \delta_1^{rs}.$$

The problem of existence is now resolved, provided companies are assumed to behave in a way that is quite far from the usual assumptions on competitive behavior. Grossman (1979) finds the same outcome, yet with another equilibrium concept, i.e., companies are able to reject some applicants (this notion will be used later in this paper, within an explicitly dynamic formulation). Nevertheless, the equilibrium which has just been obtained is not a second-best optimum if $\lambda_1/\lambda_2 < \delta_1^*(0)$. An improvement can be performed by forcing newcomers to submit pricing *policies* rather than isolated contracts.

Definition 8. An E′1 equilibrium is a set of admissible policies Z′1 such that there is no admissible policy that, were it offered jointly with Z′ 1, would yield a positive profit.

Proposition 7. The only policy that can correspond to an E′1 equilibrium is the best equitable pricing policy $Z^*(0)$. It corresponds in effect to an E′1 equilibrium, iff $Z^*(0)$ is a second-best optimum [i.e., if $\lambda_1/\lambda_2 \geqslant \delta_1^*(0)$].

Definition 9. An E′2 equilibrium (à la Miyazaki) is a set Z′2 of admissible pricing policies such that there is no admissible pricing policy that, were it offered jointly with Z′2, would yield a positive profit, after the withdrawal of policies that are in deficit (if any).

Proposition 8 (Miyazaki 1977). An E′2 equilibrium always exists. The corresponding pricing policy is unique and is given by $Z^*(0)$ if $\lambda_1/\lambda_2 \geqslant \delta_1^*(0)$. If $\lambda_1/\lambda_2 < \delta_1^*(0)$, then it is the policy preferred by low risks, among second-best optima where low risks are not subsidized. In particular, the E′2 equilibrium is always a second-best optimum.

The E′2 equilibrium first, always exists, and second, is always a second-best optimum. Two criticisms can however be leveled at it:

- First, and this stands for equilibrium E2 as well, this concept supports the assumption that companies are characterized by an "anticipating" behavior, which is difficult to admit in a purely competitive framework. We shall see in section V how this can be justified, using an explicitly dynamic description of the market.
- Second, companies must accept the possibility of losing money on some contracts, if this loss is compensated by a profit on other contracts. In section III, we see that this is possible only with a specific form of public intervention on the market.

V. An Explicitly Dynamic Formulation of the Market

Even if it leads to an existence theorem, the concept of E2 (on E′2) equilibrium is subject to criticisms, regarding is vagueness concerning the assumed behavior of companies. As for the E1 equilibrium, it corresponds exactly to the familiar concept of a Nash-Bertrand equilibrium in a two-stage sequential game defined as follows. In the first stage, companies simultaneously offer contracts and in the second one, consumers make their choices. However, as noticed before, this game may not have an equilibrium if the proportion of high risks is too low.

Hellwig (1988) suggests adding a third stage to this game, by allowing companies to simultaneously withdraw some of the contracts they just offered in the first stage (consumers rejected this way do not have any immediate recourse). This third stage complicates very much the properties of the game. Because of the choice they make, consumers reveal some information to the companies. The way companies use this information to update their estimates then has to be described. Unfortunately, there is a multitude of (Bayesian) Nash equilibria (this is a frequent problem with this kind of games). Nevertheless, by using a refinement of this concept (i.e., the stable equilibrium of Kohlberg and Mertens 1987), Hellwig shows that introducing the third stage has the effect of stabilizing a unique pricing policy, which corresponds to the E2 equilibrium.

Proposition 9 (Hellwig 1986). The three-stage sequential game defined above has a unique, stable equilibrium, corresponding to the E2 equilibrium. For insurance economists, a natural question is what is the most realistic formalization of the market? As a matter of fact, this question is not purely abstract, but, on the contrary, lies at the heart of an important debate in the French motor insurance market. Several consumer unions (cf. L'Assurance Automobile 1985) effectively requested that the insurance proposal (which French law obliges every company to deliver to any consumer asking for it) have a binding nature. The French Regulatory Board (la Direction des Assurances) firmly came out against this claim, arguing that insurance had a contractual nature. If insurance proposals were to have a binding nature, the adequate description of the market would be the two-stage game of Rothschild and Stiglitz and Wilson, which was shown not always to have an equilibrium.

However, the game of Hellwig corresponds to granting every company the opportunity to refuse to accept some consumers as would-be customers (which in other contexts is forbidden by French law), but in our case it has the merit of stabilizing a competitive market.[6] In order to proceed, that is, forcing companies to set up cross-subsidies between different categories of risks, one has to rely on yet another mode of public intervention, which we analyze in the last part of this paper.

VI. Quantitative Regulation

Our starting point is an interesting episode in the recent history of the French motor insurance market. In the mid-1970s, the use of differentiated deductibles has become generalized. This was particularly the case for young (less than 25 years) drivers, to whom companies imposed high deductibles (so called "young drivers" deductible). To justify this decision, companies relied upon statistical data on car accidents involving young drivers, which showed that a large majority of them were not subject to more accidents than the average driver, regardless of age. On the other hand, some drivers between the ages of 18 and 25, could cause 5, 6, or 7 car accidents (whereas the average probability is about one accident every 10 years for the whole population).

Companies wanted to "screen" these two categories of young drivers, by offering a premium discount to "good" drivers, on the condition that they accept the so-called "young driver deductible." "Bad drivers" (or people considering themselves as such) had the opportunity to obtain complete insurance by paying a much higher premium. After consumer unions strongly protested, the Insurance Board decided to impose ceilings on companies' premiums. Companies reacted by using an indirect strategy, rejecting insured people who seemed to be "high risks." In order to stop such behavior, the Insurance Board eventually accorded to itself the right to force companies, when necessary, to grant a full compensation contract to every consumer asking for it, with an imposed pricing policy calculated by a central pricing Bureau. To describe these arrangements, we adopt the following definitions:

Definition 10. An admissible regulated pricing policy is a pair of contracts $\{z_1, z_2\}$ such that

$$\forall i, j \qquad v_i(z_i) \geqslant v_i(z_j) \qquad \text{(self-selection)}, \tag{6}$$

$$\forall i, j \qquad \Pi_i \leqslant \Pi, \Pi_j \leqslant \Pi \qquad \text{(ceiling on premia)}, \tag{15}$$

$$q_i = D \text{ or } q_j = D \qquad \text{(full insurance is always offered)}, \tag{16}$$

$$\sum_{i=1} \lambda_i(\Pi_i - p_i q_i) \leqslant 0 \qquad \text{(positive expected profit)}. \tag{17}$$

Definition 11. A regulated market equilibrium is a set of admissible regulated policies Z, such that there does not exist another admissible regulated policy that would yield a positive profit, if proposed jointly with Z.

In this setup, we obtain a counterpart of the two fundamental theorems of welfare economics.

Proposition 10. Every regulated market equilibrium is a second-best optimum.

Proposition 11. Every second-best optimum $\{z_1, z_2\}$, where low risks are not subsidized ($\Pi_2 \geqslant p_2 q_2$), is a regulated market equilibrium for $\Pi = \Pi_1$.

One can point out that a regulated market equilibrium does not always exist. The regulatory board has to choose a ceiling Π, compatible with a second-best optimum. Actually, Π is limited by an upper bound $\beta(\lambda_1/\lambda_2)$, which is an increasing function of the ratio between a proportion of high risks and low risks. On the other hand, once this constraint is satisfied, the choice of Π provides a close to complete means of redistribution. For a sensible choice of Π, every second-best optimum is an equilibrium, with low risks not being subsidized.

Let us finally point out that it is not possible to decentralize a Pareto optimum where low risks are subsidized. As a matter of fact, if such an optimum does exist, the best equitable pricing policy is also optimal (cf. proposition 4). If a company offered such a policy, it would attract bad risks, therefore unbalancing the initial pricing policy.

Appendix

Let V^λ denote the set of utility vectors accessible through pricing policies belonging to C^λ.

$$V^\lambda = \{(V_i)i = 1, \ldots, N, \qquad \exists (z_1, \ldots, z_N) \in C^\lambda, \qquad V_i = V_i(z_i)\}.$$

We first prove the following lemma:

Lemma 1. V^λ is a convex subset of $\mathbb{R}^N$.

Proof. $V \in V^\lambda$ if and only if there exist $z_i = (\Pi_i, q_i)$ such that

$$\forall i, j \in \{1, \ldots, N\} \begin{cases} p_i u(R - D + q_j - \Pi_j) + (1 - p_i) u(R - \Pi_j) \leqslant V_i \\ p_i u(R - \Pi + q_i - \Pi_i) + (1 - p_i) u(R - \Pi_i) = V_i \end{cases} \tag{1}$$

and

$$\sum_{i=1}^{n} \lambda_i (\Pi_i - p_i q_i) \geqslant 0. \tag{2}$$

We set $x_i = u(R - D + q_i - \Pi_j)$, $y_i = u(R - \Pi_j)$, and $\varphi = u^{-1}$.
(x_i, y_i) $i = 1, \ldots, N$ such that

$$\forall i, j \in \{1, \ldots, N\} \begin{cases} p_i x_j + (1 - p_i) y_j \leqslant V_i \\ p_i x_i + (1 - p_i) y_i = V_i \end{cases} \tag{3}$$

$$\sum_{i=1}^{N} \lambda_i (p_i \varphi(x_i) + (1 - p_i)\varphi(y_i)) \leqslant R - \left(\sum_{i=1}^{n} \lambda_i p_i\right) D. \tag{4}$$

From the convexity of φ, we immediately deduce the convexity of V^λ.

From Lemma 1, we have that every local Pareto optimum of C^λ is necessarily a pricing policy of the $Z^*(\alpha)$ category (cf. proposition 2).

Given a subsidy scheme α (α is a vector having at least two coordinates of opposite sign), we denote by $\{V_i(\alpha)\}$ $i = 1, \ldots, N$ the N-set of utilities obtained through the pricing policy $Z^*(\alpha) = \{\Pi_i^*(\alpha), q_i^*(\alpha)\}$.

Let us denote

$$x_i(\alpha) = u(R - D + q_i^*(\alpha) - \Pi_i^*(\alpha)),$$

$$y_i(\alpha) = u(R - \Pi_i^*(\alpha)).$$

We have that $(1 - p_i)(1 - p_i)$

$$p_{i-1} x_i + (1 - p_{i-1}) y_i = V_{i-1}$$

$$p_i x_i + (1 - p_i) y_i = V_i$$

and

$$p_i \varphi(x_i) + (1 - p_i)\varphi(y_i) - R + p_i D = \alpha_i$$

(we set by convention $p_0 = 1$ and $v_0 = v_1$).

Hence

$$p_i \varphi\left[\frac{(1 - p_i)V_{i-1} - (1 - p_{i-1})V_i}{p_{i-1} - p_i}\right] + (1 - p_i)\varphi\left[\frac{p_{i-1}V_i - p_i V_{i-1}}{p_{i-1} - p_i}\right] - R + p_i D = \alpha_i$$

Let $\lambda \in \alpha^\perp \cap \Sigma$ be a distribution of risks which is compatible with the subsidy scheme α. The equation of the boundary of U^λ is

$$\sum_{i=1}^{N} \lambda_i \left\{ p_i - \varphi\left[\frac{(1 - p_i)V_{i-1} - (1 - p_{i-1})V_i}{p_{i-1} - p_i}\right] + (1 - p_i)\varphi\left[\frac{p_{i-1}V_i - p_i V_{i-1}}{p_{i-1} - p_i}\right]\right\} = \sum_{i=1} \lambda_i (R - p_i D)$$

We have that

$$\frac{\partial \Phi}{\partial V_i} = \lambda_i \left[\frac{(1-p_i)p_{i-1}}{p_{i-1}-p_i} \varphi'(y_i) - \frac{(1-p_{i-1})p_i}{p_{i-1}-p_i} \varphi'(x_i) \right]$$

$$-\lambda_{i+1} \frac{p_{i+1}(1-p_{i-1})}{p_i - p_{i+1}} [\varphi'(y_{i+1}) - \varphi'(x_{i+1})]$$

(Let's set by convention $\lambda_{N+1} = 0$):

$$\frac{\partial \Phi}{\partial V_i} = \lambda_i A(V_i, V_{i-1}) - \lambda_{i+1} B(V_{i+1}, V_i)$$

From the convexity of φ and from the fact that $x_i \leqslant y_i$ we have that $A(V_i, V_{i-1}) > 0$ and $B(V_{i+1}, V_i) \geqslant 0$.

Furthermore,

$$\frac{\partial \Phi}{\partial V_N} = \lambda_N A(V_N, V_{N-1}) > 0$$

We infer that V is a utility vector of U^λ, which is Pareto optimal if and only if

$$\frac{\partial \Phi}{\partial V_N} \geqslant 0 \qquad \text{for every } i = 1, \ldots, n-1$$

That is,

$$\frac{\lambda_i}{\lambda_{i+1}} \geqslant \frac{B(V_{i+1}, V_i)}{A(V_i, V_{i-1})}.$$

We then write $\delta_i(\alpha) = [B(V_{i+1}, V_i)]/[A(V_i, V_{i-1})]$ (the vector v in fact depends only on α) and this concludes the proof.

Proof of Proposition 4. For a given λ and a pricing policy $Z^*(\alpha)$ from Proposition 2, $V_1(z^*(\alpha))$ is an increasing function of α_1.

When $n = 2$, the set C^λ can be represented graphically (figure 3):

From the convexity of V^λ we have, there exists $V_1^*(\lambda)$ in $\mathbb{R}^+$ such that

$Z^*(\alpha)$ is Pareto-optimal if and only if $V_1(Z^*(\alpha)) \geqslant V_1^*$

we deduce, there exists $\alpha_1^*(\lambda)$ such that

$Z^*(\alpha)$ is Pareto-optimal if and only if $\alpha_1 \geqslant \alpha_1^*(\lambda)$.

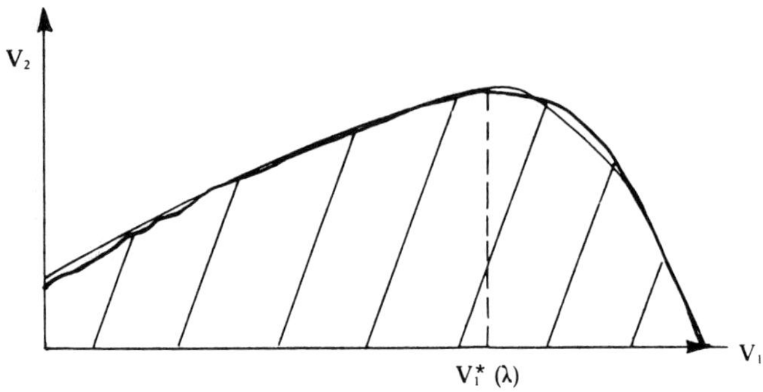

Figure 3.

Proof of Proposition 10. Let $Z = \{z_1, z_2\}$ be a regulated market equilibrium

- Z is a pricing policy of C^λ.

Actually, $V_i(z_i) \geqslant V_i(z_j)$ and $\sum_1^2 \lambda_i(\Pi_i - p_i q_i) \geqslant 0$.

- $\Pi_i \leqslant \Pi$ and $q_1 = D$.

Indeed, if $q_1 < D$ then (since $Z \in C^\lambda$) $q_2 \leqslant q_1 < D$ which is impossible.

- We conclude that Z is a pricing policy of the $z^*(\alpha)$ kind (cf. Proposition 2) satisfying $V_1(Z_i) \geqslant u(R - \Pi_1)$.
- Assuming that Z is Pareto-dominated by a policy $Z = (\Pi', q')$, then $\Pi' \leqslant \Pi_1$ and $q' = D$.

Hence Z' is an admissible regulated policy. If added to Z' it attracts both kinds of risks and Z is therefore not in equilibrium.

Proof of Proposition 11. Let Z be a second-best optimum such that

$$Z = \{(\Pi_1, D), (\Pi_2, q_2)\}, \qquad \Pi_2 \geqslant p_2 q_2$$

We show that Z is a regulated equilibrium. Let's write $\Pi = \Pi$. Let Z' be a regulated admissible policy

$$Z = \{(\Pi'_1, D), (\Pi'_2, q_2)\}, \qquad Z' \neq Z.$$

Either

$$V_1(Z') < V_1(Z) \tag{a}$$

or

$$V_2(Z') < V_2(Z) \qquad \text{(b)}$$

(a) is impossible because it would lead to $\Pi_1' > \Pi$. Therefore (using b) Z' attracts only high risks, when added to z.

Z' being different from Z, we have $\Pi_1 < \Pi$, and since $\Pi \geqslant p_1 D$ (because $\Pi_2 \geqslant p_2 q_2$), Z' will yield a deficit. Hence Z is in equilibrium.

Acknowledgment

We are grateful to Alban Thomas for translating this article into English.

Notes

1. An application of this model to credit markets can be found in Bester 1985.

2. The issue concerning the choice of relevant observable criteria is far from being simple. See Henriet and Rochet 1987b for a discussion of a complete information setup and Crocker and Snow 1986 for the case of incomplete information.

3. In the words of insurance, we oppose *a priori pricing*, which is based on variables that are observable before the contract is signed, and *a posteriori pricing*, i.e., the systems of no-claim bonuses. A posteriori pricing can provide a partial solution to problems related to asymmetric information (Henriet and Rochet 1986).

4. At any equilibrium, such indifferences are impossible.

5. This reacting equilibrium corresponds to the Pareto-dominating element of the family of signaling equilibria, à la Spence (1973).

6. Unfortunately, if consumers have the opportunity to speak first by expressing their demands, we are dealing with a signaling game à la Cho and Kreps (1986). The stable equilibria of such a game no longer correspond to the E2 equilibrium, but to Riley's reactive equilibrium (see Hellwig 1986).

References

Akerlof, G. A. (1970) "The Market for Lemons: Qualitative Uncertainty and the Market Mechanism." *Quarterly Journal of Economics* 84: 488–500.

Bester, H. (1985) "Screening VS Rationing in Credit Markets with Imperfect Information." *American Economic Review* 75(4): 850–855.

Cho, I. K. and D. Kreps (1986) Signaling Games and Stable Equilibria. Graduate School of Business, Stanford University.

Crocker, K. J. and A. Snow (1985a) "The Efficiency of Competitive Equilibria in Insurance Markets with Asymmetric Information." *Journal of Public Economics* 26 (2): 207–220.

Crocker, K. J. and A. Snow (1985b) "A Simple Tax Structure for Competitive Equilibrium and Redistribution in Insurance Markets with Asymmetric Information." *Southern Economic Journal* 51(4): 1142–1150.

Crocker, K. J. and A. Snow (1986) "The Efficiency Effects of Categorical Discrimination in the Insurance Industry." *Journal of Political Economy* 94(2): 321–344.

Grossman, H. (1979) "Adverse Selection, Dissembling and Competitive Equilibrium." *Bell Journal of Economics* 10: 336–343.

Hellwig, M. (1987) "Some Recent Developments in the Theory of Competition in Markets with Adverse Selection." *European Economic Review* 31.

Henriet, D. and J. C. Rochet (1986) "La logique des Systèmes Bonus-Malus en Assurance Automobile: Une Approche Théorique." *Annales d'Economie et de Statistique* 1: 133–152.

Henriet, D. and J. C. Rochet (1987a) "Some Reflections on Insurance Pricing." *European Economic Review* 31: 863–885.

Henriet, D. and J. C. Rochet (1987b) "Price Regulation in Insurance Markets with Asymmetric Information." *Economics Letters* 24: 327–329.

Kohlberg, E. and J. F. Mertens (1986) "On the Strategic Stability of Equilibria." *Econometrica* 54(5): 1003–1037.

"L'Assurance Automobile" (1985) Journées d'Etudes (Mars), DGRP., Ministère de l'Economie, des Finances et du Budget.

Malinvaud, E. (1971) "The Allocation of Individual Risks in Large Markets." *Journal of Economic Theory* 4: 312–328.

Malinvaud, E. (1973) "Markets for an Exchange Economy with Individual Risks." *Econometrica* 41(3): 383–410.

Miyazaki, H. (1977) "The Rat Race and Internal Labor Markets." *Bell Journal of Economics,* 8(2): 394–418.

Riley, J. G. (1979) "Informational Equilibrium." *Econometrica* 47(2): 331–359.

Rochet, J. C. (1985) "Vers une Tarification Equitable de l'Assurance?" *L'Actualité Economique* 61(4): 453–471.

Rothschild, M. and J. E. Stiglitz (1976) "Equilibrium in Competitive Insurance Markets." *Quarterly Journal of Economics* 11: 629–649.

Spence, M. (1973) "Job Market Signalling." *Quarterly Journal of Economics* 87: 355–374.

Wilson, C. (1977) "A Model of Insurance Markets with Incomplete Information." *Journal of Economic Theory* 16: 167–207.

10

The Impact of Discrimination on Contestability in a Market with Vertical Differentiation

Claude Henry

That an incumbent monopoly is contestable means that the mere threat of entry by a competitor prevents the monopoly from charging those prices that, in the absence of any threat, it would charge in order to maximize profits. According to Baumol, Panzar, and Willig (1982), there are situations where the effect of contestability is strong enough to drive prices down to competitive levels. However, as pointed out by Brock (1983) and by Spence (1983), if the monopoly is able to react with sufficient flexibility should entry actually take place, one must seriously wonder to what extent the monopoly pre-entry pricing behavior should take post-entry events into account.

On the other hand, the tougher post-entry competition is, the less attractive is entry. Having explored a variety of models, Dasgupta and Stiglitz (1988) stress that "A general principle emerges: the more competitive ex post competition, the less effective is the market discipline provided by potential competition."

These two parameters, incumbent's flexibility in price setting and intensity of post-entry competition, obviously are key determinants of the effectiveness of potential competition, i.e., of contestability. But their joint effects are not straightforward. A well-defined framework is needed in order to assess them. This is what we do in this paper, within a vertically differentiated market. Some form of differentiation is required to avoid well-known paradoxes and simplistic oppositions; vertical differentiation has been selected because it is relatively easy to handle, is frequently considered in the imperfect competition literature, and is not without relevance.

Taking into account an important point made by Brock (1983) and systematically discussed by Fudenberg and Tirole (1986), we consider flexibility in price setting as an endogenous variable, in the sense that it can be limited only in so far as the incumbent monopoly finds its interest in such a limitation. We have then three possible market configurations: no entry with or without self-imposed restrictions on behalf of the monopoly (self-imposed restrictions mean that some form of contestability is at work); or entry accommodated by the incumbent, which then is no longer a monopoly, but an actual competitor in a vertically differentiated duopoly (sections 1 and 2).

We investigate the relationship between the market configuration that obtains and the intensity of post-entry competition. Many factors may influence post-entry competition; in that respect, we pay special attention to two forms of discrimination among customers. In section 3, discrimination means that both firms operate on two separate submarkets instead of one global market. Then competition is reduced, in the sense that the set of circumstances under which the incumbent can behave as an (unconstrained) monopoly is larger. However, in those circumstances under which competition (either actual or potential) prevails notwithstanding, it is tougher, and all concerned customers are then better off. In section 4, discrimination results from a voluntary and a priori (i.e., before the market starts functioning) reduction of its market share by the entrant, provided it actually enters the market. Then competition is enlarged, in the sense that the set of circumstances under which the incumbent can behave as an (unconstrained) monopoly is smaller. However, in those circumstances under which competition (either actual or potential) prevails even in the absence of discrimination, it is softened as an effect of discrimination, and all customers are then worse off.

From a policy point of view, this shows how important it might be to precisely know how the characteristics of the market and the expected forms of post-entry competition influence the prospects of potential competition. Otherwise measures might be taken that would run against their objective. In the case of section 4, for example, it would at first sight seem that restrictive practices such as those adopted by the entrant should be opposed. Our analysis leads to more qualified conclusions, insofar as those practices may facilitate entry and therefore increase the threat that such entry represents for the incumbent monopoly. The result can be that the consumers are better off, in which case it might seem desirable not to discourage the restrictive practices. But it is not always so, because accommodating entry is made more attractive for the incumbent as the cost of deterring entry is higher; a precise assessment is thus needed.

1. Duopoly with Vertical Differentiation

We consider a market where at most two firms may be active. Each firm produces only one good: firm A produces good A and firm B produces good B. Goods A and B are produced in discrete units and consumers purchase at most one indivisible unit of one of the goods. Thus, a typical consumer[1] faces three choices: not to purchase anything, to purchase one unit of good A, or to purchase one unit of good B. Finally, we assume that A is a good of better quality than B; that is, if the price for both goods were identical, then all consumers would buy good A rather than good B; we thus can speak of vertical differentiation. Examples of such goods might be a flight between two cities at a given time, in more (A) or less (B) satisfactory conditions of speed and comfort; or a personal computer, more (A) or less (B) powerful. Corresponding examples of situations that might lead to potential competition are an airline, which is already active on a certain number of other connections, considers opening a new line between the two aforementioned cities; a firm, which is already selling minicomputers, considers entering the market of personal computers. This firm, as well as the airline, plays the role that firm B is to play throughout this chapter.

There is a continuum of consumers represented by the interval $[0, r]$. The consumer $x = r$ has reservation values a for good A and b for good B, with $a > b > 0$. The consumer $x = 0$ has the same reservation value b for good B, but his reservation value for good A is higher, namely $a + \eta$, with $\eta > 0$. As for consumers located between 0 and r, they all have b as their reservation value for good B, but their reservation value for good A is intermediate between a and $a + \eta$: the consumer x, with $0 \leqslant x \leqslant r$, has the reservation value $a + [(r - x)/r]\eta$ for good A. Thus, all consumers attach the same value to good B whereas the preference for A varies in intensity, depending on where consumers are located on the line. This variation is intrinsic; it is not due to differences in income, as in Gabsewicz and Thisse (1979) or in Shaked and Sutton (1982), but to differences in the use different consumers can make of the superiority of good A over good B, as in Gal-Or (1985).

Consumption choices will obviously depend on the prices p_A and p_B at which goods A and B are offered. Consumer x purchases nothing if $p_A > a + [(r - x)/r]\eta$ and $p_B > b$; otherwise, he purchases a unit of A if $a + [(r - x)/r]\eta - p_A$ is greater than $b - p_B$, and a unit of B in the opposite case. The total demand functions, for $p_A \leqslant a + \eta$ and $p_B \leqslant b$, will therefore be

$$d_A(p_A, p_B)$$

$$\begin{aligned} &= 0 && \text{if } p_A \geqslant p_B + \eta + a - b \\ &= \frac{r}{\eta}(\eta - p_A + a + p_B - b) && \text{if } p_B + \eta + a - b \geqslant p_A \geqslant p_B + a - b \\ &= r && \text{if } p_B + a - b \geqslant p_A \end{aligned} \tag{1.1}$$

and

$$d_B(p_A, p_B) = r - d_A(p_A, p_B). \tag{1.2}$$

In the case where $p_A \leqslant a + \eta$ but $p_B > b$, there is no demand for good B, firm A is alone serving the market and the demand function for good A is

$$d_A^m(p_A) = d_A(p_A, b). \tag{1.3}$$

In the case where $p_B \leqslant b$ but $p_A > a + \eta$, there is no demand for good A and all consumers purchase B, i.e.,

$$d_B^m(p_B) = r. \tag{1.4}$$

In this model, where an individual demand can only be of 0 or 1, the total demand for a good is equal to the total number of consumers who ask for this good at given prices.

We now consider the supply side. We assume that each firm, whether A or B, has a sunk fixed cost,[2] I_A or I_B, and a unit cost, c_A or c_B, with $c_A < a + \eta$ and $c_B < b$. Total costs are thus given by $I_A + c_A d_A$ and $I_B + c_B d_B$.

What happens when both I_A and I_B are equal to zero? Each firm will then make a profit by selling any positive amount of its product at a price greater than unit cost. Together, these two firms constitute a duopoly with vertical differentiation. We shall now examine how competition in prices[3] works within this duopoly.

Bertrand and Stackelberg[4] equilibria may be calculated from the respective reaction functions of A and B. The results are gathered in figures 1 and 2 where the following notations are used:

$\alpha = a - c_A$,

$\beta = b - c_B$,

$\delta = -\alpha + \beta$,

$P_B = p_B - c_A$,

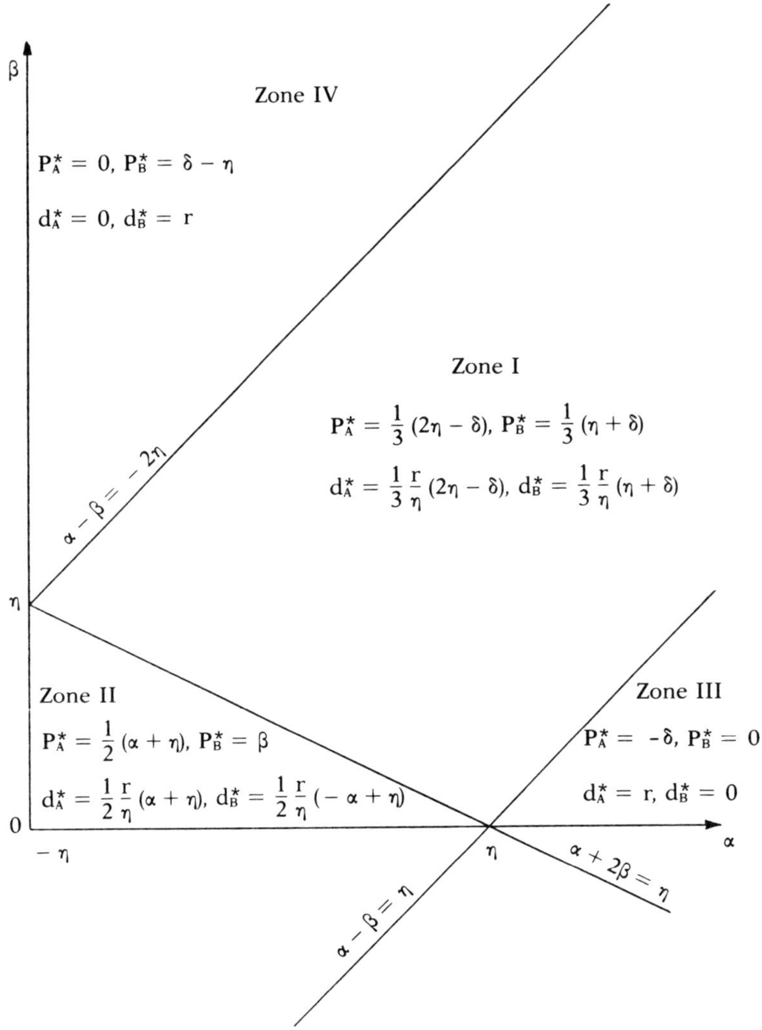
β
Zone IV
$P_A^* = 0,\ P_B^* = \delta - \eta$
$d_A^* = 0,\ d_B^* = r$
Zone I
$P_A^* = \frac{1}{3}(2\eta - \delta),\ P_B^* = \frac{1}{3}(\eta + \delta)$
$d_A^* = \frac{1}{3}\frac{r}{\eta}(2\eta - \delta),\ d_B^* = \frac{1}{3}\frac{r}{\eta}(\eta + \delta)$
$\alpha - \beta = -2\eta$
η
Zone II
$P_A^* = \frac{1}{2}(\alpha + \eta),\ P_B^* = \beta$
$d_A^* = \frac{1}{2}\frac{r}{\eta}(\alpha + \eta),\ d_B^* = \frac{1}{2}\frac{r}{\eta}(-\alpha + \eta)$
Zone III
$P_A^* = -\delta,\ P_B^* = 0$
$d_A^* = r,\ d_B^* = 0$
0
−η
η
α
$\alpha + 2\beta = \eta$
$\alpha - \beta = \eta$

Figure 1.

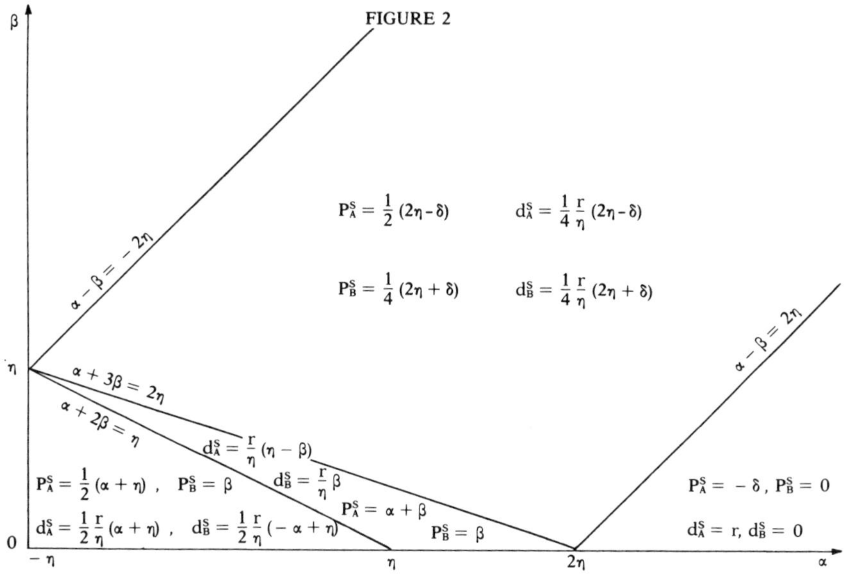

Figure 2.

$$P_B = p_B - c_B.$$

The results appear as functions of α and β, η being kept constant.

Bertrand prices P_A^* and P_B^*, and the corresponding demands d_A^* and d_B^*, are given in figure 1. The corresponding profits of course are

$$\pi_A^* = d_A^* P_A^* \qquad \text{and} \qquad \pi_B^* = d_B^* P_B^*.$$

For every pair (α, β) in area *I*, we have actual competition between the two firms, in the sense that they both have a positive market share, and these shares are the result of their interaction in the market. In areas III and IV, there is potential competition at a limit price equilibrium[5]: only one firm is active in the market, because it is in its best interest to set a price low enough to make it impossible for the other firm to sell at a profit. In area II, there is no competition at all, but coexistence of two monopolies: firm A behaves as it would in the complete absence of B, i.e., A is an unconstrained monopoly, while B gets the market share that A chooses not to serve.

Stackelberg prices P_A^s and P_B^s, and the corresponding demands d_A^s and d_B^s, are given in figure 2. The corresponding profits of course are

$$\pi_A^s = d_A^s P_A^s \qquad \text{and} \qquad \pi_B^s = d_B^s P_B^s.$$

When $\delta \leqslant 0$, firm A is a natural monopoly[6]: firm A not only can provide a higher quality product, it can also profitably sell this product at a price such that all consumers will purchase it. However, only in area III is it in the best interest of A to set a price low enough to attract all consumers away from B. Elsewhere A is better off selling at a higher price, despite the loss of consumers to B that this implies. It is clear that actual competition is better for consumers than is unconstrained monopoly; but then the greater efficiency of the natural monopoly is not fully exploited. Potential competition might be a way out of this dilemma; indeed, we shall see in the next section that it may work for pairs outside area III provided the sunk fixed cost I_B is positive.

2. Potential Competition versus Acceptance of Entry

We consider here the following case: (i) $\delta = 0$, hence firm A is a natural monopoly. (ii) A has already entered the market, i.e., has already spent I_A. (iii) B has not yet decided whether to enter the market or not, i.e., B has not yet spent I_B. B's decision depends on what it expects post-entry competition will be. If post-entry competition, as B expects it, is to result in a Bertrand equilibrium, B's profit will be π_B^*, in which case it is profitable for B to enter if and only if $I_B < \pi_B^*$.[7] If, on the other hand, B assumes that post-entry competition will result in a Stackelberg equilibrium, the comparison is between I_B and π_B^*.

When B thinks that post-entry competition results in a Bertrand equilibrium, it decides not to enter the market if $I_B > \pi_B^*$. B's decision does not depend on whether A profits little or much by its present monopoly position, provided A can change its price at will. In the present case ($I_B > \pi_B^*$), even if A were able to commit itself not to change its price in response to B's entry, it would not want to do so since that could only make entry more attractive to B.

On the other hand, if $I_B < \pi_B^*$, B will enter unless A takes some actions to reduce B's post-entry profit, by a sufficient amount to make entry unattractive. Firm A can deter entry in this way only if it can commit itself to a post-entry price, and if this price is lower than the Bertrand equilibrium price. Such a post-entry commitment usually involves a commitment to an identical pre-entry price. For example, a typical form of commitment is to sign a binding contract with customers; usually the price agreed upon in such a contract cannot be made contingent on the event of entry. The same is true for a commitment guaranteed by a public authority. Hence we take for granted that when firm A commits itself to a price, the commitment is binding whether firm B enters the market or not.

Assuming that such commitments are feasible, firm A may choose between two lines of action: (i) to commit itself to a price which will indeed deter entry; (ii) to commit itself to the Stackelberg price, which will provoke entry, albeit with a result which is better for both firms than the Bertrand equilibrium. A will choose according to whether it can have a higher profit by deterring entry or by inducing the Stackelberg equilibrium. Let us now see how these profits compare.

As soon as P_A is less than some threshold price P_A^θ, B is deterred from entering the market. P_A^θ is determined from

$$\theta^2 \pi_B^* = \pi_B(P_A^\theta, P_B(P_A^\theta)) \tag{2.1}$$

with

$$I_B = \theta^2 \pi_B^*; \tag{2.2}$$

as $0 \leqslant I_B \leqslant \pi_B^*$, $0 \leqslant \theta \leqslant 1$. We can rewrite (2.1) under the form

$$\theta^2 \pi_B^* = \frac{r}{\eta}(P_A^\theta - \tfrac{1}{2}(P_A^\theta + \delta) + \delta) \cdot \tfrac{1}{2}(P_A^\theta + \delta)$$

or equivalently

$$\theta^2 \tfrac{1}{9}\frac{r}{\eta}(\eta + \delta)^2 = \tfrac{1}{4}\frac{r}{\eta}(P_A^\theta + \delta)^2.$$

To do so, we have used the fact that $P_B(P_A) = \frac{1}{2}(P_A + \delta)$.[8] We thus have

$$P_A^\theta = \theta P_A^* - (1 - \theta)\delta. \tag{2.3}$$

If A sets the price P_A^θ, hence deterring entry, its profit is

$$\pi_A^\theta = d_A^m(P_A^\theta) \cdot P_A^\theta. \tag{2.4}$$

If A sets the price P_A^s, hence inducing entry, its profit is

$$\pi_A^s = \pi_A(P_A^s, P_B^s). \tag{2.5}$$

Comparing (2.4) and (2.5) for $\delta = 0$ leads to the following conclusion: A chooses to deter entry

if and only if $\frac{3}{4} < \theta \leqslant 1$ for $\frac{\eta}{2} \leqslant \alpha$

if and only if $\frac{3}{2}\left(1 - \frac{\alpha}{\eta}\right) < \theta \leqslant 1$ for $\frac{\eta}{3} \leqslant \alpha \leqslant \frac{\eta}{2}$.[9]

Let us denote by τ the value of θ for which both strategies are equivalent from the point of view of A, i.e., the value of θ for which (2.4) and (2.5) are equal. The above conclusion can then be reformulated in the following way:

$$\tau = \tfrac{3}{4} \qquad \text{for } \eta/2 \leqslant \alpha,$$

$$\tau = \tfrac{3}{2}(1 - \alpha/\eta) \qquad \text{for } \eta/3 \leqslant \alpha \leqslant \eta/2.$$

The complete picture of A's strategic choices is then:

- If $I_B > \pi_B^*$, A does not commit itself to any price; A is then in a position to behave as an unconstrained monopoly.
- If $\pi_B^* \geqslant I_B > \tau^2\pi_B^*$, A commits itself to the price $P_A^\theta = \theta\frac{2}{3}\eta$ in order to deter entry; A is then a constrained monopoly.
- If $\tau^2\pi_B^* \geqslant I_B$, A commits itself to the price P_A^s, and in this way A accepts entry and induces the Stackelberg equilibrium.

3. Tougher Albeit Reduced Competition

We consider here that both firms are able to perfectly discriminate between two populations of customers: on one side a minority of customers who have higher willingness to pay for good A, i.e., those customers x such that $x < \gamma r$, with $0 < \gamma < \frac{1}{2}$; on the other side, those customers x such that $x \geqslant \gamma r$. Under these circumstances two different markets are working side by side, with different Bertrand and Stackelberg equilibria. For the larger market ($x \geqslant \gamma r$), that we denote M′, Bertrand prices $P_A^{*\prime}$ and $P_B^{*\prime}$ and Stackelberg prices $P_A^{s\prime}$ and $P_B^{s\prime}$ are given in table 1; they are obtained from the results in section 1 with $(1-\gamma)\eta$ instead of η and $(1-\gamma)r$ instead of r. For the smaller market ($x < \gamma r$), that we denote M″, Bertrand prices $P_A^{*\prime\prime}$ and $P_B^{*\prime\prime}$ and Stackelberg prices $P_A^{s\prime\prime}$ and $P_B^{s\prime\prime}$ are given in table 2; they are obtained from the results in section 1 with $\alpha + (1-\gamma)\eta$ instead of α, $\gamma\eta$ instead of η, and γr instead of r.

Table 1

$P_A^{*\prime} = \frac{2}{3}(1-\gamma)\eta$	$P_B^{*\prime} = \frac{1}{3}(1-\gamma)\eta$
if $\frac{1}{3}(1-\gamma)\eta \leqslant \alpha \leqslant \frac{1}{2}(1-\gamma)\eta$	
$P_A^{s\prime} = 2\alpha$	$P_B^{s\prime} = \alpha$
if $\frac{1}{2}(1-\gamma)\eta \leqslant \alpha$	
$P_A^{s\prime} = (1-\gamma)\eta$	$P_B^{s\prime} = \frac{1}{2}(1-\gamma)\eta$

Table 2

$P_A^{*\prime\prime} = (1 - \gamma)\eta$ for $\gamma \leqslant \frac{1}{3}$	$P_B^{*\prime\prime} = 0$
$P_A^{s\prime\prime} = (1 - \gamma)\eta$ for $\gamma \geqslant \frac{1}{3}$	$P_B^{s\prime\prime} = 0$
$P_A^{s\prime\prime} = \frac{1}{2}(1 + \gamma)\eta$	$P_B^{s\prime\prime} = \frac{1}{4}(3\gamma - 1)\eta$

Let us call $\sum_1$ (deterrence) and $\sum_2$ (acceptance) the strategies between which A has to choose when it cannot take for granted that B has no intention to enter the market, i.e., when I_B is less than the profit B expects from Bertrand equilibria. As $\pi_B^{*\prime\prime} = 0$, this is equivalent to

$$I_B \leqslant \pi_B^{*\prime}. \tag{3.1}$$

Implementing $\sum_1$ requires that A commits itself to a price $P_A^{\lambda\prime}$ on the market M′, while A does not commit to any price on the market M″. Due to (3.1) and (2.3), $P_A^{\lambda\prime}$ is such that

$$P_A^{\lambda\prime} = \lambda P_A^{*\prime} \tag{3.2}$$

with

$$I_B = \lambda^2 \pi_B^{*\prime}, \qquad 0 \leqslant \lambda \leqslant 1. \tag{3.3}$$

Let $\pi_A^{\lambda\prime}$ be the corresponding profit for A on the market M′; its profit on the market M″, where it can behave as an unconstrained monopoly, is $\pi_A^{m\prime\prime}$. Therefore, the total profit that A can obtain from implementing the strategy $\sum_1$ is

$$\pi_A^1 = \pi_A^{\lambda\prime} + \pi_A^{m\prime\prime}.$$

Implementing $\sum_2$ requires that A commits itself to the Stackelberg prices $P_A^{s\prime}$ and $P_A^{s\prime\prime}$ on the respective markets M′ and M″. The corresponding total profit is

$$\pi_A^2 = \pi_A^{s\prime} + \pi_A^{s\prime\prime}.$$

Proposition 3.1. Discrimination reduces competition, in the sense that the set of circumstances under which A can behave as an unconstrained monopoly is larger. However, in those circumstances under which competition —be it actual or potential—prevails, it is tougher and all concerned customers are better off.

Proof. From (2.6) we know that

$$\theta > \tau \Leftrightarrow \pi_A^\theta > \pi_A^s.$$

Transposed to the conditions specific of the market M′, it gives

$$\lambda > \tau' \Leftrightarrow \pi_A^{\lambda'} > \pi_A^{s'}$$

with

$$\tau' = \tfrac{3}{4} \qquad \text{for } \frac{(1-\gamma)\eta}{2} \leqslant \alpha$$

$$\tau' = \frac{3}{2}\left[1 - \frac{\alpha}{(1-\gamma)\eta}\right] \qquad \text{for } \frac{(1-\gamma)\eta}{3} \leqslant \alpha \leqslant \frac{(1-\gamma)\eta}{2}$$

Comparing (2.2) and (3.2), one sees that

$$\theta = \lambda(1-\gamma).$$

Thus

$$\theta > \tau \Rightarrow \lambda > \tau'$$

and furthermore

$$\pi_A^\theta > \pi_A^s \Rightarrow \pi_A^{\lambda'} > \pi_A^{s'}.$$

On the other hand, one has

$$\pi_A^{\lambda'} > \pi_A^{s'} \Rightarrow \pi_A^1 > \pi_A^2;$$

this is because, for obvious reasons,

$$\pi_A^{m''} \geqslant \pi_A^{s''}.$$

Combining, one finally gets

$$\pi_A^\theta > \pi_A^s \Rightarrow \pi_A^1 > \pi_A^2,$$

and the proposition follows, on the basis of the results gathered in tables 1 and 2 and figure 2.

4. Enlarged Albeit Softened Competition

The Bertrand equilibrium characterized in section 1 entails the prices and demands (for $\delta = 0$)

$$P_A^* = \tfrac{2}{3}\eta \qquad \text{and} \qquad d_A^* = \tfrac{2}{3}r$$

$$P_B^* = \tfrac{1}{3}\eta \qquad \text{and} \qquad d_B^* = \tfrac{1}{3}r.$$

As in section 1, we start here by assuming $I_A = I_B = 0$. In order to increase its profit, firm B considers reducing its market share down to $(1-\gamma)r$, with $1-\gamma < \frac{1}{3}$. This would be a voluntary and a priori restriction[10] meant to soften competition so that the increase in prices would more than compensate for B the decrease in its market share.

Such compensation is possible only if A is not induced to extend its own market share beyond γr, that is, only if the new prices P_A and P_B set by A and B satisfy

$$P_A \geqslant P_B + (1-\gamma)\eta.$$

But this condition implies that A chooses P_A in such a way that

$$P_A \geqslant \alpha + (1-\gamma)\eta.$$

The only price which, given such a P_A, maximizes B's profit is

$$P_B = \alpha.$$

Then A is actually induced to extend its market share beyond γr, except when

$$d_A^m \leqslant \gamma r,$$

i.e., except when

$$\alpha \leqslant (2\gamma - 1)\eta.$$

When this condition is satisfied, B's voluntary restriction[11] leads to the situation where two monopolies coexist. When the condition is not satisfied, there is no equilibrium with voluntary restriction.

This negative conclusion is changed when the population of consumers is represented by a rectangle of length r and height h. This looks like a meaningless modification of the model: the density of consumers per unit length is now h instead of one. This does not affect the Bertrand equilibrium prices P_A^* and P_B^* and simply increases demands by a factor h. However, this modification makes available to B new ways of voluntarily restricting its market share. For example, on half[12] the height of the market, B reduces its market share down to $\frac{1}{2}h(1-\gamma)r$, while it makes no restriction at all on the other half of the market height (see figure 3).

Lemma 4.1. When $\alpha \geqslant \eta$, there exists a Bertrand equilibrium with voluntary restriction for every γ in the interval $[\frac{3}{4}, \frac{3}{4}(\alpha/\eta)]$. The corresponding

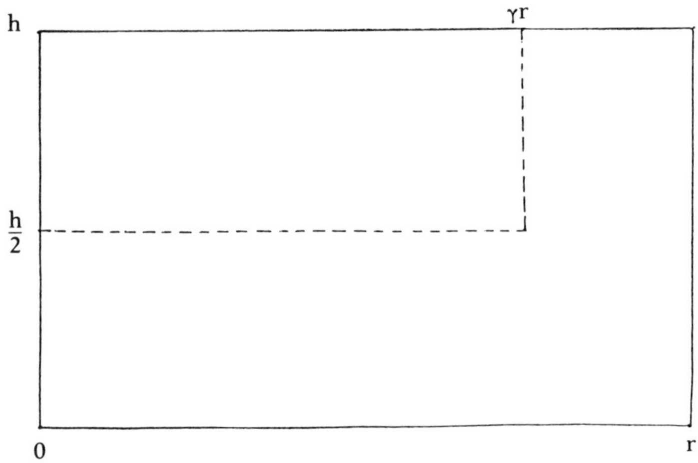

Figure 3.

equilibrium prices are

$$\tilde{P}_A = (1 + \gamma/3)\eta \text{ and } \tilde{P}_B = (1 - \gamma/3)\eta \tag{4.1}$$

and the equilibrium demands (see figure 3) are

$$\begin{aligned}\tilde{d}_A &= \tfrac{1}{2}h\gamma r + \tfrac{1}{2}hd_A(\tilde{P}_A, \tilde{P}_B) = \tfrac{1}{2}h\gamma r + \tfrac{1}{2}h(1 - \tfrac{2}{3}\gamma)r \\ \tilde{d}_B &= \tfrac{1}{2}h(1 - \gamma)r + \tfrac{1}{2}hd_B(\tilde{P}_A, \tilde{P}_B) = \tfrac{1}{2}h(1 - \gamma)r + \tfrac{1}{2}h\tfrac{2}{3}\gamma r.\end{aligned} \tag{4.2}$$

The proof is given in the appendix.

Lemma 4.2. Firm B's profit is greater at the Bertrand equilibrium with voluntary restriction than at the usual Bertrand equilibrium.

Proof. Firm B's profit at the Bertrand equilibrium with voluntary restriction is

$$\tilde{\pi}_B = \tfrac{1}{2}hr\eta(1 - \gamma/3)^2. \tag{4.3}$$

For any γ in $[\frac{3}{4}, \frac{3}{4}(\alpha/\eta)]$, one thus has

$$\tilde{\pi}_B > \pi_B^*.$$

When B is active in the market and a Bertrand equilibrium with voluntary restriction exists, it is in B's best interest to induce its implementation, rather than to accept the implementation of the usual Bertrand equilibrium. Therefore, when B has not yet entered the market, it decides to enter or not on the basis of a comparison between $\tilde{\pi}_B$ and I_B, rather than π_B^* and I_B. And firm A takes this into account for choosing, when required, between deterring B's entry (strategy $\sum_1$) or accepting B's entry (strategy $\sum_2$).

Implementing $\sum_1$ requires that A commits itself to a price P_A^θ that deters B from entering. Once A has committed itself to a particular price P_A, voluntary restriction cannot be of any interest for B. Therefore B's reaction $P_B(P_A)$ is the same as in section 1, which implies that

$$P_A^\theta = \theta P_A^*$$

with

$$I_B = \theta^2 \pi_B^*.$$

However, the maximum value of θ is no longer 1 but

$$\bar{\theta} = \left[\frac{\tilde{\pi}_B}{\pi_B^*}\right]^{1/2}.$$

Implementing $\sum_2$ requires that A does not commit itself to any price. This induces the realization of a Bertrand equilibrium with voluntary restriction, which, provided it exists, entails higher profits for both firms than the Stackelberg equilibrium.

Proposition 4.1. Voluntary restriction enlarges competition, in the sense that the set of circumstances under which A can behave as an unconstrained monopoly is smaller. However, in those circumstances under which competition—be it actual or potential—prevails even without voluntary restriction, it is softened with voluntary restriction and all customers are worse off.

Proof. Let θ^e denote the value of θ for which A is indifferent between $\sum_1$ and $\sum_2$; it is such that

$$\theta^e > 1.$$

Indeed, for $\theta = 1$, $P_A^\theta = P_A^*$, and

$$P_A^* d_A^m(P_A^*) = hr\tfrac{2}{3}\eta < \tfrac{1}{2}hr(1 + \gamma/3)^2\eta = \tilde{\pi}_A$$

for any γ in $[\frac{3}{4}, \frac{3}{4}(\alpha/\eta)]$.

How the market works with and without voluntary restriction can be summed up in the following way (see figure 4):

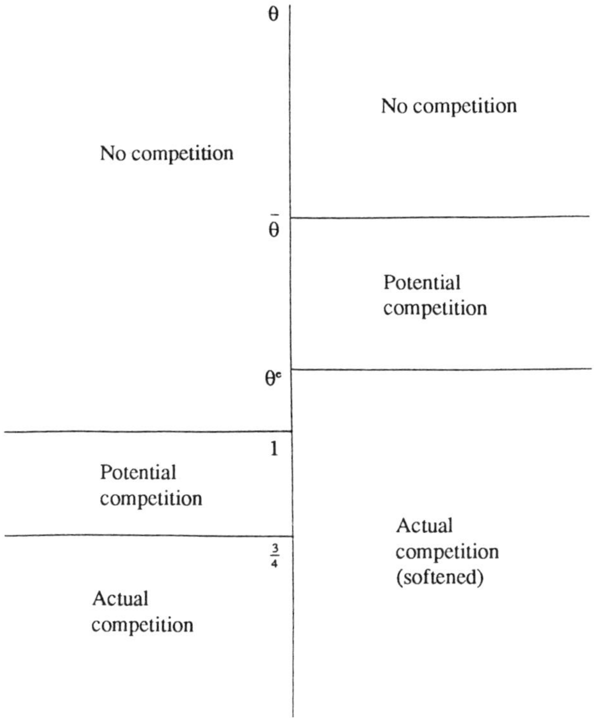

Figure 4.

- If $\theta > \bar{\theta}$, A behaves as an unconstrained monopoly on both markets.
- If $\bar{\theta} \geqslant \theta > \theta^{e}$, A behaves as an unconstrained monopoly on the market without voluntary restriction and as a constrained monopoly, deterring entry, on the market with voluntary restriction.
- If $\theta^{e} \geqslant \theta > 1$, A behaves as an unconstrained monopoly on the market without voluntary restriction, and accepts B's entry and the actual but softened competition that results on the market with voluntary restriction.
- If $1 \geqslant \theta > \frac{3}{4}$, A behaves as a constrained monopoly, deterring entry, on the market without voluntary restriction; on the market with voluntary restriction, the situation is as it is for $\theta^{e} \geqslant \theta < 1$.
- If $\frac{3}{4} \geqslant \theta$, there is entry and actual competition on both markets, but competition is tougher on the market without voluntary restriction (Stackelberg equilibrium) than on the market with voluntary restriction (Bertrand equilibrium with voluntary restriction, as for $\theta^{e} \geqslant \theta > 1$ and $1 \geqslant \theta > \frac{3}{4}$).

Appendix: Proof of Lemma 4.1

1. Faced with $\tilde{P}_B$, does A prefer $\tilde{P}_A$ rather than any other price?
1.1. Let P_A be any price in $[\tilde{P}_B, \tilde{P}_B + (1 - \gamma)\eta]$; then

$$d_A(P_A, \tilde{P}_B) \geqslant \gamma r$$

and voluntary restriction is of no consequence. Hence (see section 1), A's profit is

$$\pi_A(P_A, \tilde{P}_B) = \frac{hr}{\eta}(\eta - P_A + \tilde{P}_B)$$

$$= \frac{hr}{\eta}(\eta - P_A + (1 - \gamma/3)\eta)P_A,$$

which is maximum for

$$P_A = (1 - \gamma/6)\eta \qquad \text{if } \gamma \leqslant \tfrac{6}{7}$$

$$P_A = (2 - \tfrac{4}{3}\gamma)\eta + (1 - \gamma)\eta \qquad \text{if } \gamma \geqslant \tfrac{6}{7}$$

1.2. Let P_A be any price in $]\tilde{P}_B + (1 - \gamma)\eta, \alpha + (1 - \gamma)\eta]$; then

$$d_A(P_A, \tilde{P}_B) < \gamma r$$

and voluntary restriction has tangible effects, although all customers are still served. Then A's profit is

$$\tilde{\pi}_A(P_A, \tilde{P}_B) = \tfrac{1}{2}h\gamma r P_A + \tfrac{1}{2}\frac{hr}{\eta}(\eta - P_A + \tilde{P}_B)P_A$$

$$= \tfrac{1}{2}\frac{hr}{\eta}((2 + \tfrac{2}{3}\gamma)\eta - P_A)P_A,$$

which is maximum for

$$P_A = (1 + \gamma/3)\eta \qquad \text{if } \alpha \geqslant \tfrac{4}{3}\gamma\eta$$

$$P_B = \alpha + (1 - \gamma)\eta \qquad \text{if } \alpha \leqslant \tfrac{4}{3}\gamma\eta$$

1.3. Let P_A be any price in $]\alpha + (1 - \gamma)\eta, \alpha + \eta]$; then

$$d_A(P_A, \tilde{P}_B) < \gamma r$$

and voluntary restriction has tangible effects, with some customers not being served. Then A's profit is

$$\tilde{\pi}_{A}^{m}(P_A, \tilde{P}_B) = \tfrac{1}{2}\frac{hr}{\eta}(\eta - P_A + \alpha)P_A + \tfrac{1}{2}\frac{hr}{\eta}(\eta - P_A + \tilde{P}_B)P_A$$

$$= \tfrac{1}{2}\frac{hr}{\eta}((3 - \gamma/3)\eta + \alpha - 2P_A)P_A,$$

which is maximum for

$$P_A = \tfrac{1}{4}((3 - \gamma/3)\eta + \alpha) \qquad \text{if } \alpha \leqslant \tfrac{1}{3}(-1 + \tfrac{11}{3}\gamma)\eta$$

$$P_A = \alpha + (1 - \gamma)\eta \qquad \text{if } \alpha \geqslant \tfrac{1}{3}(-1 + \tfrac{11}{3}\gamma)\eta$$

1.4. Because

$$\tfrac{4}{3}\gamma\eta > \tfrac{1}{3}(-1 + \tfrac{11}{3}\gamma)\eta,$$

it is sufficient to compare the maxima for $P_A = (1 - \gamma/6)\eta$ and for $P_A = (1 + \gamma/3)\eta$. As $\gamma > \frac{2}{3}\eta$, this comparison leads A to prefer $P_A = (1 + \gamma/3)\eta = \tilde{P}_A$.

2. Faced with $\tilde{P}_A$, does B prefer $\tilde{P}_B$ than any other price?

2.1. Let P_B be any price in $[\max\{0, \tilde{P}_A - \eta\}, \tilde{P}_A - (1 - \gamma)\eta[$; then

$$d_B(\tilde{P}_A, P_B) > (1 - \gamma)r,$$

and voluntary restriction has tangible effects. Then B's profit is

$$\tilde{\pi}_B(\tilde{P}_A, P_B) = \tfrac{1}{2}h(1 - \gamma)rP_B + \tfrac{1}{2}\frac{hr}{\eta}(\tilde{P}_A - P_B)P_B$$

$$= \tfrac{1}{2}\frac{hr}{\eta}((2 - \tfrac{2}{3}\gamma)\eta - P_B)P_B,$$

which is maximum for

$$P_B = (1 - \gamma/3)\eta.$$

2.2. Let P_B be any price in $[\tilde{P}_A - (1 - \gamma)\eta, \alpha]$; then

$$d_B(\tilde{P}_A, P_B) \leqslant (1 - \gamma)r,$$

and voluntary restriction is of no consequence. Then B's profit is

$$\pi_B(\tilde{P}_A, P_B) = \frac{hr}{\eta}(\tilde{P}_A - P_B)P_B$$

$$= \frac{hr}{\eta}((1 + \gamma/3)\eta - P_B)P_B,$$

which is maximum for

$$P_B = \tfrac{1}{2}(1 + \gamma/3)\eta \qquad \text{if } \gamma \leqslant \tfrac{3}{7}$$

$$P_A = \tfrac{4}{3}\gamma\eta \qquad \text{if } \gamma \geqslant \tfrac{3}{7}.$$

2.3. As $\gamma \geqslant \frac{3}{4}$, the result follows immediately.

Notes

1. It would be more appropriate here to speak of a prospective consumer; however, for simplicity, we shall not explicitly distinguish between actual and prospective consumers.

2. However small the quantity of good A produced, firm A must incur the cost I_A (I_A is a fixed cost); moreover, in case of exit from the market, firm A has no possibility of recovering even a fraction of I_A (I_A is a sunk cost); the same is of course true of I_B.

3. As in Baumol et al. (1982), we concentrate on competition in prices.

4. We consider only the Stackelberg equilibrium with A playing the role of leader.

5. For similar configurations, see Demange and Ponssard (1986) and Singh and Vives (1984).

6. For a survey of the various approaches to natural monopoly, see Waterson (1987).

7. It is convenient to assume that, if $I_B = \pi_B^*$, then firm B decides not to enter the market.

8. This is true for every $P_A > -\delta$. In this section we are actually only interested in the case $\delta = 0$. But in the next section, we shall need the more general results given below.

9. For $\alpha \leqslant \eta/3$, we are in area II in figure 1, and A is indifferent to B's existence.

10. The restriction thus takes place before the market starts functioning. B can implement such voluntary and a priori restriction in sales' opportunities through various methods such as restricting the extension of its distribution network or targeting its advertising to a restricted category of customers.

11. We do not repeat that the restriction is also a priori; it always is in what follows.

12. It could be another proportion; half has been chosen for expository purposes. Such voluntary restrictions are rationing devices, albeit different from those considered in models of duopoly with differentiation by Boyer and Moreaux (1985) and by Osborne and Pitchik (1986). See also Encaoua and Moreaux (1987), although they have no differentiation in their model.

References

Baumol, W. J., J. C. Panzar and R. D. Willig (1982) *Contestable Markets and the Theory of Industry Structure.* Harcourt, Brace and Jovanovich.

Boyer, M. and M. Moreaux (1985) Rational Rationing with Differentiated Products. Southern European Economics Discussion Series No. 37.

Brock, W. A. (1983) "Contestable markets and the theory of industry structure: A review article." *Journal of Political Economy* 91: 1055–1066.

Dasgupta, P. and J. Stiglitz (1988) "Potential competition, actual competition, and economic welfare." *European Economic Review* 32: 569–577.

Demange, G. and J. P. Ponssard (1986) "Barrière de mobilité et concurrence dans un duopole." *Annales d'Economie et de Statistique* 1: 35–53.

Encaoua, D. and M. Moreaux (1987) "Concurrence et monopole naturel: une approche par la théorie des jeux." *Annales d'Economie et de Statistique* 8: 89–116.

Fudenberg, D. and J. Tirole (1986) "Dynamic models of oligopoly." In *Fundamentals of Pure and Applied Economics,* vol. 3. Harwood.

Gabsewicz, J. J. and J. F. Thisse (1979) "Price competition, quality and income disparities." *Journal of Economic Theory* 20: 340–359.

Gal-Or, E. (1985) "Differentiated industries without entry barriers." *Journal of Economic Theory* 37: 310–339.

Osborne, M. and C. Pitchik (1986) "Price competition in a capacity-constrained duopoly." *Journal of Economic Theory* 38, 238–260.

Shaked, A. and J. Sutton (1982) "Relaxing price competition through product differentiation." *Review of Economic Studies* 49: 3–13.

Singh, N. and X. Vives (1984) "Price and quantity competition in a differentiated duopoly." *Rand Journal of Economics* 15: 546–554.

Spence, M. (1983) "Contestable markets and the theory of industry structure: A review article." *Journal of Economic Literature* 21: 981–990.

Waterson, M. (1987) "Recent developments in the theory of natural monopoly." *Journal of Economic Surveys* 1, 59–80.

11 Incentives in Cooperative Research and Development

Pierre Picard and
Patrick Rey

1. Introduction

In Europe, the promotion of cooperative research and development programs has gained ground in the past few years, and in the future will probably become a major tool of EEC industrial policy. By cooperative research and development we mean the organization of a project where a public regulator invites a number of oligopolistic firms or laboratories to participate in a joint research program. In some respects, scientific knowledge is a public good that tends to be undersupplied; cooperative research agreements are thus mostly viewed as a way of speeding up invention and technical innovation by coordinating individual efforts, by making them less risky, and by creating synergetic effects through exchange of information and combination of technological abilities.

The European Strategic Program for Research and Development in Information Technology (ESPRIT) is a typical example of such cooperative research projects, whose coordination is organized by a public regulator. ESPRIT contracts bring industrial laboratories together to participate in a well-defined applied (production for market) research in the field of information technology. Each laboratory bears a part of the research costs and receives a subsidy that is equal to half its own costs. Furthermore, each laboratory may exploit all the results that have been achieved in the joint research program. The EUREKA and RACE programs are other typical examples of regulated cooperative R & D in Europe.[1]

Using cooperative programs to promote research and development activities is something relatively new in Europe, but in Japan it is already an important tool of industrial policy: MITI takes vigorous initiatives in organizing joint research projects among oligopolistic firms of the semiconductor and other high technology industries, in providing partial funding, and in assuming the role of an effective coordinator. As Yamamura

(1986) writes: "Above all, MITI evidently has no doubt of the social desirability of joint research activities among selected oligopolistic firms. MITI officials, in their public pronouncements and interviews, stress the necessity of pooling R & D efforts in order to make the most efficient use of scarce scientific manpower and research funds. MITI clearly believes its joint research projects serve the national interest." This Japanese conception, which is akin to the European one, contrasts sharply with American perceptions of what should be the role of government in promoting technological progress, since American policymakers do not seem to have reached a consensus as to the desirability of sponsoring joint research ventures among oligopolistic firms. In the United States, public sponsorship gives way to individual initiatives, possibly leading to privately organized joint research corporations such as the Microelectronics and Computer Consortium (MCC).

Be that as it may, the purpose of this paper is not to provide a comparative analysis of respective merits of sponsored joint ventures and unregulated markets in R & D activities and the desirability of promoting a research joint venture will be considered here rather as a postulate.[2] Attention will be focused on the design of contractual rules, which have to be decided upon if one aims at an efficient functioning of such a cooperative program.[3]

More precisely, we will consider a public regulator who is in charge of coordinating a joint research project and we will characterize socially optimal incentive schemes under imperfect information. It will be assumed that the regulator does not know precisely how much money each firm will be able to make from the patents and other statutory rights for inventions conceived by contractors in the execution of the cooperative program. We will also consider informational constraints arising from the inability of the regulator to verify the actual contribution of each contractor, that is, the actual effort levels when the program is implemented.

Conforming to a terminology that is now familiar in the theory of incentives, the first type of the above-mentioned informational constraints refers to "hidden knowledge" and the second one corresponds to "hidden actions." Recent contributions have simultaneously considered both types of problems in a principal-*one* agent framework, where the observation of the agent's actions is garbled by some random noise. In particular, results obtained by Laffont and Tirole (1986), Caillaud et al. (1986), McAfee and McMillan (1987), and Picard (1987) show that, in most cases, imperfect observability of the agent's actions does not entail any additional welfare loss (by comparison with the pure adverse selection problem) when the principal and the agent are both income risk-neutral. They also emphasize the potential interest of simple and intuitive (linear or quadratic) reward schemes, which are quite robust to the nature of the garbling noise.

Here, we will consider an incentive problem where a principal (the regulator) enters into contractual relations with *several* agents (firms or industrial laboratories), so that strategic interactions bear on the agents' behavior. A short methodological digression may be useful to clarify the following developments. First, in such a multi-agent setting, moral hazard can emerge from the fact that the regulator may be unable to identify individual contributions to an aggregate (observable) outcome: this gives rise to the free-rider problem in teams, as analyzed by Holmström (1982). On the other hand, optimal decision making under imperfect observability of the agents' characteristics has motivated a great deal of works on implementation of social choice rules. Informational assumptions differ among these works. In a first class of models, agents are supposed to have perfect information about others' characteristics and *Nash (or perfect Nash) implementability* is usually considered in that case. It turns out that in general it is possible for a noninformed regulator to get all information revealed by proposing "denunciation" games (see, for example, Maskin 1977 and Moore and Repullo 1988, respectively for Nash and perfect Nash implementation). In a second class of models, agents have incomplete information. The *Bayesian approach* consists in assuming that agents have prior beliefs about others' information. Once again, it may be possible to extract the private information through Bayesian incentive compatible mechanisms (see, for example, Maskin 1986); D'Aspremont and Gérard-Varet 1979, 1986; Bensaïd 1986) at least when beliefs are conveniently correlated. However, this approach requires strong assumptions and, in particular, prior beliefs must be common knowledge, which in some cases may not be an acceptable assumption. Moreover, once the information is revealed, agents may desire to change their play. This stresses the question of the durability of these mechanisms (see, for example, Holmström and Myerson 1983; Crawford 1985) and of their robustness to preplay communications (Farrell 1982; Forges 1986) and renegotiations (Cramton 1984; Dewatripont 1988, Hart and Tirole 1988). An alternative approach consists in ignoring the agents' beliefs and this leads to focusing on *dominant strategies*. Of course the decision rules which can be implemented in dominant strategies are usually much fewer than those which are Bayesian incentive compatible but, as a counterpart, implementation in dominant strategies is quite robust to "outside" communication or negotiation. From a different point of view, implementation in dominant strategies is a natural concept when the regulator has imperfect information about the agents' beliefs, since a decision rule is implementable in dominant strategies if and only if it is Bayesian implementable for any prior belief (see Dasgupta et al. 1979).

A possible way of bringing these two approaches nearer is to add a *posterior implementability* condition to the Bayesian framework (see Green and Laffont 1987): a decision rule is said to be posterior implementable if, once all agents' plays are known, no agent has any regret about his initial strategy. When using direct truthful mechanisms in adverse selection models, posterior implementability coincides with implementability in dominant strategies. As we will show, this property generalizes to all types of mechanisms, as soon as private information that is known to any given agent does not affect other agents' welfare.

Posterior implementability will be assumed here and this choice is motivated by at least two reasons. First, posterior implementability considerably reinforces the strength of Bayesian implementability (as mentioned above; in some cases, it even coincides with implementability in dominant strategies). Furthermore, posterior implementability makes sense when contractual agreements are formed in a two-step procedure. In a first step, there is a tatonnement during which agents announce the strategies they intend to play. This tatonnement terminates only when agents are satisfied with their play, taking into account the additional information which is transmitted in the messages announced by the other agents. Second, there is a signing step in which no further information is exchanged and the agreement obtained at the first step is ratified. From this point of view, posterior implementability seems to be a reasonable condition for research and development joint ventures, since oligopolistic firms will probably communicate in the process of forming such contractual arrangements

From an abstract point of view, the purpose of this paper is to show that posterior implementable decision rules, which are optimal when agents' actions are verifiable, can still be (posterior) implemented in the presence of a moral hazard. We thus aim at generalizing results that are now reasonably well understood in the one-agent case to a multi-agent setting. More precisely, in our framework of cooperative R & D, we will first characterize the optimal posterior implementable decision rule, under incomplete information about private profitability: here, the firms' contributions will be verifiable and can be contracted upon. We thus have a pure adverse selection problem, where ex post inefficiency results only from the inability of the regulator to observe contractors' private profits originated in the cooperative R & D.

Second, we will consider the case where individual contributions cannot be verified. It will be assumed that the aggregate outcome of the cooperative program can be observed by the regulator (possibly with a random noise), but the contributions of contractors are not publicly observed. In this framework, the following type of mechanism is developed. First, the regulator offers reward schemes, associated with profitability reports, which define individual subsidies as a function of the aggregate outcome. Firms then play a two-stage game. At the first stage, each firm publicly announces its profitability; at the second stage, firms choose their contributions. Under reasonable assumptions, it will be shown that the reward schemes can be chosen so that effort levels and subsidies coincide with the optimal decision rule of the pure adverse selection case, for any truthful perfect equilibrium that satisfies the posterior implementability condition. In this sense, imperfect observability of the contractors' actions entails no additional welfare loss for the regulator.

Let us finally mention that, after writing the first draft of this paper, we became aware of an unpublished paper by McAfee and McMillan (1986) in which the same questions are approached in a different context. Connections and differences will be stated precisely at the end of this paper.

The paper is organized as follows. Section 2 presents the model and characterizes the complete information solution. Section 3 considers the case where the regulator has imperfect information about the firms' profitability. In section 4 this assumption is combined with unobservability of firms' contributions. Finally, comments and concluding remarks are offered in section 5. All proofs are gathered in an appendix.

2. The Basic Framework

We consider n firms (laboratories) taking part in a joint research program organized by a regulator (central planner). Let X be the outcome of this research joint venture (X can be thought of as a cost reduction in an elementary production process, owing to improvements conceived in the execution of cooperative R & D). This outcome depends on the firms' contributions and on a random disturbance. We will write

$$X = R(a) + \varepsilon,$$

where

- $a = (a_1, \ldots, a_n) \in R_n$ and a_i denotes the firm i's (monetary) contribution;
- $R(\cdot)$ is a strictly concave function, defined and twice continuously differentiable on R^n, which satisfies, for $i, j = 1, \ldots, n$,

$$R'_i = \frac{\partial R}{\partial a_i} > 0 \qquad \text{and} \qquad R''_{ij} = \frac{\partial^2 R}{\partial a_i \partial a_j} \geqslant 0 \qquad \text{if } i \neq j.$$

Positivity of R''_{ij} for $i \neq j$ corresponds to the complementarity of contractors' contributions. This seems to be a rather natural assumption in the present context where firms are willing to cooperate.

- ε is a zero mean random variable with a variance σ^2.

By assumption, contractors derive inequal benefits from the exploitation of patents and statutory rights for invention or improvements conceived in the execution of the cooperative program. More precisely firm i is characterized by a (constant) marginal profitability θ_i. Firm i's utility, taken as expected additional profits, attributable to the research program, is given by[4]

$$u_i(a, t_i, \theta_i) = E_\varepsilon[t_i - a_i + \theta_i X] = t_i - a_i + \theta_i R(a),$$

where t_i denotes a transfer paid by the regulator to firm i. We also assume

$$\theta_i \in \Theta_i = [\theta_i^0, \theta_i^1] \subset \mathbb{R}.$$

The regulator aims at maximizing the social surplus, which is supposed to be written as

$$h(\theta)X - \sum_{i=1}^{n} t_i,$$

where $\theta = (\theta_1, \ldots, \theta_n)$ and $h(\theta) > 0$ for all θ in $\Theta = \prod_{i=1}^{n} \Theta_i$. $h(\theta)X$ stands for the effect of the outcome X on the social surplus.[5] A possible interpretation is to assume that the regulator maximizes the aggregate consumers' surplus on markets where firms $i = 1, \ldots, n$ are present. The research program both modifies firms' production costs and increases consumers' surplus. In that case, a functional relation can be derived between the consequences of the research program for the aggregate consumers' surplus and for the firms' profits.[6]

Transfers to firms are supposed to be paid by consumers through taxes and have to be deduced to obtain an evaluation of social benefits. More realistic objective functions could be introduced, for instance by assuming that the regulator maximizes a weighted sum of firms' profits and consumers' surplus, without any qualitative change in the result, at least when the weight is larger for the consumer surplus than for the firms' profits. However, we will confine ourselves to the previous formulation because of its simplicity.

Finally we will assume that the firms and the regulator are risk neutral.

In this framework an *allocation* $(a, t) = (a_1, \ldots, a_n, t_1, \ldots, t_n) \in \mathbb{R}^n \times \mathbb{R}^n$ specifies the contributions and the transfers. A *decision rule* $\varphi(\cdot)$ is a function from Θ into $\mathbb{R}^n \times \mathbb{R}^n$, which associates an allocation $\varphi(\theta) = (a(\theta), t(\theta))$ to any possible list of profitability parameters $\theta \in \Theta$. If the regulator had perfect information about the profitability parameters θ_i and if he could verify the individual levels of effort, he would choose the first best allocation $\varphi^*(\theta) = (a^*(\theta), t^*(\theta))$ which maximizes the social surplus, subject to individual rationality constraints:

$$\underset{(a,t) \in \mathbb{R}^n \times \mathbb{R}^n}{\text{Maximize}}\ h(\theta)R(a) - \sum_{i=1}^{n} t_i$$

subject to

$$u_i(a, t_i, \theta_i) \geqslant 0 \qquad i = 1, \ldots, n.$$

The first best allocation φ^* is thus characterized by

$$\left[h(\theta) + \sum_{j=1}^{n} \theta_j\right] R_i'(a^*) = 1, \tag{1}$$

$$t_i^* = a_i^* - \theta_i R(a^*). \tag{2}$$

From (1) the marginal social value (in monetary terms) of firm i's contribution is equal to one. This marginal social value is the sum of marginal profits $(\sum_j \theta_j) R_i'(a_i^*)$ and marginal social surplus $h(\theta) R_i'(a_i^*)$. From (2), firm i is reimbursed for costs a_i^* minus expected cash flows $\theta_i R(a^*)$.

3. The Pure Adverse Selection Case

We will now assume that the profitability parameters are private information (but in this section the levels of effort are still supposed to be verifiable). The characteristics are drawn from a joint distribution F, which is common knowledge, and each θ_i is only observed by the corresponding firm. In the following we will assume that the joint density f is strictly positive and continuous over the whole set Θ.

As usual in incentives theory, we will define a *mechanism* as an n-tuple of message (signal) spaces S_i and a measurable outcome function g from $S = \prod_{i=1}^{n} S_i$ into the set of allocations $\mathbb{R}^n \times \mathbb{R}^n$.

Given a mechanism (S, g), firms choose a signal $s_i \in S_i$ based on their beliefs, described by the conditional distributions $F_i(\cdot|\theta_i)$ over the other firms' characteristics $\theta_{-i} = (\theta_1, \ldots, \theta_{i-1}, \theta_{i+1}, \ldots, \theta_n)$. A *strategy* for firm i is thus a measurable function σ_i from Θ_i into S_i. The outcome associated to the mechanism (S, g) and strategies $\sigma = (\sigma_1, \ldots, \sigma_n)$ is given by the function from Θ to $\mathbb{R}^n \times \mathbb{R}^n$, defined by $\theta \to g(\sigma_1(\theta_1), \ldots, \sigma_n(\theta_n))$ and $\sigma = (\sigma_1, \ldots, \sigma_n)$ is a *Bayesian equilibrium* of the mechanism (S, g) if

$$\forall i = 1, \ldots, n,\ \forall \theta \in \Theta,\ \sigma_1(\theta_i) \in \operatorname*{Arg\,Max}_{s_i \in S_i} \int_{\Theta_{-i}} u_i(g(s_i, \sigma_{-1}(\theta_{-i})), \theta_i)\, dF_i(\theta_{-i}|\theta_i),$$

where

$$\sigma_{-i}(\theta_{-i}) = (\sigma_1(\theta_1), \ldots, \sigma_{i-1}(\theta_{i-1}), \sigma_{i+1}(\theta_{i+1}), \ldots, \sigma_n(\theta_n)).$$

Finally, a decision rule $\varphi(\cdot)$ is *Bayesian implementable* if there exists a mechanism (S, g) and a Bayesian equilibrium σ of this mechanism such that $\forall \theta \in \Theta$: $\varphi(\theta) = g(\sigma_1(\theta_1), \ldots, \sigma_n(\theta_n))$. Following Green and Laffont (1987), $\varphi(\cdot)$ is *posterior implementable* if $\varphi(\cdot)$ is Bayesian implementable and it is common knowledge that firms will remain satisfied with their play, given the play of all others. Let $\tilde{F}_i(\theta_{-i}|\theta_i, s_{-i})$ be the conditional distribution that firm i holds about θ_{-i}, after having observed the others' choices $s_{-i} \in \Theta_{-i}$. Posterior implementability requires that equilibrium strategy rules satisfy

$$\forall i = 1, \ldots, n,\ \forall \theta_1 \in \Theta_i,\ \forall s_{-i} \in \sigma_{-i}(\Theta_{-i}) = \prod_{j \neq i} \sigma_j(\Theta_j):$$

$$\sigma_1(\theta_i) \in \operatorname*{Arg\,Max}_{s_i \in S_i} \int_{\Theta_{-i}} u_i(g(s_i, s_{-i}), \theta_i)\, d\tilde{F}_i(\theta_{-i}|\theta_i, s_{-i}).$$

Since the expected profit of firm i does not depend on θ_{-i}, the posterior implementability condition is equivalent to

$$\sigma_i(\theta_i) \in \operatorname*{Arg\,Max}_{s_i \in S_i} u_i(g(s_i, s_{-i}), \theta_i)$$

for all s_{-i} in $\sigma_{-i}(\Theta_{-i})$; that is, $\sigma_i(\theta_i)$ is a dominant strategy for the mechanism $\{S', g\}$ with $S' = \prod_{i=1}^n S'_i$ and $S'_i = \sigma_1(\Theta_i) \subset S_i$. Thus, from the revelation principle, there exists a direct mechanism $\{\Theta, g'\}$, i.e., a mechanism in which strategies are profitability reports, for which truthtelling is a dominant strategy and which satisfies $g'(\theta) = \varphi(\theta)$ for all θ. In other words, to conclude this methodological digression, under our assumptions, a decision rule that can be posterior implemented through a mechanism with abstract strategy sets can also be implemented truthfully through a direct mechanism. Thus, there is no generality loss in restricting the design of decision rules, by assuming that truthtelling is a dominant strategy in the corresponding direct mechanism. The individual rationality constraint also has to be introduced to ensure the feasibility of allocations. These conditions are summarized up in the following definition.

Definition 1. The decision rule $\phi: \theta \to (\hat{a}(\theta), \hat{t}(\theta))$ is incentive compatible if $\forall i = 1, \ldots, n$, $\forall \theta \in \Theta$:

$$\theta_i \in \operatorname*{Arg\,Max}_{\theta_i \in \Theta_i} u_i(\phi(\hat{\theta}_i, \theta_{-i}), \theta_i) \tag{3}$$

and

$$u_i(\phi(\theta), \theta_i) \geqslant 0. \tag{4}$$

Incentive compatible decision rules are characterized in the following proposition.

Proposition 1. A function $\phi = \{\hat{a}, \hat{t}\}: \Theta \to \mathbb{R}^n \times \mathbb{R}^n$ is an incentive-compatible decision rule if and only if $\forall i = 1, \ldots, n$, $\forall \theta \in \Theta$:

$$\hat{t}_i(\theta) = \hat{a}_i(\theta) - \theta_i R(\hat{a}(\theta)) + \int_{\theta_i^0}^{\theta_i} R(\hat{a}(s_i, \theta_{-i}))\, ds_i + \pi_i(\theta_{-i}), \tag{5}$$

$\theta \to R(\hat{a}(\theta))$ is weakly increasing and $\pi_i(\cdot)$ is an arbitrary function of θ_{-i} that satisfies $\pi_i(\theta_{-i}) \geqslant 0$ $\forall \theta_{-i} \in \Theta_{-i}$.

Such conditions are familiar from the literature on incentive compatibility in dominant strategies. Condition (5) defines the rent that the regulator has to pay to induce truthful revelation: the profit of firm i is equal to

$$\int_{\theta_i^0}^{\theta_i} R(\hat{a}(s_i, \theta_{-i}))\, ds_i + \pi_i(\theta_{-i}), \tag{6}$$

so that high profitability firms get larger profits than low profitability ones. Furthermore, from the monotonicity condition, the expected outcome $R(\hat{a}(\theta))$ is a nondecreasing function of the profitability parameters θ_i.

The regulator is risk neutral and selects the incentive compatible decision rule that maximizes expected social surplus. A preliminary lemma will characterize the expected social surplus.

Lemma. For any incentive-compatible decision rule $\phi = \{\hat{a}, \hat{t}\}$, the expected social surplus W may be written as

$$W = \int_{\Theta} \{\Psi(\theta)R(\hat{a}(\theta)) - \sum_{i=1}^{n} (\hat{a}_i(\theta) + \pi_i(\theta_{-i}))\}\, dF(\theta), \tag{7}$$

where $\pi_i(\cdot)$ satisfies (5) and

$$\Psi(\theta) = h(\theta) + \sum_{i=1}^{n} \theta_i - \sum_{i=1}^{n} \left[\frac{1 - F_i(\theta_{-i}|\theta_i}{f_i(\theta_{-i}|\theta_i}\right]. \tag{8}$$

We now are in a position to characterize the optimal decision rule.

Proposition 2. If the function $\Psi(\theta)$ is positive and increasing, the optimal decision rule $\hat{\phi} = \{\hat{a}, \hat{t}\}$ is continuous and satisfies for all θ in Θ and $i = 1, \ldots, n$:

$$\Psi(\theta)R_i'(\hat{a}(\theta)) = 1 \tag{9}$$

$$\hat{t}_i(\theta) = \hat{a}_i(\theta) - \theta_i R(\hat{a}(\theta)) + \int_{\theta_i^0}^{\theta_i} R(\hat{a}(s_i, \theta_{-i}))\, ds_i \tag{10}$$

and the functions $\hat{a}_i(\theta)$, $i = 1, \ldots, n$, are increasing.

Conditions (8) and (9) define the optimal contributions of firms that take part in the cooperative program. The marginal social value $[h(\theta) + \sum_j \theta_j]R_i'$ is now less than one, which shows that imperfect information entails an efficiency loss, except when the firms have the highest profitability parameters ($\theta_i = \theta_i^1, i = 1, \ldots, n$). From (10), profits are strictly positive except for the firms with the lowest profitability parameter (i.e., $\theta_i = \theta_i^0$). By proposition 1, the expected outcome associated to any incentive-compatible decision rule is a weakly increasing function defined over Θ. Proposition 2 reinforces this property for the optimal decision rule [when $\Psi(\theta)$ is positive and increasing], since all functions $\hat{a}_i(\theta)$ are increasing functions of the profitability parameters θ_i.

For incentive-compatible decision rules, the profits of all firms are almost surely strictly positive. This informational rent marks up the cost of effort for the regulator and, in turn, as stated in the following corollary, it leads to suboptimal levels of effort.

Corollary. If function $\Psi(\theta)$ is positive and increasing, the optimal decision rule $\hat{\phi} = \{\hat{a}, \hat{t}\}$ satisfies

$\hat{a}(\theta) = a^*(\theta)$ if $\theta = (\theta_1^1, \ldots, \theta_n^1)$

$\hat{a}_i(\theta) < a_i^*(\theta)$ for all i, otherwise

4. Adverse Selection and Moral Hazard

We now assume that individual contributions are not verifiable. Only the outcome X is publicly known and can be contracted upon. However, we will show that the decision rule ϕ which was optimal when effort was verifiable can still be implemented through a two-stage mechanism.

This mechanism can be described as follows. Let $T = (T_1, \dots, T_n)$ with $T_i = T_i(\tilde{\theta}, X)$ be an incentive scheme which specifies the transfers received by each firm i as a function of profitability reports $\tilde{\theta} = (\tilde{\theta}_1, \dots, \tilde{\theta}_n)$ and ex-post outcome X. We consider a two-stage sequential game. Each firm i sends a profitability report $\tilde{\theta}_i$ to the regulator at stage 1 and chooses a contribution a_i at stage 2. The regulator commits to pay a transfer $T_i(\tilde{\theta}, X) = T_i(\tilde{\theta}, R(a) + \varepsilon)$.

In this sequential game, firm i's strategy is a pair (σ_i, α_i), where σ_i: $\Theta_i \to \Theta_i$ specifies the profitability report of the firm, as a function of its true characteristic, and $\alpha_i(\theta_i, \tilde{\theta})$: $\Theta_i \times \Theta \to \mathbb{R}_+$ specifies its contribution a_i as a function of its characteristic θ_i and of the reports $\tilde{\theta}$ observed at stage 1. Let $\tilde{F}_i(\theta_{-i} | \theta_i, \tilde{\theta}_{-i})$ be the posterior conditional distribution that firm i holds about θ_{-i}, after having observed the reports $\tilde{\theta}_{-i}$.

Strategies (σ, α) and posterior beliefs $\tilde{F}$, where $\sigma = (\sigma_1, \dots, \sigma_n)$, $\alpha = (\alpha_1, \dots, \alpha_n)$, and $\tilde{F} = (\tilde{F}_1, \dots, \tilde{F}_n)$, define a *perfect Bayesian equilibrium* of the game induced by the incentive scheme $T(\cdot)$ if, for all $i = 1, \dots, n$, the following three conditions are satisfied:

Condition 1. σ is a Bayesian equilibrium of the game defined by $T(\cdot)$, α, and prior beliefs F, i.e., $\forall i = 1, \dots, n$, $\forall \theta_1 \in \Theta_i$:

$$\sigma_1(\theta_i) \in \operatorname*{Arg\,Max}_{\theta_i \in \Theta_i} \int_{\Theta_{-i}} \{E_\varepsilon[T_i(\tilde{\theta}_i, \sigma_{-i}(\theta_{-i}), R(\dots, \alpha_j(\theta_j, \tilde{\theta}_i, \sigma_{-i}(\theta_{-i})), \dots) + \varepsilon)] - \alpha_i(\theta_i, \tilde{\theta}_i, \sigma_{-i}(\theta_{-i})) + \theta_i R(\dots, \alpha_j(\theta_j, \tilde{\theta}_i, \sigma_{-i}(\theta_{-i})), \dots)\} \times dF_i(\theta_{-i} | \theta_i).$$

Condition 2. For all possible reports $\tilde{\theta}$, $\{(\alpha_1(\cdot, \tilde{\theta}), \dots, \alpha_n(\cdot, \tilde{\theta})\}$ is a Bayesian equilibrium of the corresponding subgame, for posterior beliefs $\tilde{F}$, i.e., $\forall i = 1, \dots, n$, $\forall \theta_i \in \Theta_i$, $\forall \tilde{\theta} \in \sigma(\Theta)$:

$$\alpha_i(\theta_i, \tilde{\theta}) \in \operatorname*{Arg\,Max}_{a_i \in \mathbb{R}^n} \int_{\Theta_{-i}} \{E_\varepsilon[T_i(\tilde{\theta}, R(a_i, \dots, \alpha_j(\theta_j, \tilde{\theta}), \dots) + \varepsilon)] - a_i + \theta_i R(a_i, \dots, \alpha_j(\theta_j, \tilde{\theta}), \dots)\} \, d\tilde{F}_i(\theta_{-i} | \theta_i, \tilde{\theta}_{-i}).$$

Condition 3. Posterior beliefs $\tilde{F}$ are updated from prior F and are consistent with Bayes' rule and strategies σ.

We will say that $(\sigma, \alpha, \tilde{F})$ is a *posterior perfect Bayesian equilibrium* if it is a perfect Bayesian equilibrium and if it moreover satisfies:

Condition 1a. For all possible reports $\tilde{\theta}$, σ is a Bayesian equilibrium of the game defined by $T(\cdot)$, α, and posterior beliefs $\tilde{F}$, i.e., $\forall i = 1, \ldots, n$, $\forall \theta_i \in \Theta_i, \forall \tilde{\theta}_{-i} \in \sigma_{-i}(\Theta_{-i})$,

$$\sigma_i(\theta_i) \in \operatorname*{Arg\,Max}_{\tilde{\theta}_i \in \Theta_i} \int_{\Theta_{-i}} \{E_\varepsilon[T_i(\tilde{\theta}_i, \tilde{\theta}_{-i}, R(\ldots, \alpha_j(\theta_j, \tilde{\theta}_i, \tilde{\theta}_{-i}), \ldots) + \varepsilon)]$$
$$- \alpha_i(\theta_i, \tilde{\theta}_i, \tilde{\theta}_{-i}) + \theta_i R(\ldots, \alpha_j(\theta_j, \tilde{\theta}_i, \tilde{\theta}_{-i}), \ldots)\}\, d\tilde{F}_i(\theta_{-i} | \theta_i, \tilde{\theta}_{-i}).$$

From condition 1a, at stage 1 each firm i remains satisfied with its play $\sigma_i(\theta_i)$, given any possible play of all others $\tilde{\theta}_{-i} \in \sigma_{-i}(\Theta_{-i})$ and given its posterior beliefs $\tilde{F}_i$. When posterior beliefs are constrained to be consistent with Bayes' rule, condition 1a is much more stringent than condition 1. This point is rigorously stated in Proposition 3 and leads to Definitions 2 and 3.

Proposition 3. Conditions 1a and 3 imply condition 1.

Definition 2. A vector of strategy rules (σ, α) and beliefs $\tilde{F}$ define a posterior perfect Bayesian equilibrium if, for all $i = 1, \ldots, n$, conditions 1a, 2, and 3 are satisfied.

Definition 3. The incentive scheme T is said to truthfully (posterior) implement the decision rule $\varphi = \{\hat{a}, \hat{t}\}$ if it defines a sequential game for which

a. there exists a posterior perfect Bayesian equilibrium $(\sigma, \alpha, \tilde{F})$ such that $\forall \theta \in \Theta$: $\sigma(\theta) = \theta$,

b. for any posterior perfect Bayesian equilibrium $(\sigma, \alpha, \tilde{F})$ such that $\sigma(\theta) = \theta$, we have $\alpha_i(\theta_i, \theta) = \hat{a}_i(\theta)$ $\forall i = 1, \ldots, n$, $\forall \theta \in \Theta$,

c. $\forall i = 1, \ldots, n$, $\forall \theta \in \Theta$: $E_\varepsilon T_i(\theta, R(\hat{a}(\theta)) + \varepsilon) = \hat{t}_i(\theta)$.

Truthful posterior implementation means that there exists a posterior perfect Bayesian equilibrium such that at stage 1 all firms tell the truth and at stage 2 they choose the contributions and they receive the expected transfers as specified by function ϕ.

At first sight, turning one's attention to truthful equilibria may seem unduly restrictive here, since the revelation principle does not hold for the class of posterior implementable mechanisms (see Green and Laffont 1987). However, it will turn out that the optimal decision rule $\hat{\varphi}$ described in Proposition 2 can actually be implemented through such a truthful equilibrium: there is thus no actual loss of generality here. Of course, restricting attention to truthful equilibria does not mean that there does not exist other equilibria in the sequential game under consideration; moreover, a nontruthful equilibrium, if any, might lead to suboptimal decisions. Such a possibility occurs in many models, even when the revelation principle applies, but it certainly sets limits to the relevance of our results.

Revelation problems here mix adverse selection and moral hazard. The following proposition confirms the intuition that the set of implementable allocations is a part of the set of the allocations which could be obtained in the pure adverse selection setting.

Proposition 4. If $\hat{\varphi}$ is an individually rational decision rule which can be truthfully implemented through an incentive scheme $T(\cdot)$, then $\hat{\varphi}$ is incentive compatible (in the sense of Definition 1).

In fact, we aim here at proving a symmetrical result: under suitable assumptions, there exists an incentive scheme which truthfully posterior implements the optimal decision rule defined in Proposition 2. This is the purpose of Proposition 5.

Proposition 5. Assume $\Psi(\theta)$ is positive and increasing. Then there exists a nonpositive parameter $\bar{H}$ such that, for any $H \leqslant \bar{H}$, the optimal decision rule $\hat{\varphi} = \{\hat{a}, \hat{t}\}$ defined in Proposition 2 is truthfully (posterior) implemented through quadratic incentive schemes $T^H = (T_i^H)$, defined by

$$T_i^H(\tilde{\theta}, X) = \frac{H}{2}[X - R(\hat{a}(\tilde{\theta}))]^2 + (\Psi(\tilde{\theta}) - \tilde{\theta}_i)[X - R(\hat{a}(\tilde{\theta}))]$$

$$+ \hat{t}_i(\tilde{\theta}) - \frac{H\sigma^2}{2}.$$

Furthermore, one can choose $\bar{H} = 0$ if $\Psi(\theta) - \sum_i \theta_i$ is weakly increasing and, in that case, $\hat{\varphi}$ can be truthfully (posterior) implemented through an incentive scheme which is linear in ex post outcome X.

5. Comments and Concluding Remarks

Proposition 5 is the main result of this paper and deserves a number of comments. First, it should be stressed that this proposition extends results obtained by Laffont and Tirole (1986), Caillaud et al. (1986), McAfee and McMillan (1987), and Picard (1987), in the framework of a one agent model. In these papers, the optimal allocation can be implemented through a menu of linear or quadratic compensation schedules which define the agent's reward as a function of realized outcome. It is also the case here: the family of compensation schedules takes the form of a simple penalty-bonus scheme, where $R(\hat{a}(\tilde{\theta}))$ should be interpreted as the targeted outcome associated with vectors of messages $\tilde{\theta}$ sent to the regulator. These compensation schedules are thus fairly simple and, furthermore, they require only the knowledge of the variance of the random noise ε: it is thus unnecessary for the regulator to know the exact distribution of ε.

Under a more restrictive assumption, i.e., $\Psi(\theta) - \sum_i \theta_i$ weakly increasing, the optimal decision rule can even be implemented through a menu of linear compensation schedules. In that case, the agents' compensation includes a fixed fee $\hat{t}_i(\theta)$ and a variable transfer. From (5) the fixed fee satisfies

$$\hat{t}_i(\tilde{\theta}) = \hat{a}_i(\tilde{\theta}) - \tilde{\theta}_i R(\hat{a}(\tilde{\theta})) + \int_{\theta_i^0}^{\tilde{\theta}_i} R(\hat{a}(s_i, \tilde{\theta}_{-i}))\, ds_i.$$

The fixed fee includes the reimbursement of firm i's contribution $\hat{a}_i(\tilde{\theta})$ minus expected cashflows $\tilde{\theta}_i R(\hat{a}(\tilde{\theta}))$. It also includes a term that increases with the announced profitability parameter $\tilde{\theta}_i$, in order to induce truthful revelation. The variable transfer $[\Psi(\tilde{\theta}) - \tilde{\theta}_i][X - R(\hat{a}(\tilde{\theta}))]$ is proportional to the difference $X - R(\hat{a}(\tilde{\theta}))$ between realized and expected outcome and the penalty coefficient $\Psi(\tilde{\theta}) - \tilde{\theta}_i$ is higher for firms that announce a low profitability than for firms announcing a large profitability. Nevertheless penalty coefficients $\Psi(\tilde{\theta}) - \tilde{\theta}_i$ are all increasing when any profitability announcement $\tilde{\theta}_j$ increases. Under less restrictive assumption [$\Psi(\theta)$ increasing], the optimal decision rule is implemented through quadratic incentive schemes, the constant coefficient $-H\sigma^2/2$ being chosen so as to satisfy the individual rationality constraint.

The proof of Proposition 5 is rather tedious but a good intuition of the results can be developed as follows. *Assume first that effort is verifiable.* Let $P_i = t_i - a_i$ be the "net transfer" to firm i. The optimal decision rule $\phi = \{\hat{a}, \hat{t}\}$ described in Proposition 2 gives functions $\hat{P}_i(\theta)$, $i = 1, \ldots, n$ and $\hat{R}(\theta)$:

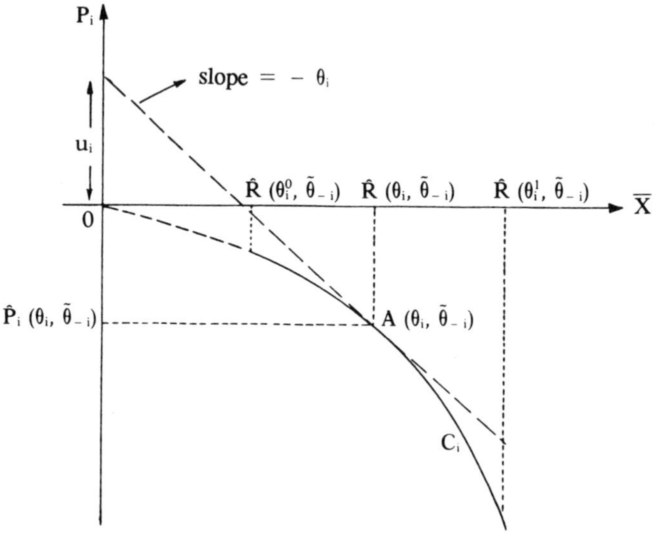

Figure 1.

$$\hat{P}_i(\theta) = \hat{t}_i(\theta) - \hat{a}_i(\theta) \qquad i = 1, \ldots, n.$$

$$\hat{R}(\theta) = R(\hat{a}(\theta))$$

For all $i = 1, \ldots, n$ and for given reports $\tilde{\theta}_{-i}$, the functions $\theta_i \to \hat{P}_i(\theta_i, \tilde{\theta}_{-i})$ and $\theta_i \to \hat{R}(\theta_i, \tilde{\theta}_{-i})$ define a smooth concave curve C_i in the $(\overline{X}, P_i)$ plane, where $\overline{X}$ is the expected outcome (see figure 1). The expected profit of firm i can be written as $u_i = P_i + \theta_i \overline{X}$ and isoprofit curves are straightlines with slope $-\theta_i$.

For firm i, announcing a profitability report $\tilde{\theta}_i$ amounts to selecting a point $A(\tilde{\theta}_i, \tilde{\theta}_{-i})$ on curve C_i. From incentive compatibility, profit maximization leads firm i to choose $A(\theta_i, \tilde{\theta}_{-i})$ when the true profitability parameter is θ_i. Furthermore, optimal expected profits u_i cancel out when $\theta_i = \theta_i^0$ and are strictly positive when $\theta_i > \theta_i^0$.

Assume now that effort is not verifiable. Suppose that firm i *believes* that other firms abide by strategies (σ_j, α_j), $j \neq i$, which satisfy

(i) $\sigma_j(\theta_j) = \theta_j, \qquad \forall j \neq i, \forall \theta \in \Theta$

(ii) $\alpha_j(\theta_j, \theta) = \hat{a}_j(\theta), \qquad \forall j \neq i, \forall \theta \in \Theta.$

Now, let $\ell_i(\overline{X}, a_{-i})$ be defined by

$$R(\ell_i, a_{-i}) = \overline{X}$$

and let

$$\Gamma_i(\tilde{\theta}, \bar{X}) = E_\varepsilon[T_i(\tilde{\theta}, \bar{X} + \varepsilon)] - \ell_i(\bar{X}, \hat{a}_{-i}(\tilde{\theta}))$$

Γ_i is a function from $\Theta \times R$ to R which specifies the expected net transfer to firm i as a function of profitability reports $\tilde{\theta}_1, \ldots, \tilde{\theta}_n$ and of the expected outcome $\bar{X}$. When the firms j, $j \neq i$, announce $\tilde{\theta}_j$ at stage 1, firm i infers that these firms will choose levels of effort $\alpha_j(\tilde{\theta}_j, \tilde{\theta})$ with probability 1 at the second stage, since from (i) firm i thinks that other firms tell the truth at the first stage. From (ii), we have

$$\alpha_j(\tilde{\theta}_j, \tilde{\theta}) = \hat{a}_j(\tilde{\theta}) \qquad \forall j \neq i.$$

Then, from the definition of $\ell_i(\cdot)$, $\ell_i(\bar{X}, \hat{a}_{-i}(\tilde{\theta}))$ is the contribution that is viewed as necessary by firm i to achieve an expected outcome $\bar{X}$. Consequently, $\Gamma_i(\tilde{\theta}, \bar{X})$ is the expected net transfer to firm i, from the point of view of this firm, when firm i chooses its own contribution so as to achieve an expected outcome $\bar{X}$ after profitability reports $\tilde{\theta}_1, \ldots, \tilde{\theta}_n$ have been announced at stage 1.

For the quadratic or linear incentive schemes defined in Proposition 5, the curve C_i and the image of the function $\bar{X} \to \Gamma_i(\theta_i, \tilde{\theta}_{-i}, \bar{X})$ are tangent at point $A(\theta_i, \tilde{\theta}_{-i})$. For these incentive schemes, $\Gamma_i(\theta, \bar{X})$ is concave with respect to $\bar{X}$ and, for $H \leqslant \bar{H}$, its curvature is large enough for C_i to be the upper envelope of curves $\Gamma_i(\theta_i, \tilde{\theta}_{-i}, \bar{X})$, $\theta_i \in \Theta_i$. This family defines a menu of contracts offered to firm i, contingent on $\tilde{\theta}_{-i}$. Firm i has first, to choose a contract by announcing $\tilde{\theta}_i$ and second, to select an expected outcome $\bar{X}$. At stage 1, firm i's optimal choice consists in announcing $\tilde{\theta}_i = \theta_i$: $\sigma_i(\theta_i) = \theta_i$ is its optimal strategy. At stage 2, for any announcement $\tilde{\theta}$, firm i chooses a level of effort $\alpha_i(\theta_i, \tilde{\theta})$ which maximizes expected profits; we thus have

$$\alpha_i(\theta_i, \tilde{\theta}) = \ell_i[v_i(\theta_i, \tilde{\theta}), \hat{a}_{-i}(\tilde{\theta})] \tag{11}$$

where

$$v_i(\theta_i, \tilde{\theta}) \in \operatorname*{Arg\,Max}_{\bar{X}} \{\Gamma_i(\tilde{\theta}, \bar{X}) + \theta_i \bar{X}\}. \tag{12}$$

Since function v_i satisfies

$$v_i(\theta_i, \theta) = \hat{R}(\theta)$$

we have

$$\alpha_i(\theta_i, \theta) = \ell_i[\hat{R}(\theta), \qquad \hat{a}_{-i}(\theta)] = \hat{a}_i(\theta). \tag{13}$$

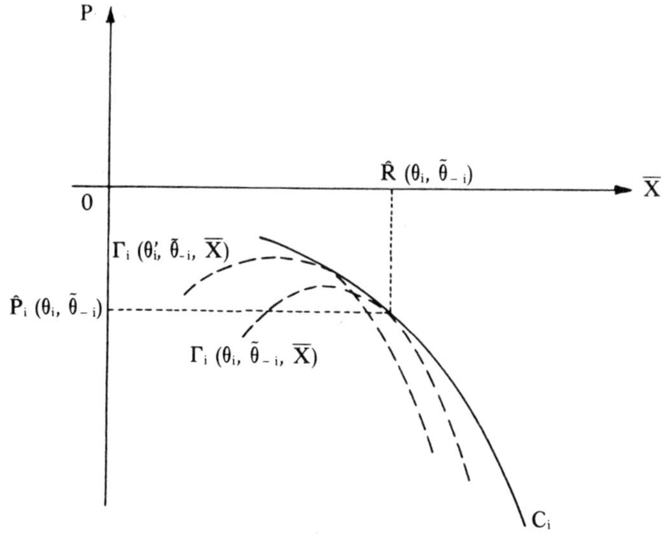

Figure 2.

Conditions (i) and (ii) are thus satisfied for firm i. The same argument holds for all firms. Consequently, telling the truth at stage 1, following the strategy $\alpha_i(\cdot)$, $i = 1, \ldots, n$, defined in (11) and (12) at stage 2 and relying on "degenerated" updated beliefs, which assign probability one to announced parameters, define a posterior implementable perfect Bayesian equilibrium (figure 2).

Let us finally state precisely the connection between proposition 5 and the work of McAfee and McMillan (1986). These authors analyze similar issues in a pure Bayesian setting, which thus differs from our posterior implementability requirement.[7] They exhibit conditions under which Bayesian incentive-compatible decision rules can still be implemented through linear schemes, when individual contributions cannot be observed. However, they rule out, by assumption, correlation among the agents' characteristics. The principal then has the same prior information as any agent j, $j \neq i$ about the characteristic of agent i and, in such a case, substituting implementation in dominant strategies for the Bayesian approach would not entail any welfare loss for the principal: individual contributions, expected transfers, and the expected outcome would be unchanged in the adverse selection model and, as shown in this paper, it could still be implemented when contributions are not verifiable. This would not be the same with correlated characteristics. In that case, assuming that agents play optimal Bayesian strategies and using the information that each agent has about all others would usually be welfare improving for the principal, by comparison with implementation in dominant strategies. In that sense, by keeping to dominant strategies, proposition 5 shows how the results of McAfee and McMillan can be extended to take into account correlation among characteristics. This proposition moreover emphasizes the potential usefulness of nonlinear schemes, since it shows that quadratic schemes are sometimes more efficient than linear ones.

Appendix

Proof of Proposition 1. Consider a decision rule $\phi = \{\hat{a}, \hat{t}\}$ and let $U_i(\theta_i, \tilde{\theta}_i, \theta_{-i}) = u_i(\phi(\tilde{\theta}_i, \theta_{-i}), \theta_i)$. Let us first assume that ϕ is incentive compatible. From (3), we have $\forall \theta \in \Theta$, $\forall \tilde{\theta}_i \in \Theta_i$:

$$\begin{aligned} U_i(\theta_i, \tilde{\theta}_i, \theta_{-i}) &= t_i(\tilde{\theta}_i, \theta_{-i}) - \hat{a}_i(\tilde{\theta}_i, \theta_{-i}) + \theta_i R(\hat{a}_i(\tilde{\theta}_i, \theta_{-i})) \\ &= U_i(\tilde{\theta}_i, \tilde{\theta}_i, \theta_{-i}) + (\theta_i - \tilde{\theta}_i) R(\hat{a}(\tilde{\theta}_i, \theta_{-i})) \\ &\leqslant U_i(\theta_i, \theta_i, \theta_{-i}). \end{aligned}$$

and thus

$$U_i(\tilde{\theta}_i, \tilde{\theta}_i, \theta_{-i}) - U_i(\theta_i, \theta_i, \theta_{-i}) \leqslant (\tilde{\theta}_i - \theta_i) R(\hat{a}(\tilde{\theta}_i, \theta_{-i})).$$

Symmetrically, we have

$$U_i(\theta_i, \theta_i, \theta_{-i}) - U_i(\tilde{\theta}_i, \tilde{\theta}_i, \theta_{-i}) \leqslant (\theta_i - \tilde{\theta}_i) R(\hat{a}(\theta_i, \theta_{-i})).$$

Consequently, $\forall \theta \in \Theta$, $\forall \tilde{\theta}_i \in \Theta_i$

$$\begin{aligned} (\theta_i - \tilde{\theta}_i) R(\hat{a}(\tilde{\theta}_i, \theta_{-i})) &\leqslant U_i(\theta_i, \theta_i, \theta_{-i}) - U_i(\tilde{\theta}_i, \tilde{\theta}_i, \theta_{-i}) \\ &\leqslant (\theta_i - \tilde{\theta}_i) R(\hat{a}(\theta_i, \theta_{-i})) \end{aligned} \tag{14}$$

so that the function $\theta_i \to R(\hat{a}(\theta_i, \theta_{-i}))$ is nondecreasing for all θ_{-i} in Θ_{-i}. The function $R(\hat{a}(\theta))$ is thus weakly increasing. Furthermore, from (14) the function $\theta_i \to U_i(\theta_i, \theta)$ is convex (and thus almost everywhere differentiable) and its derivative is equal to $R(\hat{a}(\theta))$. Let $\pi_i(\theta_{-i}) = U_i(\theta_i^0, \theta_i^0, \theta_{-i})$; we then have

$$U_i(\theta_i, \theta) = \pi_i(\theta_{-i}) + \int_{\theta_i^0}^{\theta_i} R(\hat{a}(s_i, \theta_{-i}))\, ds_i$$

which shows that (5) is satisfied. Last, we have $\pi_i(\theta_{-i}) \geqslant$ from (4).

Conversely, let us assume that (5) is satisfied, with a nonnegative function $\pi_i(\theta_{-i})$, and let $R(\hat{a}(\theta))$ be a weakly increasing function. We then have $\forall \theta \in \Theta$, $\forall \tilde{\theta}_i \in \Theta_i$:

$$U_i(\theta_i, \tilde{\theta}_i, \theta_{-i}) = U_i(\tilde{\theta}_i, \tilde{\theta}_i, \theta_{-i}) + (\theta_i - \tilde{\theta}_i)R(\hat{a}(\tilde{\theta}_i, \theta_{-i})) \tag{15}$$

and from (5)

$$U_i(\theta_i, \theta) = \int_{\theta_i^0}^{\theta_i} R(\hat{a}(s_i, \theta_{-i}))\, ds_i + \pi_i(\theta_{-i}) \tag{16}$$

so that (15) and (16) imply

$$\begin{aligned} U_i(\theta_i, \tilde{\theta}_i, \theta_{-i}) &= U_i(\theta_i, \theta) + \int_{\theta_i}^{\tilde{\theta}_i} R(\hat{a}(s_i, \theta_{-i}))\, ds_i + (\theta_i - \tilde{\theta}_i)R(\hat{a}(\tilde{\theta}_i, \theta_{-i})) \\ &= U_i(\theta_i, \theta) + \int_{\theta_i}^{\tilde{\theta}_i} [R(\hat{a}(s_i, \theta_{-i})) - R(\hat{a}(\tilde{\theta}_i, \theta_{-i}))]\, ds_i \\ &\leqslant U_i(\theta_i, \theta) \end{aligned}$$

This last inequality results from the weak monotonicity of the function $\theta_i \to R(\hat{a}(\theta_i, \theta_{-i}))$ and it implies (3). Furthermore, (4) is satisfied from (16) and $\pi_i(\theta_{-i}) \geqslant 0$. QED

Proof of the Lemma. We have

$$W = \int_{\Theta} \left\{ h(\theta)R(\hat{a}(\theta)) - \sum_i \hat{t}_i(\theta) \right\} dF(\theta)$$

and (5) gives

$$\begin{aligned} \int_{\Theta} \hat{t}_i(\theta)\, dF(\theta) = &\int_{\Theta} \left[\int_{\theta_i^0}^{\theta_i} R(\hat{a}(s_i, \theta_{-i}))\, ds_i \right] dF(\theta) \\ &+ \int_{\Theta} \{\hat{a}_i(\theta) - \theta_i R(\hat{a}(\theta)) + \pi_i(\theta_{-i})\}\, dF(\theta). \end{aligned} \tag{17}$$

We have

$$\int_{\Theta} \left[\int_{\theta_i^0}^{\theta_i} R(\hat{a}(s_i, \theta_{-i}))\, ds_i \right] dF(\theta) = \int_{\Theta_{-i}} \int_{\Theta_i} \int_{\theta_i^0}^{\theta_i} R(\hat{a}(s_i, \theta_{-i}))\, ds_i\, dF(\theta)$$

and integrating by parts yields

$$\begin{aligned} &\int_{\Theta} \left[\int_{\theta_i^0}^{\theta_i} R(\hat{a}(s_i, \theta_{-i}))\, ds_i \right] dF(\theta) \\ &\quad = \int_{\Theta} ([1 - F_i(\theta_i|\theta_{-i})]R(\hat{a}(\theta))\, d\theta_i) \left(\int_{\Theta_i} f(s_i, \theta_{-i})\, ds_i \right) d\theta_{-i} \end{aligned}$$

where

$$dF_i(\theta_i|\theta_{-i}) = \frac{f(\theta_i, \theta_{-i})}{\int_{\Theta_i} f(s_i, \theta_{-i})\, ds_i} d\theta_i = f_i(\theta_i|\theta_{-i})\, d\theta_i.$$

We thus have

$$\int_{\Theta} \left[\left[\int_{\theta_i^0}^{\theta_i} R(\hat{a}(s_i, \theta_{-i}))\, ds_i \right] dF(\theta) = \int_{\Theta} \frac{1 - F_i(\theta_i|\theta_{-i})}{f_i(\theta_i|\theta_{-i})} R(\hat{a}(\theta))\, dF(\theta). \qquad (18)$$

Then (17) and (18) give the result.

Proof of Proposition 2. From the lemma, maximizing W yields

$$\hat{a}(\theta) \in \operatorname*{Arg\,Max}_{a \in R} \left\{ \Psi(\theta) R(a) - \sum_{i=1}^{n} a_i \right\} \text{ for all } \theta \text{ in } \Theta$$

which gives (9). Functions $\pi_i(\theta_{-i})$ are nonnegative and at the optimum we have $\pi_i(\theta_{-i}) = 0$ for all θ_{-i} in Θ_{-i}. Then (5) gives (10). Furthermore, $\hat{a}(\theta)$ is continuous from the maximum theorem and, from (10), the continuity of $\hat{t}(\theta)$ results from the continuity of $\hat{a}(\theta)$. It remains to be checked that functions $\hat{a}_i(\theta)$ are increasing [which will imply that $R(\hat{a}(\theta)$ is increasing] so that the function $\hat{\varphi}$ defined in (9)–(10) is actually an incentive-compatible decision rule. From (9) we have

$$\Psi(\theta) R'(\hat{a}) = e$$

where $R' = (R_i')$ and $e = (1, 1, \ldots, 1)^t$ are column vectors. Differentiating gives

$$\left(\sum_i \Psi_i' \, d\theta_i \right) R' = -\Psi R'' \, d\hat{a} \qquad \text{a.e.}$$

and thus

$$d\hat{a} = -\frac{1}{\Psi} \left(\sum_i \Psi_i' \, d\theta_i \right) R''^{-1} R' \qquad \text{a.e.}$$

The result follows from the fact that R''^{-1} has nonpositive coefficients (since it is the inverse of a negative semidefinite matrix with nonnegative nondiagonal terms[8]) and from the monotonicity of function $\Psi(\theta)$. QED

Proof of the Corollary. Let $x \in R_+$ and $\tilde{a}_i(x) \in R_n$, $i = 1, \ldots, n$, be defined by the following equation:

$$xR'(\tilde{a}) = e$$

where $e = (1, 1, \ldots, 1)^t$.

Using an argument similar to the one developed in the proof of Proposition 2, $\tilde{a}_i(x)$, $i = 1, \ldots, n$, are increasing functions. Furthermore, we have

$$\hat{a}(\theta) = \tilde{a}(\Psi(\theta))$$

$$a^*(\theta) = \tilde{a}\left(h(\theta) + \sum_{j=1}^{n} \theta_j\right)$$

for all θ in Θ. The result follows from the fact that

$$\Psi(\theta) = h(\theta) + \sum_{j=1}^{n} \theta_j \qquad \text{if } \theta = (\theta_1^1, \theta_2^1, \ldots, \theta_n^1)$$

$$\Psi(\theta) < h(\theta) + \sum_{j=1}^{n} \theta_j \qquad \text{otherwise.}$$

Proof of Proposition 3. Let $g_i(\tilde{\theta}_i, \theta_{-i}, \theta_i)$ and $h_i(\tilde{\theta}_i, \tilde{\theta}_{-i}, \theta_i, \theta_{-i})$ be, respectively, the functions under the integral in conditions 1 and 1a. We thus have

$$g_i(\tilde{\theta}_i, \theta_{-i}, \theta_i) = h_i(\tilde{\theta}_i, \sigma_{-i}(\theta_{-i}), \theta_i, \theta_{-i}).$$

Assume that conditions 1a and 3 hold. Condition 1a writes as

$$\sigma_i(\theta_i) \in \operatorname*{Arg\,Max}_{\tilde{\theta}_i \in \Theta_i} \int_{\Theta_{-i}} h_i(\tilde{\theta}_i, \tilde{\theta}_{-i}, \theta_i, \theta_{-i})\, d\tilde{F}_i(\theta_{-i} | \theta_i, \tilde{\theta}_{-i})$$

for all $i = 1, \ldots, n$ and for all $\tilde{\theta}_{-i}$ in $\sigma_{-i}(\Theta_{-i})$.

Let $G_i(\tilde{\theta}_{-i} | \theta_i)$ be the conditional distribution of reports $\tilde{\theta}_{-i}$ which result from the conditional distribution of types $F_i(\theta_{-i} | \theta_i)$ and strategy rules σ_{-i}, i.e.,

$$G_i(\tilde{\theta}_{-i} | \theta_i) = \int_{A(\tilde{\theta}_i)} dF_i(\theta_{-i} | \theta_i)$$

with

$$A(\tilde{\theta}_i) = \{\theta_{-i} \in \Theta_{-i} | \sigma_{-i}(\theta_{-i}) \leqslant \tilde{\theta}_{-i}\}.$$

We have

$$F_i(\theta_{-i} | \theta_i) = \int_{\Theta_{-i}} \tilde{F}_i(\theta_{-i} | \theta_i, \tilde{\theta}_{-i})\, dG_i(\tilde{\theta}_{-i} | \theta_i)$$

so that condition 1 is written as

$$\sigma_i(\theta_i) \in \operatorname*{Arg\,Max}_{\tilde{\theta}_i \in \Theta_i} \int_{\Theta_{-i} x \Theta_{-i}} h_i(\tilde{\theta}_i, \sigma_{-i}(\theta_{-i}), \theta_i, \theta_{-i})\, d\tilde{F}_i(\theta_{-i}|\theta_i, \tilde{\theta}_{-i})\, dG_i(\tilde{\theta}_{-i}|\theta_i).$$

But from condition 3, $\tilde{F}_i(\cdot\,|\theta_i, \tilde{\theta}_{-i})$ assigns probability zero to types θ_{-i} such that $\sigma_i(\theta_{-i}) \neq \tilde{\theta}_{-i}$. Consequently, condition 1 can be rewritten as

$$\sigma_i(\theta_i) \in \operatorname*{Arg\,Max}_{\tilde{\theta}_i \in \Theta_i} \int_{\Theta_{-i} x \Theta_{-i}} [h_i(\tilde{\theta}_i, \tilde{\theta}_{-i}, \theta_i, \theta_{-i})\, d\tilde{F}_i(\theta_{-i}|\theta_i, \tilde{\theta}_{-i})]\, dG_i(\tilde{\theta}_{-i}|\theta_i)$$

which is implied by condition 1a.

Proof of Proposition 4. Assume that $T(\cdot)$ implements $\varphi = \{\hat{a}, \hat{t}\}$ truthfully. Then, from (a), there exists a posterior perfect Bayesian equilibrium $(\sigma, \alpha, \tilde{F})$ of the game defined by T such that $\sigma(\theta) = \theta\ \forall\theta \in \Theta$. For such an equilibrium, updated beliefs $\tilde{F}_i(\theta_{-i}|\theta_i, \tilde{\theta}_{-i})$ are degenerate distributions and conditions 1a and 2 may be, respectively, written as $\forall\theta_i \in \Theta_i$, $\forall\tilde{\theta}_{-i} \in \Theta_{-i}$, $\forall i = 1, \ldots, n$,

$$\theta_i \in \operatorname*{Arg\,Max}_{\tilde{\theta}_i \in \Theta_i} \{E_\varepsilon[T_i(\tilde{\theta}, R(\alpha_i(\theta_i, \tilde{\theta}), \ldots, \alpha_j(\tilde{\theta}_j, \tilde{\theta}), \ldots) + \varepsilon)]$$
$$- \alpha_i(\theta_i, \tilde{\theta}) + \theta_i R(\alpha_i(\theta_i, \tilde{\theta}), \ldots, \alpha_j(\tilde{\theta}_j, \tilde{\theta}), \ldots)\}$$

and

$$\alpha_i(\theta_i, \tilde{\theta}) \in \operatorname*{Arg\,Max}_{a_i \in R} \{E_\varepsilon[T_i(\tilde{\theta}, R(a_i, \ldots, \alpha_j(\tilde{\theta}_j, \tilde{\theta}), \ldots) + \varepsilon)]$$
$$- a_i + \theta_i R(a_i, \ldots, \alpha_j(\tilde{\theta}_j, \tilde{\theta}), \ldots)\}.$$

Using (b), these conditions simultaneously imply

$$(\theta_i, \hat{a}_i(\theta_i, \tilde{\theta}_{-i})) \in \operatorname*{Arg\,Max}_{\substack{\tilde{\theta}_i \in \Theta_i \\ a_i \in R}} \{E_\varepsilon[T_i(\tilde{\theta}, R(a_i, \hat{a}_{-i}(\tilde{\theta})) + \varepsilon)] - a_i + \theta_i R(a_i, \hat{a}_{-i}(\tilde{\theta})\}$$

and thus

$$\theta_i \in \operatorname*{Arg\,Max}_{\tilde{\theta}_i \in \Theta_i} \{E_\varepsilon[T_i(\tilde{\theta}, R(\hat{a}(\tilde{\theta}) + \varepsilon)] - \hat{a}_i(\tilde{\theta}) + \theta_i R(\hat{a}(\tilde{\theta}))\}.$$

Finally, using (c) we deduce

$$\theta_i \in \operatorname*{Arg\,Max}_{\tilde{\theta}_i \in \Theta_i} \{\hat{t}_i(\tilde{\theta}) - \hat{a}_i(\tilde{\theta})) + \theta_i R(\hat{a}(\tilde{\theta}))\}$$

for all θ_i and $\tilde{\theta}$, which means that the individually rational decision rule $\varphi = \{\hat{a}, \hat{t}\}$ is incentive compatible.

Proof of Proposition 5. (a) Assume that $\Psi(\theta)$ is positive and increasing. Let $\hat{R}(\theta) = R(\hat{a}(\theta))$ and, for $i = 1, \ldots, n$, let $K_i(\tilde{\theta}) = \Psi(\tilde{\theta}) - \tilde{\theta}_i$ and

$$\alpha_i(\theta_i, \tilde{\theta}) \in \operatorname*{Arg\,Max}_{a_i \in R^n} \left\{ \frac{H}{2}(R(a_i, \hat{a}_{-i}(\tilde{\theta})) - \hat{R}(\tilde{\theta}))^2 + (K_i(\tilde{\theta}) + \theta_i)R(a_i, \hat{a}_{-i}(\tilde{\theta})) - a_i \right\},$$

which implies

$$\alpha_i(\theta_i, \theta) = \hat{a}_i(\theta) \quad \forall \theta \in \Theta \qquad \text{if } H \leqslant 0. \tag{19}$$

Let $\sigma(\theta) = \theta \quad \forall \theta \in \Theta$ and let $\tilde{F}_i(\theta_{-i}|\theta_i, \tilde{\theta}_{-i})$, $i = 1, \ldots, n$, be degenerated distributions that assign probability one to $\theta_{-i} = \tilde{\theta}_{-i}$. We will show that $(\sigma, \alpha, \tilde{F})$ is a posterior perfect Bayesian equilibrium of the game defined by T. For such strategy rules and updated beliefs, condition 1a is written as

$$\theta_i \in \operatorname*{Arg\,Max}_{\tilde{\theta}_i \in \Theta_i} V_i(\theta_i, \tilde{\theta}_i, \tilde{\theta}_{-i}, \tilde{\theta}_{-i}) = \bar{U}_i(\theta_i, \tilde{\theta}) \; \forall \theta_i, \forall \tilde{\theta}_{-i} \tag{20}$$

where

$$\begin{aligned} V_i(\theta_i, \tilde{\theta}_i, \theta_{-i}, \tilde{\theta}_{-i}) = \frac{H}{2}[R(\ldots, \alpha_j(\theta_j, \tilde{\theta}), \ldots) - \hat{R}(\tilde{\theta})]^2 \\ + (K_i(\tilde{\theta}) + \theta_i)R(\ldots, \alpha_j(\theta_j, \tilde{\theta}), \ldots) \\ - K_i(\tilde{\theta})\hat{R}(\tilde{\theta}) + \hat{t}_i(\tilde{\theta}) - \alpha_i(\theta_i, \tilde{\theta}). \end{aligned} \tag{21}$$

Using (19) we have:

$$\begin{aligned} \bar{U}_i(\theta_i, \tilde{\theta}) = \frac{H}{2}[R(\alpha_i(\theta_i, \tilde{\theta}), \hat{a}_{-i}(\tilde{\theta})) - \hat{R}(\tilde{\theta})]^2 \\ + (K_i(\tilde{\theta}) + \theta_i)R(\alpha_i(\theta_i, \tilde{\theta}), \hat{a}_{-i}(\tilde{\theta})) \\ - K_i(\tilde{\theta})\hat{R}(\tilde{\theta}) + \hat{t}_i(\tilde{\theta}) - \alpha_i(\theta_i, \tilde{\theta}). \end{aligned} \tag{22}$$

Using the first-order condition which defines $\alpha_i(\theta_i, \tilde{\theta})$, we have

$$\begin{aligned} \frac{\partial \bar{U}_i}{\partial \tilde{\theta}_i}(\theta_i, \tilde{\theta}) = [H(R(a^1) - R(a^2)) + K_i(\tilde{\theta})]\left[\sum_{j \neq i} R_j'(a^1)\frac{\partial \hat{a}_j}{\partial \tilde{\theta}_i} - \sum_j R_j'(a^2)\frac{\partial \hat{a}_j}{\partial \tilde{\theta}_i}\right] \\ + \frac{\partial K_i}{\partial \tilde{\theta}_i}(\tilde{\theta})[R(a^1) - R(a^2)] \\ + \frac{\partial \hat{t}_i}{\partial \tilde{\theta}_i}(\tilde{\theta}) + \theta_i \sum_{j \neq i} R_j'(a^1)\frac{\partial \hat{a}_j}{\partial \tilde{\theta}_i}, \end{aligned} \tag{23}$$

with

$a^1 = (\alpha_i(\theta_i, \tilde{\theta}), \hat{a}_{-i}(\tilde{\theta})), a^2 = \hat{a}(\tilde{\theta})$.

From (9), (10), and (23), we get $(\partial \bar{U}_i/\partial \tilde{\theta}_i)(\theta_i, \tilde{\theta}) = 0$ if $\tilde{\theta}_i = \theta_i$, and using the continuity of $\hat{a}(\cdot)$, (20) will be satisfied if $(\partial \bar{U}_i/\partial \tilde{\theta}_i)(\theta_i, \tilde{\theta})$ is positive (respectively negative) when $\tilde{\theta}_i < \theta_i$ (respectively $\tilde{\theta}_i > \theta_i$).

Assume $\exists \tilde{\theta}_i > \theta_i$ such that $(\partial \bar{U}_i/\partial \tilde{\theta}_i)(\theta_i, \tilde{\theta}) > 0$. Then, we would have

$$\frac{\partial \bar{U}_i}{\partial \tilde{\theta}_i}(\theta_i, \tilde{\theta}) > \frac{\partial \bar{U}_i}{\partial \tilde{\theta}_i}(\theta_i, \theta_i, \tilde{\theta}_{-i}) = \frac{\partial \bar{U}_i}{\partial \tilde{\theta}_i}(\tilde{\theta}_i, \tilde{\theta}) = 0. \tag{24}$$

We also have from (23)

$$\begin{aligned}\frac{\partial^2 \bar{U}_i}{\partial \tilde{\theta}_i \partial \theta_i}(\theta_i, \tilde{\theta}) &= H\left[\sum_{j \neq i} R_j'(a^1)\frac{\partial \hat{a}_j}{\partial \tilde{\theta}_i} - \sum_j R_j'(a^2)\frac{\partial \hat{a}_j}{\partial \tilde{\theta}_i}\right] R_i'(a^1)\frac{\partial \alpha_i}{\partial \theta_i} \\ &\quad + [H(R(a^1) - R(a^2)) + K_i(\tilde{\theta}) + \theta_i] \sum_{j \neq i} R_{ji}''(a^1)\frac{\partial \hat{a}_j}{\partial \tilde{\theta}_i}\frac{\partial \alpha_i}{\partial \theta_i} \\ &\quad + \frac{\partial K_i}{\partial \tilde{\theta}_i}(\tilde{\theta}) R_i'(a^1)\frac{\partial \alpha_i}{\partial \theta_i} + \sum_{j \neq i} R_j'(a^1)\frac{\partial \hat{a}_j}{\partial \tilde{\theta}_i}.\end{aligned} \tag{25}$$

From proposition 2, we know that $\partial \hat{a}_j/\partial \tilde{\theta}_i > 0\ \forall i, j$. Then, one easily checks that the term that multiplies H in (25) is strictly negative. Thus, there exists $\hat{H}_i(\theta_i, \tilde{\theta})$ such that

$$\frac{\partial^2 \bar{U}_i}{\partial \tilde{\theta}_i \partial \theta_i}(\theta_i, \tilde{\theta}) > 0 \qquad \text{if } H \leqslant \hat{H}_i(\theta_i, \tilde{\theta}).$$

Define $\hat{H} = \mathrm{Min}_{i=1,\ldots,n}\{\mathrm{Inf}\{\hat{H}_i(\theta_i, \tilde{\theta}) | \theta_i \in \Theta_i, \tilde{\theta} \in \Theta\}, 0\}$. If we let $H \leqslant \hat{H}$, (24) cannot be satisfied and we have

$$\frac{\partial \bar{U}_i}{\partial \tilde{\theta}_i}(\theta_i, \tilde{\theta}) \leqslant 0 \qquad \text{if } \tilde{\theta}_i > \theta_i.$$

Symmetrically, we also have

$$\frac{\partial \bar{U}_i}{\partial \tilde{\theta}_i}(\theta_i, \tilde{\theta}) \geqslant 0 \qquad \text{if } \tilde{\theta}_i < \theta_i$$

so that (20) is fulfilled in that case.

It can also be observed that a sufficient condition for $\partial^2 \bar{U}_i/\partial \tilde{\theta}_i \partial \theta_i$, to be positive with $H \leqslant 0$ may be written as $\partial K_i/\partial \tilde{\theta}_i \geqslant 0$, which is satisfied for all i if function $\Psi(\theta) - \sum_i \theta_i$ is weakly increasing.

Consequently, (20) is satisfied when $H \leqslant \bar{H}$, where $\bar{H} = 0$ if $\Psi(\theta) - \sum_i \theta_i$ is weakly increasing and $\bar{H} = \hat{H} \leqslant 0$ otherwise. Condition 1a is thus satisfied. Furthermore, condition 2 is also satisfied, from the definition of strategy rules $\alpha_i(\theta_i, \tilde{\theta})$ and updated beliefs $\tilde{F}$. $(\sigma, \alpha, \tilde{F})$ is thus a posterior perfect Bayesian equilibrium.

(b) We also have to prove that $\forall\theta$, $\forall i$, $\alpha_i(\theta_i, \theta) = \hat{a}_i(\theta)$ for any posterior perfect Bayesian equilibrium $(\sigma, \alpha, \tilde{F})$ such that $\sigma(\theta) = \theta$. In that case, from condition 2 and 3 we have $\forall\theta_i \in \Theta_i$, $\forall\tilde{\theta} \in \Theta$, $\forall i = 1, \ldots, n$:

$$\alpha_i(\theta_i, \tilde{\theta}) \in \operatorname*{Arg\,Max}_{a_i \in R^n} \left\{ \frac{H}{2} [R(a_i, \ldots, \alpha_j(\tilde{\theta}_j, \tilde{\theta}), \ldots) - \hat{R}(\tilde{\theta})]^2 \right.$$
$$\left. + (K_i(\tilde{\theta}) + \theta_i) R(a_i, \ldots, \alpha_j(\tilde{\theta}_j, \tilde{\theta}), \ldots) - a_i \right\}$$

and thus, for $\tilde{\theta} = \theta$

$$[H(R(\ldots, \alpha_j(\theta_j, \theta), \ldots) - \hat{R}(\theta)) + (K_i(\theta) + \theta_i)] R_i'(\ldots, \alpha_j(\theta_j, \theta), \ldots) = 1$$

which means that

$$(\alpha_1(\theta_1, \theta), \ldots, \alpha_n(\theta_n, \theta)) \in$$
$$\operatorname*{Arg\,Max}_{a \in R^n} \left\{ \frac{H}{2} [R(a) - \hat{R}(\theta)]^2 + \Psi(\theta) R(a) - \sum_i a_i \right\},$$

which in turn implies

$$(\alpha_1(\theta_1, \theta), \ldots, \alpha_n(\theta_n, \theta)) = \hat{a}(\theta).$$

(c) Finally, one immediately checks that

$\forall i$, $\forall\theta \in \Theta$, $E_\varepsilon T_i(\theta, \hat{R}(\theta) + \varepsilon) = \hat{t}_i(\theta)$. Q.E.D.

Acknowledgments

We thank Dilip Mookherjee, Roland Benabou, two referees, and workshop participants at Toulouse, Paris, and Stanford for helpful comments. Thanks are also due to CNET (Centre National d'Etudes des Télécommunications) for financial support.

Notes

1. However, there is an important difference between these programs: for ESPRIT and RACE, the European strategy is to promote transnational cooperative research

at the precompetitive stage, while EUREKA is intended to lead to a joint industrial exploitation of results. On cooperative research in Europe, see Jacquemin and Spinoit 1986 and Jacquemin 1987.

2. For a different approach of cooperative R & D, more from an industrial organization standpoint, see d'Aspremont and Jacquemin 1987 and Katz 1987.

3. After developing potential advantages of cooperative R & D, Jacquemin and Spinoit (1986) write: "A cooperative agreement is a compromise between a desire for collaboration and an intention of maintaining independence, so that the organizational structure reflecting such an ambiguity is usually complex. Various clauses of the legal structure express this concern and imply heavy transaction costs of negotiation, especially for transnational ventures. Partner selection and the possibility of defining well-balanced contributions is the first barrier.... At the second stage, the management of existing cooperative agreements is also costly, especially in R & D where technological conditions are changing rapidly and unpredictably. As it is not possible to maintain complete control over the functioning of the cooperation, it is necessary to construct complex contracts containing explicit clauses concerning confidentiality and transmission of information.... Finally, it is not easy to divide the benefits of a cooperative agreement in R & D, given that scientific knowledge has many aspects of a public good and that its results are not often easily incorporated.... All of these elements suggest that even in the context of a very tolerant antitrust policy, without positive public actions, European cooperation in R & D will remain a limited and unstable phenomenon."

4. In the following $E_\varepsilon(\cdot)$ denotes expectation with respect to the random variable ε.

5. The results of this paper can be easily extended to the case where the benefits of firm i are written as $B_i(\theta_i, X)$ with $\partial B_i/\partial\theta_i > 0$ and $\partial^2 B_i/\partial\theta_i\partial X > 0$ so that θ_i would still be interpreted as a profitability parameter.

6. To simplify matters, the social value of the cooperative program is supposed to be linear with respect to the outcome X but this assumption is not essential. To interpret this social value assume, for instance, that firms are monopolists in independent markets and, for simplicity, assume $n = 2$. Let $P_i(q_i) = b - q_i$, $C_i(q_i) = (c - k_i X)q_i$ for $i = 1, 2$, where $P_i(q_i)$, $C_i(q_i)$, and q_i are, respectively, the inverse demand function, the cost function, and the production of firm i ($b > c$). Firm i's profit π_i and consumers surplus S are, respectively, given by

$$\pi_i = (b - c + k_i X)^2/4$$

and

$$S = [(b - c + k_1 X)^2 + (b - c + k_2 X)^2]/8.$$

Using a first-order approximation, we have

$$\theta_i = \frac{\partial \pi_i}{\partial X} | X = 0 = (b - c)k_i/2$$

and

$$h(\theta) = \frac{\partial S}{\partial X} | X = 0 = (b - c)(k_1 + k_2)/4 = (\theta_1 + \theta_2)/2.$$

7. The modeling options also are slightly different: in the model of McAfee and McMillan, the unknown characteristics are productivity parameters.

8. See, for example, Arrow and Hurwicz 1977, pp. 326 and 371. Using this property of negative semidefinite matrices with nonnegative nondiagonal terms has been suggested to us by the paper of McAfee and McMillan (1986).

References

Arrow, K., and L. Hurwicz (1977) *Studies in Resource Allocation Processes.* Cambridge University Press.

Bensaïd, B. (1986) Bayesian Incentive Compatible Mechanisms under a Negative Dependence Assumption. Mimeo, Université de Paris I, Groupe de Mathématiques Economiques.

Caillaud, B., R. Guesnerie, and P. Rey (1986) Noisy Observation in Adverse Selection Models. INSEE discussion paper No. 8602.

Cramton, P. (1984) "Sequential Bargaining Mechanisms." In Two Papers on Sequential Bargaining, IMSSS Technical Report No. 444, Stanford University.

Crawford, V. (1985) "Efficient and Durable Decision Rules: A Reformulation." *Econometrica* 53: 817–836.

D'Aspremont, C., and L. A. Gérard-Varet (1979) "Incentives and Incomplete Information." *Journal of Public Economics* 11: 25–45.

D'Aspremont, C., and L. A. Gérard-Varet (1986) "Bayesian Incentive Compatible Beliefs." *Journal of Mathematical Economics* 10: 83–103.

D'Aspremont, C., and A. Jacquemin (1987) A Note in Cooperative R & D in Duopoly. CORE DP No. 8742.

Dasgupta, P. S., P. J. Hammond, and E. S. Maskin (1979) "The Implementation of Social Choice Rules: Some General Results on Incentive Compatibility." *Review of Economic Studies* 46(2): 185–216.

Dewatripont, M. (1988) "Commitment through Renegotiation Proof Contracts with Third Parties." *Review of Economic Studies* 55(3): 377–389.

Farrell, J. (1982) Communication in Games. Mimeo, MIT.

Forges, F. (1986) "An Approach to Communication Equilibria." *Econometrica* 54(6): 1375–1385.

Green, J., and J. J. Laffont (1987) "Posterior Implementability in a Two-Person Decision Problem." *Econometrica* 55(1): 95–115.

Hart, O., and J. Tirole (1988) "Contracts Renegotiation and Coasian Dynamics." *Review of Economic Studies* 55(4): 509–540.

Holmström, B. (1982) "Moral Hazard in Teams." *Bell Journal of Economics* 13(2).

Holmström, B., and R. B. Myerson (1983) "Efficient and Durable Decision Rules with Incomplete Information." *Econometrica* 51: 1799–1920.

Jacquemin, A. (1987) "Collusive Behaviour, R & D and European Policy." *Economic Papers,* Commission of the European Communities, Directorate-General for Economic and Financial Affairs.

Jacquemin, A., and B. Spinoit (1986) "Economic and Legal Aspects of Cooperative Research: A European View." In Annual Proceedings of the Fordham Corporate Law Institute.

Katz, M. (1987) "An Analysis of Cooperative Research and Development." *Rand Journal of Economics,* 17(4): 527–543.

Laffont, J. J., and J. Tirole (1986) "Using Cost Observation to Regulate Firms." *Journal of Political Economy* 94(3): 614–641.

Maskin, E. S. (1977) Nash Equilibrium and Welfare Optimality. Mimeo, MIT.

Maskin, E. S. (1986) "Optimal Bayesian Mechanisms." In *Essays in Honor of Kenneth J. Arrow,* vol. 3, ed. W. P. Heller, R. M. Starr, and D. A. Starrett. Cambridge University Press.

McAfee, R. P., and J. McMillan (1986) Optimal Contracts for Teams. Mimeo, University of Western Ontario.

McAfee, R. P., and J. McMillan (1987) "Competition for Agency Contracts." *Rand Journal of Economics* 18(2): 287–307.

Moore, J., and R. Repullo (1988) "Subgame Perfect Implementation." *Econometrica* 56(5): 1191–1220.

Picard, P. (1987) "On the Design of Incentive Schemes under Moral Hazard and Adverse Selection." *Journal of Public Economics* 33: 305–331.

Yamamura, K. (1986) "Caveat Emptor: The Industrial Policy of Japan." In *Strategic Trade Policy and the New International Economics,* ed. P. R. Krugman. MIT Press.